State Interests and Public Spheres

State Interests and Public Spheres

The International Politics of Jordan's Identity

Marc Lynch

COLUMBIA UNIVERSITY PRESS   NEW YORK

COLUMBIA UNIVERSITY PRESS
Publishers Since 1893
New York, Chichester, West Sussex
Copyright © 1999 Columbia University Press

Library of Congress Cataloging-in-Publication Data

Lynch, Marc,
    State interests and public spheres : the international politics of
Jordan's identity / Marc Lynch.
        p.   cm.
    Includes bibliographical references and index.
    ISBN 0–231–11322–6 (cl.). —ISBN 0–231–11323–4 (pa.)
    1. Jordan—Politics and government—1952–   2. Jordan—Foreign
relations.   3. Arabism.   4. Civil society—Jordan.   I. Title.
DS154.55.L89   1999
956.9504′3—dc21   99–12186
                                                                      CIP

c 10 9 8 7 6 5 4 3 2 1
p 10 9 8 7 6 5 4 3 2 1

*to my grandfather, Samuel Edelson, and
to the memory of my grandmothers, Ida and Marie*

Contents

Preface and Acknowledgments

On February 7, 1999, Hussein ibn Talal died after 46 years on the throne of the Hashemite Kingdom of Jordan. In the eyes of many observers, his passing marked not only the end of an era, but potentially also the end of Jordan. Viewing Jordanian politics through the prism of one extraordinary man, they could not envision a Jordan without him. While Hussein was certainly central to the Jordanian political system, Jordan is not and has never been reducible to one man. This book, written before the King's death, focuses on the interplay of the regime's preferences and the identities and interests articulated by important segments of Jordanian society. The emergence of a Jordanian public sphere in the 1990s, which allowed these actors to express and argue for their conceptions of Jordan, and the monarchy's struggle to maintain its freedom of maneuver, produced a far more complex and intriguing political situation than was often appreciated. I argue that a clear and powerful Jordanian national identity has emerged, locating Jordanian interests firmly on the East Bank and precluding a return to the West Bank. I also argue that the failure to embed the peace treaty with Israel in a domestic consensus renders it less stable than the strategic logic and presumed shared interests behind it might suggest. The passing of Hussein from the scene and the ascension to the throne of his son, Abdullah, offers both an opportunity and a danger for the Jordanian public. It also highlights the significance of the political and public dynamics discussed in this book. An inexperienced King, dependent on external supporters and most comfortable with military interests, might move to repress contrary public opinion and reassure his foreign patrons. On the other hand, Abdullah could choose to engage with the Jordanian public sphere, seeking to secure legitimacy, shared identity, and popular support through public deliberation. While such questions are beyond the scope of this book, I hope that the arguments developed here will be of use to those who now ponder them.

As with any project that has evolved over a long period of time, this book has developed though an ongoing dialogue with numerous people. As usual, they have much to do with its strengths and bear no responsibility for its mistakes.

By far my greatest debt goes to Peter Katzenstein and Shibley Telhami, who took the unusual step of agreeing to be co-chairs of a rather odd dissertation, and were model advisers: committed, reliable, supportive, and critical. Without their faith, combined with close reading, this book could never have been written. Sid Tarrow helped shape the dissertation by constantly forcing me to express my ideas more clearly and to engage with empirical questions. Cornell's exceptional intellectual environment shaped my approach to the project; my thanks go out to all the participants in the Peace Studies Colloquium, the Advanced Graduate Student Colloquium, and the Dissertation Support Group. Christian Reus-Smit and Richard Price, in particular, introduced me to a new way of thinking about International Relations.

Outside of Cornell, a number of people read all or part of the manuscript. Lisa Anderson was involved in this project at an early stage. Her sharp critiques and good humor helped me focus on the project; her willingness to spend long hours with a graduate student from another university during her sabbatical year showed me the meaning of dedicated scholarship. Michael Barnett read many versions of this project and helped provide the space for my arguments. Alex Wendt read the entire manuscript and identified crucial missing points in the argument. Indeed, this book can be read as an ongoing dialogue between my dissertation and Alex's provocative criticisms. Ian Lustick brought me in to a collective Social Science Research Council project, "Rightsizing the state," which allowed me to explore and develop the comparative implications of Jordan's experience. I received useful comments and criticisms while presenting parts of this work at the annual meetings of the Middle East Studies Association, the International Studies Association, and the American Political Science Association, as well as at the Social Science Research Council, Cornell University's Peace Studies Colloquium, and the University of Maryland.

As I went from graduate school to the job market, several people and institutions quite literally kept me alive. Thanks to Princeton University, particularly John Waterbury and the Politics Department, for hosting me in the fall of 1993. Judith Reppy, director of the Peace Studies Program at Cornell, intervened on my behalf at more than one critical moment. For financial support, I thank the Social Science Research Council's International Predissertation Fellowship Program; the MacArthur Foundation grant administered by the Cornell Peace Studies Program; the United States Information Agency Dissertation Fellowship program administered by the American Center for Oriental Research in Jordan; the Mellon Foundation Dissertation Completion Fellowship; and the MacArthur Foundation postdoctoral fellowship on ethnic conflict administered by the Institute for International Studies at the University of California, Berkeley.

John Kozlowicz, chair of the Political Science Department at the University of Wisconsin, Whitewater, gave me my first teaching position before I had finished my dissertation. Thanks to John and the department for a wonderful year and an exhilarating introduction to the world of teaching. John Rapp and the faculty of Beloit College were extremely helpful during my year in Wisconsin and I warmly thank everyone there. I rewrote the book during a postdoctoral fellowship year in the Political Science Department at the University of California, Berkeley. Among the many people at Berkeley that I would like to thank for their friendship and advice are Robert Price, Kiren Chaudhry, Elizabeth Kier, Bob Powell, Kirsten Rodine, Beth Simmons, and Steve Weber. I finished my revisions at Williams College, and I thank Michael MacDonald and the entire Political Science Department for their support.

In Jordan, a number of institutions and individuals supported my research. I particularly thank Mustafa Hamarneh, director of the Center for Strategic Studies at the University of Jordan, where I was a visiting fellow from 1994 to 1995. Mustafa, Nahla, and the staff helped me with everything from access to the University library to arranging interviews; Mustafa's generosity, enthusiasm, and sharp analysis of Jordanian politics will always be deeply appreciated. I stayed at the American Center for Oriental Research in Amman for six months in 1995, and would like to thank Pierre Bikai and the entire staff. Jillian Schwedler, Joseph Massad, Pete Moore, and Cathy Hanaman contributed immensely to both my understanding of Jordan and to my mental health. Beth Dougherty lived through a lot of this book with me, and I will always be grateful. I can not begin to thank the many Jordanians who gave generously of their time and insight, and whose arguments shaped my understanding of Jordanian politics. Lauren Posner entered my life late in the writing of this book, and helped me to complete it. Her love and support, as well as her patience, have changed my life.

Kate Wittenberg at Columbia University Press has been a model editor, making clear what was expected every step of the way and offering outstanding advice. Leslie Bialler made the copy-editing process both smooth and enjoyable; his appreciation of the finer points of the semi-colon set him apart.

My love goes to my sisters, Karen and Elizabeth, and my parents, Marian and Jeremy. I dedicate the book to my grandfather, Samuel Edelson, and to the memory of my grandmothers, Ida and Marie.

Marc Lynch
Williamstown, Massachusetts
April 1999

State Interests and Public Spheres

1 State Interests and Public Spheres

In July 1988, the Hashemite Kingdom of Jordan surrendered its claim to the West Bank after twenty-one years of intense diplomatic efforts to regain the territory it lost in war. This Jordanian reversal caught nearly everyone by surprise. For strategic as well as normative reasons, the West Bank was assumed to be an integral, fundamental, and primary component of Jordanian state interests. Because of this deeply held interest in the West Bank, Jordan's decision was widely interpreted as a tactical gambit to be reversed at the first opportunity. Nevertheless, the severing of ties has become deeply institutionalized in Jordanian behavior and discourse. Jordan came to view political unity with the West Bank as a threat rather than an interest, and to support the creation of the Palestinian state which had long been considered its deepest fear. Jordan has undergone a fundamental transformation in a first order preference over an outcome vital to the state's identity, security, and foreign policy behavior. Why did Jordan sever its ties with the West Bank? Why did Jordan not reassert its claim when circumstances shifted in its favor? Does the change in Jordanian behavior toward the West Bank signify a shift in positions based on changing incentives in the international arena, or does it represent a deeper change in Jordanian conceptions of identity and interests?

In August 1990, Iraq invaded Kuwait, forcing Jordan into excruciating political decisions of a rather different nature. With the exception of Kuwait and Iraq themselves, no state was more deeply affected, nor more existentially threatened, than Jordan. Despite its traditional alliance with the West,

Jordan became one of the few states that refused to join the American coalition against Iraq, thereby suffering severe economic dislocation, political isolation, the threat of Israeli intervention, and the influx of hundreds of thousands of refugees. International Relations theory has had little to say about this surprising and important decision. Power and threat balancing arguments do not convincingly explain why Jordan refused to join an almost certainly winning coalition led by its traditional international patron against a powerful neighbor which manifestly threatened small states. Rent seeking does not explain why Jordan turned down the huge financial incentives offered by the coalition. Suggestions that the democratization process constrained state policymakers beg more questions than they answer. Why did popular opinion matter so much in 1991 and so little in past and future foreign policy decisions? Why did Jordan identify so strongly with Iraq? In 1995 Jordan shifted alignments, abandoning Iraq in favor of Israel and the United States. How can this decision be reconciled with the theoretical and empirical conclusions drawn from the Gulf crisis? How did popular opposition affect state behavior?

In October 1994, Jordan signed a peace treaty with Israel. On first view, there is little puzzling in this decision. Jordan seemed to have made a rational decision based upon new international and regional power realities. Jordan and Israel were assumed to have broadly consistent strategic interests, and their long history of cooperation on functional issues and secret meetings between leaders seemed to mean that little had changed other than publicity. Did a formal peace treaty matter in any "real" way for international relations? The Jordanian regime, especially the King, demonstrated exceptional enthusiasm for the peace treaty, calling for regional transformation and a warm peace. Had Jordan been forced to sign by a preponderance of power, or had it been persuaded that the peace process best served state interests? Important currents within the Jordanian public equated the peace treaty with an identity project aimed at transforming the character of the Jordanian polity. Did the treaty represent an alignment with Israel at the expense of Jordan's Arab identity? As regime and society clashed over the definition of Jordanian interests in relation to Israel, the relationship between contested identity and contested interests became starkly apparent. Why was the treaty so unpopular? Why did the regime and most Jordanians hold such divergent conceptions of Jordan's interests? The tension between the competing visions escalated as the peace process collapsed on the Syrian and Palestinian fronts, the Likud assumed the leadership of Israel, and the Jordanian regime became increasingly repressive. Would Jordan's "interests" in relations with Israel survive the failure of regional transformation and the absence of domestic support?

Each of these pivotal events in recent Jordanian political history points to the importance of the public contestation of identity and interests for international behavior. Rapid change and successive foreign policy crises coincided with an unprecedented liberalization in Jordan, in which for the first time in decades an open public sphere allowed for public deliberation over foreign policy. Jordanian interests assumed to be deeply embedded and stable became the subject of explicit public debate. These struggles some-times—but not always—produced significant change in official and/or public conceptions of state interests. In official discourse, close ties to the West Bank, long seen as a fundamental interest, came to be portrayed as a serious threat; Israel, long a threat, became a strategic ally; Iraq, long a pillar of Jordanian security, became a threat. In some cases, sharply divergent conceptions of Jordanian interests emerged, as societal forces challenged government policies and the interpretations of interests used to justify them; the public contested the redefinition of Jordan's relationship with both Iraq and Israel. In others, public deliberation produced a new consensus around official policy; most of the public came to accept the severing of ties with the West Bank and support for a Palestinian state.

I argue that state interests should be understood in terms of the interaction between the preferences of state actors and public deliberation within multiple public spheres, which do not necessarily correspond to state borders (Calhoun 1992, 1995; Habermas 1996; Somers 1994, 1995a, b). In so doing, I argue for placing communication at the center of International Relations theory. This does not imply slighting power or strategic interaction. Indeed, recent rationalist work on the dynamics of incomplete information games has moved rationalist theory toward a concern with proxies for communication such as signaling, cheap talk, and updating of information (Fearon 1994b, 1997). An approach based on both strategic interaction and communicative action focuses attention on dialogue, deliberation, and persuasion without slighting the centrality of power and interest in political behavior.

Jurgen Habermas's concepts of communicative action and the public sphere provide the theoretical foundations for this project. By offering a conceptual framework for bridging strategic and communicative action, public sphere theory holds out the prospect for a productive synthesis of rationalist and constructivist arguments. The use of Habermas's social theory in international relations has been to this point largely confined to the philosophical critique of positivism and to normative theorizing about the foundations for a cosmopolitan world order (Linklater 1990, 1998; Haacke 1996). The communicative approach to social action offers important insights for an empirically engaged constructivist theory of international politics (Reus-Smit 1997; Adler 1997). The attempt to take both strategic interaction and communicative action seriously offers one of the most promising avenues of engagement between rationalist and constructivist social theories (Bates, et al 1998). Political theorists and sociologists have applied Habermas's ideas to a growing array of empirical and theoretical issues. In particular, the debate over "deliberative democracy" has brought together rational choice theorists and public sphere theory (Elster 1998; Bohman and Rehg 1997). These applications of Habermas can recast current debates in International Relations over the questions of communication, cultural norms, identity and preference formation.

I argue for the value of a public sphere approach through an empirical investigation of Jordanian behavior and Arab order. The case for public sphere theory rests both on a theoretical bid to integrate key constructivist and rationalist insights and on an empirical claim to best explain an important case. Rather than once again asserting that "norms matter" or that "rationalism can not account for preferences," or refighting old battles over epistemology, I concentrate on theory building and testing. The cases I explore lie firmly within the arena of security; the hypotheses tested include Realist and non-Realist rationalist approaches, constructivist approaches, and the public sphere approach. The cases of Jordanian foreign policy studied are commonly accepted as important and controversial, and directly involve the major Realist concerns: war and peace, security and alliances. Despite the prominence of identity questions in Jordan , Jordanian behavior has been to this point primarily explained by rationalists (Brand 1992, 1994; Brynen 1991a,b; Mufti 1996; Harknett and VanDenBerg 1997). Jordanian foreign policy is a challenging case for constructivists, as the intense security dilemma that characterizes Middle Eastern politics should force states to conform to neorealist assumptions. The dominance over foreign policy by one leader, King Hussein, who has been in power for more than four decades, should produce considerable preference stability. I argue that there has been significant change in the conception of Jordanian identity and interests; that this change is the result of public sphere contestation; and that this has produced changes in Jordanian behavior which cannot be adequately explained in rationalist terms.

Contested Identity, Contested Security

From Europe to Asia, from the Democratic Peace to the war in Yugoslavia, identity has been used to explain important dimensions of state behavior (Chafetz 1998; Katzenstein 1996a; Lapid and Kratochwil 1996). Arab states have faced multiple domestic and international potential identities, embedded within an unusually strong collective sense of regional identity. Since the mobilization of local and Arab nationalism against the Ottoman Empire, European colonialism, and Zionism, political behavior has been justified in terms of conflicting claims to national identity. The tension between self-interested state behavior and norms of Arab unity has long fascinated observers of Arab politics. Analysis has alternately overstated the importance of Arab norms by asserting the uniqueness of Arab politics and understated it by focusing solely upon the manipulation of norms by Arab elites. Both extremes fail to appreciate how the articulation of identity constituted the interests for which elites struggled and how the structure of the Arabist public sphere and Arabist norms shaped strategic interaction. Arabist norms affect state behavior in ways that are theoretically consistent with the relationship between norms and interests in other parts of the world, and should be studied with the same concepts and methodologies used for other regions and issues. International Relations theory should change through engaging with this important case, rather than the Arab experience either being dismissed as unique or being forced into existing Realist theoretical models.

The tension between *qawmiya* (Arab nationalism) and *wataniya* (local nationalism) in Arab political thought and practice has structural underpinnings in the public sphere. More than most other regions, the Arab state system possessed a public sphere that transcended state borders and which often trumped domestic public spheres. Political elites debated questions of collective identity and shared interest before an Arabist audience and in pursuit of an Arabist consensus. Each Arab state was forced to justify its behavior not only before a domestic public but also before an Arabist public. The relative power of this transnational public sphere structures the strategic interaction of Arab states, leaders, and contenders for political power. Indeed, the production and manipulation of an Arab consensus was a crucial manifestation of power in the Arab order. This public sphere provides the frame of meaning and reference within which actors understand the purpose of interaction, shaping first order preferences as well as strategies. This should not be taken as an endorsement of the sincerity or principles of Arab leaders, who are famously self-interested and repressive of public discourse. Neither, however, should the pragmatic behavior and domestic repressiveness of many Arab regimes divert attention from the very real political implications of the Arab public sphere and its norms, expectations, and demand for consensus.

The case studies in this project each represent not only major international issues, but also points of fierce contention in the Jordanian polity. The relationship between the international and the domestic deliberation is a key focus of international public sphere theory. The extent to which international and domestic debate produces consensus, and whether these public spheres reinforce or oppose each other, are key variables for determining the durability of behavioral change. If deliberation changes preferences, then change will likely endure even if systemic incentives change; if not, then policy will likely shift once the systemic incentives shift. For example, the disengagement from the West Bank generated a domestic crisis, debate in an opening public sphere, and a new consensus which became institutionalized. The Jordan-Israel peace treaty, by contrast, provoked debate and an international consensus, but no domestic consensus. Each case puts the theoretical questions into sharp empirical focus. Did identity debates affect state behavior? Which debates mattered more, international or domestic? How did publicly articulated conceptions of interest relate to externally imputed, "objective" strategic interests? Did identity and interests change?

Jepperson, Wendt, and Katzenstein (1996) propose five causal pathways for the relationship among identity, public discourse, interests, and behavior: (1) norms directly shape interests; (2) norms shape identity; (3) variations in identity affect interests; (4) configurations of identity shape international structures; (5) state policies reproduce or reconstruct norms or institutions. International public sphere theory follows several of these causal pathways. For example, state engagement in international public spheres drives states to "construct and project" identities that fit with international norms (Path 2). Jordanian struggles in the 1950s to manifest an "Arab" state identity responded to the increasing importance of the Arabist public sphere, while its efforts in the 1980s to demonstrate a "real" national identity responded to the Israeli argument that "Jordan is Palestine." The second part of my argument follows Path 3, in which "variation in state identity can affect interests or policies of states" or "state policy may be a direct enactment or reflection of [domestic] identity politics." In each case, political outcomes directly reflect the struggles to redefine Jordan's identity and interests: East Bank Jordan or unitary Jordan? Arab Jordan or Peace Camp Jordan? Finally, the debate over normalization with Israel involved a struggle over the principles and institutions of international order (Path 4): Arab order or New Middle East?

A public sphere approach has not received sustained attention in the International Relations literature. Kratochwil (1989, 1994, 1995, 1996) has drawn attention to the role of public justifications in the development and efficacy of norms, situating state behavior within intersubjective structures of meaning (Hall 1999). Linklater (1990, 1996a,b, 1998) has developed Habermas's critical theory as a philosophical alternative to existing theories of International Relations, with dialogic communities serving as the foundation for world order. Critical theorists have participated in the ongoing debate over universalism and the philosophical foundations of International Relations theory (George 1993; Hoffman 1987; Brown 1992; Haacke 1996). In a more empirical vein, several approaches have studied changes in the meaning of state sovereignty by analyzing shifts in the public justifications of intervention (Weber 1995; Biersteker and Thomson 1996; Lyons and Mastanduno 1993). An emerging "global civil society" has been a topic of significant research interest, as constructivists examine the mechanisms by which international norms are constructed and spread (Lipshutz 1992; Koslowski and Kratochwil 1994; Finnemore 1996a; Price 1998). Such attention to the institutional underpinnings of international society supports an analytical move toward the public sphere (Reus-Smit 1997). Risse-Kappen (1995, 1996, 1997) has most directly attempted to apply a communicative action framework to international relations, in his studies of the European Union, relations among democratic allies, and transnational networks. The potential existence of a global public sphere, and its implications for sovereignty, citizenship, and cultural pluralism has engaged normative and empirical theorists alike (Bohman and Lutz-Bachmann 1998; Bohman 1998; Habermas 1998). From a rationalist perspective, Fearon (1994a,b, 1996, 1997, 1998) has focused on the impact of communication on strategic interaction, deploying concepts such as signaling, audience costs, and commitment, which direct attention to questions of public communication. Building on these contributions, I begin to develop an international public sphere theory based on communicative action, public sphere structure, and the constitution of identity and interests through public deliberation.

While I have chosen Jordan as the case to explore the significance of international and domestic public spheres, other Arab states experience similar concerns. The debates over Jordan's identity have parallels in virtually every other Arab state, as each state has searched for legitimacy, stability, and national identity (Hudson 1977). Lebanon, for example, has been torn since its creation between competing conceptions of Lebanon's identity, Western or Arab (Picard 1996). Egypt has engaged in ongoing debates about the relative weight of its African, Arab, Phaoronic, Mediterranean, and Islamic identities (Jankowski and Gershoni 1997). Syria, the "beating heart of Arabism," struggles between competing definitions of Arab identity, Greater Syria, and Syria in its present boundaries (Hinnebusch 1996; Lawson 1996). Palestinians have struggled to reconcile Arabist convictions and a territorially defined claim to national identity, and over the scope of such territorial claims (Gresh 1989, Khalidi 1996). Should "Palestine" include the East Bank or Israel inside the Green Line? Should "Jordan" include the West Bank? Should "Syria" incorporate Lebanon, Jordan, Palestine? Should "Iraq" include its nineteenth province of Kuwait? Should Arab states seek cooperation between sovereign states or should they dissolve "illegitimate" boundaries and unify? Should the allegiance of Arab states automatically go to Arab Iraq in its war with Persian Iran? Can Arab states make peace with Israel and remain "Arab"?

Internal identity debates reflect region-wide debates about the meaning and identity of the international order. The Arab identity of each state could be manifested only within a community of Arab states. The Arab order rested on shared understandings of what Reus-Smit (1997) calls the "moral purpose of the state," by which the Arab state was seen as specifically and distinctively Arab, essentially unlike non-Arab states. While each state had individual interests and different conceptions of the collective interest, they shared a consensus on the necessity of maintaining the community itself. Interactions between Arab and non-Arab states were understood, contrary to Waltzian minimalism, as relations between like and unlike units. Identity debates cast and recast the collective purpose of Arab states; since the Gulf War and the Madrid peace process, deliberation has directly challenged the existence of this Arab community and proposed alternative regional identities (Barnett 1998; Khuli 1995; Salamah 1995). Jordan, challenged to justify its existence by Arabism and by Revisionist Zionism, its relations with Israel, and its competition with Palestinian nationalism, has been deeply engaged in public deliberation at the domestic and the international levels. Jordan's behavior involves debates over the meaning of Arab identity, the definition of state interests, and Jordan's place within an Arab regional order.

The Constructivist-Rationalist Debate

The *origin* of interests represents a crucial point of theoretical contention between rationalist and constructivist approaches (Wendt 1994; Katzenstein 1996a; Adler 1997; Checkel 1997, 1998; Clark 1998; Kimura and Welch 1998). Can identity and interests be taken as exogenous, allowing state behavior to be modeled as strategic interaction, or should identity and interests be taken as variable, contingent upon practice? Are interests systemically derived from objective security and economic concerns, or are they articulated based on identity? It seems best to not make any prior decision about such issues, but instead to formulate them as research questions. Does the contestation of state identity in public spheres, international or domestic, affect state formulations of interests? Does public sphere debate produce behavior different from what would be predicted by rationalist models?

Rationalist theories assume that actor identity can be held constant, while interests are stable and exogenous to interaction (Powell 1994; Baldwin 1993; Oye 1986). Neorealism and neoliberalism agree on the basic definition of international relations as the behavior of unitary rational states facing a security dilemma under anarchy (Powell 1994). Norms and institutions matter to the extent that they change the incentive structure of states, making certain behaviors more or less costly. An actor's identity can be reduced to its *type*—a set of preferences, risk propensity and aggregation rules—without reference to culture, history, or values. Increasingly, rationalist approaches have abandoned the "state as unitary actor" assumption, attempting to establish state preferences in terms of the preferences of societal actors and the decision rules of political institutions (Milner 1997; Morrow 1997). This modeling of domestic politics offers the potential to explain changing state preferences without abandoning the rationalist assumption of stable actor preferences.

Constructivists counter that collective identity is produced through political action and through public performance, and that interests cannot be attributed without taking into account the actor's identity. Identity involves frames of reference of meaning, constitutive of the understanding of the purpose of political activity and of the interests of the individual or the collective. The shared concern with the construction of identity and the importance of public discourse provides a hard core for a constructivist research program. Wendt has been perhaps the most influential in defining constructivism, by focusing on the mutual constitution of state actors and the international system (Wendt 1987, 1992, 1994; Katzenstein 1996a). Wendt emphasizes the intersubjective practices—norms, discourse—which give meaning to material structure. Because actors' identities and interests are endogenous to systemic interaction, the potential for change is inherent in the process of strategic interaction.

The programmatic statement of constructivism's approach to identity and interests is Wendt's (1994): "what 'we' want depends upon who 'we' are." This simple, compelling assertion profoundly challenges the rationalist assumption that the interests of actors can be derived from their structural position. If the definition of interests depends upon the articulation of a collective identity, then it is necessary to theorize and empirically study the construction of identities and the process by which these identities produce interests (Weldes 1996). The contested nature of both identity and interest is essential to constructivism. It challenges the direct inference of interests from any theoretically prioritized quality: social class, gender, ethnicity, power position. Instead, collective identity can be constructed out of any or all of these possible categories, as actors confront choices among multiple potential identities. Given the existence of multiple possible identities, constructivism asks why one identity triumphs over others, or how multiple identities coexist, and how the articulation of one identity rather than another informs the articulation of interests. Identity does not directly produce a single, coherent set of interests. On the contrary, actors who share a collective identity compete to interpret and frame the interests of the collective: while "we" are all Americans, "we" have very different conceptions of American foreign policy interests. "What 'we' want depends upon who 'we' are" represents a theoretical beginning rather than an end, a question rather than an answer. Public deliberation provides one route toward answering these political questions.

The *stability* of preferences is another key axis of the rationalist-constructivist debate (Elster 1998; Bohman 1996; Knight and Johnson 1994). Rationalists argue that actors change their strategies in response to changing circumstances, but not their underlying preferences over outcomes (Clark 1998; Lake and Powell forthcoming; Powell 1994). If preferences change in the course of strategic interaction, then it becomes virtually impossible to model behavior. Constructivism argues that the underlying preferences themselves can change in the process of interaction, as actors articulate and deliberate over their interests. The major claim of "deliberative democracy" theorists is that deliberation can lead actors to change their preferences, reduce (but not eliminate) the need for aggregative decisions, and thereby enhance the legitimacy of decisions (Elster 1998). By identifying the structural preconditions, the mechanisms, and the significance of change, a public sphere approach can bridge constructivist and rationalist arguments. Identifying the conditions for the initiation of communicative action should allow for the specification of the applicability of rationalist and constructivist theories. I identify three necessary conditions for the initiation of communicative action on state identity and preferences: perception of crisis, the presence of a public sphere, and a will to consensus. During periods of crisis in which a public sphere offers the potential for communicative action, change in actor identity and interests becomes possible. Once underway, a dialogue involves dynamics of persuasion and strategic framing which could result either in change or in the reinforcement of the status quo. During periods of "normal politics," or where an effective public sphere does not exist, actor identity and interests are likely to be relatively stable, and rationalist models of strategic interaction should apply.

Public sphere theory engages with both rationalism and constructivism around the themes of identity and interests. Defined as "a contested participatory site in which actors with overlapping identities . . . engage in negotiations and contestations over political and social life," the public sphere is that site of interaction in which actors routinely reach understandings about norms, identities, and interests through the public exchange of discourse (Calhoun 1993). This functional definition of the public sphere makes no assumptions about either its location (with regard to the state) or its content (with regard to rational-critical discourse). By making the public sphere a component of structure, it becomes possible to account for significant variation in the institutional and social content of political behavior (see chapter 2). The public sphere is a dimension of a social structure that has both material and normative elements, involving sites of communication and contestation that can be identified independently of outcomes (Habermas 1996; Ruggie and Kratochwil 1986).

A public sphere approach builds on a conception of action in which a public claim on identity or an argument made in the public sphere is an action. In a very real sense, in diplomacy, words are deeds: positions, resolutions, condemnations, assurances, declarations of friendship, warnings. For the rationalist, talk is only talk, sharply distinguished from action, and talk is cheap (Elster 1998; Johnson 1993, 1998). Because international politics is assumed to be asocial and competitive, an actor can never trust the sincerity of another actor, and therefore can only judge capabilities and concrete actions (Fearon 1998). While political actors often use talk to mask their real intentions or to substitute for more concrete measures, this does not diminish the extent to which words constitute the substance of international politics. Public discourse shapes the political significance of action: Do arms sales constitute an alliance or only a business transaction? Is the provision of foreign aid tied to human rights compliance? Is trade with South Africa an endorsement of Apartheid? Is the deployment of nuclear weapons in a neighboring state a threat? Is the political merger of two Arab states an annexation or a unification? Public discourse is the action by which behavior is interpreted and rendered sensible, and persuading others to accept a particular interpretive frame is an important component of strategic interaction. Consistent public interpretation of a policy can, over time, shape an actor's own understanding of the policy and its significance, in what Elster (1997) has called "the civilizing force of hypocrisy."

In terms of its approach to identity, public sphere theory can therefore be compatible with both rationalism and constructivism. Rather than assuming the stability of state identity and interests, a public sphere approach focuses on the construction of identity and the political struggle to define state interests (Weldes 1996; Koslowski and Kratochwil 1994; Lapid and Kratochwil 1996; Katzenstein 1996a). Habermas has been criticized for taking actor identities and interests as given and exogenous to the public sphere (Somers 1995; Calhoun 1992). Within public sphere theory, however, it is now widely argued that under certain conditions deliberation can produce change (Bohman 1996; Benhabib 1996). Constructivists view deliberation as constitutive, allowing actors to reconceptualize their identities and interests; rationalists view deliberation as a mechanism for coordinating preferences and reducing uncertainty (Knight and Johnson 1994; Elster 1997). Constructivists and rationalists increasingly converge on the importance of persuasion, which could be defined as bringing others to change their preferences through the force of argument.

This is not to say that interests and identity change continuously or fluidly, however. Identities and interests change primarily during moments of crisis, when they lose their "taken for granted" quality and become the subject of explicit public debate. During periods of "normal politics," interests are likely to be relatively stable. For example, Jordan's interest in reclaiming the West Bank drove its behavior for twenty years after the 1967 war, despite Arab and Palestinian criticism, little support on the West Bank, domestic opposition inside of Jordan, and substantial incentives to abandon its claim. It is this stability of deeply held interests that makes their change theoretically and empirically interesting and important. This approach to interests, which attempts to explain the relationship between objectively ascribed and publicly constructed interests on the one hand and the potential and direction of change of interests on the other, holds out the potential for moving beyond rationalist-constructivist opposition toward theoretically productive synthesis.

Rationalism and Identity

While I have followed Wendt in drawing the lines of debate between rationalists who do not look at questions of identity and constructivists who do, rationalists do employ an implicit theory of state identity. Realism specifies the sovereign state as the primary actor in international politics; other rationalist approaches incorporate domestic politics, economic sectors, ethnic groups, and other non-state actors. More central for rationalism is the relative stability of identity and interests, which allows the modeling of strategic behavior to proceed without the complication of changing preferences. While the unit of analysis designated as the actor varies, that designated actor can then be held constant: whatever the specified actor, its identity and its preferences remain constant, and its boundaries are not in question. Rationalism depends on the persistence of a will to independence among the units, which implies a clear conception of identity and difference (Nau 1993). With the rise of identity politics, ethnic and nationalist conflict, state breakdown, and transnational movements, rationalist International Relations theorists have increasingly recognized the need to explain these phenomena.

Rationalist theory has developed a number of arguments to explain this observable significance of identity. First, many rationalists have argued that change in identity and interests can be accounted for exogenously and then held constant for the purposes of modeling strategic behavior. For example, Ferejohn (1991) proposes using interpretive methods to determine the identity and interests of actors, before incorporating these insights into the rational actor model (Bates, et al., 1998). North (1990) suggests that institutional change follows a model of punctuated equilibrium, so that during any specific period the relevant actor identities and interests can be identified and held stable. In each case, change is sufficiently slow and uncommon that it can be effectively held out of the model. Interpretive analysis can provide important insights into the distinctive preference rankings of different actors, which can then enrich rationalist models of strategic behavior. Constructivists, in this view, provide an approach to preference formation, but do not challenge the rationalist account of behavior.

The ongoing process of interest formation challenges this division of labor between rationalist theories of behavior and interpretivist theories of preference formation. Constructivism should not be relegated to an account of preference formation outside models of strategic interaction, precisely because much political behavior involves a struggle over contested norms, identity, and interests. Identity and interests can change when they become the subject of public sphere contestation. At such moments, accepted truths become open to question, shared convictions about the role and purpose of the state become contentious, and new ideas and interpretations compete for hegemonic status. The struggle to establish new interpretive frames should become part of accounts of behavior rather than being relegated to an exogenous source of preferences. The proposed division of labor is only possible once a compelling explanation has been developed of when and how preferences become unstable.

Second, many rationalists have adopted a situational, "portfolio" model of identity, in which actors select strategically from an available menu of possible identities. For Elster's "multiple self," identity is a function of the situation: when in the classroom he is a teacher, when at home a father. While navigating these different situations, however, his autonomous Self remains intact, coherent, and exogenous, choosing from a menu of identities. Hardin (1995) argues that political identity is chosen strategically from a range of possible identities in order to maximize security or other goods. The outbreak of ethnic conflict, for example, might be explained by a combination of the ability of ethnic entrepreneurs to overcome collective action problems, the security dilemma faced by individuals, and a tipping effect affecting individual calculations (Lake and Rothchild 1998). Political identity represents a rational choice based on the incentive structure. Studies of political identity in the Middle East have often implicitly relied on such a model of rational choice of identity, arguing that actors chose Arab or statist identities based upon their likelihood of exercising social power within each community: Sunni Arabs in Iraq favor "Arabist" identities in order to maximize their social weight in the larger imagined political community, while Iraqi Kurds and Shi'a favor "Iraqist" identities in order to maximize their weight in the restricted state boundaries (Mufti 1996; Kienle 1995). Thus, Jordanians of Palestinian origin would be expected to favor ties to the West

Bank in order to increase their overall weight inside of Jordan, while Jordanians of Transjordanian origin would be expected to favor severing ties to the West Bank in order to maximize their social power within the smaller Jordan.

Some institutionalists have developed a variation of the portfolio model, in the guise of role theory (S. Walker 1987; Barnett 1993). As with the portfolio model, actors choose from among a set of possible roles. Role theory assumes the existence of an autonomous Self making strategic decisions. While role theory allows for the possibility that the demands of a role can change an actor's conception of identity, as the actor internalizes the role (which would make it a constructivist argument), the portfolio model generally posits an actor navigating multiple institutional roles without being affected by them. Barnett (1993, 1995) explains Arab international order in terms of the competition between the two institutions of state sovereignty and Arabism. The role conflict between these conflicting roles and expectations for Arab states generates behavioral instability. Posing the question as one of states embedded in competing institutions diverts attention away from the action by which Arabist norms are redeemed. This focus conceals the ways in which the identity of actors and the content of the norms changes in the process of contesting these norms (Barnett 1998 recognizes this). In that sense, Barnett comes closer to the rationalist conception of the multiple self than to a constructivist account of identity and interests.

Some Realists have argued that despite the constructed nature of identity and interests, the anarchical international system tends overwhelmingly to produce egoistic forms of identity and interest. Mercer (1995), for example, draws upon in-group/out-group experiments in social psychology to argue that under anarchy the constructed identity of states will tend to reproduce the self-help, relative gains profile of Realist theory. Attempting to turn constructivism against itself, he claims that "the more carefully one examines the question of state identity in anarchy, the stronger the assumption of egoism becomes." (Mercer 1995: 230) Such findings would reduce the constructivist claim to purely theoretical interest. Mercer fails to grapple with the heart of the constructivist challenge, however. By insisting on the assumptions of anarchy and autonomous states, Mercer ignores the fundamental constructivist argument that state identity is shaped by the quality of the international society. In the presence of a strong international public sphere or institutions, states would not confront the simple anarchy of the realist model and would not necessarily produce the same patterns. Shared understandings and communicative action—rather than an artificial isolation and silence—could produce different patterns of identity formation and behavior. Reproducing neorealist assumptions about anarchy unsurprisingly reproduces neorealist conclusions.

Social psychology has provided a competing, non-rationalist approach to identity in international relations (Chafetz 1997, 1998; Herrmann 1997). For this approach, relationships between state actors are social relationships, in which the identification of other states as "friends" or "enemies" underlies all other calculations of threat and opportunity. Chafetz demonstrates widely varying levels of positive and negative identification, rather than a uniform tendency toward the assumption of self-help, zero-sum, competitive relations. Identification informs state responses to other states, so that the behavior or power of a friend seems less threatening than the identical behavior or power of an enemy. This approach provides important theoretical foundations for understanding the development of international identity. Such processes need to be grounded in public sphere structures, which shape the possibility of interaction and the articulation of shared identity and interests.

The dominant account of the role of Arabist norms in foreign policy remains Hudson's (1977) description of the legitimation shortfalls of most Arab regimes. While not fully theorized, Hudson's argument fits neatly into a rationalist conception of norms as a strategic resource. The reliance of each legitimacy-deficient state on Arabist norms leaves them vulnerable to the strategic manipulation of these norms by other actors (Telhami 1994). State actors, with stable identities and exogenously determined interests, draw on norms as resources in strategic interaction with other states and with their societies. The existence of multiple public spheres makes it problematic to assume that the state level is the only one of importance for legitimation, and that action in the Arab arena is primarily for domestic consumption, however. This approach assumes a body of free-standing, unchanging Arabist norms upon which state policymakers draw, and locates the tension at the international level on this shared reliance on the same "legitimation" resource. After all, everybody can't be the greatest defender of Palestine, which is how each regime wants to be viewed by its domestic public. Lost in this static vision is a sense of how the norms are constituted by practice, interpreted by actors, and change in the process of discursive interaction. Barnett (1998) develops an intriguing argument that the competition over the symbols of unity drives the fragmentation of the Arab order; drawing on Goffmann, he emphasizes symbolic interaction and performance in inter-Arab relations. This study of dialogues and strategic framing offers a far more nuanced and dynamic conception of norms, consistent with the public sphere approach advanced here.

Domestic and International Sources of Interests

The assumption of international preference stability rests on a sharp distinction between the realms of national politics and international relations. While there might exist a national public sphere in which various sectors of society debate the public good for domestic affairs, "politics ends at the water's edge" and the harsh exigencies of international anarchy and the security dilemma preclude public participation in the formation of international interests. Realism views civil society as primarily "a constraint on . . . the pursuit of interests which are defined independently of civil society input" (Cox 1981: 134). State interests are based on objective considerations of power, strategy, security and economic wealth, not on the transient passions of the citizenry (Krasner 1978). Because foreign policy is based on objective considerations of the national interest derived from international structure, it seems plausible to postulate a set of consistent preferences. These preferences would not be likely to change in the course of domestic or international political debates, precisely because of the relative autonomy of the state and the systemic derivation of the national interest (Telhami 1990).

The conception of interests developed here argues that even seemingly objective, overriding interests are constructed based on an actor's identity, norms, and interpretation of threat and opportunity (Wendt 1994). Shared interests and conflictual interests alike are articulated in social terms. For example, a common interpretation of Jordanian foreign policy is predicated upon the assumption that Jordan's "real" interests lie in cooperation with Israel, both over functional issue areas and in order to prevent the emergence of a Palestinian state (see chapter 6). Jordan's public assertions of support for the Palestinian cause or of Arab unity against a Zionist threat are dismissed as cheap talk, lip service to protect Jordan against Arab attacks but in no way expressive of "real" Jordanian concerns. This approach fails to appreciate the constitutive, as well as constraining, impact of Arabist norms and the Arabist public sphere. The opposite approach, that Jordanian public assertions of its interests are "real," is equally unconvincing; the long history of contacts between the Israeli and Jordanian leaderships and the reality of cooperation demonstrate quite clearly that a pure conflict model does not suffice (Lukacs 1997; Garfinkle 1992). Shared strategic interests exist, but they could not be publicly avowed or defended, either at home or in the Arab arena. This tension sharply demonstrates the theoretical and empirical stakes in choosing between externally ascribed "interests" and those interests articulated in the public sphere. Israel remained a publicly identified "enemy" until 1994, sharply constraining cooperation and making any increase in Israeli power be interpreted as threatening, but it also provided important strategic benefits. It is a fallacy to assume that the strategic interest is "real," and the avowed interests are therefore "false." The approach to interests advanced here attempts to consider the interaction between private and public conceptions of interest, and thus the difference that a public sphere makes for state behavior. Actors seek to determine their interests and to frame them with public justifications which enact the identity and moral purpose of the state. Both the strategic demands of Jordan's position and the public assertions of Arabist identity and interests matter; the question is how their coexistence affects state behavior. How do actors reconcile these competing identities and competing conceptions of interest? Which interests, under which conditions, matter for behavior?

The identities and norms that inform the articulation of state interests are both domestic and international. Public sphere theory is not necessarily a second-image theory, and should not be equated with the study of domestic public opinion. It is not only the balance of power and threat that constitute the international sources of state interest; international institutions form the social content of international structure. Arab state identity and interests are deeply shaped by the existence of an Arab order, constructed upon an Arabist public sphere, an Arab identity, and shared Arab institutions. Were a different regional identity to be constructed, this would provide a different social content to the relationships between regional states, both in their domestic identities and in their international identities.

International Sources of Interests

International Relations theories have made a determined effort to identify the international sources of state interests. This effort has been driven by the desire to avoid the Waltzian (1979) charge of reductionism, that no domestic level argument can account for variation in international outcomes. Neorealism posits that the most basic and essential state interests can be deduced from the state's position in the international system, rather than being contingent upon variation in domestic systems or personal leaderships. Realists argue that all states, whether democratic, Communist, monarchical, or authoritarian, tend to balance and bandwagon in predictable and rational ways. States tend to respond to incentives, threats, and opportunities in consistent, rational ways regardless of their ideology or political system. While the findings of a "democratic peace" have sharply challenged this Realist consensus, the emphasis on the systemic derivation of interests remains a fundamental component of theory (Russett 1995; Elman 1998; Owen 1997).

Institutionalism also argues that actors derive identities from international structures, in this case from their embeddedness in international institutions (Powell and DiMaggio 1991; Strang 1994). Variation in state behavior can be explained by the variable institutional context structuring the environment. Rather than facing threats and opportunities within anarchy, states face more or less dense institutional structures. In a dense institutional environment, such as the European Union, states face far less of a security dilemma and can therefore pursue more cooperative strategies. Their preferences are affected by the institutional environment, rather than being solely the product of domestic structures. The international institutional environment can shape the domestic institutions of states (Katzenstein 1985; Gourevitch 1986).

Wendt has proposed grounding constructivist theory, as well, in systemic interaction. Interests change or are reproduced through interaction, as states produce collective meanings and interpretations of the situation, as well as interpretations of themselves and others. By restricting theory to international interaction and excluding domestic politics, Wendt accepts Waltz's definition of structural international theory while contesting his Realist conclusions. This attempt to produce a structural constructivism has been quite controversial. Wendt's desire to adhere to the "state as actor" assumption cuts off attention rather arbitrarily from other, nonsystemic sources of identity and interests. Why assume that the international system is the only site of participation in which states form interests and identities?

A more compelling constructivist theory should not arbitrarily privilege the domestic or the international. Instead, it should establish relationships between the multiple arenas in which interests are constituted. Wendt's insights into the role of interaction should be broadened to consider the different fields within which actors interact. This is a task for which Habermas's concepts are uniquely useful, although they have not to this point been so applied (Cohen and Arato 1984). If interests can change in the process of interaction, under what conditions does domestic or international interaction most influence the articulation of interests?

The Arab system makes it unusually clear that the priority of the domestic as the site of contestation of state identity and interests cannot be taken for granted. While every Arab state had strategic interests, each remained embedded in an ongoing public deliberation over shared Arab identity and collective interests. The preference for an outcome within an Arab consensus over any outcome outside the Arab consensus, and the definition of collective identity and interests prevents state interests from being articulated purely in terms of the individual autonomous state. If identity and interests are constructed and contested, then it becomes necessary to consider where and how they are contested. Sovereignty traditionally demarcates a qualitative line between political community inside and anarchic competition outside, but the existence of international public spheres blurs these sharp lines bounding political community. Public spheres have no necessary correlation with state borders; the formation of identity and interests should similarly not be arbitrarily restricted to one level of analysis.

Domestic Sources of Interests

While much of International Relations theory privileges the international sources of interests, foreign policy research locates interest formation within domestic institutions, political competition, and norms. Theoretical and empirical studies demonstrate the causal links between public opinion, state structures, and foreign policy (Holsti 1995). State strength, the organization of interest groups, and issue area are frequently cited to account for variation in the impact of public opinion on state behavior (Risse-Kappen 1991). Political economists deductively determine state and societal preferences based on the insight that different domestic sectors have different interests in terms of state policy toward the international economy. Rationalist approaches increasingly incorporate domestic politics, defined as decision rules for the aggregation of individual preferences (Morrow 1997; Milner 1997). In one of the most far-reaching critiques, Moravcsik (1997) argues for making domestic preferences the primary building block of International Relations theory. Variation in state preference gives content to the question of cooperation and conflict under any set of structural conditions, from pure anarchy to a highly institutionalized environment. While international structure and institutions play an important role in shaping these preferences, the primary unit of analysis is the actors and their preferences, not the structural environment. Preferences, whether identified deductively or inductively, are the basic theoretical building block.

It is important to distinguish between public opinion, as conventionally employed by foreign policy analysts, and the public sphere (Habermas 1996). The public sphere involves the exchange of arguments oriented toward producing consensus, which can have a constitutive rather than only a constraining impact. Public opinion, by contrast, implies an external constraint and an objectively existing quantity, rather than the outcome of public deliberation. I am not simply arguing that state actors are more responsive to domestic public opinion than is often assumed (public opinion as constraint). Instead, I argue that the process of formulating justifications in the public sphere, and of articulating the relationship between identity and interests, establishes the meaning and range of legitimate action (public sphere as constitutive). Rather than simply being a question of the extent to which public opinion constrains state policy, the issue is the extent to which public sphere discourse constitutes the state's articulation of interests.

The public sphere is an important institutional variable in the domestic articulation of interests. While the impact of public deliberation in framing the national interest is usually stressed more in the study of liberal democracies than in the study of Third World autocracies, the case of Jordan demonstrates that the public sphere can have significant impact even under conditions of less than full formal democracy. The ability of various sectors to articulate and express their interests depends on the existence of the institutional means for such expression. Habermas (1996) explicitly distinguishes the public sphere from the formal political decision making institutions. Public deliberation can frame issues, articulate alternatives, interpret the meaning of policy for identity. In the absence of an effective public sphere, it seems plausible to assume that the state will enjoy a considerable degree of autonomy in the definition of the national interest, subject only to the constraint imposed by the fear of "the street." The more developed a public sphere, however, the more the state will be forced to articulate and justify its conception of the national interest against the counter-arguments of politically important forces.

There is a tendency among observers of Jordan, as with many Arab states, to reduce foreign policy to the personal preferences of King Hussein. Given his personal control over foreign policy, Hussein's decisions seem to be largely autonomous from domestic forces. One of the major objectives of this study is to challenge this assumption, or at least to put it into context. King Hussein makes Jordanian foreign policy, to be sure, but he does so from a position deeply embedded within the Jordanian and Arab political systems. Hussein pays close attention to the domestic and Arab implications of foreign policy. Elite opinion is transmitted to the Palace both through the public sphere and through private channels; public uprisings and riots, such as those in 1989, 1996 and 1998, represent an extreme form of public expression in the face of the breakdown of other forms of communication. The liberalization in 1989, in response to popular uprisings and demands for greater political participation, opened the public sphere to deliberation over state identity and state interests. Hussein engages in a regular dialogue over Jordanian identity and interests. His ability to act against the expressed will of the Jordanian public at key points in no way implies the nonexistence or insignificance of that opinion. As the cases in this book make clear, the Palace recognizes the importance of persuasion and the instability of policies based purely on the repressive application of state power. The King decides, but Jordan deliberates.

The relationship between identity politics and the definition of interests emerges powerfully in Jordan. Any definition of Jordanian interests necessarily rests on a definition of Jordanian identity in relation to the Arab order and in relation to the Palestinian nationalism. When King Hussein asserts that the peace treaty with Israel serves Jordanian interests , many citizens of Palestinian origin respond: "the interests of which Jordanians? Are we not equally citizens?" As Ashley (1987) suggests, foreign policy involves a "boundary producing political performance." By negotiating for narrowly defined state interests, or by abandoning its claim to the West Bank, the Jordanian government defines the identity of the Jordanian state in new ways. The proposed separation between the internal and the external defines a pressing interest of a majority of the population [Palestine] as external. The legitimacy of any such articulation of interests depends upon the outcome of the discursive struggle about the identity of the state and of the nation.

Katzenstein (1996a) argues for a constitutive relationship between domestic norms and state interests. In his study of Japan and Germany, he concludes that cultural norms embedded in domestic institutions profoundly shape international behavior. The prevailing conception of national identity constitutes how each state understands the meaning and purpose of regional and international organizations, the role the state should play in the world, and the kinds of interests worth pursuing. In Jordan, similar arguments could be made for a correlation between domestic and international norms and structures on the one hand. The most obvious example of the embedding of an international identity into domestic norms is the Hashemite commitment to Arab unity. Jordanian discourse justifies the creation of the state in terms of the Great Arab Revolt and Arab identity. While the Hashemite rulers of Jordan pursue state interests and regime interests which often sharply contrast with the Arab consensus, they not only accept but proclaim the primacy of Arab identity. This normative stance is not tactical, and is not compelled by external pressures. On the contrary, it is deeply constitutive of the sense of purpose of the state and the regime.

Another important norm that guides Jordanian state behavior in both domestic and international arenas is "dialogue" (*hiwar*). Jordan's first instinct in a political crisis is always to call for *hiwar* in order to find collective solutions to conflicts of interests. Countless examples could be offered, since this norm permeates Jordanian political life; I offer here one example from each arena. When faced with the threat of an electoral boycott by opposition parties in 1997, the Jordanian government called for a national *hiwar* over the boycott; the opposition parties accepted the appeal, only dropping out and affirming the boycott after the dialogue failed to change government policy. After tensions in the Jordanian political system peaked in the summer of 1998, Hussein appointed a new Prime Minister, who immediately announced a serious and wide-ranging "*hiwar*" with all sectors of society, established a "*hiwar* committee" made up of the senior members of his cabinet, and began a regular series of "*hiwar* meetings" with civil society representatives. When Iraq invaded Kuwait in 1990, Jordan appealed for *hiwar* at the Arab level in order to arrive at an Arab solution and prevent the outbreak of war. Indeed, Jordan has always been among the leading advocates of Arab summitry and has on numerous occasions accepted Arab consensus resolutions sharply contrary to its preferences. In the ongoing crisis between the United States and Iraq in the mid-1990s, Jordan called for the opening of direct American-Iraqi dialogue, despite its own conflicts with the Iraqi regime. While these Jordanian positions might be attributed to its weak position, its need for the goodwill of its neighbors, or to hypocrisy, the fundamental consistency across domestic and international behavior suggest the constitutive importance of this cultural norm. The centrality of *hiwar* and the search for consensus in Jordanian norms might well contribute to the applicability of the public sphere approach developed in this book.

Jordan's Identity

While this book focuses on the period after 1988, Jordanian history offers many examples of publicly contested identity and interests. This brief review is not intended to be a comprehensive exposition of Jordanian history, but only to introduce some of the major examples of this tension and to provide context. Since its creation as Transjordan in 1922, the Hashemite state faced a particularly tortured encounter between publicly avowed identity and strategic interests. Emir (later King) Abdullah accepted the throne of the newly created entity on the expectation that this small Emirate would serve as the launching pad for the creation of a larger Arab entity. Abdullah saw his rightful sphere of power as including Syria and Palestine as well as Transjordan, and worked tirelessly to advance and pursue this claim (Nevo 1996; Wilson 1987). In pursuit of these ambitions, Abdullah contributed immensely to the articulation of Arabism in an emerging Arabist public sphere; although most Arab nationalists rejected the Hashemite claim to leadership and resisted Abdullah's Greater Syria plans, by engaging Hashemite Arabism in debate they defined their own conceptions of Arabism (Seale 1986). Inside of Transjordan, a small nationalist movement oriented to the emerging Arabist norms coexisted uneasily with Abdullah's Hashemite version of Arabism; while this nationalist movement did not compare in strength or influence with its Syrian and Palestinian counterparts, it did hold several National Conferences, issue declarations, and at some level constrain Abdullah's behavior (Wilson 1987; Hattar 1986; Muhafiza 1990).

One of the most controversial dimensions of Abdullah's conception of interests lay in his relations with the Zionist movement in Palestine (Shlaim 1987). Unlike most Arab leaders, Abdullah saw the Zionists as a potential ally and cultivated relations with representatives of the Yishuv. These relations could not be justified before the Arabist public sphere, as they offended Transjordanian nationalists as well as the wider Arab public. At the same time, they were not entirely secret; denunciations in the Palestinian or Syrian press occasionally generated political firestorms which forced Abdullah to cool his activities for short periods. The secrecy of these relations carries important implications for the development of Arabist norms and for Jordan's place within them, since the normative stigma attached to such contacts was strengthened with each wave of denunciations. These contacts involved extensive negotiations over the partition of Palestine between Transjordan and the Zionist movement. While historical controversy continues to rage over whether these negotiations came to fruition in 1948 (Shlaim 1987; Sela 1990; Karsh 1997), the outcome of the war generally followed the contours of the Hashemite-Zionist discussions: the Arab portions of the Palestine Mandate joined with Transjordan to constitute the Hashemite Kingdom of Jordan. The union between the Palestinians and Transjordan followed a "national conference" in Jericho; the characterization of these events as "annexation" or as "unification" is an important part of the identity framing that followed. In 1951, Abdullah was assassinated in Jerusalem by a Palestinian nationalist. After a period of turmoil, in which a regency maintained stability and deposed Abdullah's son Talal (Satloff 1994), Abdullah's grandson Hussein ascended the throne, where he remains to the present day.

Hussein's ascension to the throne coincided with the transformation of the Arabist public sphere, as the rise of Gamal Abd al-Nasir (hereafter Nasser) in Egypt initiated a period of intense public contestation and demands for physical unification of Arab states. Between 1955 and 1958, Arabism threatened the survival of both the Jordanian regime and the state (Dann 1989; Shwadran 1959). Nasser's Arabism portrayed Jordan as a particularly illegitimate division of the Arab world, a buffer state for British interests and a guarantor of Israeli security rather than an authentic Arab state. These charges often accurately reflected Jordanian strategic interests, but framed them as inherently illegitimate and forced Jordan to publicly disavow them. Invoking a norm of distinctly Arab independence, Arabists argued that Jordan as constituted did not qualify as an "Arab state." To the extent that these arguments persuaded Jordanians, they pushed in the direction of the voluntary dissolution of the state. This denial of Jordanian identity inspired oppositional political activity which forced a steady shift in Jordanian behavior, from the dismissal of the British Commander of the Arab Legion to the refusal to join the Baghdad Pact. Egyptian broadcasting worked because of the orientation of political publics toward this Arabist public sphere, the consolidation of its norms as the only acceptable justification for political action, and the binding of political identity to this public sphere and its norms. Military power played no appreciable role in the Arabist challenge to Jordan. The public argumentation involved more than the exertion of power as constraint, however; real persuasion took place over the nature of Arab identity and interests. To a considerable extent, Hussein was persuaded of the need for Arab unity, and many of his concrete steps reflected attempts to manifest this identity without compromising the survival of the state or the regime (Hussein 1962). Only when the throne itself came into question did Hussein assert state power and end the liberal era.

Throughout the 1960s, Jordan engaged in argumentation over its Arab identity while also working control Palestinian nationalism and to keep the Israeli border quiet in order to prevent retaliatory Israeli attacks (Morris 1991; Shemesh 1996). The tension between Arab norms and these security needs kept Jordan constantly on the defensive. In 1967, Jordan entered the war with Israel and suffered a catastrophic defeat, losing the West Bank to Israeli occupation. The decision to enter the war has been interpreted variously as opportunism based on Egyptian misinformation about the course of the war; a necessary act after Israel attacked Egypt and invoked the Arab Collective Security Agreement; and the only way Hussein could prevent an uprising among his own people had he stayed out of the war (Mutawi 1987). Whatever the motivation, the outcome was devastating: military humiliation, economic destruction, the occupation of the West Bank, a second wave of refugees. Hussein along with Nasser advocated entering into peace negotiations, based on the return of occupied territory to Syria, Egypt, and Jordan in exchange for peace.

After 1967, the rise of Palestinian nationalism challenged Jordanian sovereignty, identity, and claim to the West Bank. The reconstituted PLO implicitly laid claim to representing up to two-thirds of Jordan's population and at times vetted a claim to Jordan itself. As the *fida'yin* engaged Israel in guerrilla activities and captured the public banner of Arab action, they also established increasingly autonomous areas of influence on the East Bank. The Arab order attempted to mediate between the Jordanian government and the Palestine Resistance (PRM), but by 1970 Hussein could no longer tolerate the challenge to Jordanian sovereignty and in September unleashed the army. By brutally expelling the Palestinian resistance from the country, Jordan's regime forcefully established its identity as a Jordanian, not Palestinian, state. The Arab order, forced to choose between recognition of the right of states to defend sovereignty from internal challenge and the normative value accorded to the Palestinian cause, chose the former. Their "betrayal" of the Palestinians in Black September stood as a decisive turning point in the Arabist public sphere, as Arab leaders turned to a more conservative, state-centric conception of Arabism.

Despite condemnation and sanctions, and an abortive Syrian intervention, Jordan emerged victorious from Black September. Paradoxically, however, its military victory weakened its Arabist argumentation, as the Jordanian claim to represent the Palestinian people could no longer be credited. In the struggle for Palestinian representation in the Arabist arena, Black September won Jordan the East Bank but lost it any Arabist support against the PLO for the right to rule Palestine. In 1974, the Arab summit at Rabat declared the PLO the sole legitimate representative of the Palestinian people, rejecting the Jordanian claim, while the PLO shifted the territorial location of Palestinian national demands to the 1967 occupied territories. From 1974 to 1993, the "peace process" involved strategic interaction among Jordan, Israel, and the PLO over the dispensation of the West Bank and Gaza.

The rise during the 1980s of the Israeli claim that "Jordan is Palestine" offers an example of the relationship among security, identity, and international public sphere argumentation outside of the Arab arena. Israel's refusal to recognize or deal with the PLO strengthened Jordan's international position, even as the Arab affirmation of the PLO role weakened Jordanian leverage. A Revisionist trend in Israel proposed a Palestinian identity for Jordan as the best solution to the Israeli-Palestinian conflict. This argument rose from the fringe to the political mainstream in the 1980s (Tessler 1989; Lustick 1993; Shindler 1995). The primary threat to Jordan came not from Israeli military action but from the possibility that such arguments would prove convincing in the international public sphere and undercut support for Jordanian sovereignty. To the extent that Jordan was viewed as an illegitimate state by influential international publics, the idea that with a new political system it could serve as an alternative homeland for Palestinians gained plausibility. Jordan's responses to this threat included the domestic encouragement of a "national identity" on the premise that the way to overcome this challenge to its sovereignty in the international public sphere was to more closely conform to the nation-state ideal (Layne 1993).

Research Design

While such basic questions of social theory as the relationship among identity, interests, and behavior defy easy empirical testing, Jordan offers a remarkably useful opportunity. Between 1988 and 1998 a significant change in the quantity, quality, and location of public discussion of Jordanian identity took place, as the public sphere opened and identity shifted from a near-taboo to a veritable obsession in the Jordanian public sphere. At the same time, international events forced the articulation of Jordanian interests within changing structural circumstances. I have identified four cases of major foreign policy change in which competing rationalist and constructivist explanations can be evaluated. In addition to these four cases—the disengagement with Palestine, the peace treaty with Israel, the Gulf crisis, and the 1995 turn against Iraq—subsequent challenges to each policy provide additional behavioral observations: opportunities for Jordan to reassert its claim to the West Bank; relations with Israel during the collapse of the Palestinian-Israeli peace process; American-Iraqi confrontations. In this way, I have generated a number of observations of Jordanian behavior. Obviously, Jordan alone can neither prove nor disprove the public sphere case, but it can serve as an initial empirical test and as a demonstration of the value-added of the approach.

Identity and interests are not at stake in every issue of foreign policy and international politics. In these cases, identity and interests were at stake to an exceptional degree, however. with varying outcomes in terms of change and continuity. Therefore, I have selected on the independent variable—the thematization of identity and interests—rather than on the dependent variable—change or continuity. The liberalization process beginning in 1989 created an open public sphere, dramatically changing the public sphere structure for the contestation of Jordan's identity and interests. In earlier periods of Jordanian political history, the primary public contestation of Jordan's identity came in the Arabist public sphere, not from the closed Jordanian public sphere. It was only the severing of ties and the opening of the public sphere that allowed the initiation of public deliberation.

Critics of constructivism often contend that its findings are restricted to countries that do not face serious security threats or are restricted to relatively unimportant issue areas (Katzenstein 1996a; Checkel 1998). While this challenge has been met with an increasing body of empirical studies, it is still often heard. This study directly confronts these criticisms. Jordan is a small state in a nasty part of the world (to borrow a journalistic cliché). The Middle East is hardly known for a dense institutional network of cooperative regimes or for democratic systems of government. Surrounded by powerful, aggressive states such as Syria, Iraq, and Israel, and intimately involved in the most destabilizing of regional issues, Jordan faces acute security concerns. As a small, threatened state, Jordan should reasonably be expected to conform to Realist precepts. Jordan's highly centralized foreign policy process and relatively stable political system should demonstrate considerable preference stability.

Throughout this book, rather than engaging with a broadly defined, moving target of "Realism" or "rationalism," I prefer to engage with concrete competing hypotheses derived from their assumptions, that have been used to explain Jordanian behavior. In addition to the strategic interaction approaches, which have been the primary focus of the theoretical discussion in this and the next chapter, other approaches share rationalist assumptions. While these explanations have not always been fleshed out for each case, their theoretical presumptions and application to other cases allow me to reconstruct clear competing hypotheses. While other rationalist theories obviously exist, I have chosen those which either are most applicable to the cases at hand or which enjoy widespread currency for explaining Jordanian behavior.

The first such rationalist hypothesis is *threat balancing*. Drawing on Walt

(1987), a balance of threat perspective argues that states tend to balance against the most threatening, rather than the most powerful, state. Walt identifies a number of objective criteria by which a state would determine threat, including aggregate power, geographic proximity, offensive power, and perceived aggressive intentions (Walt 1987, p. 22). While I generally critique this approach for ignoring the processes by which threat is constructed, and argue that it consistently underdetermines outcomes, it does provide clear hypotheses about Jordanian behavior.

The second rationalist hypothesis is *omnibalancing*, or regime-survival. The study of foreign policy in the Third World, and in the Arab Middle East in particular, has argued that leaders choose alliances based not only on external threat, but also on internal threats to their power (Korany, Brynen, and Noble 1993; Harknett and VanDenBerg 1997; David 1991; Ayoob 1991). King Hussein therefore guides Jordanian foreign policy with an eye toward maintaining his throne, rather than only being concerned with protecting Jordan from international threats. This has been among the most influential and common interpretations of Jordanian foreign policy: the severing of ties was intended to prevent the Intifada from spreading to Jordan; the Gulf war decision was made out of fear of a domestic uprising; the peace treaty gave a guarantee of the Hashemite regime.

A third rationalist hypothesis is *rent-seeking*, a specific hypothesis drawing on more broadly defined political economy explanations. Brand (1994) has most persuasively argued that Jordanian policy is driven not by threat or by norms, but by the need to secure sufficient external financing to maintain its neopatrimonial state. Alliances are chosen in terms of access to valued economic resources; relations with the Gulf, Iraq, or Syria provide not only military security or political power, but also economic security. Rent-seeking models become more sophisticated when the conflicting preferences of state actors and various economic sectors are taken into account. A rationalist rent-seeking model would suggest fluid changes in policy, as states shift behavior in pursuit of the highest payoffs; a constructivist variant suggests that some kinds of interaction produce networks of trade that might evolve into communities of identity and shared interest.

The empirical chapters in this book fall into two categories. The first group are those which focus on explaining a specific, discrete foreign policy decision: the severing of ties, the peace treaty with Israel, the Gulf War neutrality, and the turn against Iraq. In these chapters (3, 5, 6, and 8), I engage competing hypotheses about the decisions: first, evaluating competing rationalist explanations for the behavior; second, presenting a detailed reading of public sphere structure and processes; third, considering evidence for the thematization and potential change of identity and interests; and finally, considering subsequent behavior for evidence of change or continuity.

The second group of chapters (4, 7, and 8) examines the implications of and the public deliberation over each of these actions, to determine the extent to which a domestic, Arabist, or international consensus emerged. Here I focus on the question of changing preferences: to what extent, and how, did these critical decisions change Jordanian identity, interests, or preferences? Were these changes institutionalized? Did they become part of the identity of the state, or did they continue to be contested?

Rationalist approaches are most useful at those points in which identity and interests are not thematized, and a consensus has been embedded in institutions. At these points, actors do strategically pursue relatively fixed preferences. Such approaches are less useful at those points where identity and interests have become focal points of public debate. If state policymakers must defend, justify, and explain their positions before a public sphere, behavior will tend to closely conform to the arguments being advanced, as each side attempts to establish its frame. If the state resorts to repression in order to enforce its interpretation, then I expect tension and erratic behavior as the state struggles to establish some operating principle. If a new consensus is achieved and institutionalized, then I would expect behavior to again conform to rationalist models, but with a new set of interests and preferences.

If the consensus on identity is challenged primarily in international public spheres, I would expect very different outcomes than when the primary site of contestation is a national public sphere. International contestation is likely to produce defensive argumentation and increased domestic repression if the argumentation is viewed as hostile or threatening. If the international public sphere is viewed as a legitimate site of deliberation over collective identity and interests, then the articulation of a consensus can persuade a state of the need to change its behavior and even its preferences. In the absence of domestic deliberation, such change is likely to be temporary, however, contingent upon changes in power or discourse, since it involves only the top decisionmakers. If the domestic public sphere is a primary site of contestation, then there is the potential for—though not a certainty of—change. Where a change in policy commands a communicatively secured consensus, and becomes institutionalized in state preferences, then the identity and interests of the actor can be said to have changed.

Chapter 2 develops the concept of the public sphere for international relations theory, with particular attention to its role in Arab politics. The rest of the book then examines the four cases from the perspective of the theoretical argument. Inevitably, a book aimed at two audiences has the potential to frustrate both. International Relations specialists may wonder at the amount of discussion of domestic politics, or the attention to public discourse. Middle East or Jordan specialists may question the value of seemingly esoteric theoretical debates, and wish for more detail on Jordanian political structures and struggles. It is important, therefore, to stress what this book is not. It is not a comprehensive political history of Jordan, or an overview of the Jordanian political system. It is not a biography of King Hussein; nor is it an insider's account of the politics of the Royal Court, nor of Jordanian diplomacy. These cases are designed to explore and to test specific questions about political behavior from within an ongoing debate in the International Relations literature. The book maintains a tight focus on these theoretical and empirical questions, perhaps to the exclusion of other, equally interesting questions. My goals are both less and more ambitious: to answer puzzling questions about Jordanian behavior, while also advancing International Relations theory.

Note on Sources

I collected information during eighteen months of fieldwork in Jordan in 1992, 1994–95, and 1997, in addition to shorter visits to Egypt, Jerusalem, and the West Bank. While I conducted a large number of interviews, the book refers to the public record wherever possible. Since my emphasis is on public deliberation and public discourse, the statements and arguments advanced in public take on great importance. I draw primarily on the Arabic press in Jordan and elsewhere, as well as on extensive interviews and observation of public and private political debate in Jordan. Since the liberalization of 1989, political discussion in Jordan has become remarkably free and open on even the most sensitive topics, which allows considerable access to Jordanian political developments. I also rely on published collections of documents, including publications of the Jordanian Ministry of Information, the Center for Arab Unity Studies, the Israeli Foreign Ministry, and the Palestinian Research Center. The Center for Strategic Studies at the University of Jordan has carried out a number of important opinion surveys, and its director, Mustafa Hamarneh, has kindly made their findings available to me. The University of Jordan maintains useful newspaper archives, and a number of Jordanian journalists and editors gave me access to their archives and to their time. I have collected close to the universe of commentary within the Jordanian press, daily and weekly, for 1988–1997. My interpretation of these sources is heavily influenced by ongoing, often informal, discussions with journalists, politicians, and other Jordanian and Palestinian actors. All translations, unless otherwise noted, are mine.

2   The Public Sphere Structure of International Politics

In the first chapter, I located the source of state interests in public sphere debate. The theoretical foundations of such debate must be unpacked, however. The location of this public sphere represents an important structural variable for International Relations. While the paradigm case has generally been that of a state engaging with a domestic public sphere, public spheres are not necessarily bounded by state borders. I argue that state behavior will differ depending upon whether or not a public sphere is present. In this chapter, I develop an international public sphere theory, discuss its relationship to constructivism and rationalism, and present a series of indicators for empirical research on international public spheres. I also provide an overview of the development of the Jordanian and Arab public spheres, which provides a foundation for the case studies to follow.

The Arab order is both a strong and a problematic case for developing international public sphere theory. While the existence of a potent transnational identity, with high levels of political interaction framed around shared identity and interests, suggests the existence of an unusually strong international public sphere, the theory has generally been applied in liberal democratic states, and is commonly associated with liberalism and Western models. Adapting the concept to the Middle East, with its repressive governments, different cultural norms and traditions, and high levels of military and political conflict, challenges many of these assumptions. International relations theory has rarely looked to the Middle East for theory building; despite wide recognition of the importance of identity and norms in Arab politics, few constructivists have focused upon its experience (but see Barnett 1993, 1995, 1998). Theoretically driven study of the international politics of the Middle East in recent years has downplayed the significance of Arabist norms and collective identities in order to render state behavior more amenable to rationalist models (Walt 1987; Telhami 1990; Mufti 1996). Area studies and historical literature have focused on Arabism and its competitors, but without explicit theory and with little impact on wider debates. My goal is not to reassert the cultural difference or uniqueness of Arab states, but rather to argue that the behavior of Arab states should be explained with the same concepts and theories used in other parts of the world. These theories are not necessarily rationalist, however; arguing against Orientalism or cultural exceptionalism does not have to mean accepting rationalism as the only available model of political behavior. Rather than viewing the Arab order as an exception, to be explained with unique theories, I argue that the Arab experience should inform a generalizable international public sphere theory.

International Society and the Public Sphere: Structure

The focus upon international norms and institutions was once associated with the International Society tradition (Bull 1977; Vincent and Miller 1991). Bull famously distinguished between a state system, "formed when two or more states have sufficient contact between them and sufficient impact on one another's decisions, to cause them to behave as parts of a whole," and a society of states, which "exists when a group of states, conscious of certain common interests and common values, forms a society in the sense that they conceive themselves to be bound by a common set of rules in their relations with one another and share in the working of common institutions" (Bull 1977: 10–13). Bull made the extent of normative understanding and institutions within an international system a constitutive variable. In an international society, an overarching set of shared norms and expectations guide state behavior even as the system remained a formal anarchy. States in an international society felt like part of a community and behaved accordingly. Instead of only reflecting convergences of interest, institutions involve the evolution of communities of identity.

Bull's emphasis on shared norms, expectations, and institutions involves communicative action and the public sphere dimensions of structure. This approach to international society drives the constructivist critique of neoliberal regime theory, drawing attention to the intersubjective structures that give meaning to interaction (Ruggie and Kratochwil 1986). The structural dimension lies in the distinction between "system" and "lifeworld." This basic variation in structure mirrors Elster's (1997) distinction between "the market and the forum." The bargaining appropriate in the market, based on the pursuit of self-interest and power, is inappropriate in the forum, where persuasion and deliberation are the norm. The application of public sphere theory to international relations builds upon this basic observation of structural variation. Some international structures more resemble the market, with its strategic bargaining behavior, while others more resemble the forum, with communicative action and persuasion. The public sphere is the dimension of social structure which constitutes the "forum."

Strategic interaction, as conceptualized by formal IR theory, takes place within an international "system," anarchical structures characterized by little shared identity and minimal participation in any shared public sphere. Action is mediated through nonlinguistic steering media, such as money or power, which do not require or permit communicative contact between actors. Action is cut off from public justification, as states must pursue their own survival and self-interest in a competitive system. This dimension of structure roughly corresponds to the neorealist image of states as atomistic actors, isolated from communicative interaction, calculating purely in terms of interest and power, and unable to have access to the perceptions, interpretations, and fears of other actors. Rationalist modeling of behavior assumes a "system" structure, reducing state action to the strategic pursuit of predefined preferences in the absence of communication. Neoliberalism relaxes the anarchy assumption by demonstrating the ways in which international institutions can reduce transaction costs and uncertainty, increase transparency and predictability, and generate incentives for cooperative behavior. The basic assumptions of strategic interaction remain, however (Keohane 1984, 1988; Oye 1986; Baldwin 1993).

The lifeworld, on the other hand, is that dimension of structure characterized by communicative action, directly mediated by language and intersubjective understandings. Action is "socially integrated through interpretations of a normatively secured or communicatively created consensus" (Cohen and Arato 1992: 427). Within the lifeworld, actors share meanings and understandings which facilitate communicative rather than instrumental strategic behavior. This allows for the possibility of action geared to consensus rather than the naked power struggle of the Realist world. Where there is an expectation of and an institutional basis for the public interpretation and justification of action, behavior differs. Action could, at least po-

tentially, be justified before a recognized community and according to
shared norms. The lifeworld dimension of structure corresponds to those
institutionalist or constructivist theories which emphasize the social dimension of international relations (Ruggie 1993, 1997).

The distinction between system and lifeworld focuses attention upon the
presence or absence of a public sphere within which actors can communi-
cate and produce shared frames, norms, and identities (Habermas 1996:
359). Communicative action, the routine exchange of argumentation oriented toward achieving consensus within a set of shared norms, defines
public sphere sites. These sites are not necessarily identical with state boundaries or formal international institutions: "the public sphere comes into existence whenever and wherever all affected by general social and political
norms of action engage in a practical discourse, evaluating their validity"
(Benhabib 1992: 87). Public spheres exist when action is coordinated
through discourse oriented to the achievement of consensus. Arab states, no
matter how competitive, continuously exchange interpretations and arguments in pursuit of the goal of an Arab consensus. Dense interaction, with
regular explanations of state positions framed in terms of the Arab interest,
ensure that the interactions among Arab states involve communicative,
rather than exclusively strategic, dimensions. No conception of the structure
of Arab international politics is complete without this public sphere dimension; even sophisticated realists are forced to smuggle Arabism into their
accounts in order to explain state behavior (Walt 1987; Telhami 1990, 1994).
The presence or absence of a public sphere in which action is routinely
justified, interpreted, and contested, is an integral element of any characterization of political structure, not only Arab or international structure.

Critics of the system/lifeworld dichotomy question the extent to which
these constitute separate realms. Action in virtually every sphere, no matter
how "systemic," involves some degree of linguistic interaction (Berger 1983).
Bourdieu (1977) sees violence in the most discursively mediated exchange.
Even the intimate sphere of the family, which Habermas locates as the
exemplar of communicative lifeworld, involves domination and power struggles (Fraser 1989). If systems are characterized by communication, and the
lifeworld is penetrated by power, then what is the basis for the distinction?
How can communicative action be relevant in the international arena which
is generally seen as the most power-centric of fields? These arguments are
persuasive, especially because few institutional structures fully meet either
ideal type. Not even the most strategic, competitive international relationship is completely free of communication; during the Cold War, unspoken

and negotiated agreements about spheres of influence, arms control, and crisis management helped to regularize interaction. Not even the most co-operative, institutionalized relationships are free of power and calculation of relative gain; within the European Union, states seek to maximize their gains within a shared identity and common interests. Therefore, I do not rely on a strict system/lifeworld dichotomy, but instead look to identify public spheres within the international structure, as the institutional form that per-mits communicative action.

Habermas distinguishes the public sphere from the political system, de-fined as the official, institutionalized decisionmaking system (Habermas 1996: 361–63). The political subsystem entails administrative and state bu-reaucracies that make and enforce binding decisions (McCarthy 1988). While the public sphere thematizes issues, frames and interprets their sig-nificance, and identifies alternative solutions, only the political system can act by taking authoritative decisions. The literature on deliberative democ-racy generally respects this differentiation. Deliberation does not itself pro-duce decisions, even in the unlikely event of a perfect consensus. Some decision rule must, in the end, aggregate the preferences of actors at the end of the deliberative process (Knight and Johnson 1994). This division of re-sponsibilities between a public sphere for deliberation and a political sub-system for decisions takes on rather different connotations in the interna-tional arena, where no sovereign decisionmaking body can enforce binding decisions. International public spheres serve as locations for norm formation and for deliberation over the shared interests of international communities, but in the absence of an authoritative political subsystem. In such an insti-tutional structure, the international public sphere potentially carries sub-stantial weight. Without centralized political institutions to act, the creation and manipulation of a public consensus in an international public sphere takes on significance in its own right. At the same time, the absence of a central decisionmaking body to influence might mean that public sphere deliberation is less weighty, since in the end every state maintains its sov-ereign decisionmaking capacity and can reject an international decision. This tension between international deliberation and formal anarchy, in which deliberation can produce only a nonbinding consensus, stands at the heart of the international public sphere theory. The absence of a fully dif-ferentiated political subsystem does not mean that the international public sphere does not exist; it does mean, however, a constitutive difference be-tween international and domestic public spheres. The difference between international and domestic is more a continuum than a hard dichotomy:

the more institutionalized the international society, the more that consensus can produce legitimate political decisions. Where an international consensus produces a Security Council Resolution which is enforced, such as the sanctions regime on Iraq, the international public sphere looks rather more like a domestic public sphere. The differentiation of an international political subsystem is not a necessary condition for the existence of an international public sphere, however. The forum itself changes the structural context of strategic interaction.

Public sphere dimensions of structure allow for specification of international change independent of shifts in the number or relative power of powerful actors and without presuming a change in the constitutive ordering principle of anarchy (Waltz 1979). International structure changes with the development or decline of public spheres. The rise in the 1950s of an Arabist public sphere or its decline in salience in the 1980s should be seen as structural changes tied to, but not reducible to, shifts in power relations. A public sphere provides the space for communicative action, embodying lifeworld aspects of international politics where actors strive to arrive at consensus. Each public sphere is a bounded sphere of communication characterized by a specific set of norms and practices, which authorizes particular kinds of entities as actors, and which defines the stakes of competition and cooperation. Variation in "anarchy" can take the form of variation in the degree of lifeworld aspects of structure and the extent of communicative action. Such a conceptualization of political order challenges the increasingly besieged idea that the international and the domestic comprise constitutively distinct realms of political life. International relations theory should respect the structural significance of the forum, without abandoning the strategic interaction of the market.

International Society and Public Sphere: Action

Public sphere theory emphasizes the articulation, contestation, and redemption of validity claims (Kratochwil 1990). For all the talk of international politics as the site of naked struggle, the pursuit of the self-interest, and the amoral exercise of power, states spend an inordinate amount of time justifying their behavior. Even when decisions plainly reflect the self-interest of a state, they are presented within a language appropriate to the normative expectations of international and domestic publics. "Statesmen," argued Inis Claude (1966), "take collective legitimacy seriously as a factor in international politics" (Franck 1990; Brilmayer 1989). Actions are accompanied by, and in a sense inseparable from, justifications offered to some public sphere. It is from these justifications and the counter-arguments presented by competing actors, that actions are interpreted and become social acts. The empirical observation of state justifications offered to other states and to an international community demonstrates the existence of an international public sphere. Where state actors feel that they must justify and explain, then they are acting in the forum, with different expectations for strategic interaction.

This is emphatically not to say that public justifications necessarily represent the "true" motivations behind actions. Justifications often involve strategic calculations and cynical manipulation of normative structures. It is common knowledge that actors struggling to manipulate public opinion will say anything to win. But the strategic dimension of public discourse should not hide the fundamentally communicative nature of the act of offering justifications. Where there is an expectation and demand that the legitimacy of an action should be secured discursively through the exchange of justifications, there are very different constraints on and opportunities for action than in a structure where no justification is expected or needed. In a public sphere, "not all interests can be publicly advocated" (Habermas 1996: 340). Interests must be generalizable to the community, not selfish. Behavior that cannot be justified must be either concealed or abandoned, or else the actor must be willing to pay the price of community sanctions (Elster 1995, 1997).

Even cynical actors can become bound by their public discourse, forced to live up to their public commitments. This is especially the case during periods of competitive framing, in which actors strive to prove the sincerity of their discourse and the credibility of their claims against the challenges of other actors. In order to demonstrate credibility, action must match discourse; the more costly and irreversible the action taken, the more credible the argument (Fearon 1994b). At least in the short term, actors can be tightly bound by their argumentation: releasing dissidents to prove commitment to human rights; demobilizing troops in order to prove commitment to a ceasefire; deploying aircraft carriers in order to prove commitment to deterrence. Over time, particularly when engaged in ongoing rather than episodic deliberation, the defense of positions, norms, and identities can change the actor's conception of her positions, norms, and identities, in what Elster (1997) calls "the civilizing force of hypocrisy."

Rationalist uses of the public sphere emphasize the constraining force of norms and discourse rather than their constitutive potential (Checkel 1997). Fearon (1994b, 1997), for example, argues that leaders face the problem of demonstrating credible commitments in their strategic interactions with other states. One way of enhancing credibility is through generating "audience costs," or by raising the costs of backing down from a position by going public with the position and investing political capital in its achievement. If other states can observe that a leader has staked his domestic political future on a position, they are more likely to believe in his sincerity. Such an argument conceptualizes the public sphere in instrumental terms, as a constraint upon behavior. Leaders act, "generating" audience costs by invoking the force of public opinion. The "audience" is entirely passive, despite its implied sanctioning force; the leader pursues predefined preferences which are not affected by his performance before the audience. This conceptualization contrasts sharply with the public sphere approach, in which leaders engage in argumentation with public actors over the definition of interests. Rather than leaders deploying audience costs in pursuit of predefined goals, leaders and publics engage in collective deliberation. Their public discourse produces shared conceptions of collective identity and interests, which in turn guide behavior. The rationalist emphasis on public sphere as constraint, while a weaker claim than the constructivist argument that public deliberation constitutes identity and interests, does demonstrate the difference that a public sphere makes for behavior: the more active and autonomous the public sphere, the more credible will be the generated audience costs.

The relevance of communicative action can be seen not in the irrelevance of power but in the mediation of power through structures in which action must be justified and legitimated. The point is not to find interest-free, power-free behavior but rather to identify the conditions under which the need for public justification oriented to shared norms, goals or identity produces behavior different from behavior absent such demands. Most action combines communicative and strategic elements. Frequently the talk accompanying action involves little effort to reach consensus, with justification only serving as a "fig leaf" over naked power. But where realists view this scenario as the norm and communicative action as exceptional, I would argue that the balance between strategic and communicative action varies dramatically across regions, issue areas, and time. The more that a public sphere provides the expectation of ongoing deliberation, and the greater the sense of belonging to shared identity and institutions, the more that states must justify their behavior with reference to shared norms. The Arab order was characterized by such ongoing communicative interaction over collective identity and interests; every action by every state had to be justified and explained before an Arab public sphere. States might act against Arab norms, but at such points they were clearly recognized as outside the Arab consensus and suffered material and normative sanctions: Egypt in Camp David; Jordan in the Gulf War. Strong domestic public sphere support for the "deviant" interpretation, such as the Jordanian public support for Iraq in the Gulf crisis, can deflect the international consensus by providing an alternate public sphere seen as more legitimate.

The relationship between compulsion and persuasion is a difficult one, because of the overlapping strategic and communicative action in almost every real international interaction. If material power directly determines victory in public argumentation, then Realists could convincingly challenge the value of the public sphere concept. Habermas's ideal of communicative action would exclude power from the exercise of reason: a rational consensus is one to which all affected parties would agree in the absence of compulsion. This ideal presents a critical baseline for the evaluation of political behavior, but is not intended as an empirical description of any political reality. Justifications succeed where they satisfy the procedural rules of consensus formation and the demands of rational argumentation oriented toward mutually held norms (Bohman 1996). Cynical or not, the proffered justification represents a potentially redeemable validity claim which is judged, accepted, rejected, or contested by other communicatively competent members of the society. These procedural requirements at least in principle ensure that reasoned argument rather than power produces decisions. The structure of a particular public sphere, particularly the norms and interpretive frames available within it, determines the relevant power resources. Public deliberation allows for creative performances and potent articulations of shared identity, norms, and interests that can overcome imbalances of material power and persuade others of a course of action.

Justifications and argumentation appeal to the force of the better argument, but what counts as a powerful argument depends upon the ability to frame a validity claim in terms of shared norms, identities, and goals. Deliberation seeks to recast conflicts of interest into potential cooperation toward some higher, shared interest. Deliberation produces shared identities by establishing a common frame of reference and by asserting common membership and belonging. The goal of deliberation is to transform preferences through persuasion—or at least change strategies through an appeal to different preferences, rather than simply to aggregate preferences through voting or to impose preferences through the exercise of power.

The nature of justifications is of great importance for analyzing the status of a norm (Beirstecker and Weber 1996; Weber 1996). Kratochwil (1990) distinguishes between those justifications which accept the validity of a norm, those which reject its applicability, and those which reject its status and seek to change it. Justifications that admit violation of a rule but offer excuses for the violation actually reinforce the norm by demonstrating its general acceptance: for example, when a state claims that an intervention was justified, it accepts and reinforces the basic norm against intervention. Rejecting a norm's applicability—"this action was not an intervention"— has ambiguous implications, tending to evolve in the course of contestation into acceptance of the norm or an attempt to change it. Justifications that contest the status of a rule or norm are more basic, representing a bid to change the norm. Egyptian arguments that the international norm of non-intervention could not apply to two Arab states because they were a single nation would mean a fundamental reinterpretation of sovereignty norms. Finally, a justification could simply repudiate a public sphere as the relevant site for contestation.

For a public sphere to have significant impact on behavior, actors must share a "will to consensus," or a commitment to maintain the conditions for interaction (Bohman 1996). The will to consensus does not contradict the fact that every actor hopes to achieve its own interests within that consensus, nor does it assume that every actor will be fully convinced of every collective decision. The minimalist definition of the will to consensus might be that an objectively worse outcome within consensus is preferred to an objectively better outcome outside of it. By "consensus," therefore, I do not mean a fully hegemonic discourse in which no other position is conceivable; I mean only that all actors accept an outcome reached through legitimate procedures. The "consensus" on the severing of ties, for example, does not mean that every Jordanian accepts and embraces the separation between Jordan and Palestine, or even that the separation is never challenged in public discourse; it means that all actors accept that the separation best serves their interests. Within the Arab arena, King Hussein accepted the Rabat Summit resolutions of 1974 declaring the PLO the representative of the Palestinian people, despite deep reservations and real fears, rather than be outside the Arab consensus. The preference to maintain the process of deliberation and the institutions of regional order outweighed the preference over the outcome on even this issue, which struck at the very heart of Jordanian identity, security, and even survival. No outcome could be legitimate or stable outside of this consensus. The commitment to consensus represented a constitutive norm of the Arabist order. Even Walt, who does not theorize consensus formation, admits that "regimes have gained power and legitimacy if they have been seen as loyal to accepted Arab goals, and they have lost these assets if they have appeared to stray outside the Arab consensus" (Walt 1987: 146). The formation and manipulation of this consensus, within an Arabist public sphere, is a fundamental structural characteristic of the Arab order, which observably shapes state behavior.

An example of the policy importance of the theoretical arguments developed to this point can be seen in the debates over containment of or engagement with "rogue states" (Lake 1994). Would political and economic engagement with China, for example, strengthen a hostile regime or moderate that regime and socialize it into international society? Realists, who argue that preferences will not change and that competition is structurally determined, argue that engagement simply strengthens an inevitable future enemy. Such "backlash" states should instead by contained, and their behavior influenced through the manipulation of sanctions and incentives. The election of the moderate reformer Mohamed Khatemi in Iran in 1997 energized an already simmering debate over American policy toward Iran, again posing the question of whether engagement in dialogue might moderate and socialize Iranian foreign policy behavior. Similar debates about Cuba, North Korea, Libya, and other repressive regimes have been heard. Each of these debates refers back to an implicit theoretical issue: can dialogue transform the preferences of these regimes in the direction of shared identity, norms, and interests; or is dialogue only a cover for the harsh realities of the struggle for power, such that any political concession will only strengthen a future enemy rather than moderate the reasons for enmity. Public sphere theory firmly supports the first view: given the proper conditions, engagement in public deliberation can change state identities and interests, and facilitate cooperation.

Power and the Public Sphere

Constructivists are aware of the importance of power in international politics, but seek to reconceptualize it in terms of the social structures in which it is exercised (Mearsheimer 1996, Wendt 1994/95). As Kratochwil suggests, "the embeddedness of the power-game in a shared normative structure shows that the alleged antimony between power politics and following the rules of the international game is largely mistaken" (1990: 52). While Habermas proposes an ideal in which power can not influence outcomes, empirical application of public sphere theory does not make any such assumptions. The procedural conditions for the legitimation of power matter, however. Agreements seen as compelled by power are perceived as illegitimate, as violations of the rules of deliberation and therefore unjust.

Most states in the modern international system do not seriously have the option of ignoring the international public sphere; those states designated as "rogue states" by the international community are the exception which confirm the membership of "normal states" in that community. In a public sphere structure such as the Arab order of the 1950–1960s, Arab states exercised power in large part by advancing claims in the Arabist public sphere which challenged the target to justify its deviance from this interpretation of Arabist norm or else to comply. The targeted state simply did not have the option of ignoring such accusations or claims, and had to either defend or modify its behavior. At the same time, "the usefulness of military and economic capabilities as bases of power was clearly restricted" (Noble 1991: 61). The threat to Jordan in the 1950s had little to do with a prospective Egyptian military invasion or economic sanctions, and much to do with persuasion, delegitimation, and the encouragement of domestic opposition. To account for such variation in the utility of power resources, international theory should recognize the social dimensions of structure.

Realists dismiss public justifications as empty talk, with no impact on the actual pursuit of policy. If material power determines outcomes, then what is gained by adding the complexities of discourse? The answer to this standard question must be that the initial premise is flawed: power cannot be usefully defined solely in terms of material resources (Baldwin 1989). When Walt's neorealist explanation of Arab alliances asserts that "the most important source of power has been the ability to manipulate one's own image and the image of one's rivals in the minds of other Arab elites," serious questions arise as to the coherence of neorealist power analysis (Walt 1987: 149). What has happened to material power? What is it about the Arab system which makes "the manipulation of images" a meaningful power resource?

Ideas and norms embody power resources within specific public sphere structures. Neither material power resources nor norms alone can explain outcomes. A powerful state might seem to have less of a need to seek international legitimation for its exertion of power, but it may well have more interest in doing so (Kratochwil 1993; Ikenberry 1998). An exertion of power that is viewed as illegitimate is far harder to sustain than one which the international community, however cynically, publicly ratifies as legitimate. For example, why did the United States perceive a vital interest in constructing a consensus at the United Nations for its actions against Iraq during the Gulf Crisis? The securing of legitimacy is in many ways a superior indicator of power than is a military victory: the American formation of the international coalition was a far more impressive demonstration of power than its subsequent military victory. The shifting perception of the international community toward the sanctions regime offers an example of the importance of legitimation: as long as the sanctions could be justified in terms of international interests and norms, they commanded widespread diplomatic support. As states came to perceive the sanctions as an instrument of American policy exceeding the international mandate, international support eroded (Brzezinski, Scowcroft and Murphy 1997). By the mid-1990s, only the exercise of American power or artificially generated crises kept the sanctions in place, and in November 1997 the United States could not find a single Arab ally, not even Kuwait, for a military attack against Iraq. The exertion of power, even at the international level, involves a communicative, discursive activity in which material capabilities play an important but mediated role. The exercise of military power, like repressive force domestically, tends to indicate a failure of power. Power involves the ability to establish rules and norms and to convince others of their legitimacy, as much as it involves the application of the means of coercion.

Because his framework does not take into account the specificities of multiple public spheres, Habermas fails to suggest how actors navigate the different power relations and structural conditions of different public spheres (Calhoun 1995). Each public sphere is composed of very different stakes, rules, and power resources. Bourdieu (1989) begins from the premise that each actor embodies competencies and power resources specific to distinct fields. Resources are specific to a given field, not necessarily fungible across fields, and encompassing both the material and discursive bases of power. Social structure involves a network of relatively autonomous fields, each characterized by specific modes of power resources, norms, and stakes.

Bourdieu's description of power as symbolic capital specific to the normative and institutional structures of a field applies to power relations across multiple public spheres. Simply put, changing the place of the public sphere represents a shift in power relations by privileging different forms of capital. When the location of the struggle for consensus leaves the Arab arena and enters the international arena or the domestic Jordanian arena, Egypt loses very real power. The power commanded by Egypt relative to other Arab actors in the 1950s simply did not exist when Egypt acted in other, non-Arab, arenas. Egyptian power depended upon the maintenance of the Arabist public sphere. Similarly, when the place of the public sphere moved away from the Arab into the international arena, the power relations between Jordan and the PLO changed dramatically. This approach to multiple public spheres opens up a way of thinking about international power that captures the ways in which normative structures shape power relations.

A second dimension of the public sphere approach to power is the concept of interpretive frames (McAdam, Tarrow, and Tilly 1996; Tarrow 1995). By defining the stakes and the meaning of interaction, framers confer significant power. All interaction takes place against a background of historical experience, institutionalized norms, and entrenched beliefs. Actors compete to mobilize powerful cultural symbols into an interpretive frame which defines the meaning and stakes of a political struggle. In the public sphere struggle, the actor "that succeeds in identifying itself with the interest of the collective . . . has framed the terms of political discourse and debate, and thus the limits of legitimate policy" (Gagnon 1994: 136). The ability of Islamists to frame their political agenda in terms of religion and authenticity within Arab public spheres confers great power—who wants to be "against Islam?" King Hussein might warn against politicizing religion, or complain that "violence and extremism and closed-mindedness are not how I understand Islam," but this accepts the validity of Islam as a frame. The competition to establish a dominant frame for the struggle is crucial in determining its outcome. In the Gulf crisis, for example, the emergence of an interpretive frame of "United States/Israel vs. Arabs" rather than "Iraq vs. Kuwait" profoundly influenced subsequent behavior. The relationship between framing and power should not be described in the abstract; in each of the empirical chapters, I demonstrate the interaction between material and public sphere structures and the process of public argumentation which produces interpretive frames.

Public Spheres and States

Public sphere theory, like liberal theory in general, has implicitly accepted the ordering principle of sovereignty (Latham 1996; Walker 1994). Analysis of the public sphere has rarely been extended to explicit consideration of the international structure of the public sphere. For example, in his analysis of the future of Europe, Habermas notes that despite the growth of European bureaucracy, "so far the political public sphere is fragmented into national units . . . [and] by and large the national public spheres are culturally isolated from one another" (Habermas 1992). Whatever the empirical

validity of this statement, it reveals Habermas's state-centric assumptions. I
have reservations at two levels. First, the cultural isolation of national public
spheres is a contingent phenomenon subject to empirical analysis and
should be a variable. In the Arab world, the opposite of Habermas's characterization seems to be the case: an early period of cultural unity across
state public spheres, with a secular trend toward increased isolation and
insulation of the national public spheres. Second, this argument underrates
the importance of legitimation of policies and debates at the international
level even when state-centric public spheres are strong. The need to construct justifications for foreign policy—in other words, the tension between
the pursuit of national interest and the need to fit into the international
normative structure—and the shifting relevance of different public spheres
should be taken into account.

Habermas's concern with the development of the bourgeois print public
sphere in specific states led him to assume the existence of a single public
sphere in each country. Instead of conceptualizing the public sphere as a
single, unified arena in which a unified public debates the affairs of a single
state, it is possible to think about public sphere structure as a network of
overlapping and competing publics, which are not necessarily bounded by
state borders. Empirical public sphere theory often reveals the changing
boundaries between these public spheres (Somers 1994; Benhabib 1996).

Can a concept developed to explain the processes by which individuals
established democratic constraints on the state meaningfully be adapted to
the interaction of states? In conventional levels of analysis formulations, the
constitutive boundary between international and domestic politics is the lack
of an international state able to make and enforce decisions. The concept
of the public sphere can usefully be stripped down to its function as an
institutional site of discursive communicative interaction, with a set of in-
tersubjectively shared norms, an imagined site of consensus, and a set of
media specific to public debate in that arena. In other words, the existence
of a public sphere is not contingent upon a state taking authoritative decisions. The manipulation and contestation of an international consensus
takes the place of the effort to influence state policy as the defining characteristic of public activity.

One of the most developed applications of public sphere theory to international relations has been in normative theory, with the attempt to develop
the theoretical foundations of a cosmopolitan internationalism (Linklater
1998). The emergence of a "global civil society" would allow the articulation
of global, rather than national, interests. While this does not necessarily

imply the emergence of world government, it often leans toward the idea that such an international public sphere could serve as the foundation for "perpetual peace," as states engage in deliberation rather than military competition and discover common interests and norms in this deliberation (Bohman and Lutz-Bachmann 1997). While this normative international theory holds out great promise, the international public sphere theory advanced here does not necessarily support this line of argument. Rather than the emergence of a single "international public sphere," I argue for the existence of multiple public spheres, across regions and issue areas. While a truly universal international public sphere may exist around certain issues and at certain times, this is only a small part of the much richer network of public spheres. I do not assume that the existence of a public sphere necessarily reduces the prospects of war or competition. Public spheres change the structural context of strategic interaction, and could in principle offer the prospects for the articulation of shared identities and interests; but at other times, public deliberation could produce hostile, negative identification. An effective Arabist public sphere could, for example, produce shared Arab identities and interests that identify Israel, Turkey, Iran, or other non-Arab powers as enemies, thereby raising the dangers of war rather than reducing them. Perhaps a truly cosmopolitan, universal international public sphere could avoid this danger, but absent the assumption of a such a single institution the argument for "perpetual peace" does not follow.

With states embedded in multiple public spheres, the production of identity and interests takes place through multiple, overlapping dialogues. Jordanian debates over identity are interwoven with regional debates over Arab identity, just as German debates over state identity and interests interact with European debates over regional order (Katzenstein 1997b). The articulation of a specifically Jordanian identity in the 1990s depended upon shifts in Arab norms, as each Arab state has since the early 1970s advanced increasingly state-centric nationalisms and Arabism has been defined increasingly in terms of interstate cooperation. Jordan's advances in the peace process were tightly interrelated with the expectation of regional transformation; since the peace process was seen as inevitable, Jordan's peace treaty would secure the state's position in a new regional order. The failure of the peace process on the Syrian and Palestinian tracks left Jordan in limbo, with a peace treaty and normalized relations with Israel that went rather beyond any other Arab state. These relations could be justified and even valued given a transition to a "Middle Eastern" identity, with a public sphere open to Israelis and framed around the pursuit of cooperative economic and political relations; these relations could not be justified given the reassertion of an "Arab" identity, with a public sphere closed to Israelis and framed around Israeli hostility and aggression. While the Jordanian public deliberated over Jordanian identity and interests, it also followed the debates in the Arab public sphere: when the peace process seemed to be advancing, many Jordanians remained open to the potential benefits of peace; when an Arab consensus emerged on the failure of the process, the Jordanian public easily tied their own positions to this consensus.

Because the state is embedded in multiple public spheres, its conception of identity and interests might well diverge from the dominant beliefs of the domestic public. A state engaged in deliberation over regional or international order can acquire an international identity that has not been secured in dialogue with the domestic public sphere. Public debates over American pursuit of international free trade agreements or the necessity for military intervention abroad, for example, often demonstrate a sharp contradiction between official and popular conceptions of American interests. Official Jordanian commitment to regional transformation failed to convince the majority of the Jordanian public sphere, which opposed these policies as contrary to Jordan's Arab identity and detrimental to Jordan's interests. Where consensus runs together in multiple important public spheres, such as the Arab, Palestinian, and Jordanian support for the severing of ties, they can powerfully reinforce and stabilize policy. When the consensus in important public spheres sharply diverge, however, states can find themselves forced to exercise power in one arena, often in the form of repression of the domestic public sphere or unilateral international action.

The Public Sphere and the Rationalist-Constructivist Debate

Rationalist models of incomplete information, signaling, and cheap talk have directed attention toward communication (Fearon 1996, Morrow 1997). The concept of deliberative democracy has generated a particularly productive engagement between rationalists and public sphere theorists (Elster 1998; Bohman and Rehg 1997; Johnson and Knight 1996). As discussed in chapter 1, deliberation and the stability of preferences represent an important point of convergence for a rationalist-constructivist dialogue.

Rationalism can incorporate the public sphere by conceptualizing public opinion as a constraint on action, and by introducing proxies for communication into their models. Conventional analysis of Arab public opinion, for example, takes an almost pure form of rationalist conceptions of public opinion. In most analysis of the "Arab street," public opinion acts only as a constraint upon the pragmatism of Arab leaders (Pollock 1992; Telhami 1992a). State leaders calculate how far they can go without "the street" erupting in violent riots and threatening the stability of the regime. Leaders use propaganda and a mobilizational media as a unidirectional conveyor of opinion, information, and frames, attempting to impose rather than to deliberate or persuade. The failure of the Arab street to erupt during the Gulf War is explained by the successful control of information, the application of repressive power, or perhaps even that state policies were broadly congruent with societal preferences. The "street" is not a public sphere, however. It allows for no deliberation, no equal participation, no persuasion. Public opinion is almost purely a constraint in this understanding.

"Soft" rationalists are comfortable with the idea of norms as constraints. Henry Kissinger, no constructivist, recognized the role of normative structures as a constraint for Jordan in the 1970 crisis when he "feared that intervention on behalf of Hussein would totally discredit him in the Arab world" (Dowty 1984: 124). Language like "discredit" reveals the importance participants attribute to the ability to produce acceptable interpretations of actions. Within the Arab order, actors took the potential for justification and the likely reception of validity claims within an imagined Arab consensus into account. But this alone does not rule out rationalist approaches. Neoliberal regime theory, for example, conceived of norms as intervening variables that constrained states pursuing their preconceived interests. Norms affect behavior through their structuring of the environment in which states interacted, as an external force, not though an impact on the preference structures of the states themselves (Ruggie and Kratochwil 1986).

The constructivist claim is that norms are constitutive of actor identities and interests, and that interaction can change these identities and interests. Norms and regimes should be conceptualized as intersubjective practices constitutive of actor identity and interest. In other words, the norms of the international structure in which a state is embedded enter the political process at the point of the formation of identity and interests, as internalized norms, rather than solely at the level of action and external constraint. What distinguishes public sphere theory from either rationalism or constructivism is the the claim that the process of deliberation contributes to shaping actor identity and interests. It is here, in the process of argumentation, that norms are redeemed, actions are legitimated, and identities and interests are reshaped. This points to the production of identity and the articulation of interests through communicative practice. Interests are not read directly off of identities, any more than they are read directly off of structure. Instead they are contested, interpreted, and articulated in public spheres.

Constructivists who have studied norms and regimes as constitutive of identity and interest have paid little attention to the structures in which norms are redeemed (for exceptions see Reus-Smit 1997; Risse-Kappen 1995; Keck and Sikkink 1998). The structure of the public sphere should be seen as a variable: the locus and importance of justificatory practices in the international system are different at the turn of the century than in 1955. While the collapse of bipolarity has been the most evident factor in the structural changes of the international system, attention must also be paid to the transformation in information technologies and media, the spread of a truly international communications infrastructure (Rosenau 1990; Thompson 1995; Dreisler 1997). Public sphere analysis directs attention both to the changes in the structures of international political communication, and to the change in the underlying normative structure of world politics.

Habermas's formulation of public sphere theory does not thematize identity (Habermas 1996). On the contrary, Habermas considers it to be a constitutive norm of the public sphere that the identity of participants must be bracketed. For consensual decisions to be reached in communicative action, appeal must be made to the strength of an argument, not to the identity and status of the individual making the argument or according to the distribution of power. This "bracketing" condition expressly discourages the thematizing of identity. To the extent that Habermas does not see identity as at stake in public sphere interaction and maintains that identity is formed in the intimate sphere of the lifeworld, he is consistent with rationalists who bracket identity as external to interaction. Where communicative action and lifeworld structures are prominent, however, actors' interpretations of action are intersubjective rather than subjective, socially constructed rather than dependent purely on individual perception. Once the undefended assumption of the autonomous actor secure in his identity is opened to question, the constructivist implications of deliberation and the public sphere become unavoidable.

The choice between the rationalist and constructivist approaches to public sphere interaction and identity has high stakes for International Relations theory. In the former case, the public sphere would contribute to a structural theory in which public spheres of communicative action supplement the system structures of anarchy as a set of constraints on rational action. The identities and interests of those actors, formed in the intimate sphere and brought stable and fixed into public life, would remain outside the scope of the theory. In the latter case, the identity and interests of the actors are at stake in public interaction. While a rationalist public sphere account which focuses on the constraining role of norms and public opinion can help explain state behavior, a constructivist theory of international politics based on a theory of communicative action is needed to explain change. Holding actor identity and interests outside the process of interaction blinds analysis to a crucial pathway to political change.

Specifying the Public Sphere

The conceptual history of the public sphere is such that it cannot be uncritically adopted as a concept for International Relations theory. The ideal type of the bourgeois public sphere, according to Habermas (1989), emerged in modern Europe as an arena of rational-critical discourse irreducible to the state, the economy, or private intimate life. The institutional function of the public sphere, rather than its historical specificity, guides my adaptation of the concept. The public sphere is the site in which members of a society exchange justifications and arguments oriented toward establishing a political consensus. Public action is held accountable before some recognized and articulated public opinion, embodied in the critical commentary of the participating subjects.

The analogy cannot be stretched too far, of course. Where the bourgeois public sphere primarily attempted to hold the state accountable to its citizens, the international public sphere primarily aims at holding the participants (states) accountable to a set of norms which are the contested but shared foundations of international society. An imagined consensus without institutional manifestation obviously differs from a sovereign state, which is a way of restating the familiar domestic/international dichotomy. The functional similarity is crucial, though: the international public sphere, like the national public sphere, provides a site for the formation and contestation of norms, identities, and interests even where it does not mediate before an authoritative sovereign center.

The variance in the influence, locus, and content of justifications points to an operational definition of the public sphere as an element of international structure. The variation in public sphere structure can perhaps be best presented through a comparison of two ideal types. The Arab order of the 1950–1960s might be characterized as one ideal type, close to Elster's "forum": a strong international public sphere whose norms, media, and imagined consensus dominate the national public. The normative framework to which actions must be justified was located at the regional level. The pursuit of state interests never ceased, but a powerful norm of behavior, a will to consensus, insisted that inter-Arab action should be oriented toward achieving consensus. In contrast, the "Realist ideal type" international structure, like Elster's "market," involves a very weak public sphere, in which actions do not require justification beyond the self-evident assumption of the pursuit of self-interest. The dominant norm is the pursuit of national self-interest defined within a state apparatus insulated from society. Neither ideal type fully captures any empirically existing structure: as much as power permeated the Arabist arena, so did communication and norms structure the classical European balance of power.

This brief contrast between the idealized Arabist public sphere and the idealized Realist public sphere highlights the most important indicators for analyzing the public sphere: the place of the public sphere [to what imagined consensus are claims directed?]; the media of argumentation [how are arguments brought to the public?]; the efficacy of the imperative to justification [to what extent do actors modify their behavior? to what extent does contestation affect actors identities and interests?]; the nature of participation [who can legitimately speak?]; the quality of discourse [what constitutes a good argument?]; and decision rules [how does deliberation affect outcomes?].

1. The Place of the Public Sphere

The most basic variable in public sphere structure is the relationship between the public sphere and the state. The place of the public sphere should be established empirically through quantitative, institutional, and interpretive indicators. The structure of public communication has been empirically measured by researchers such as Karl Deutsch, Ernst Haas, and Bruce Russett: media density, transaction flows, and the relative levels of interaction within and across borders and regions. Patterns of political interaction can be seen in the use of particular media as sites for argumentation. For example, the rise of the Jordanian public sphere in the 1990s can be measured in part by the increasing volume of Jordanian newspapers publishing political analysis and commentary on local issues. The prominence of the Arabist public sphere in the 1960s can partially be seen in the circulation of newspapers across borders and the density of international broadcasting.

Quantitative indicators only partially captures the sense of this variable, however. Location also refers to the "imagined consensus" to which actors direct claims. Participants in a particular public sphere implicitly buy into a specific identity and normative structure. Since public debate aims at swaying some public opinion, the operational question should be "who is the imagined public?" In the Jordanian experience, the imagined public for argumentation during the 1950s was an Arabist public. By contrast, the 1994 debate over the peace treaty revealed a primary locus of argumentation in the Jordanian public sphere. The authors publishing in the 1990s Jordanian print public sphere orient their argumentation toward Jordanian identity, Jordanian interests, Jordanian norms. In each case, public sphere structure is characterized by a clear ranking of public spheres as relevant sites of contestation, in terms of the arguments and justifications presented. The shift from an Arabist to a Jordanian public sphere does not mean that the former ceases to exist, or that the latter emerged out of nothingness. The key question for the researcher can be formulated as such: to what imagined consensus must actors direct justifications in order to establish an authoritative interpretation?

Communicative action in the Arabist public sphere involved three principal fora: the Arab League, international media (broadcasting and the press), and Arab summit meetings. The Arab League never fully filled its intended function as an Arabist forum because of institutional limitations evident from its creation. During the constitutional negotiations over the form of the Arab League, proposals which gave more power to the regional organization were blocked by states anxious to protect their sovereignty. The decision rule of consensus was established specifically in order to prevent the enforcement of Arab decisions (MacDonald 1965; Maddy-Weitzman 1993). While it had symbolic resonance as the institutional manifestation of Arab regional order, the League never played a particularly active role. The Arab League failed to emerge as an authoritative site for the negotiation, contestation and ratification for Arabist norms. Debate within the League remained at a low level, either repeating hollow formulas or concentrating on the details of minor regional cooperative endeavors. The frequent appeals for the reform and revitalization of the League indicate the desire among many intellectuals and political activists for some such public institution that could serve as a differentiated, effective political system, but all such proposals have failed.

Arab summit meetings, from the time of their inception in 1964, played an ambiguous role as the embodiment of the Arab consensus: more effective at producing consensus but also more deeply entrenching the privileged position of states as actors and distancing the consensus from the participation of mass publics. These gatherings of Arab leaders to deal with specific crises became a signally important site for the contestation and evaluation of regional norms (Barnett 1998). The tremendous pressure to arrive at a consensus document at the end of every summit led states who knew that their position could not be reconciled with the Arab consensus to boycott the session rather than prevent consensus. The very act of convening a summit and its attendance took precedence over the contents of its resolutions. For example, "the fact that every single Arab League member except Egypt took part in the Baghdad summit meeting [after Camp David] turned its very convention . . . into an all-Arab court trying Egypt in absentia and unanimously finding it guilty" (MECS 1979: 5).

The emergent centrality of summit meetings had serious implications for the Arabist public sphere. Summit meetings exclude Arab publics, relying on the most rigidly exclusive of participation criteria: only states [and the PLO] and only their sovereign leaders. With the exclusion of non-state actors, the insulation of decision from the mobilized publics of the radio-dominant public sphere, and the secrecy of much of the proceedings, state leaders become far less bound by public norms. In Elster's (1995) terms, the institutions of the Arab summit allowed a move from "open arguing" to "secret bargaining," with the attendant reduction of the dangers of outbidding but also the decline in potency of the "civilizing force" of publicity. With each summit, Arab leaders could emerge with a consensus that redefined Arab norms, with public participation only entering as a latent constraint. Closed meetings of a relatively small number of leaders allowed for more bargaining, fewer audience costs, and less public posturing and denunciation over violations of norms. This allowed for more pragmatic decisionmaking, at the expense of the wide-ranging feelings of belonging through participation. Where the summit meetings served to facilitate consensus among Arab states, they also neutered the Arabist public sphere and contributed to its decline. The rise of the summit is therefore directly related to the increased "Realism" of Arab politics in the 1980s.

The public sphere created by international radio broadcasting represented the primary arena in the 1950–60s for the interpretation of action within a shared normative structure (Boyd 1993; Brown 1975; McDaniel 1980). An extremely dense web of broadcasting from every country, as well as from numerous non-state actors, constituted a forum for the exchange of justifications and interpretations of action. Between 1955 and 1970, radio broadcasting arguably stood as the most relevant site of political communication for the negotiation of consensus on norms, identities, and collective interests. The radio-centric public sphere invited mass participation in politics by speaking directly to mass publics, bypassing state control and the constraints of literacy and wealth associated with the press, and seeking to mobilize mass publics into political action as the instrument for translating discourse into political power. The radio-centric public sphere encouraged argument rather than bargaining, and carried powerful incentives towards outbidding and rhetorical appeals (Elster 1995). After the Arab defeat in 1967, radio broadcasting took substantial blame for distorting the reporting of the war, for misleading Arab publics about their states' capabilities, and for inciting a war for which the states were manifestly unprepared. This critique delegitimized the radio-based public sphere. Radio broadcasting continued, but it lost its privileged normative position as the site of the Arab public dialogue.

Within Jordan, multiple sites of public consensus formation shaped patterns of integration and contestation. In the 1950s, the press located on the West Bank tended to invoke norms and identity claims at odds with those of the Jordanian state. The West Bank public oriented its discourse to the Arabist public sphere, struggling to bring the Jordanian polity into line with Arabist norms and goals and to break the general isolation and insularity that had characterized Transjordan prior to 1950. The political struggles of the 1950s can be characterized as a struggle over the place of the public sphere: would there be an efficacious public sphere?; would it be centered in the relatively autonomous West Bank press or in the state-dominated East Bank media?; and would it be oriented toward the emerging Arabist public sphere? In 1957, after elections won by proponents of Arabism, the regime carried out a coup from above and forcefully repressed political action (Mishal 1978; Dann 1989).

In the 1980s, the struggle over the place of the public sphere inflamed issues inside of the Jordanian state. One survey by a Jordanian academic found a significant difference among urban, rural, and bedouin Jordanians in terms of the media from which they obtained information about candidates in the 1989 elections (Sari 1991). Among urban citizens, 58 percent paid significant attention to the press, compared to 28 percent of those outside the cities. There has been tension between the state and the Islamist movement over the development of mosques into a political public space outside of state control. Equally important is the tension between national and local publics, as tribal leaders resented the usurping of their role in the expression and formation of public opinion at the local level (Layne 1993; Jureidini and McLaurin 1984; Day 1986). The Information Minister resigned, and the debates faded away, but the underlying issues persisted: what should be the balance between a national print public sphere and the traditional private lines of communication and patronage?

The importance of the Palestinian public sphere for many Jordanian citizens as a site of political identity formation and norm contestation complicated the development of any autonomous Jordanian public sphere centered upon Jordanian identity and concerns. The Palestinians after 1967 developed a nonterritorial public sphere in which the independent Palestinian identity emerged as the fundamental, constitutive frame of reference. This public sphere became an active site for the contestation of Palestinian identity, goals, practices, and ideals. "Palestinians" manifested their political identity through participation in the Palestinian public debates. The Palestinian public sphere became distinct precisely when actors began to orient argumentation toward a specifically Palestinian identity and interests, through a set of media created by and for actors espousing the Palestinian identity. A dense field of publications and radio stations provided the media for the exchange of arguments. The PLO and especially the Palestinian National Council represented an institutional manifestation for the authoritative ratification of the norms and goals that developed through public debates. The Palestinian public sphere is an exceptional example of the constitution of political identity through the process of public debate. Many Jordanians, and not only those of Palestinian origin, took this Palestinian public sphere as their primary source of identity and interests, especially in the absence of any compelling, open Jordanian public sphere. The Palestinian public sphere therefore represented a powerful competitor to the emergence of any distinctly Jordanian site for identity and interest formation; only after 1988 would this reality begin to change.

2. Dominant Media of Participation

The dominant media play an important role in both the structure and processes of the public sphere. The relative weight of press, radio, TV, and face to face interaction affects the nature of participation, the content of discourse, the process of deliberation, and the extent of the normative consensus. While I do not make a technological determinist argument, I do argue that the characteristics of the primary media of public discourse profoundly structure that discourse (Dreisler 1997; Thompson 1995). Different media forms create different relations between participants in discourse, and privilege different kinds of arguments. The radio-dominant public sphere of the 1950–1960s empowered mass participation, outbidding in the rapid exchange of claims and counterclaims, and strong Arabist identification. Television, at least in the Arab world, is a more state-centric media. The high startup costs virtually eliminate the possibility of clandestine broadcasting, which contributed to centralizing the position of the sovereign state. Television discourages mass participation, rapid exchange of argument, and direct engagement, instead offering a more unidirectional flow of information and discourse. Underground, clandestine media, whether Xeroxed Samizdat publications or pirated cassettes of Khomeini's sermons, encouraged the emergence of underground, oppositional publics outside the discourse and observation of the state.

Because it was central to the unusually powerful international public sphere of the 1950s–1960s, radio broadcasting merits more attention. The rise of Nasser and the initiation, several years later, of wide scale political broadcasting, represented a structural change in the Arabist public sphere. Radio broadcasting replaced the press as the primary carrier of Arabist public contestation, immensely widening the scope of participation in, or at least consumption of, the political public sphere. From a small elite with very similar ideas about Arab unity, the public now expanded to include the recently mobilized classes. By the early 1960s, most Arab states had their own transmitters and were able to participate in the constant exchange of normative appeals, justifications, accusations, and argumentation which characterized Arabist public debate. This "contributed to a substantial change in the style of conducting international relations in the Arab world" which is inexplicable in neorealist terms (Dawisha 1976). The radio formed a strong sense of relationship among members of this public and enabled the imagined consensus to which claims were addressed. Shifts in the imagined audience of justificatory claims, in the relationship between publics and discourse, in the density of communicative action were independent of shifts in material power capabilities. Arab summitry was begun in the mid-1960s directly in order to remove inter-Arab dialogue from the radio public sphere and to stop the outbidding which was driving Arab conflicts. The radio ceasefire did not last long, primarily because of the power generated by this broadcasting, the temptation to use it, and the need to respond once challenged.

Press, arguably the most amenable media to reasoned discourse, is also the medium most effectively controlled across borders. The circulation of the press across Arab states has generally been small-scaled, unbalanced, and restricted by political censorship (Rugh 1987; Khalidi 1996). Nevertheless, the Arab political press has a long and important history, playing a major role in many of the anticolonial struggles (Khalidi 1996; Ayalon 1995). Virtually every Arab political party or movement has attempted to publish a magazine or newspaper in order to have a voice in the Arabist public sphere and thereby be recognized as an Arab actor. In 1990, according to one survey, 64 percent of Jordanians cited the press as their primary source of political opinion and debate, rather than radio or television (Muhadin 1992). This represents a huge change from the heyday of Arabist radio broadcasting in the 1950s, when large majorities of the public were oriented primarily to the news and heated exchange of opinion over the airwaves.

In the 1980s an Arab emigrant press based primarily in Europe emerged, as Saudi Arabia or Kuwait purchased leading publications, which openly encouraged a new style of discourse characterized by moderation, pragmatism, and abstention from inflammatory rhetoric (Khazen and Atwan 1996). Openly ideological discourse was deemphasized in favor of a pragmatism heavily biased toward the political status quo. This is not to say that this press abandoned norms or ideology—far from it. Instead, it advanced a competing model of the Arabist public sphere, complete with reinterpreted norms, style of discourse, and media. The conservative control of the international Arab press aimed at spreading a distinctive pattern of norms and an interpretation of political reality no less than had the "ideological" press.

Each of these forms of media must be contrasted with face to face communication. In the international arena, Arab summits emerged as an instrument for overcoming the distancing effects of politicized radio broadcasting. By meeting face to face, Arab heads of state sought a new dynamic for the exchange of ideas and arguments, explicitly hoping to bypass the inflammatory rhetoric of the media. These meetings proved far more effective at producing working consensus than did the exchange of accusation and defense over the airwaves. As noted above, however, this pragmatism came at the expense of participation.

Inside of Jordan, the emergence of the print public sphere brought politically important changes to established structures of face to face political communication such as private salons, tribal gatherings, and the royal court. A 1996 survey confirmed the growth of the national press: 52 percent of Jordanians reported regularly reading the daily press and 39 percent read at least one weekly newspaper (Hamarneh 1996a). This might be compared to Lerner's 1950 findings in which a Jordanian sample found 44 percent reading newspapers, but "prefer[ring] newspapers, magazines and books from the more advanced Arab countries to the local product" (Lerner 1958: 310). As government repression of the press increased, readership plummeted in a rational response to the decreasing potential for real public sphere deliberation. In the 1997 survey, overall readership of the daily press fell to 34 percent and readership of the weeklies fell to 17 percent; in the 1998 survey readership fell even further. The fall in readership directly corresponded with increased repression; in 1997 the government passed a "temporary law" in the absence of Parliament which sharply limited the press and drove most of the weeklies out of print (Human Rights Watch 1997; MERIP special report 1998 for details).

The press coexisted uneasily with the *salon*, long the primary site of political debate in Jordan. These gatherings at private homes were the site of relatively unrestrained discourse. After a marked convergence in the early 1990s, the difference between unconstrained salon discourse and relatively bound press discourse rebounded after the peace treaty, to the dismay of liberals. Trends as varied as Transjordanian exclusivism, PLO-Jordanian cooperation, moves to peace with Israel, and political liberalization have all gestated within salons (Sha'ir 1987, 1995; Majali 1995; Sayigh 1997). The private audience with the King had long been the most important route toward efficacy in the Jordanian system. Rather than engaging in public debate through media available to all members of the polity, individuals or groups would directly present their positions to the King and seek to influence his decisions. The emergence of the print public sphere has produced an interesting hybrid of the salon and the private audience. On numerous occasions, King Hussein or Prince Hassan has convened public figures for discussions of particularly contentious issues. These sessions range from meetings with editors and writers to assemblies of politicians and public figures, to hear complaints and explain regime policies. Frank and open discussions focus on the most contentious of issues. They are widely reported in the press, offering a unique combination of face-to-face communication and press publicity. The King regularly holds open meetings and press conferences which are far more open and contentious than most counterparts in the Arab world.

Finally, attention must be paid to the mosque as a site of political communication. As one seasoned observer of the Jordanian polity pointed out in a conference on the media, "the mosque . . . is stronger than all other media.. there are more than 2000 mosques and the number of attendees at the smallest of them probably exceeds the number of readers of many news-

papers or the viewers of most television programs" (Ayesh 1994). Throughout the 1990s, the liberalization of the press has coincided with state efforts
to control the mosques. Members of the Islamic Action Front, including
Parliamentarians, have been banned from delivering *khutba*, the Friday ser-
mon to the gathered worshippers. The King has frequently warned of the
politicization of mosques, but the centrality of the mosque to political communication for a large number of Jordanians is a political fact. The mosque
has become a major dimension of the public sphere in Jordan as in other
Arab states, serving as a location for the creation and defense of identity and
norms and the articulation of interests.

3. Participation

One of the crucial questions in any public sphere, and especially in
international public sphere theory, is the question of who participates. Is an
international public sphere strictly an interstate affair (Barnett 1998), or does
it primarily involve transnational discourse among nongovernmental actors
(Lipschutz 1992)? Every public sphere specifies certain actors as legitimate
participants while explicitly or implicitly excluding others (Benhabib 1996).
Modern international relations uniquely specifies the sovereign state as the
legitimate actor in international institutions, with the idea of the nation-state
legitimating the notion that the state speaks for the nation. Domestic politics
produces a leadership which then speaks in the voice of the people in the
international arena. The proliferation of transnational and nongovernmental
organizations, citizens advocacy campaigns, ethnic and subnational groups,
and other nonstate actors in the international arena challenges this formal
requirement of sovereignty. Studies of international norm formation,
whether of anti-Apartheid (Klotz 1995), chemical weapons (Price 1996),
land mines (Price 1998), or human rights (Keck and Sikkink 1998) demonstrate the powerful voices of nonstate actors in international public
spheres. I take as an empirical question the participation rules and norms
of any public sphere.

Participation in the Arabist radio public sphere was relatively open, in
that radio transmitters were inexpensive, easy to acquire, and cheap to operate. Besides the states, each of which by the early 1960s had at least one
domestic and one foreign broadcast frequency, a wide array of clandestine
radio stations contributed to produce an impressive density of communications. Palestinian broadcasting, from Lebanon and from various friendly
states, was particularly important in contesting the norms of this emergent

mass public (Browne 1975). This is not to say that broadcasting capabilities were evenly divided among actors. Egypt enjoyed a large advantage in broadcasting over most other Arab states. During the 1958 crisis between Jordan and Egypt, Hussein complained bitterly about the imbalance of resources, that Radio Cairo was heard in every coffeehouse in Amman while Radio Amman could barely sustain a 30 mile radius (Hussein 1962: 173). Richard Parker (1996) notes that the United States tried to help Jordan overcome this imbalance, but even providing a stronger transmitter, which was eventually accomplished, "could not supply them with their own Ahmed Sa'id [the popular editorialist of Voice of the Arabs]." As Parker points out, "no one would tune in to Jordan radio except maybe to find out what was going on in Amman." The huge popularity of Egypt's Voice of the Arabs, the wide acceptance of the Nasserist interpretation of Arabism, and, not least, cultural dominance gave Egypt significant power resources. This coincidence between ideology and dominance in public sphere media represented real power, which Nasser well recognized: asked by the UN to rein in Egyptian broadcasting after a Lebanese complaint, he responded: "If you ask me for radio disarmament, you are asking for complete disarmament" (Haykal 1973; Boyd 1977).

Despite the imbalance of resources, participation in the radio public sphere constituted actors as equals at the level of discursive contestation. Access to radio broadcasting equipment was relatively easy, with low capital requirements and few technical demands, which allowed a bewildering array of state and non-state actors to register their voices. Participation in this Arabist public sphere has several characteristics. First, by virtue of having a voice in the public sphere, groups were constituted as actors. Participation itself defined the identity of these groups, and this played an underestimated role in the consolidation of the Palestinian identity. Having a voice, participating in public debate connotes the reality of the group and its recognition by others in their responses to that voice. Second, some degree of formal equality governed this participation, in that a statement by a Palestinian group, when broadcast, took on roughly the same weight as an Egyptian broadcast, in the sense that Jordan felt obligated to respond and offer explanations. A voice heard over the radio challenging King Hussein to justify his decision not to arm the villagers of the West Bank demanded a response over the airwaves. While the source mattered, even the smaller voices could hardly be ignored. Once arguments were put out into the public sphere they demanded a response before the imagined Arab consensus. These three elements of the Arabist radio public sphere are crucially important: the constitution of actors through participation, the formal equality in argumentative status, and the norm of responding to claims.

Participation in the public sphere is intimately tied to the question of sovereignty. Who is authorized to speak in an international public sphere: heads of sovereign states? private individuals? social movements? Arab summits explicitly authorize only heads of state to participate, effectively excluding all other prospective actors. The radio public sphere, by contrast, enabled virtually anyone to register a political opinion and be taken seriously by other participants. Norms of sovereignty designated only states as actors in international society. But this is contingent rather than essential. Any kind of actor could be recognized as such through participation and the acceptance of others. Palestinian participation in the Arabist public sphere was extremely significant for their recognition as an international actor despite their lack of a sovereign state. Public sphere structure specifies which actors can legitimately participate, and whether exclusions are constitutive or incidental.

Participation in the Jordanian public sphere has changed significantly. Prior to 1990, the press was carefully controlled, with a limited number of opinionmakers in the major dailies offering a very narrow range of differences. The independent weekly press of the 1990s opened up dozens of opinion columns a week, which were filled by serious and influential writers and politicians of widely diverse views. Both the number of voices and their quality radically increased. The print public sphere allowed a wide, broadly representative spectrum of opinion to regularly engage in debate about specifically Jordanian issues. Furthermore, it could be reasonably assumed that all public sphere participants and many government decisionmakers regularly read this weekly press and took it seriously. The same cannot be said for the Jordanian electronic media, which remained tightly controlled and restricted to a narrow range of pro-government positions.

Critics of the Jordanian public sphere often attacked its alleged nonrepresentativeness. Particularly since the peace treaty with Israel and the growing conflict between regime and society, official spokesmen have argued that the public sphere does not articulate the beliefs of most Jordanians. King Hussein regularly asserted that the vast majority of Jordanians supported his policies, "no matter what the elite in Amman say." The public sphere expressed the beliefs of a very narrow stratum of elites in the capital, whose political influence and articulate opposition masked their small numbers. At particularly tense moments, Hussein bitterly complained that "there are no media in Jordan that identify with Jordan and its concerns." Such claims are notoriously difficult to prove: it is no easier in Jordan than in the

United States to know whether a "liberal media" misrepresents the real preferences of "the silent majority." Nevertheless, the regular electoral victories of the opposition in the Professional Associations, student organizations, and other civil society institutions gives some credibility to the claim that the public sphere consensus broadly represents the opinions of at least the politicized sectors of society.

4. Efficacy

Describing the location, media, and participation of the public sphere is not sufficient without evaluating its political efficacy. In the 1970s, for example, the Third World succeeded spectacularly at transforming the United Nations into an international forum for political debate and norm formation, but it was relatively ineffective in compelling the powerful states of the North to comply with these the norms and principles in material ways (Krasner 1985). This lack of efficacy, of course, has always been at the heart of the Realist critique of international organizations and norms. But the relationship between public sphere argumentation and material power must be seen as a variable rather than as a constant. It varies with power balances, but also with the legitimacy of the site, the kind of issue, the actors participating.

The efficacy of the Arab public sphere could be seen both in behavior and in the priority granted it by political actors. During the "Arab Cold War," Arabist attacks leveled against Jordan and Lebanon led to domestic uprisings, political mobilization, and a real fear of regime collapse. Egyptian and Syrian broadcasting, mobilizing people as "Arabs" in pursuit of collective Arab identity and interests, had real power. What is often not sufficiently appreciated is that this mobilization was not a simple reflection of material power relations. Arab publics judged arguments, not only power relations. Actors advanced competing frames based on Arab identity and interests, and publics judged these frames rationally. The common picture of inflamed masses responding to emotional appeals does not fully capture the extent to which politicians weighed competing claims and attempted to determine the best way to achieve Arab interests. Jordan's response to an Egyptian broadcast had to be framed as a reasoned argument defending Jordan's position, or at least as a counterattack contesting Egypt's interpretation or sincerity. Even Egypt, by far the most powerful Arab state, could be compelled into action by well-conceived broadcasts by weaker rivals. Most analysts agree that the Egyptian actions in 1967 which led to the Six Day War were in large part driven by the challenges to Nasser's Arabism leveled by Syrian and Jordanian radio broadcasting. Needing to respond convincingly, Nasser took increasingly costly and provocative steps toward Israel, contributing to the spiral of crisis behavior culminating in the Israeli surprise attack.

The efficacy of the public sphere should be broken down into two analytical categories: constraining and enabling. This distinction becomes crucial for comparing rationalist and constructivist public sphere theories. The public sphere as constraint marks the modified rationalist conception: to what extent does public opinion constrain the behavior of state actors? Efficacy would be defined as the extent to which a publicly articulated position succeeds in forcing state actors to act contrary to their interpretation of their interests. In the Gulf crisis, for example, many rationalist analysts accept that the intensity and unanimity of Jordanian public opinion's support for Iraq compelled King Hussein to refuse to join the American coalition against state interests. The constructivist conception of efficacy incorporates an enabling dimension: to what extent does participation in public sphere discourse change actors' conception of their identity and/or interests? Did engagement with this Jordanian public opinion persuade Jordanian policymakers of the appropriate course of action?

5. Quality of Discourse

It is also necessary to consider the actual discourse within these structures (Habermas 1996: 304). Is there communicative action oriented toward achieving consensus, or is there only strategic action? An effective public sphere is one in which rational-critical debate oriented toward consensus is carried out within the structures of public discourse. In other words, it is not sufficient to only note "media proliferation" (Calhoun 1992: 276). It is also necessary to analyze the rational-critical potential, even if unrealized, of the discourse within these media. How do these media structures contribute to the constitution of community and to collective will-formation? To what extent are norms subject to rational criticism? What are the criteria for judging between arguments? Is consensus achieved through rational debate or compelled by power?

In terms of the quality of discourse, the communicative practices of international relations in the Arab world have often been characterized by a large gap between programmatic appeals to Arab unity and self-interested state behavior. Since 1967 this divergence has led to a reevaluation of the structural features of Arab politics by Arab critics, as well as by Western commentators, who rather smugly point to the divergence between Arabist proclamations and state-centric action in order to dismiss the significance of Arabism (Ajami 1991). Many observers have been content to explain this feature of Arab politics purely in terms of Arab culture or, even more prob- lematical, in terms of unique features of the "Arab mind" (Said 1979, 1994). Journalistic and scholarly accounts of Arab politics alike attribute the gap between action and words to deeply rooted cultural history, to religion, to the distinctiveness of the Arabic language. Innovative social theory in the Arab world itself is devoted to explaining the formation of a uniquely Arab reason and its shortcomings in the field of public discourse (Jabiri 1992; Ghalyun 1985). A structural approach based on the public sphere can offer an alternative explanation for these observations. Divergence between jus- tificatory claims in the public sphere and self-interested action is a funda- mental characteristic of politics: the difference between Arab and Western international relations is one of degree, not of kind, and this difference can be explained by structural variables. The failure of most American politicians to deliver on their campaign promises is rarely taken to mean a unique American mind incapable of matching words and deeds. Arabism should be analyzed as a discourse specific to and rational within a particular public sphere structure, rather than as an aberration from "normal" politics.

The critique from within the Arab public sphere of the pathologies of Arab discourse highlights the political relevance of this issue. The selling of the state's Realist agenda in Jordan, as in much of the Arab world, has been predicated upon the devaluation of the norms of Arabism. Most recent anal- ysis of interaction within the Arab public sphere has focused on "patholo- gies," the tendencies toward "outbidding, ideological grandstanding, accu- sations, impracticality, threats, zero-sum mentalities" and irrationality which supposedly characterize Arab discourse. And yet, most Arab leaders are seen by other policymakers as extremely shrewd, calculating, and rational in their behavior. This strongly indicates that the so-called irrationality of Arab be- havior has more to do with the public sphere structures in which Arab lead- ers must justify their actions than with individual psychology or cultural pathology.

An example of the quality of discourse as a public sphere variable can be seen in one of the most pressing questions Jordanians have faced in their construction of a public sphere: "intellectual terrorism." Many critics com- plain that Jordanian public debate has tended to be dampened by the brow- beating tactics of opinion leaders who prevent the expression of independent critical thought. As direct state repression retreated, societal pressure to con- formity took its place. Can a public discourse characterized by rigidly enforced unities of thought really be considered a public sphere? While the concerns about the potential repression inherent in the demand for consensus are valid, I would contest this description of the Jordanian public sphere. Despite the complaints of many writers who feel persecuted for their views, the evidence does not suggest that intellectual terrorism rules the Jordanian public sphere. Those authors who have expressed controversial opinions in the press have met with little retaliation; even the most extreme have only on rare occasions failed to find an outlet for their ideas. This is particularly the case since the popular consensus has often run against the will of the state, meaning that the means of coercion do not support the "intellectual" pressures. The "excesses" of the weekly press, and their alleged abdication of the responsibility which comes with freedom, became the major justification for the regime crackdown after 1995. American observers seem drawn to this idea of social compulsion; the assumption that such attitudes are the artificial product of indoctrination and the enforcement of political correctness protects them from being forced to grapple with the possibility that such positions have rational or reasonable bases (J. Miller 1996). The extent to which intellectual terrorism deters effective public sphere debate is nevertheless an important variable for assessing the quality of discourse, and as such should be taken seriously.

6. Decision Rules

No matter how effective the deliberative process, it is unlikely to produce a universal consensus, and eventually a decision will have to be made (Johnson and Knight 1997). Unresolvable differences of interest, time constraints, and other well-known problems intervene in the production of consensus. Indeed, even the demand for consensus can be seen as oppressive of difference and individual autonomy (Young 1996; Rescher 1993). While the point of deliberation is at least in part to transform preferences by producing shared frames of reference and shared conceptions of interest, it is unrealistic—and not necessarily desirable—to expect that all actors will adopt identical preferences. Therefore, as Habermas recognizes as well as do rationalist commentators, the political system must at some point end deliberation and make a decision. This decision can more or less accurately reflect the outcome of deliberation, but as rational choice theory has effectively demonstrated, will never transparently reflect actor preferences. Decision rules, or the procedure by which individual preferences are aggregated into a collective decision, have a strong independent impact on outcomes.

In the Arab arena, the decision rule has been consensus. This strong decision rule has often been blamed for the weakness of Arab institutions, since any consensus will reflect a lowest common denominator and will tend to avoid decisive action. Nevertheless, Arab League decisions are only binding upon those who accept them. Therefore, participation in an Arab Summit is tantamount to accepting the consensus achieved therein; where an unacceptable consensus is expected, Arab states prefer to boycott the Summit. While persuasion is often enhanced by the provision of positive sanctions, especially financial incentives from Gulf states, pure coercion and threats are excluded from this discourse. Negative sanctions can be applied against defectors, with the most prominent example being the expulsion of Egypt from the Arab League after its independent peace with Israel. In that case, Iraq drove the production of the Arab consensus; Iraqi and Gulf money provided material incentives to the frontline states (Jordan, Syria) to not join Egypt; and analysis of Camp David convinced the Arab public sphere that its provisions did not serve Arab interests. The failure of the 1990 Cairo Summit to find an Arab consensus on a response to the Iraqi invasion of Kuwait effectively destroyed Arab institutions for years.

Jordanian decision rules represent a more familiar example: an authoritarian system which is relatively open to public deliberation but retains executive power. As a constitutional monarchy, the Jordanian political system is designed to concentrate power in the throne, while also maintaining consultative bodies and an institutional structure of modern government. In 1989, the push to liberalization energized Parliament as well as the public sphere, generating a tremendous amount of public deliberation on controversial issues. As long as this deliberation produced broadly acceptable results—support for the severing of ties, support for Iraq, a National Charter— the government accepted and encouraged debate. When public deliberation began producing results contrary to the preferences of the King—over the peace process, relations with Iraq, and economic reforms—the executive branch reasserted its autonomy. Despite the furious resistance of the public sphere, little could be done to resist executive decisions within the bounds of Jordanian political rules, and few expressed an interest in extralegal or violent opposition. In the summer of 1996, for example, the decision to increase the price of bread was preceded by a spirited, reasoned, high quality debate, in which Prime Minister Kabariti actively engaged with opposition arguments. However, when this dialogue rejected the increased bread prices, Kabariti abruptly implemented his prior decision and ended the dialogue. The riots which followed could be traced as much to the violation of the rules of deliberation as to the increased prices themselves, which were compensated and had few immediate effects on the cost of living. The important point is that executive (monarchical) power carried the expectation of legitimation through *hiwar*.

Conclusion

The Arab and Jordanian public spheres underwent profound structural changes in the period covered by this book. The Arabist arena had been experiencing a relatively consensual period in the late 1980s, with the formation of the Arab Cooperation Council (Iraq, Egypt, Jordan, and Yemen) in 1989 signaling the apparent emergence of a new subregional axis in the Arab heartland and the reintegration of Egypt into the Arab order. In 1990, the foundations of the Arabist public sphere were shattered, perhaps irrevocably, by the Iraqi invasion of Kuwait and the failure of Arab summitry to find an Arab solution to the conflict. The Gulf crisis effectively ended Arab summits, creating deep rifts between Arab states and shattering the belief in both the will to Arab consensus and the meaning of Arab norms (Sayigh 1991). In terms of the Arab public sphere, Iraq became a pariah state, as most Arab states honored the international sanctions regime and refused to reintegrate Iraq into the Arab order. Huge popular sympathy for the suffering of the Iraqi people was expressed throughout most Arab public sphere platforms, but this did not translate into state action. Indeed, the contrast between official positions and popular sympathies encouraged the repression of the moves toward liberalization seen in many Arab states in the late 1980s. Only with the near-collapse of the Arab-Israeli peace process after the election of Benjamin Netanyahu in the summer of 1996 did some semblance of an Arabist order begin to re-emerge.

The Jordanian public sphere underwent equally dramatic transformation in this period. The uprisings of 1989 led to an unprecedented liberalization, including relatively free Parliamentary elections, the legalization of political parties, and a remarkably open and contentious press. After Jordan's position in the Gulf crisis led to its ostracization from the mainstream Arab public sphere, the Jordanian public sphere became even more central to Jordanian political deliberation. The open and contentious press flourished until 1994, when the Jordanian government began its moves toward a peace treaty with Israel. During the negotiations and the conclusion of the peace treaty, the government became increasingly repressive of the press, but did not shut it down completely. Indeed, the struggles by politicians and journalists to

maintain an open public sphere became a central feature in the configu-
ration of that public sphere, as actors avowed the value of their participation
in this Jordanian public deliberation, even where they disagreed about the
issues under deliberation. Nevertheless, as deliberation produced and reflected public opinion hostile to government policies toward Israel, Iraq,
political freedoms, and the economy, the state clamped down even harder.
In 1997, the government issued a repressive new Press and Publications
Law—eventually found unconstitutional by the Jordanian Supreme
Court—and used it to shut down a number of the most outspoken independent political newspapers. This temporary law was followed by the passage
of a hugely contentious new permanent Press and Publications Law in 1998,
institutionalizing the relative closure of the public sphere. By the fall of 1998,
however, the regime relaxed its grip, appointing a relatively liberal Prime
Minister and initiating a new round of *hiwar*.

These structural changes in the Arab and Jordanian public spheres therefore frame the public deliberations discussed in the rest of the book. The
collapse of the Arabist public sphere and the rise, and subsequent attempts
to close, the Jordanian public sphere constitute the social structure of international politics of the period. I argue in the remainder of this book that the
shift in the location and efficacy of deliberation, between and within public
spheres, powerfully affect Jordan's articulation of state interests and its strategic choices.

3 Who Says Jordan Is Palestine?

King Hussein announced on July 31, 1988 that he had de-
cided to sever administrative ties between Jordan and the West Bank, officially accepting the permanent loss of half the kingdom. This decision
shocked most observers, who assumed that a dominant position in the West
Bank represented a primary interest governing Jordanian foreign policy.
While Jordan routinely changed its strategies toward the West Bank in response to shifts in threat, power, and opportunity, change in Jordanian preferences with regard to the final status of the West Bank hardly seemed
conceivable. The severing of ties was interpreted as part of the ongoing
strategic interaction with Israel and the PLO. Nevertheless, despite predictions that Jordan would renew its bid for the West Bank when the opportunity arose, it did not. This chapter explores the decision to sever ties,
evaluating rationalist and constructivist hypotheses; chapter 4 explores the
question of whether Jordan's identity and interests changed.

I advance a public sphere explanation for the decision and its consequences based on both strategic interaction and communicative action. The
decision to sever ties followed strategic logic, in which the stakes and the
opportunities were shaped by shifts in public conceptions of Jordanian and
Palestinian identity. The reception of the decision within the Arabist public
sphere involved communicative deliberation aimed at securing an Arabist
consensus about the meaning of the decision. Over the course of this competitive framing, Jordan sent increasingly costly signals, behavioral and discursive, to confirm the sincerity of the severing of ties, culminating in the

decision to recognize the declaration of a Palestinian state. Jordanian policy became bound when the Arabist deliberation produced a consensus interpretation favorable to Jordan. After 1989, debate about Jordanian state and national identity after the severing of ties erupted inside a reconfigured Jordanian public sphere. This deliberation produced a powerful consensus around a Jordanian state identity separate from Palestine, generating dramatically different conceptions of Jordanian interests in the West Bank and facilitating the Jordanian move to a peace treaty with Israel. The initial strategic decision thus became the object of a communicative dialogue, first in the Arabist and then in the Jordanian public sphere, which produced a substantively new consensus on Jordanian identity and interests.

The second crucial issue is the stability of preferences: did the severing of ties change Jordanian interests in the West Bank? I argue that this case represents a major example of change of underlying preferences over outcomes in the process of strategic interaction, with extremely significant empirical and theoretical implications. Rationalism and constructivism offer substantively different predictions about subsequent Jordanian behavior, based primarily on the core claims about change in identity and interests. From a rationalist perspective, the severing of ties changed the strategies of various actors, but did not fundamentally affect their interests or identities. Jordan stepped back from the struggle over the West Bank in order to better achieve its underlying preferences, but did not change in any real sense. The constructivist position, in contrast, argues that the severing of ties between Jordan and the West Bank produced a major turning point in the political life of Jordan which went beyond positions, affecting basic identity and interests. Close ties to the West Bank, long considered a basic and primary interest, came to be interpreted as a threat. A Palestinian state, long seen as a threat, came to be seen as an essential partner for maintaining stability. Both theoretical approaches make specific and falsifiable predictions about behavior. The rationalist position suggests that Jordan would reverse its disengagement from the West Bank should the opportunity present itself. The constructivist position suggests that if a new consensus has been secured on Jordanian identity, then Jordan would not reassert its claim to the West Bank even if circumstances turned in its favor. In chapter 4 I evaluate converging streams of evidence, including changes in Jordanian institutions, shifts in identity discourse, and Jordanian behavior toward the West Bank and the PLO as a test of these hypotheses.

This change in Jordanian preferences does not offer support for fluidly changing identity or interests. Indeed, what makes the change so interesting and important is precisely the consistency of Jordanian concerns in the preceding decades. The West Bank was a fundamental part of Jordan's avowed state identity, posited as essential to Jordanian interests, and a major dimension of all Jordanian foreign policy strategies. Despite intense Arab pressures, uninterest among Palestinians, and serious internal challenges, the Jordanian regime maintained its preference for a leading position in the West Bank. While Jordan altered its strategies in response to changing circumstances, its interests remained the same. The rise of the PLO, the Israeli capture of the West Bank, Black September, and repeated expressions of the Arab consensus all failed to change Jordan's preferences. The West Bank, constructed as a fundamental part of Jordanian identity, stood as the centerpiece of Jordanian interests. Between 1967 and 1988, Jordanian behavior conformed to what would be expected on the basis of this stable preference; even when Jordan backed away from its claim on the West Bank, such as in 1974, it always sought an opening for a reassertion of influence. The burden of proof, therefore, is on my argument that after 1988—unlike all earlier periods— Jordanian preferences changed.

Severing ties required a struggle to establish interpretive frames within multiple public spheres: Jordanian, Arabist, international. By 1988, the international consensus clearly accepted the difference between Palestine and Jordan and the artificiality of their union. Decades of Arab and Palestinian persuasion had succeeded in establishing this consensus for virtually everyone except for Israel—and for Jordan. The severing of ties, and the communicative deliberation which it initiated, aimed above all at demonstrating Jordan's sincere commitment to this evident international consensus. The disengagement took on meaning as a political act through public debate in these interconnected and competitive public spheres. Within each, actors struggled to render competing interpretations authoritative by imposing a frame. During the course of competitive framing, Jordan was bound by its discourse and its arguments. This interpretive struggle did not simply complement the "real" disengagement: to the extent that actors made decisions based on them, the interpretations were the reality. Since the Israeli occupation of the West Bank remained unaffected by the claims and counterclaims of Jordan and the PLO, the situation on the ground scarcely changed. At stake in the severing of ties were claims to represent the Palestinian people, claims largely without empirical referent. To a large degree, the severing of ties and what followed nvolved only claims, interpretations, and understandings. For these struggles, material power is important but not determinate. The ability to produce a consensus frame, to draw effectively on the norms of a particular public sphere, to claim to speak in the name of a collectivity, and to construct effective arguments, should be considered real power resources.

To anticipate the argument of chapter 4, the move from deliberation in the Arabist arena to the Jordanian public sphere was the decisive point in transforming Jordan's preferences. The 1988 severing of ties with the West Bank, combined with the unprecedented opening of the Jordanian public sphere in 1989, unleashed the first serious public discussion of Jordanian identity in the history of the Jordanian public sphere. This public debate transformed prevailing conceptions of Jordanian identity and interests. By the early 1990s, this debate produced an effective consensus on the formula of "Jordan is Jordan and Palestine is Palestine," with Jordan defined in terms of East Bank borders. Conceptions of interests shifted in response to this change in identity, strongly supporting the constructivist position on interests. This changing sense of identity and interests best explains Jordanian positions on Palestinian-Israeli final status issues, including the high levels of coordination between Jordan and the Palestine National Authority (PNA) and Jordan's outspoken support for a Palestinian state. This consensus did not extend to the question of internal identity, however, with the status of Jordanians of Palestinian origin remaining a crucial unresolved question for the Jordanian political system.

In the first section of this chapter, I establish the consistency and centrality of Jordan's preference for a leading role in the West Bank, demonstrating that this role was a fundamental component of Jordan's conception of interests, deeply rooted in identity, institutions, and norms. In the second section, I analyze several earlier controversies over Jordan's relations with the West Bank, and demonstrate both the strategic nature of Jordan's actions—in that its preferences toward the West Bank remained stable—and the ways in which the public sphere shaped Jordan's discursive strategies. In the final section, I analyze the severing of ties and show why the Arabist dialogue in 1988 produced a dramatic change in Jordan's strategies, which later led to a transformation in Jordanian preferences.

Jordanian-Palestinian Relations in the Arabist Public Sphere

The annexation of the West Bank in 1950 transformed Transjordan into the Hashemite Kingdom of Jordan, composed of two national communities with potentially divergent understandings of state interests. While some ethnic differences divided the two communal groups, such as the largely bedouin character of Transjordanian society, they were not divided by language, religion, or culture. Integration into a single Jordanian identity within shared state institutions was encouraged by the Arabist discourse of the Hashemite regime, which did not belong to either ethnic/national group. The national identity of the communal groups was reinforced by the demands of international argumentation, however, especially the drive to develop the Palestinian national identity. Both Jordan and the PLO actively constructed national identities, with the loyalties of the Palestinian citizens of Jordan falling between the competing claims. Each wave of Palestinian refugees altered communal identities and relations. Debate over Jordan's identity overlapped between domestic and international public spheres, despite Jordanian efforts to remove its national identity from the realm of legitimate international debate. The purpose of this section is not to present a detailed political history of the Jordanian-Palestinian relationship (Bailey 1984; Day 1986), but to explore two issues: first, the development of Jordanian discourse about the relationship between the West Bank and Jordanian identity; second, Arabist deliberation about this relationship.

Jordan's identity was deeply interwoven with international debates about Palestinian and Arab identity. Palestinians developed a strong sense of distinctive identity within the broader framework of Arabism in their confrontation with the Zionist movement and the British mandate (Khalidi 1996). After the merger in 1950, the state attempted to merge Transjordanian and Palestinian identities into a single unitary Jordanian identity. As the Palestinian identity submerged into Arabism in the 1950s and 1960s, this project could be plausibly framed in Arabist terms as a normatively valued "unification" rather than an imposed "annexation." However critical most Arabists were of Jordanian policies with regard to Israel and the West, Arabist unity discourse made it very difficult to justify calls for the division of an Arab state into two smaller units. Political opposition tended to be cast in ideological, rather than communal, terms; even resentment over the dominant position of Transjordanians or of the relative underdevelopment of the West Bank was largely expressed in terms of distributional demands within the framework of a single entity (Mishal 1977, Cohen 1982, Plascov 1981, Dann 1989). Challenges to Jordan's borders called not for the creation of a smaller Palestinian entity but for Jordan's dissolution and merger into a larger Arab entity. After Jordan lost control of the West Bank in 1967, the integrationist position became increasingly untenable. Rather than a call to separate the West Bank from Jordan, appeals could now be framed in terms of liberating the West Bank from Israel. Jordan's increasing need to articulate and defend the principle of a single political identity in the early 1970s served notice on the breakdown of the unitary identity claim. By 1974, Jordan had been forced to recognize the Arab consensus in favor of the PLO claim to represent the Palestinian people.

Because of the centrality of the Palestine issue to the Arabist public sphere, the Jordanian-Palestinian relationship represented a major issue in Arabist argumentation. Jordan constantly needed to justify and defend its position in the Arabist public sphere, with important implications both for foreign policy—the need to live up to its proclaimed beliefs to maintain credibility—and for domestic politics—the need to maintain control of the internal arena to avoid undermining the unitary Jordanian voice in the Arabist arena. The official discourse of the Jordanian state toward the Jordanian-Palestinian relationship passed through several identifiable stages in the ongoing process of political struggle and dialogue, each based on a different conception of state identity: from a recognition of difference; to formal unity and the denial of difference; to a federal scheme and a competition for representation; to a confederal proposal in cooperation with the PLO; to recognition of two distinct sovereignties.

Prior to 1948, Transjordanian discourse recognized the difference between the Palestinian and Transjordanian entities. While Abdullah looked to Palestine as an outlet for his Greater Syria ambitions, he did not consider Jordan and Palestine to be a single entity, or Jordanians and Palestinians to be a single people (Wilson 1987, Nevo 1996). Many authors have argued that Transjordan lacked a nationalist movement in this time period, primarily because it did not have the urban centers with the notable classes which tended to lead these movements; Wilson (1987) claims that the British even tried to create a nationalist movement to pressure Abdullah. Jordanian nationalist scholarship has attempted to refute this historical claim, pointing to national congresses and political parties formed in the late 1920s as evidence of the national consciousness of the Transjordanian population under the mandate (Hattar 1985; Muhafiza 1990; Rogan and Tell 1994; T. Tal 1996). The evidence suggests that Transjordanian actors supported the Palestinian struggle, but recognized the distinctiveness of the two arenas.

The annexation of the West Bank followed from the Arab Legion's success in occupying many of the portions of the Palestine mandate assigned to the Arabs by the UN partition plan. Abdullah convened a national conference in Jericho which voted to unite the Palestinian areas under the control of the Arab Legion with Transjordan. In the unitary constitutional framework of the new state, shared institutions were meant to produce a single Jordanian identity. All citizens were to be considered Jordanian and expressions of Palestinian identity were repressed. The unity of the two banks became deeply embedded in the identity and institutions of the state, underlying its discourse and behavior, and shaping Jordanian understandings of Arabism. Because the dominant conceptions of Arabism discouraged the assertion of any *wataniya* identity, including Palestinian, it provided Jordan with a powerful discursive tool for justifying the incorporation of Palestinians. The merger could be normatively defended as a successful example of Arabist unification, while calls to end it could be dismissed as illegitimate separatism. On the other hand, the perceived illegitimacy of Hashemite Arabism and the suspicion of their collusion with Israel left Jordan always on the defensive.

The formation of the PLO, following discussions of a Palestinian entity in the early 1960s, came in the context of Arabist public sphere competition (Farsoun and Zacharia 1997; Cobban 1984; Tessler 1994; Gresh 1989; Shemesh 1996). As Egypt and Iraq advanced competing proposals, the idea emerged that a Palestinian entity should be created out of Egyptian controlled Gaza and Jordanian controlled West Bank. Jordan strongly objected, arguing that the West Bank was now a fully equal part of the Hashemite Kingdom. Palestinian activism should be oriented toward Israel, not toward an Arab state with which they had freely unified. Egypt rejected the unification, arguing that Jordan only held the West Bank in trust for the Palestinian people. In the context of this Arabist argumentation, Jordan needed to tightly control internal debate in order to prevent any appeals for the separation of the West Bank from Jordan. Jordan appealed to potent Arab unity norms, asking how the division of an Arab state into two Arab states could possibly meet Egyptian norms of Arab unity. Given the Arab decision rule of consensus, the assumed Jordanian veto prevented the realization of the Palestinian Entity. No conception of Jordanian interests, whether statist, Hashemite, or Arabist, could be reconciled with allowing the West Bank to be detached from the Kingdom and made into a Palestinian Entity.

The PLO was created by an Arab summit in 1964. Whatever the instrumental functions of the PLO's creation in enhancing the control of Palestinian action by Arab states, its impact was to articulate a particular national claim for the Palestinians. Jordan's acceptance of the Arab consensus in support of the PLO rested on an agreement not to locate Palestinian national demands in the West Bank or Jordan, and on Jordanian hopes that it could use its large concentration of Palestinians as leverage to gain control of the

PLO. In its early stages, the PLO adopted an Arabist approach to the struggle for Palestinian liberation. While Shuqayri clashed with King Hussein, the PLO at this time generally oriented its policy toward Palestinian self-determination in Israel and maintained an uneasy modus vivendi with regard to Jordan. Jordan would support the struggle for Palestinian self-determination inside of Israel, as long as the PLO did not challenge the Jordanian identity of its Palestinian citizens. This uneasy compromise never stabilized, but facilitated short-term coexistence.

Although the loss of the West Bank to Israel in 1967 forced Jordan to reconfigure its strategy, the regime resisted efforts to reconfigure state identity or its preferences over outcomes. Rather than accept the PLO claim to hold the right to struggle for the liberation of the West Bank, Jordan fought to maintain its claim to the occupied territories. Jordanian arguments foundered against the growing popularity of the PLO, but were strengthened by the Israeli and American refusal to accept the PLO as a partner in negotiations. In the postwar environment, the Palestinian Resistance emerged as the most potent expression of nationalism in the Arab world, carrying Jordan in its wake. Jordan emerged as the primary location of Palestinian institutions and armed struggle. The Arab order attempted to mediate the growing tension between Jordanian sovereignty and Palestinian institutions, most notably in the Cairo Agreement. The fundamental question came down to one of sovereignty: was this an internal Jordanian affair having to do with civil order, as Jordan claimed, or was it an Arab affair having to do with the survival of the Palestinian issue? This debate, unlike most, Jordan effectively won: state sovereignty outweighed the normative commitment to the Palestinian struggle.

In September 1970, the Jordanian state reasserted its authority, violently expelling the PLO. Black September has been framed as a Jordanian-Palestinian civil war, an interpretation that has shaped all subsequent interactions between the two national groups. In fact, significant numbers of Transjordanians participated in the Resistance, while important parts of the established Palestinian elite at least tacitly supported the state's reassertion of control. The communal conflict did drive rising *iqlimiya* (communal chauvinism) in both the Palestinian and Jordanian communities, generating collective fear and mistrust as well as stronger communal identities (Sayigh 1997). Black September effectively ended the PLO challenge to the internal power structure of Jordan, and deeply affected all future political calculations of every Palestinian and Jordanian citizen. On the other hand, by delegitimating Jordan's claim to represent the will of the Palestinians, Black

September weakened Jordanian argumentation in the Arabist public sphere. The use of military force demonstrated the absence of any uncoerced Jordanian identity inclusive of Palestinians, and thus increased the power of the PLO claim to represent a distinctive Palestinian identity.

In March 1972, King Hussein outlined a new Jordanian position: the United Arab Kingdom. The UAK offered a federal constitutional structure, with self-governing Palestinian and Jordanian regions and a central federal government based in Amman under the Hashemite monarchy. While maintaining federal unity, the UAK clearly recognized the distinction between the West and East Banks, which earlier Jordanian discourse had rejected. The UAK still envisioned the West Bank as an integral part of Jordan, and the Palestinians as part of the Jordanian people. The UAK was almost unanimously denounced, with a firm consensus expressed by Palestinian factions and by the key Arab states against the proposal (Shemesh 1996; Hassan 1972; Maqsoud 1972). Public debate was almost exclusively located in the Arabist arena, despite Hussein's assertions of widespread Jordanian and Palestinian support. While King Hussein consulted members of the Jordanian political elite, the proposal did not become a topic of public debate in an open Jordanian public sphere (S. Tal 1994). Instead, argumentation was oriented toward an Arabist consensus, with the Jordanian state speaking as a unitary actor, engaging in dialogue with Palestinian factions and Arab states. Black September was repeatedly invoked in these debates as evidence of Hussein's intention to "liquidate" the Palestinian issue, or of Palestinian intentions to take over Jordan. In the aftermath of those traumatic conflicts, who could have faith in Hussein's good intentions or his legitimacy among Palestinians?

The 1974 Rabat summit, which confirmed the PLO as the sole legitimate representative of the Palestinian people, involved significant argumentation at the Arabist level. The Jordanian public remained an audience, not a participant, in these debates about their identity. That Rabat coincided with an intense internal Palestinian debate over whether to pursue a policy oriented toward the West Bank and Gaza rather than all of Palestine is of obvious importance, as the Arabist consensus responded not only to shifting evaluations of Jordan's claims but also to the changing PLO discourse (Muharrib 1975).[1] Palestinians engaged in deep deliberation over the lessons of Black September, which shaped their approach to their national struggle (Hindi 1971; Allush 1972; Hassan 1972). Jordan's acceptance of the Rabat decision was compelled by strategic, rather than persuaded by communicative, action. Jordan nevertheless preferred to remain inside an undesirable consensus than to be outside it. Jordan adhered to the Rabat resolutions while continuing to compete with the PLO wherever possible. Again, Jordan's strategies changed, but not its preferences over outcomes. Since the Rabat discourse took place at the state level, and was not then embedded in Jordanian institutions, discourse, or practice, it failed to bring about any significant change in Jordanian identity or interests.

The 1985 Jordanian-Palestinian agreement proposed a confederation between two independent states, rather than the federal formula of the UAK. Unlike the UAK, confederation was negotiated and proposed by Jordan and the PLO jointly, with Arafat winning PNC consent over strong internal objections (Hassan 1985). Confederation was presented as a formula that might minimally satisfy Palestinian desire for sovereignty, Jordanian preferences for close links to the West Bank, and Israeli fears of a Palestinian state. Confederation recognized a much greater degree of difference and independence between two distinct political units than did the UAK, while maintaining the idea that a special relationship bound the two units. The West Bank maintained its position in Jordanian identity discourse, however, despite some institutional reform and public discussion of Jordanian identity (Day 1986). In February 1986, Jordan suspended its cooperation with the PLO, arguing that Arafat had failed to deliver on his promises to change Palestinian policy in order to enter the peace process. Hussein blamed the PLO and declared that Jordan would pursue its own options for peace. Jordan's new strategy included the launching of a major development plan for the West Bank, intended to win popular support for the Jordanian role, and secret negotiations with Foreign Minister Shimon Peres about the possibility of an Israeli/Jordanian condominium over the West Bank. The return to Jordanian claims on the West Bank in 1986 demonstrate the strategic nature of Jordan's strategy in the 1985 agreement. The negotiations with the PLO had not put Jordan's identity at stake, and had not generated significant communicative action within a Jordanian public sphere about the implications for Jordan's identity. When the Intifada broke out in late 1987, Jordan was again engaged in strategic competition with the PLO over influence in the West Bank.

The changing meaning of the idea that "Jordan is Palestine" helps to illuminate the complex relationship between struggles over state identity and international strategic interaction. Prior to 1967, "Jordan is Palestine" was an integral part of the Hashemite effort to assimilate the West Bank. In the period of crisis with the PRM, the Hashemites found this slogan turned against them by Palestinian groups who suggested that the Jordanian claim to Palestine justified their seizure of power in Jordan. Building on old Revisionist themes, prominent Israelis also suggested that creating a Palestinian state in the East Bank might solve Israel's problems. Israel's entry into the discursive fray fundamentally changed the concept, by shifting the public sphere in which the question was debated and the stakes of the debate. Sharon's "Jordan is Palestine" carried a very different connotation than did Hussein's invocation of the same words. By the early 1980s, the equivalence between Jordan and Palestine which had been such an important part of Jordanian argumentation a decade earlier had now become a threat to be fiercely rejected in every setting. While Israelis pointed to earlier Hashemite statements to justify their own argument, this misappropriation more demonstrates the importance of public sphere structure for shaping discourse than it does the "truth" of Israeli arguments. Between the 1960s and the 1980s, then, the claim that "Jordan is Palestine" changed from a weapon in the hands of the Hashemites against "separatists"; to a weapon in the hands of Palestinians against the Hashemites; to a weapon in the hands of the Israelis against the PLO.

The Severing of Ties

King Hussein's framing of the severing of ties stressed Jordan's determination to strengthen the Palestinian position in the international arena and to implement the Arab consensus. The severing of ties meant that Jordan no longer claimed sovereignty over the West Bank, would no longer seek to negotiate on its behalf, and would no longer compete for influence among West Bank Palestinians. Despite speculation about the possibility of such a step after the June 1988 Algiers Arab summit, which had reendorsed PLO representation of the Palestinians and pledged support for the Intifada without Jordanian participation, the disengagement still took nearly everyone by surprise. Analysis remained guided by the assumption of Jordan's permanent, unchanging interest in the West Bank: "Jordan will remain condemned by its geography . . . there is no way [it] can opt out."[2] Shimon Peres (1995, p. 304), for example, believes that "even after he opted out, the King still expected to be invited back in."

The uncertainty caused by the Jordanian disengagement cannot be overemphasized. Some Jordanian role, whether advocated or rejected, had been a basic component of virtually every actor's positions toward the West Bank. Strategic framing assumes particular importance in crisis situations in which actors cannot comfortably rely upon preconceived ideas about their interests (Bohman 1996). The decision to sever ties was such a disruptive moment, significantly altering expectations and understandings: "It is forcing open all the congealed assumptions, confronting Palestinians, Israelis and outside players with a whole new set of questions."[3] Cultivated ambiguity, the sheer complexity of the situation, and the conflicting interests of numerous actors hindered any simple interpretation. Only after a raucous emergency session did the PLO leadership welcome the Jordanian decision. Many Arab states took a wait-and-see attitude, unconvinced of Jordan's sincerity. In Israel, the Labor Party attempted to minimize the move and keep the Jordan Option alive. Some elements of the Likud took the decision as an invitation to annexation of the Territories, while others, including Prime Minister Shamir, argued that nothing had really changed.[4] The United States downplayed the decision, suggesting that it simply represented an attempt to spur the peace process along. In sum, the initial response was divided and confused.

The practical measures involved were rather out of proportion to the political significance of the act (Robbins 1989; Susser 1990). Jordan stopped paying the salaries of about 24,000 West Bank public servants, but it maintained its role in West Bank Islamic institutions and pensioned off most of the affected employees. The bridges between Jordan and the West Bank remained open for travel and trade, maintaining the major economic connection. Jordan canceled its controversial West Bank development plan, although this initiative had been dead on the ground for some time due to lack of funds and lack of interest. The citizenship of West Bank residents was revoked, but Jordan replaced passports with temporary travel documents. As Jordan's intentions were challenged in the Arabist public sphere, however, Jordan began to take increasingly dramatic practical measures in order to reinforce its interpretation of its action. The Ministry of Occupied Territories Affairs was abolished, replaced with a division in the Foreign Ministry; administrative documents such as drivers licenses came under a new regime, requiring applicants to come in person to Amman; a new quota system was established for Palestinian university students; Parliament was dissolved. The increasingly costly signals culminated with Jordan's recognition of the PLO's declaration of a Palestinian state in November.

The Jordanian frame primarily addressed the Arab public sphere, which was viewed as the most important site of consensus formation. A major issue in the framing struggle was whether the Jordanian actions had been intended to hurt or to help the PLO and the Intifada. While the intention of Jordanian policymakers may well have been the former, to challenge the PLO and set it up to fail (see below), the policy could not be publicly framed or justified in that way. Jordanian discourse inside of Jordan no less than abroad justified the disengagement in terms of Palestinian interests and Arab collective interests, not in terms of Jordanian interests. Jordanian spokesmen emphasized that the disengagement aimed at strengthening the Palestinian identity, and that it represented a voluntary response to the Arab consensus. Justifications based on Jordanian interests were conspicuously absent. While many observers are justifiably cynical about the sincerity of these explanations, it is clear that the high normative value accorded to the Palestinian national identity claim and to the Arab consensus shaped Jordanian discourse. I am not claiming that the decision was not meant to serve Jordanian interests, but rather that it could not be explained or justified in those terms. Claims based on Jordanian interests would not have been viewed as legitimate or convincing by the relevant publics. As Jordan framed its action for the purposes of public argumentation, it bound itself to behave accordingly, at least in the short term (Habermas 1996; Bohman 1996; Elster 1998).

Placing the decision in public sphere context does not exclude strategic concerns. The immediate motivations for the decision were the demands of strategic interaction within the context of public argumentation. To prove that the Jordanian action represented a real decision and not simply "cheap talk," Jordan had to live up to its discourse by taking the mandated practical steps (Fearon 1997; Elster 1998). Jordan consistently maintained that the point of the decision to sever ties was to "end [Arab and Palestinian] doubts about Jordanian intentions."[5] At first, the reaction in the Arab public sphere convinced Jordanian leaders of the need to maintain the disengagement. Later, the 1989 uprisings and the consequent liberalization of the political system, shifted the site of contention to the Jordanian arena.

Despite the efforts to deny any connection between the disengagement and citizens of Palestinian origin, the redefinition of state borders could not be segregated from questions about national identity. As one member of the inner circle observed: "the severing of ties was taken with specific political considerations, related to the PLO, but then [unfortunately] this decision came to be applied step by step upon Jordan itself and on its internal institutions."[6] The bid to define a new Jordan restricted to the East Bank required a sharp distinction between Jordanians and Palestinians, a major departure in identity norms. As long as the state claimed an identity including the West Bank, Jordanians could blur the issue of national identity, stress the common rather than the unique, and encourage the appeal of unity over division. The Jordanian frame now sought to decouple the issues of state identity and national identity by developing a sharp distinction between the

Palestinian issue and the question of Palestinians living in Jordan: one a question of foreign policy, the other a question of domestic politics.

Rationalist Explanations

Rationalist arguments share the assumption that preferences are stable and exogenous to interaction. Consistently articulated Jordanian preferences over outcomes in the West Bank have observably motivated behavior over an extended period of time. These preferences also follow deductively from Jordan's position in the regional order. Economic, geographic, demographic, and political "realities" compel Jordan's preference for a role in the West Bank, regardless of discourse, identity, or ideas. Rent-seeking offers one explanation for Jordan's defense of its role in the West Bank and the peace process (Brand 1994). Jordan's "role," or its willingness to negotiate over the final dispensation of the West Bank, represented a major source of external financial and political support. Because both the United States and Israel viewed Jordan as important primarily in regard to its presumed role in the West Bank and in competition with the PLO, this role represented a major economic and political asset. Surrendering this role would mean not only the loss of these external rents, but also exposure to serious American and Israeli pressure. The combination of international rent-seeking, strategic interaction with the PLO, and material interests provides a solid foundation for the assumption of an enduring Jordanian preference for a role in the West Bank. Because systemically derivable preferences, behavior, and discourse converge, the assumption of a constant Jordanian preference for a dominant position in the West Bank seems plausible. For the same reason, however, rent-seeking offers little purchase on the Jordanian decision to sever ties. No offer of financial support preceded, or followed, the severing of ties.

The other three rationalist hypotheses introduced enjoy wide circulation and credibility at both the academic and public level: threat balancing, omnibalancing, and strategic interaction. The strategic interpretation tended to be advanced either by those who prefer negotiations with Jordan over negotiations with the PLO, or by those directly involved in Jordanian-Palestinian rivalry. The PLO presented a fundamental challenge to the Jordanian role, as well as to the legitimacy and even survival of the Hashemite regime. Decades of conflict locked Jordan and the PLO into a competitive, zero-sum relationship which guided the Jordanian calculation of threat and opportunity. While the PLO had abandoned its aims on Jordan itself, the relationship remained highly competitive, full of suspicions and mutual doubts. Supporters of the "Jordan option" minimized the significance of the disengagement in order to keep these peace proposals alive and avoid dealing with the PLO. If Jordanian interests had not really changed, and the disengagement only responded to the rise of PLO power in the West Bank, then the weakening of the PLO would quickly bring Jordan back into play. Jordanians and Palestinians who viewed the relationship as competitive and zero-sum also propounded this viewpoint. The balance of threat position tended to be argued by those who opposed a negotiated settlement in the West Bank. The idea was to emphasize Jordanian instability, fragility, and above all its intimate ties to Palestine. Based on the asserted identity of Jordan and Palestine, it only made sense that an uprising on the West Bank would travel east. Each approach assumes continuity in identity and interests. The latter claim is that Jordan was Palestine before and continues to be; the former position sees Jordan as having had an interest in the West Bank which has not changed.

Balance of Threat and Regime Survival

The main threat-balancing explanation is that King Hussein preferred to surrender his claims to the West Bank rather than lose his immanently threatened throne, rather than an international threat balancing argument. However powerful Jordan's interest in the West Bank, regime survival took priority: "The disengagement did not become imperative . . . until it became clear that other alternatives could constitute a serious threat to the regime and to the existence of the state" (Andoni 1991: 167). This interpretation has become widely accepted, among policymakers as well as academics (Nevo and Pappe 1994; Arens 1995; Shamir 1994). The burden of this argument is to show that Jordanian decisionmakers did in fact perceive an existential threat emanating from the claim to the West Bank, and that they believed that severing of ties would best protect Jordan from that threat.

The omnibalancing hypothesis stresses Palestinian nationalism which might challenge Hussein's regime; the threat balancing hypothesis emphasizes Israeli threats to make Jordan into the Palestinian state. The Palestinian threat lies in the possibility that Palestinians resident in Jordan, inspired by the uprising across the river, would see an equivalence between Israeli occupation and Jordanian authoritarianism and act accordingly.[7] The Jordanian regime evidently feared this, severely restricting public expressions of support for the Intifada.[8] The relative success of these repressive measures casts doubt upon the degree to which fear of this threat motivated the Jordanian decision. Jordanian security services seemed to have societal unrest under control during the summer of 1988. Furthermore, while Intifada discourse rejected Jordanian influence in the West Bank, at no time did it call for an uprising in Jordan. PLO leaders recognized that Palestinian unrest in Jordan would likely divert world attention from the Intifada and thus weaken its political gains, and most leaders of the Palestinian community in Jordan shared this analysis.[9] During the April 1989 uprisings in Jordan among the Transjordanian cities of the south, the PLO advised Palestinians not to join in, indicating their belief that Palestinian interests were best served if the Intifada did not spread to Jordan. With no calls for the spread of the Intifada to Jordan, and effective security controls minimizing the risks of spontaneous outbursts, Palestinian activity does not seem to provide enough threat to the Jordanian regime to justify the disengagement.

The international threat emerged from Israeli debates about possible solutions to their predicament (Sharara 1990; Lustick 1994). The Intifada energized the campaign to impose a solution to their Palestinian problem at Jordan's expense, as Israeli public opinion became more hawkish (Arian 1997, Dowty 1998). Major figures along the Israeli political spectrum publicly raised the idea, and the crisis atmosphere raised the possibility that drastic measures might be taken by the Israeli government. One frequently cited opinion poll indicated that 49 percent of Israelis would consider a policy of transfer (Tessler 1994: 709). This Israeli threat held a high place in Jordanian discourse—probably more so than in Israel itself. Jordanians highlighted this discourse to the point that "every Jordanian official is haunted by . . . the argument that Jordan is Palestine."[10]

Despite the Israeli public discourse, there does not seem to have been any serious escalation in the Israeli threat immediately prior to the Jordanian decision. Such an Israeli action continued to be unlikely, and Jordanians were well aware of the powerful counter arguments in the Israeli public sphere and the international constraints on such extreme action. As Prime Minister Zayd Rifa'i bluntly explained, "This is mere talk which is difficult for Israel to carry out. To deport the entire Arab population from the West Bank, Israel would have to wage a new war."[11] Such statements undermine the argument for the centrality of this threat for explaining the disengagement.

An argument based on the Israeli threat also has serious difficulty with the timing of the decision. With Israeli elections approaching, Labor and Likud were nearly deadlocked. If the threat of "Jordan is Palestine" motivated Hussein, then the timing of the disengagement seems spectacularly ill-considered. The move shattered Shimon Peres's peace plan based on the Jordan option and thereby removed Labor's strongest card against Shamir. By harming Labor's electoral chances, the disengagement strengthened rather than weakened this threat. Jordanians were quite aware of Israeli domestic politics. The fact that the timing of the disengagement helped the electoral prospects of the party most identified with the "Jordan is Palestine" policy strongly undermines the Israel version of the threat-balancing explanation. Why would King Hussein help elect the party whose policies threatened his throne?

While the threat-balancing approach concentrates attention on perception, rather than material power, it does not really help to differentiate among different threats (Harknett and VanDenBerg 1997). For example, most analysts thought that Jordan could not afford to disengage from the West Bank because its large Palestinian population would be enraged and would rise up against the regime. After the disengagement, analysts agreed that Jordan felt threatened by the effects of the continued ties to the West Bank on its Palestinian population. What happened to the original threat? Threat is subject to contestation and interpretation. An explanation that does not take this contingency into account risks an easy slide into tautology. Overall, despite the emergence of the regime survival thesis as the conventional wisdom, little evidence exists to support it. The threat is not specified, and the solution is not obvious.

Strategic Interaction and the Balance of Power

Realism, for which variations in material power drive changes in behavior, is not particularly useful for explaining the severing of ties. Few changes in the balance of power occurred at the correct time to explain such a dramatic behavioral change, however. The great changes in the international system caused by the end of the Cold War lay in the near future. At the regional level, the Iran-Iraq war was close to exhaustion, but had not yet officially terminated. No major arms deals or financial booms or busts predated the decision. No grand alliance of Arab states threatened Jordan, and Israeli pressure had not noticeably increased. In short, changes in the distribution of material power among states do not explain the Jordanian disengagement.

A strategic interaction model based on Realist assumptions offers more purchase on the decision. The power struggle between Jordan and the PLO

for the right to represent the West Bank, and between those two actors and
Israel for final control of the West Bank, defines the situation. The disengagement responded to shifting incentives caused by a shift in the regional
balance of power brought about by the Palestinian Intifada (Robins 1989:
173). Support for the PLO expressed by the mobilized Palestinians seriously
undermined Jordanian claims to represent the West Bank and contributed
to PLO ascendancy within the Arab and international arenas (Susser 1990:
606; Tessler 1994). The Algiers Arab summit then pledged Arab aid to the
Intifada by way of the PLO, specifically bypassing Jordan, driving home the
new power realities. The shift in the balance of power between Jordan and
the PLO, by this argument, led Jordan to the decision to temporarily disengage from the West Bank. Jordan's interest in influence in the West Bank
did not change. What did change was its position based on the balance of
power. The severing of ties was a tactical maneuver aimed at reversing this
power shift, and would be reversed as soon as the balance of power again
favored Jordan.

With both Israel and Jordan weakened relative to the PLO, the disengagement came as a tactical move to starve the Intifada and undercut the
PLO's new strength. Since the Intifada placed considerable economic pressure on the Palestinians of the West Bank, Jordan's move might push the
Palestinian economy over the edge, by removing the salaries of civil servants
and by restricting the flow of money across the bridge. The PLO would be
compelled to devote more time and attention to administering the West
Bank. This strain on its administrative capabilities would take its toll on its
ability to exploit its new international power, and perhaps prove that it did
not in reality have the capability to replace Jordan. As many observers at the
time concluded, "King Hussein is setting the PLO up to fail." The disengagement was a move against the PLO in the game of representation. For
a strategic interaction model, the severing of ties is therefore a change in
strategy, not a change in preferences: Jordan would restake its claim to the
West Bank once the PLO position weakened.

Considerable evidence supports the argument that competition with the
PLO drove Jordanian behavior, but it does not follow from the existence of
strategic interaction that communicative action and public sphere structures
do not matter. The decisionmakers involved in the disengagement were well-
known for their orchestration over the years of Jordanian competition with
the PLO and their personal dislike for the PLO: "the fact that all the key
members [in the decision] were involved in the period of conflict with the
PLO in 1986 indicates that this is a continuation and not a break in the

Jordan/PLO confrontation."[12] Almost every member of that small group of advisers has stated explicitly, both at the time and in later interviews and articles, that the decision was directed at the PLO, although they disagree as to whether it was meant to help or to hurt their long-time rival.[13] The way in which the decision was taken is often cited as evidence that it was intended as a blow against the PLO: Jordan did not consult with or warn the PLO before acting, and it did not cooperate with the PLO to smooth the transition.[14] For advocates of this argument, many of the steps taken could be interpreted as punitive, making life more difficult on the West Bank, rather than as signals to confirm sincerity.

The form of power involved in this strategic interaction, based only marginally on material resources, had far more to do with public sphere argumentation. For the Realist, power is a function of aggregate material capabilities. The changes in the balance of power observed here, on the other hand, refer to the power of claims to leadership of the Palestinians of the West Bank, which in turn relied on three major factors: the willingness to put forward the public claim, the willingness of other public sphere participants to accept the claim, and the ability to mobilize West Bank Palestinians in support of the claim. While material power might play a role in each of these, the relationship is neither direct nor obvious. During the Intifada, the Palestinian declarations of allegiance to the PLO increased its ability to claim leadership: PLO wealth, military power, or alliances did not change. Power flows from the public recognition of claims, not from material capabilities. A public sphere synthesis, in which strategic interaction between the PLO and Jordan takes place within contested normative and communicative structures, better explains the changes in power relations. The rest of this chapter develops such a synthesis.

Constructivism, Strategic Deliberation and the Public Sphere

A standard constructivist account would also be of little help in predicting or explaining the decision to sever ties. One prominent form of norms-based theory would expect continuity in Jordanian foreign policy in the face of structural change (Katzenstein 1996; Kier 1997). The Jordanian commitment to the West Bank represented a fundamental component of Jordanian identity, deeply embedded in domestic institutions and in the discourse of Jordanian foreign policy, constitutive of Jordanian interests. A process-oriented constructivism, rather than a structural norms-based account, is needed to explain this dramatic change (Wendt 1995). I argue that the demands of argumentation in the Arabist and international public sphere, a communicative dialogue in which Jordan had to engage in order to achieve its strategic goals, bound Jordan to a particular interpretation of the severing of ties. After this frame had been consolidated at the international and Arabist levels, a dialogue inside an opened Jordanian public sphere after 1989 forced a major reconstruction of domestic institutions around the new conception of Jordanian identity. Public deliberation, rather than deeply embedded norms, explains change.

Perhaps the best entry into a public sphere account of the disengagement lies in a comparison with the Rabat Summit, where years of fierce political battle between Jordan and the PLO culminated in the Arab consensus that the PLO was to be considered the "sole legitimate representative of the Palestinian people." King Hussein, despite serious reservations, accepted this consensus. Over the next few months, Jordan made gestures in the direction of "Jordanizing" the political system and disengaging from the negotiations (Sha'ir 1987; Day 1986). Within a relatively short time, however, Jordan returned to the fray. As rationalists would predict, the 1974 disengagement changed Jordanian strategy, with nothing fundamental changing in Jordanian interests. This contrasts sharply with the 1988 disengagement, which, I argue, did involve a significant change in Jordanian identity and interests.

This difference can be traced to the changing relationship between the state, the Arab and international public spheres, and the domestic political arena. In 1974, Jordanian legitimacy as a sovereign state remained an actively contested question. Discourse between the PLO and Jordan was harsh, hostile, and fierce, tinged by the memories of the 1970–1971 Black September wars. Claims were existential, contesting the very existence of the other. The PLO was still fighting for recognition as an equal, full participant and was not beyond asserting a claim to Jordan itself. By 1988, the Arabist sphere had come to be characterized by lesser efficacy relative to participating states, and by a more rationalized style of discourse. Private bargaining, rather than public argumentation, drove Arab consensus formation. The primary challenge to the legitimacy and identity of Jordan as a sovereign state now came from Israel rather than from Arab or Palestinian radicals, and most Palestinians now recognized an interest in Jordan's survival. The Jordanian frame in the Arabist arena emphasized the needs of the Palestinians rather than Jordanian self-interest, with clear recognition of the difference between the two entities. The PLO was firmly entrenched as a recognized international actor enjoying wide support in international bodies such as the UN. The response to the Algiers resolutions was taken in a less defensive and more considered way, after relatively rational deliberation, in which arguments over the best way to serve collective interests in the Intifada predominated. Its acceptance and application of the 1988 decision was far more of a choice, expressing Jordanian decision, than was its acceptance of the 1974 decision.

Following the Algiers summit, Jordan made repeated efforts to convince the Arab and Palestinian public sphere that it sincerely supported the Arab consensus. In private meetings and public statements, Jordanian officials argued that Jordanian policy had changed in line with the summit resolutions: "Jordan will not be an alternative to the PLO and will not speak as a representative of the Palestinian people on . . . the Palestine issue."[15] Such statements alone could not convince a skeptical Arab and Palestinian audience, which had decades of experience of Jordanian tactical maneuvering within the bounds of its consistent ambitions. Such talk appeared rather cheap to the Arabist public. The severing of ties can be thought of as a costly signal, an action with real consequences whose reversal would be difficult (Fearon 1997). Jordan needed to persuade the other participants in the Arab public sphere of its frame in order to reap the benefits of its action.

Jordan's decision to sever ties with the West Bank responded more to the competitive dynamics within the Arabist public sphere than it did to direct considerations of power or threat. Jordanian explanations for the decision consistently stressed a number of factors: the threat posed by Israeli claims that Jordan should be seen as Palestine; the need to support the Intifada; and the demands of the Arab consensus. These factors, discussed above in terms of threat, should instead be interpreted in terms of public sphere interaction and competitive framing.

"Jordan Is Palestine"

The Israeli "Alternative Homeland" discourse threatened Jordan by making Jordanian identity contestable in the international public sphere. This virtually forces the theorist to a public sphere approach: power operates within discursive structures, threat emerges from the debates within them, and norms must be secured and defended through public deliberation. While Israeli military power stood behind the threat, Israel could act only if it succeeded in forging a consensus on the validity of its interpretation. In the aftermath of the Lebanon war, which had damaged Israeli standing in the world and at home, the use of military force to expel the Palestinians would have been extremely difficult without such a normative consensus. The Israeli claim that Jordan was already the Palestinian state directly tied

Jordanian security to Jordanian identity. Security threats based on identity cannot be solved by purchasing more guns or by improving the economy, however. Addressing an identity-based security threat depends upon the ability to present a more convincing identity claim. But what constitutes a convincing identity claim? Who must be convinced? It is these questions, rather than the conventional questions about power or threat, which are raised by the "Jordan is Palestine" issue and which the severing of ties sought to address. This threat assumed its distinctive potency in the 1980s by shifting the site of the contestation of Jordanian sovereignty away from the Arabist public sphere, where the question had effectively been settled, into an Israeli-American public sphere with different stakes and argumentative norms. The dominant position of Israeli interpretations within the American public sphere represented a tremendous power resource independent of the military balance.

Variants of this threat ranged from the Labor vision of a Jordanian-Palestinian confederation peacefully transforming into a Palestinian state, to the extreme right vision of a mass expulsion of Palestinians into Jordan.[16] The argument was not restricted to fringe groups like the Molodet party, or even to confrontational hard-liners like Ariel Sharon. In a numerous official statements and interviews, Prime Minister Shamir and Foreign Minister Arens claimed that Jordan was a Palestinian state and that the solution to the Palestinian problem could come only through the establishment of a Palestinian state on the East Bank.[17] Only the persistence of the Hashemite monarchy blocked the creation of a Palestinian state east of the river.[18] If the Palestinian state emerged in Jordan, the international community would then presumably be willing to accept the Israeli annexation of the West Bank. That no Palestinian or Jordanian group expressed any interest in the proposal did not seem to matter. The Likud justified this argument with an odd mix of historical and identity-based political claims. First, they argued that greater Israel had always included both banks of the river, so that their surrender of the East Bank represented a major concession. Second, the British mandate had briefly included Jordan and Palestine under the same administration, which was taken as evidence of their political unity in the Sykes-Picot framework. Third, the large Palestinian population of Jordan alone represented a satisfactory reason to put the Palestinian state there, with the historical origin of this Palestinian population in Jordan because of Israeli military activity forgotten or denied. As one Israeli commentator argued: "The moment questions arise about the legitimacy of the Hashemite claim to a separate Jordanian identity, the hook that King Hussein believes he has now escaped will ensnare him again."[19]

These historical arguments constitute a theory of identity and international relations sharply at odds with established international norms. The argument sought to delegitimize the Jordanian state by denying the Jordanian identity. Since the majority of Jordanians are "really" Palestinian, and there is no real independent or coherent Jordanian identity, there is no justification for the existence of the Jordanian state: "Jordan is Palestine in all but name." From this perspective the legitimacy of the sovereign state requires justification beyond international recognition or empirical control, the two standard measures of sovereignty in international society (Hinsley 1968; Jackson 1990). A state's existence must further be justified as an expression of some higher moral purpose or of a legitimate nationalism. This assertion contradicts a fundamental pillar of the international negative sovereignty regime, in which recognition by the international community alone confers sovereignty (Jackson 1990). The Israeli argument proposed that an existing state, an internally stable member of the UN, with the longest sitting head of state in the world, could be delegitimized and its sovereignty challenged on the basis of its weak national identity, even though no secessionist or rebel group inside of the target state or irredentist group outside it advanced such a claim.

The PLO rejected the "Alternative Homeland" project, despite persistent attempts to attribute such aspirations to it, as a profound threat to Palestinian national interests. Palestinians did debate the identity of Jordan and the possibility of political action there in the 1960s and 1970s, but by the 1980s a Palestinian consensus rejected any aspirations on the East Bank. Palestinians universally considered the idea to be an Israeli interest rather than a Palestinian interest, providing the basis for a convergence of interests between Jordan and the PLO on the question of Palestinian political activity in the East Bank. The reality of PLO influence on the East Bank did not translate into ambitions to establish a Palestinian state there. This consensus encompassed all major Palestinian figures and movements, including the leftist groups which had most fervently called for Jordanian-Palestinian unity against the Hashemite regime in the 1970s. As a prominent Palestinian intellectual explained, "if it appeared that any Palestinian faction wanted, openly or secretly, to establish an 'Alternative Homeland' . . . this would have been rejected by the Palestinian people in idea and practice."[20] Khalidi is even more forthright, asking how his national aspirations, based on generations in Jerusalem, could be resolved in Amman: "The point is that as far as the Palestinians themselves are concerned, their homeland is Palestine, west of the river. . . . It is not the East Bank of the Jordan" (1988: 9).

The international argumentation forced many unresolved contradictions of Jordanian identity to the surface. Jordan needed both to convincingly present a Jordanian identity and to reconcile the place of Palestinians within it without denying the political reality of the Palestinian identity. Since at least the early 1970s, an "East Bank-first" movement urged the regime to concentrate its energies on developing the East Bank and the Transjordanian community and to abandon its ambitions in the West Bank. Despite this powerful trend, Jordan continued to aspire toward regaining the West Bank.[21] The assertion of a Jordanian "tribal identity" in the mid-1980s never succeeded in capturing a normative consensus in Jordan. Such a limited ethnic identity claim excluded too many citizens, too poorly represented the reality of Jordanian society, and too blatantly contradicted the emergent norms of citizenship.[22] The struggle with the PLO for representation of the West Bank perpetually complicated the Jordanian position. Arguments in the Arabist public sphere about Jordanian/Palestinian unity or identity could be appropriated by Israel to support their argument for a Palestinian position on the East Bank. The need to define Jordanian particularity in the international public space could not be isolated from either the Arab or domestic spheres.

Finally, one should not underestimate the extent to which the Jordanian regime found this threat useful. Decisionmakers may have felt some real threat, especially since Hussein did not have the working relationship with the Likud leadership that had facilitated his dealings with the Labor Party, and even more so with the influx of Soviet Jews which seemed to be creating greater Israeli demand for territorial expansion. Shamir reportedly assured Hussein privately that such threats should not be taken seriously (Baker 1995: 386; Harkabi 1990: 25). "Jordan is Palestine" became a crucial gambit as a justificatory strategy in the Jordanian politics of identity. The state's appropriation of the threat became a master stroke binding the hands of Jordanians of Palestinian origin, empowering Jordanian state elites against challenges from a growing middle class which was largely of Palestinian origin. Any sign of Palestinian political assertiveness could be stifled by the argument that "Palestinian political activity will make it possible for Israel to implement its threat."[23] The usefulness of the foreign threat for the domestic political concerns of Jordanian elites points toward the construction of the threat and its public sphere deployment.

The Intifada

Many analysts place great weight on the Jordanian regime's fear that the Palestinian Intifada could spread to the East Bank. While this emphasis is correct, the causal logic generally remains under specified. The demands of public sphere argumentation played an important role in linking the Intifada to Jordanian action. If Jordan denied the distinction between the West and East Banks, then the Intifada might inspire the Palestinians in Jordan who felt oppressed by the undemocratic regime in Jordan. The Jordanian regime needed some formula by which the Intifada in the Occupied Territories could be separated from the political and social demands of Jordanians of Palestinian origin. The disengagement provided such a formula. If the West Bank, Palestine, were recognized as distinct and separate from the East Bank, Jordan, then Jordanians could legitimately support the Intifada as an external event—and thereby satisfy the Arab consensus—while delegitimizing Palestinian political activity in the East Bank. After 1989, Jordan permitted rallies expressing solidarity with the Intifada, in sharp contrast with its repression of the observances of its first anniversary, demonstrating the value of the severing of ties consensus.[24]

It is necessary to go beyond the simple calculation of threat and interest in explaining the Jordanian response to the Intifada. The depth of popular identification with the Palestinian struggle forced Jordanian decisionmakers to directly confront questions of identity, not only of interest. From a rationalist perspective, Jordan's interests seemed to coincide with those of Israel: to stop the Intifada as quickly as possible.[25] The uprising undermined Jordanian influence in the West Bank and strengthened the PLO, while also threatening to decisively end the Jordanian role in the peace process. Further, its spread to the East Bank could destabilize the Jordanian political system. From a simple calculation of interests, then, it made sense to cooperate with Israel to shut down the Intifada and keep the PLO out of the process. But as the Intifada escalated, making its scale as a social revolution apparent, Jordanians could not avoid stark questions of identity: would they stand with or against this manifestation of Arab identity and resistance, with or against its huge popularity among Arab publics? Could Jordanian interests be set starkly, diametrically against Arabist norms? While tacit collusion with Israel over the 1986 West Bank development plan had been marginally justifiable as a way to improve the lives of Palestinians under occupation, direct collusion with Israel against the Intifada would be a stark repudiation of Arab norms, a final exit from the imagined Arab consensus.

The severing of ties therefore responded not only to the threat the Intifada posed, but also to the transformation of Palestinian identity that it sparked. As the Palestinians in the Occupied Territories engaged in collective action, articulating a clear rejection of a Jordanian role, Jordan needed to establish a new relationship. Hani al-Khasawneh, one of the leading advocates of the severing of ties, claims that his support was not based on competition with the PLO, but rather on the need "for establishing healthy relations between the two Jordanian-Palestinian peoples" and for "building a cohesive and independent Jordan."[26] This appeal to generalizable, higher shared interests marks an important stage in the deliberative process. This dimension of the severing of ties cannot be reduced either to "losing" the strategic interaction with the PLO or to the demands of the Arab and international consensus.

The Arab Consensus

The Arab summit convened in Algiers in June 1988 to consider the implications of the Intifada established the consensus to which Jordan acceded. After offering an impassioned defense of the Jordanian position, Hussein asserted that "we are prepared to agree to anything that our brother leaders reach consensus about."[27] The Arab leaders pledged full support for the Palestinian struggle and again authorized the PLO as the representative of this national struggle. Why would Jordan accept an Arab consensus which it believed to be wrong and counter to its interests? The argument that the balance of power compelled Jordan to accept the decision is not satisfactory. Arab decisions are notoriously unenforceable, and the Algiers resolutions conveyed no particular threat of sanctions. Jordan's behavior is better explained by its preference for an outcome within the Arab consensus, and its acceptance of the collective interests expressed in that consensus.

The Arab consensus played an important role in the severing of ties by establishing the authoritative frame by which the act was interpreted. The Arabist public sphere was the most relevant site of interpretive struggle. Jordanian decisionmakers gave little thought to the domestic public sphere at this point, and in late 1988 effectively shut it down. The international public sphere received less attention in contesting the meaning of the disengagement, primarily because of Hussein's frustration with American policy (Quandt 1993; Shultz 1994; Susser 1990). The international and the Arabist public spheres worked at cross purposes: the United States and Israel attempted to minimize the significance of the decision and tried to convince Hussein to change his mind, while Arabs and Palestinians tried to consolidate the decision and make it irrevocable. Jordanian arguments consistently emphasized that Jordan's decision came in response to the Arab consensus on Palestinian independence and to the expressed wishes of the PLO, demonstrating the priority of the Arab consensus.

The strongly positive public response in the Arabist public sphere played an important role in consolidating the severing of ties in the short to medium term. The participants in the Arabist public sphere quickly reached consensus that Jordan had done the right thing. The initial response was heavily tinged with traditional suspicion of Jordanian motives. Debate revolved around the idea that Jordan hoped to strangle the Intifada and thereby weaken the PLO and reassert its claim to represent the West Bank in international negotiations. "The Jordanian step," this position suggested, "should be considered a form of conspiracy against the Palestinian revolution" (Ghoul 1990: 419). However, a consensus quickly formed that regardless of King Hussein's intentions, the severing of ties objectively helped the Palestinian cause and therefore should be supported. Egypt declared that "King Hussein's decision . . . represents a significant turning point in the struggle for the Palestinian cause."[28] Numerous members of the Palestinian leadership publicly welcomed the decision, regardless of its intentions.[29] A crucial meeting between high ranking Jordanian and Palestinian delegations in mid-August produced a common interpretative frame: "the objective of the decision is to serve the Palestinian cause, highlight the national identity of the Palestinian people, and underline the PLO's role. . . . the Palestinian side affirmed its full concern for Jordan's stability, sovereignty and domestic national unity."[30]

Jordanian discourse rejected any reference to Jordanian interests, insisting on framing its action in terms of Arab and Palestinian interests. The effort to frame the disengagement in terms of Jordanian interests came from Jordan's opponents, who recognized that imposing such an frame would prevent the securing of an Arab consensus favorable to Jordan. The fact that Jordan framed its actions in terms of support for the Palestinians and respect for the Arab consensus rather than in terms of Jordanian interests had a definite impact on the outcome. The success of the disengagement depended on securing a consensus in the Arab public sphere that Jordan had in fact acted in the collective Arab and Palestinian interest. It became imperative for Jordan to justify the action in the strongest possible terms of support for rather than competition with the Palestinians. This need clearly guided the steps taken, even if it did not motivate the initial decision. Jordanian behavior had to conform to the frame it advanced in the Arabist public sphere in order to make its explanations credible; hence the steady sequence of increasingly costly steps, often taken in direct responses to public challenges. Once this frame had been established, Jordan's support for the declaration of the Palestinian state, long anathema, became unavoidable, in order to maintain the integrity of the frame. The combination of the

Palestinian and Arab embrace of the disengagement and the demands of frame consistency blocked any short-term reversal of the decision. This Arab consensus might not have been sufficient to transform Jordanian interests over the long term without the domestic changes described in chapter 4, but it did secure the shift through the short term.

The capitulation to the Arab consensus in a sense liberated Jordan from the demands of participation in the Arabist public sphere by insulating it from criticism. A prominent theme in Jordanian discourse was that the severing of ties put an end to all doubts about the Jordanian position, responded to all criticism of the Jordanian role, and clarified Jordanian intentions. Few could deny that Jordan had both in word and deed done exactly as the Arab consensus and Palestinian discourse demanded. As long as Jordan did not reverse its position, it stood beyond reproach. This respite from attack on Arabist grounds made the turn inward of 1989, the construction of a specifically Jordanian public sphere, more plausible and justifiable.

In the international public sphere, a campaign to cast doubt upon the long-term sincerity of Jordan's disengagement followed, in an attempt to keep the Jordan Option alive. Analysts essentially argued that the severing of ties was a change in strategy, not a change in preferences. Richard Murphy, testifying before Congress, argued that "Jordan has not disengaged itself from the peace process. . . . the King's action . . . did change the immediate dynamics, but it did not change . . . his concern, his interest, or his expectations to be fully involved in the process."[31] Israeli discourse minimized the severing of ties, attempting to portray it as nothing but King Hussein's frightened gambit to protect himself from the PLO. Nevertheless, as Jordanian behavior and the Arabist consensus stabilized and consolidated the new situation, Arens conceded that "this option no longer exists, because King Hussein changed his position . . . [and] a realistic perspective on our part requires us to take this statement seriously. Hussein does not represent this population."[32] As the hope for a Jordanian return faded, the Reagan Administration finally agreed to commence a dialogue with the PLO as the only realistic party to a negotiated settlement. The Arabist consensus helped to overcome the power imbalances in the international public sphere, shielding Jordan from these pressures.

Conclusion

The initial decision to sever ties with the West Bank followed a strategic logic based upon the demands of argumentation in the Arabist public sphere. The significance of the decision cannot be inferred from Jordanian policy intentions, however, because it only took on meaning in the process of dialogue. In order for the severing of ties to achieve Jordanian interests, Jordan had to secure an Arab consensus. Once it achieved this consensus, however, it was bound, at least in the short term, to match its actions with its discourse. Several weeks of deliberation, including both public interpretive struggle and a series of meetings between Jordanian officials and representatives of the PLO and Arab states, established a consensus favorable to the severing of ties. From that point, "it goes without saying that Jordan's decision cannot be rescinded."[33]

If the interaction had remained at this level, it is entirely plausible that the severing of ties might have been reversed once international and Arab circumstances changed. Jordanian material interests in the West Bank remained, and the demands of the peace process would almost certainly return to a Jordanian role. What made this action fundamentally different from other policy decisions was the domestic impact. In chapter 4, I turn to the domestic politics of the severing of ties, and argue that the contestation of Jordanian identity in the Jordanian public sphere institutionalized a new conception of Jordanian identity and interests which became embedded in Jordanian state and civil society institutions as well as in political discourse.

4 Jordan Is Jordan: Jordanian Debates over Jordanian-Palestinian Relations

> "There was talk about return to the former union . . . I lived it all these years, but I found it was all wrong because each side is attached to its own identity."
>
> — King Hussein, August 7, 1991.[1]

Despite the importance of Arab and international public spheres on Jordanian conceptions of identity and interest, the severing of ties would not have produced the enduring reconception of Jordanian identity and interests without the remarkable emergence of the Jordanian public sphere. Jordan's need to secure and then maintain an Arab consensus bound its behavior after July 1988, and produced a new context for strategic interaction over the future of the West Bank: a change in preferences over strategies (Powell 1994). Change in Jordanian identity and interests—a change in preferences over outcomes—could only be produced by a domestic dialogue and the reconfiguration of domestic institutions. The emergence of the Jordanian public sphere in the 1990s provided a site for such deliberation. The severing of ties set in motion public deliberation over state identity and interests which produced a profoundly new conception of Jordan's interests in the West Bank. Jordan reached a consensus on the revision of the borders of the state which was institutionalized in discourse, state and civil society institutions, and which have produced consistent behavioral patterns. The Jordanian public sphere failed to produce such a consensus on the question of internal identity and the place of citizens of Palestinian origin in the political system, however. The internal Jordanian deliberation is profoundly linked to regional and international processes: Jordan's identity will not be fully institutionalized without a final status agreement between Israel and the Palestinians. The most important change is that most Jordanians came to believe that the interests of the downsized Jordanian state are best served by the establishment of a Palestinian state.

In this chapter, I make two arguments. First, I argue that Jordan has undergone a change in preferences over outcomes, not simply a change in strategies (Powell 1994). After long viewing unity with the West Bank as a core component of state identity and a fundamental interest, a Jordanian consensus emerged in the early 1990s that unity with the West Bank threatened Jordanian survival, identity, and interests. What had been the least preferable outcome—a Palestinian state in the West Bank and Gaza—became the most preferable outcome. This change in preferences is important both empirically, in that it is essential for understanding Jordanian behavior along a wide range of issues, and theoretically, in that it represents an observable change in first-order preferences on a central foreign policy issue. Second, I argue that Jordan's understanding of state identity and interests changed through the process of public deliberation across multiple public spheres. Public debate inside of Jordan produced the new consensus on Jordan's territorial scope, but these debates did not take place in isolation from regional developments. The emergence of the Palestinian National Authority in Gaza and parts of the West Bank, along with the Jordanian-Israeli peace treaty, helped to entrench the East Bank boundaries of Jordan.

The Disengagement in the Jordanian Public Sphere

Dialogues in the Jordanian and the Arab public spheres could never be fully insulated from one another. While Jordanian officials proclaimed in 1988 that "we do not accept any interpretation for our move other than the explanation and the interpretation that we present," Jordan's position in multiple public spheres belied such claims of interpretive power.[2] Discourse from one public sphere reinforced or challenged positions in another. Nevertheless, two distinct dialogues clearly emerged, each oriented toward a different imagined consensus, focusing on different dimensions of interests, and producing different outcomes. The Arabist dialogue produced a firm consensus in favor of the severing of ties. While it would have been difficult to find anyone outside of Jordan or Israel by 1988 who thought that the return of the West Bank to Jordanian rule represented a viable option, the internal Jordanian consensus on this remained publicly unchallenged. For Jordanian public discourse, the West Bank remained naturally a part of Jordan until the public deliberation which followed the severing of ties (Lustick 1994). The domestic dialogue produced a consensus on new borders which underlay the contentious debates over Jordanian interests in the peace process, but failed to achieve consensus on the place of Palestinian-origin citizens in the political order.

Most contemporary discussion of the severing of ties focused on the Jordanian role in the West Bank, not on internal Jordanian politics. The focus on the international dialogue accurately reflects the priorities of the Jordanian regime, which privileged the Arabist consensus as the most important arena for communicative and strategic interaction. Even those analysts who gave some attention to the domestic political implications for Jordan slighted the significance of Jordanian public debate.[3] In fact, for most of August 1988 the Jordanian press formed an arena for vigorous public debate, as the public struggled to reach some consensus about the new political situation. The regime exerted state power to prevent public debate only after several weeks of debate, but before even a tentative consensus could emerge. The government shut down the nascent identity politics by reorganizing the press: forcing the private ownership of the dailies to sell their shares to the state, replacing their editorial boards, and stifling the expression of opinion. This repression and failure to achieve public consensus quickly became a major source of instability and tension in the political system, contributing directly to the uprisings of 1989.

The public deliberation in those few weeks vividly reveals the uncertainty that the severing of ties wrought among Jordanians and their eagerness to discuss it publicly. The issue was understood not simply as difference over strategies—whether the disengagement served Jordanian self-interest—but as a deeper deliberation over Jordanian identity. If Jordan had always been conceived as an Arabist entity uniting the two banks under a Hashemite throne, what was a Jordan with only one bank? Most Jordanians, socialized into the discourse defending the unity of the two banks, found it difficult to readjust to defend separation. Unity with the West Bank and the existence of a single Jordanian-Palestinian people represented fundamental, constitutive normative principles of Jordanian discourse and institutions. Despite the widespread sympathy with the Palestinian cause, the public sphere itself retained these Jordanian focal points. Columnists at first cautiously repeated the justifications offered by Hussein in his speech, musing that perhaps the step would help the PLO and end unjustified doubts about Jordanian intentions, and at the least it responded to PLO and Arab wishes. On August 3, Fahd al-Rimawi published a pathbreaking essay stressing the need for open, public debate about the decision. Scorning the surface calm, Rimawi argued simply, "let us make open what is now whispered."[4] George Haddad, a prominent Arabist, responded with a remarkable outburst: "You want to open debate on the severing of ties and 'Jordastinian' unity . . . but I reply that I am not yet in any condition to write calmly. . . . I consider this one of the darkest days in the history of Jordan."[5]

Pointed analysis then burst into the public sphere, revealing sharp differences of interpretation. Even regime loyalists expressed dissatisfaction: "Despite all justifications, the severing of ties is a danger and is hurtful to all those who believe in unity."[6] While this critique blamed the PLO for demanding the separation, rather than directly criticizing the king, the implications of the criticism were apparent: no unity among the political elite could be assumed on this issue. The press balanced the anger of pro-unity writers with the basic theme that the disengagement came as a Jordanian response to the Arab consensus and PLO demands and therefore stood beyond reproach.

The critics drew on a normative structure relying on the unity of the two banks, which had been the cornerstone of the Jordanian position for decades. Their position drew on Jordanian norms, identity, and discourse, eschewing the Arabist and leftist denunciations of Jordanian policy which the state traditionally found threatening. The dissenters were defending Jordanian unity norms, not challenging them. However, this was hardly the point. In August 1988, the regime was primarily concerned with Arabist and international deliberation and the need to convince other actors of Jordanian sincerity and conviction. Achieving Arabist consensus took significantly higher priority than did engaging with Jordanian political society. Doubts expressed at home, or difficulty in institutionalizing the decision in the domestic sphere, would only undermine the Jordanian attempt to convey sincerity and irreversibility in the Arabist public sphere. The closure of the domestic debate therefore served the demands of international argumentation. The costly steps taken by the state in order to prove its sincerity to the Arabist public—the dissolution of Parliament, the recognition of the Declaration of the Palestinian State—were accompanied by very little deliberation in the Jordanian public sphere.

The reorganization of the press in late August removed the editorial boards of the daily newspapers and installed strict censorship. The state assault on the press has generally been seen as a strike against any manifestation of societal criticism at a time of deepening economic and political crisis, combined with Prime Minister Rifa'i's notoriously low threshold of toleration. But there is more to it than that, and it has to do with the entry of identity concerns into the debate. While the government repeatedly denied any connection between the severing of ties and the reorganization of the press, few Jordanians or Arab observers doubted the relationship.[7] Following the abandonment of claims to the West Bank, the discussion of identity would seem to be inevitable. The statist conception of debate was of the press explaining and legitimating the state decision to the people rather than effective dialogue: "the major responsibility [of the press is] communicating the guidelines of the national leadership to the citizens, explaining the government's mission and policies."[8] In other words, the press should offer one-way tutelage, not public debate.

Identity politics between the disengagement and the 1989 uprisings reveal the constraints exercised by the structure of the public sphere upon actors. Despite the impetus to debate, actors remained bound by the available media and the existing normative and discursive boundaries. The political turning point was not yet accompanied by the opening of the public sphere necessary for public identity politics. Public closure did not prevent people from interpreting the significance of the disengagement in private salons, but it prevented them from the public interaction from which new consensual understandings might emerge. The public sphere simply could not handle the introduction of identity at this highly politicized level. In short, the severing of ties made the public contestation of identity politics necessary. It took the upheavals of 1989 to make that debate possible.

In the context of uncertainty and enforced public silence between the press reorganization and the April uprisings, three noteworthy phenomena emerged. First, many Palestinians began to transfer their capital out of the country in anticipation of a move to strip them of their citizenship rights. Palestinian workers abroad similarly began to avoid Jordanian banks when remitting their wages to families in Jordan or in the West Bank. Together, these uncoordinated but widespread measures proved disastrous for the Jordanian economy. The value of the Dinar collapsed in half against foreign currencies. The economic impact of the disengagement is not nearly as straightforward as it is made out in retrospect, however. Economic analysts in the daily press minimized the probable economic impact of the move.[9] The closure of the public sphere directly influenced the economic impact of the severing of ties. The disengagement appeared to be, at least possibly, the prelude to disenfranchisement of Palestinians. True or not, there was no open forum in which these fears could be meaningfully discussed. The economic impact of the disengagement depended upon its interpretation, which was shaped by the government's repression and refusal to engage with public questioning.

The second phenomenon, the spread of rumors and underground pamphlets, took on great significance as an alternative to the tomblike silence of the official public sphere. While both rumors and pamphlets are well-entrenched features of Jordanian society, this period saw an unprecedented level of such activity. In the absence of credible information, people felt great uncertainty, complementing their historically grounded distrust of the regime's intentions. The normative structure of this counter-public played an extremely significant role in defining the new public sphere. The absence of any national public sphere forced people to rely on foreign media, which in practice often meant Israeli radio, for coverage of Jordanian news.[10] "Black pamphlets" circulated widely in the streets of Amman, accusing public officials of corruption and calling for public freedoms. As a deputy explained during a 1989 Parliament debate: "Corruption . . . forced the citizen to exit from his silence and express his outrage.. and the pamphlets appeared.. to expose it."[11] The exposure of corruption at the highest levels at a time of harsh economic recession seriously undermined the credibility not only of Rifai's government, but of the system as a whole. The emphasis on press reforms in the 1989 liberalization should be understood in this context. By surrendering some margins of control, the regime sought to relegitimate the dominant public sphere.

Third, the severing of ties emboldened the Jordanian exclusivist trend. Transjordanian political entrepreneurs seized the new opportunities to advance a claim to legitimize and advance their social power at the expense of the Palestinian-origin economic elite. This exclusivist position encountered strong opposition, but increasingly set the terms of debate. These Transjordanians saw that the disengagement represented a victory and an opportunity. Even as Hussein called for an inclusionary, identity-blind discourse, the logic of the emergent public sphere encouraged the Jordanian chauvinists. With the polity defined in terms of the East Bank, and the loyalties of Palestinian-origin citizens implicitly in doubt, the Jordanian nationalists held the upper hand in the politicization of identity. The severing of ties and the thematization of identity empowered such trends at the expense of any form of mobilization based either on Palestinian identity or on claims blind to identity.

After the severing of ties, most elites of Palestinian origin accepted an implicit bargain, largely abstaining from political activity as the price of Jordanian support for the PLO and a Palestinian state. This bargain was secured through persuasion more than through coercion. In the context of the Intifada, the Israeli "Jordan is Palestine" discourse, and the Jordanian decision to sever ties with the West Bank, most Palestinians came to agree that Palestinian, as well as Jordanian, essential interests were best served by their abstention from Jordanian politics. Despite the official discourse that "all citizens share equal rights and responsibilities," Palestinians and Transjordanians alike perceived an implicit expectation that Palestinian citizens would avoid the exercise of political power inside of Jordan. This crucial bargain on domestic order underlay the consensus on borders that "Jordan is Jordan and Palestine is Palestine." After the severing of ties, Palestinian identity could be accommodated within the Jordanian political system by sharply distinguishing the Palestinian cause as "foreign policy" from Palestinian mobilization inside of Jordan.

The Disengagement and the April 1989 Uprisings

The severing of ties and the regime's turn to repression of dissent directly led to the uprisings of April 1989. The disengagement from the West Bank shook the intersubjective norms governing Jordanian identity, but no new norms had yet emerged to replace them. The regime met the threat of instability with increased repression rather than with dialogue. The sudden, major change in the identity of the state, combined with the absence of a public space within which to negotiate new norms, directly led to the 1989 uprisings.

This explanation departs from the conventional explanation of the riots as a direct reaction to IMF austerity measures (Brand 1992; Satloff 1992; Brynen 1991). The conventional wisdom ["the people asked for bread and the regime gave them democracy"] relies on assumptions about the dominance of economic rationality over political ideas and identities. In the 1989 bread riots, this approach fails to account for important evidence. The deteriorating Jordanian economic situation played an important role in the increasing instability, but the economic problems had profoundly political roots. The closure of the public sphere was one of the main complaints of the uprising, judging by the statements released by its leaders (Hamarneh 1995a: 145–146; al-Urdun al-Jadid 1989). When asked their opinion of the causes of the April uprisings, 78 percent of Jordanians mentioned the absence of press freedoms, 81 percent pointed to the absence of a representative Parliament, and 89 percent cited the absence of dialogue between citizens and officials (Muhadin 1992). Concern for public freedoms dominated the 1989 Parliamentary electoral campaigns, and the first confidence debate in that Parliament heavily emphasized public freedoms and public participation.[12] Citizens complained that lines of communication between the government and the people no longer functioned. This condition became particularly dangerous in the conditions of radical uncertainty brought on by the severing of ties. As the identity of the state and the meaning of citizenship shifted, the system needed new publicly negotiated consensus norms of legitimation. The crisis followed directly from change in the structures of identity and the absence of a national public sphere within which new identities could be secured. Without these, the economic crisis alone would not have led to this kind of societal response.

If identity and the structure of the public sphere helped to bring on the April 1989 uprisings, they also influenced their impact. Citizens of Palestinian origin remained notably inactive, preventing the spread of the uprisings into Amman or the camps and quite possibly saving the regime. Their inactivity prevented the state from mobilizing the discourse of Palestinian disloyalty, severely constraining its ability to exert repressive force. The inactivity of the Palestinian population has been explained in a number of ways: the orders of the PLO, which did not want to destabilize Jordan during the Intifada; the concentration of security personnel in Palestinian areas; the general alienation of Palestinians who felt that local economic issues were not their problem; fear of being singled out for punishment. Palestinians in Jordan lacked a framework within which they could organize for political action. Equally importantly, most Palestinian citizens recognized the implicit bargain of the severing of ties and did not want to endanger it with active mobilization. The consensus that Palestinian interests during the Intifada were ill-served by instability in Jordan powerfully constrained their behavior in the crisis. Their choice to abstain from the April uprisings disappointed many Transjordanian political activists, who later used their inaction to question their commitment to the Jordanian political system (Hourani and Abd al-Rahman 1995). Palestinian decisions to not participate in the uprisings follow rationally from their interpretation of the severing of ties.

In response to the upheaval, the Jordanian regime began a democratization process which included elections, increased public freedoms, and a real wave of public enthusiasm and popular participation. The combination of elections to a marginally effective parliament, reining in of Public Security Directorate abuses, and widened press freedoms did not produce anything recognizably democratic, given the realities of monarchy. It did, on the other hand, entrench the norm of democracy as central to regime legitimacy. And it opened up a domestic print public sphere dominated by the questions of

Jordanian–Palestinian identity that had long been suppressed. This opening finally allowed the contradictions of the severing of ties to be worked out in public. Cautiously at first, and then bursting into the semi-official daily press and into the proliferating independent weekly press, open discussion of identity transformed the Jordanian public sphere. Always the most taboo of red lines, identity now came to permeate virtually all public issues. Instead of orienting claims toward an Arab public which favored Palestinian claims, or toward an international public sphere interested in Jordan primarily for its role in Palestinian-Israeli relations, claims were now oriented toward the Jordanian political community.

The 1991 National Charter represented a formal consensus on the East Bank identity of Jordan and the foreign policy implications of that identity: "Jordan is Jordan and Palestine is Palestine" (Hourani 1997; Rimoni 1991; Sha'ir 1990). The former Prime Minister Ahmed Obaydat, who had long been associated with an "East Bank-first" political trend, chaired a Royal Commission including representatives of most major political parties and trends. Negotiation of the Charter involved public deliberation similar to that seen in the negotiation of Constitutions (Elster 1993, 1995), in which actors recognized the need to produce a viable, publicly defended consensus transcending self-interest. Charter deliberations were generously covered in the daily press, and involved much of Jordanian political society in a dialogue over the most basic principles of Jordanian political order. Since the Charter was to establish general norms of Jordanian behavior, actors took the identity and interests of the collective as the frame of reference. It provided the framework for "national action" in all spheres of political life, drawing sharp lines between Jordanian and non-Jordanian, and succeeded to a large degree in obtaining consensus around these principles. Most observers have identified the crucial dimension of the Charter to be the regime acceptance of liberalization in exchange for societal recognition of the Hashemite monarchy, but the Charter was equally important in articulating the new Jordanian state identity. By declaring unequivocally that "Jordan is Jordan and Palestine is Palestine," the Charter ratified the distinction between Jordanian politics on the Inside and Palestinian politics on the Outside. The Charter maintained that both the Jordanian and the Palestinian national identities were legitimate and real, and that they were not in conflict with one another but rather stood together against the common Israeli enemy and the threat of "the Alternative Homeland." The Charter called for a Palestinian state, which would hopefully be united with Jordan by the free will of both sides after the achievement of Palestinian sovereignty. It also guaranteed the full citizenship rights of all Jordanians of all origins. While many Jordanians bemoan the failure of the Charter to become a central reference point for political life, it does stand as a powerful expression of formal consensus.

In the following section, I examine the preferences and positions of the major political and identity groups in the Jordanian public sphere and demonstrate how they came to converge on this particular formula in the process of public deliberation; and how their acceptance of this conception of identity reshaped political parties, state and civil society institutions, and articulation of national interests.

The dynamics of competitive framing provided clear incentives for entrepreneurs to take ever more extreme positions in a bid to draw attention and support (Lake and Rothchild 1998; Snyder and Ballantine 1997). Jordanian nationalists, the first to take advantage of the new freedoms, tended to drive and dominate the political debate. Because of the general Palestinian unwillingness to publicly identify as Palestinian within Jordan, Jordanian identity extremists possessed an inherent advantage. Since the severing of ties made the East Bank the exclusive focus of state identity, "native" East Bankers seized the initiative in interpreting the change. Indeed, framing issues in terms of identity strengthened Transjordanians; Palestinians generally preferred to avoid identity frames. As one Palestinian activist complained, "there is a Satanic spirit in the press. . . . [they] write in an attempt to arouse differences."[13] Whether it is better to discuss identity-based conflicts, and thereby possibly inflame them, or to ignore them and thereby allow them to fester, is a central topic in the Jordanian debate as in liberal theory more generally (Benhabib 1996). I argue that such deliberation, however dangerous, is necessary for the production of new identity norms. Without ignoring the danger that public discourse can lead to polarization and extremism, it is also only through public deliberation that preferences can change in the direction of a shared interpretive frame.

The monarchy has generally been understood as providing the ultimate guarantee against ethnic conflict in Jordan. Since the Black September civil war in 1970, all groups in Jordan have recognized the power of the state and the army against such mobilization. Furthermore, all groups have been sobered by the Lebanese experience. By serving as a balancer between the competing demands of the various groups in Jordanian society, the throne prevents the escalation of ethnic conflict and the descent into anarchy. The Hijazi origins of the Hashemite family, which only arrived in Transjordan in 1922, hinders the monarchy from articulating an ethnic Jordanian identity. King Hussein adopted a public position based on two key assertions: first, that "Jordan is the country of the *muhajarin* and *insar*"—a reference to the early days of Islam; and second, that "whoever harms our national unity will be my enemy until judgment day." All Jordanian citizens "regardless of roots or origins have all the rights and bear all the responsibilities of citizenship." Hussein articulated an inclusivist frame, in which Palestinians could participate as full citizens without endangering the Jordanian identity of the state. Hussein often intervened to prevent the escalation of identity debates, appealing for national unity in the face of difficult times.

Despite this inclusionary discourse, the monarchy has often been the source of division as well, manipulating tensions and mistrust between ethnic groups in order to prevent the consolidation of a united popular opposition (Brand 1988, 1995; Abu Odeh 1997). Since Black September, the regime has encouraged Transjordanian sentiment in order to guarantee a social base for the regime and to prevent opposition alliances across communal lines. Ethnic preferences in the state apparatus and the army, along with direct ties between the monarchy and the tribes, provide material benefits. The adoption of a "one-vote" electoral law, with districts carefully drawn to overrepresent the Transjordanian community, provide political benefits; this law has drawn fire as fomenting ethnic conflict and division. The tension between Hussein's inclusivist discourse and his governments' resort to exclusivist practices shapes the public space for Jordanian identity politics.

Jordanian exclusivists, more powerful within an identity frame, drove the debate. Prominent writers such as Fahd al-Fanik provided the intellectual support, arguing for the reconceptualization of Jordanian foreign policy interests and domestic political structures along a wide range of issues. Abd al-Hadi al-Majali, head of the largest Jordanian exclusivist party, *al-Ahd*, represented the major political party advancing this position. *Al-Ahd* quickly acquired a reputation as the "state's party." While it is often misinterpreted as a "tribal" party, *al-Ahd* advocates a state-centric nationalism in which political loyalty is more important than ethnic identity. Identity must be clearly defined and manifested in political behavior: everybody carrying a Jordanian passport must have a Jordanian political identity. As Fanik puts it, "national unity depends upon there existing a single national identity. . . . there can not be two national identities in Jordan" (in Hourani 1996: 168).[14] Jordanian identity means "accepting the political form of the Jordanian state . . . whoever lives on Jordanian land is Jordanian as long as he [sic] accepts the constitution and the Jordanian identity."[15] Whatever one's private sense of identity, one must publicly profess a Jordanian identity: "Jordan . . . is a homeland for all Jordanians and all Palestinians who choose to live in it. . . . all of us are citizens of the Jordanian state except the one who wants to incite events and declare openly his Palestinian identity."[16] In June 1997, *al-Ahd* formed the core of a new party, the National Constitutional Party, which brought together eight centrist parties. The NCP offers a more ambiguous version of exclusivism, and its spokesmen have contested efforts to portray it as an exclusivist party.[17] The NCP publicly identifies with the state and with the regime, rather than with the Transjordanian community and the tribes. The NCP and its symbols have moderated their identity discourse under the pressure of public argument, although it is difficult to say whether this represents a tactical retreat or a change in their preferences.[18] Its poor electoral performance in 1997 raised doubts about the power of such an identification, but in late 1998 Abd al-Hadi al-Majali became the first political party leader to be elected speaker of the House of Representatives.

Competition between different strands of Jordanian exclusivism is a major component of the strategic framing process. A radical exclusivism based on a tribal Jordanian national identity also asserted itself after the severing of ties. Ahmed Awidi al-Abaddi, Member of Parliament from 1989–1993 and re-elected in 1997, has been among the most assertive public voices, advocating a primal Jordanian claim on the land and the state.[19] Abaddi's ideology expresses ethnic hostility to Palestinians and non-Jordanians regardless of their political positions. Unlike *al-Ahd*, which relies upon a sharp public/private distinction and will accept all who are loyal to the Jordanian state, Abaddi refuses to permit any deviation from criteria of blood and tribe. Abaddi questioned the Jordan-Israel peace treaty, which *al-Ahd* supported, because it contained no provision for the return of the Palestinians who, in his mind, corrupted and threatened Jordan. In June 1998, Abaddi's declarations about Palestinian disloyalty in a Gulf TV roundtable led to calls to strip him of Parliamentary immunity and prosecute him for harming national unity. In November 1996, Nahid Hattar, a prominent intellectual of this trend, sparked a public outcry with an article entitled "Who is the Jordanian?"[20] In the firestorm that followed, Hattar was harassed, arrested, and accused of political subversion, even as all parties struggled to answer his question. Hattar's newspaper, *al-Mithaq*, relentlessly drove home the opposition of this trend to any plans that involved the resettlement of Palestinian refugees in Jordan. Many Jordanian public figures—even those associated with the conservative Jordanian exclusivist trend—express fear of, and often contempt for, radical Jordanian exclusivism; but the increasing power of these ideas should not be underestimated. Indeed, *al-Mithaq* is one of

the most outspoken opposition newspapers, despite its Transjordanian identification. Radical exclusivism has an increasingly legitimate place in the
public sphere, and thrives within the salons. The harsh criticism of any
moves toward ties with the West Bank or toward resettlement of the Palestinian refugees in Jordan has powerfully influenced the Jordanian debate
and clearly constrains state behavior. "*Iqlimiyya*" remains a normatively
charged insult, however, and the exclusivists have not succeeded in establishing a consensus on their vision of the national community.

On the Palestinian side, *Hashd*, an offshoot party of the DFLP, advanced
a forceful inclusivist identity claim within the boundaries of the East Bank.
This is not an extreme of Palestinian exclusivism to match the Jordanian
extreme: no party could legitimately take such a position in the new Jordan.
The assertion of a Palestinian identity for Jordan would be equated with the
Israeli assertion that "Jordan is Palestine"; the assertion of binationalism
would be similarly interpreted, at least by Jordanian nationalists. While
Hashd does not command a large mass following, its contribution to Jordanian public debate has been disproportionately large. *Hashd* sees the "call
to establish special Palestinian organizations in Jordan . . . [as] a call to
divide the ranks of the national [*wataniyya*] movement in the country"
(*Hashd* 1992a). The severing of ties "prepared the way for reordering the
relations between the two brotherly Jordanian and Palestinian peoples on
the basis of equality and brotherhood and independence . . . [and] solidarity
against the common enemy."[21] In other words, *Hashd* endorsed the East
Bank borders, but called for a legitimate place for Palestinian-origin citizens
in the new political order. Palestinians in Jordan are both an integral part
of the Palestinian people and an indivisible part of Jordan, and no conception of identity unable to resolve both of these facts can prove satisfactory.
Palestinians in Jordan have legitimate rights and face real discrimination,
requiring political action. *Hashd* fought for the ability both to hold a Palestinian identity and to act as a Jordanian citizen. This position has proven
difficult to maintain, and Palestinian citizens have largely refrained from
such political action. A more moderate Palestinian-identified party, the
Democratic Party, hoping to represent the interests of the Palestinian elite,
failed almost completely to advance a coherent political project.

The Islamist movement, the largest and best organized political movement in Jordan, rejected the emphasis on Jordanian/Palestinian cleavages,
presenting an inclusivist identity claim that did not recognize the separation
from the West Bank. Claiming to be the only party "not worm-ridden with
the disease of chauvinism," the Islamist movement attempted to downplay

identity problems. Islamism offered an ideology in which Palestinians could participate in oppositional politics (Robinson 1997a). In the 1993 elections, the IAF claimed half of the Palestinian origin members of Parliament, although they attempted to downplay the significance. Invoking the traditional Muslim response to sedition, the Islamists declaim regularly: "*Fitna* [anarchy, civil strife] sleeps, and woe unto he who awakens it." Because of their close relations with Hamas, the Jordanian Islamist movement often criticized the Palestinian Authority even as it argued for inclusivist Jordanian politics. At one point, the Islamist weekly *al-Sabil* denounced the "Arafatist Fifth Column" for instigating Palestinian identity mobilization inside of Jordan.[22] The Islamists were the political movement least convinced by the severing of ties, but in practice they recognized the distinction between the two political entities. The Islamist boycott of the 1997 elections led to a serious split in the movement, partially along communal lines; many of the Islamist leaders who preferred to participate in the political system ["doves"] were of Jordanian origin, while many of the most adamant in support of the boycott ["hawks"] were of Palestinian origin.

Arabists similarly decried the separation of Jordan and Palestine as an artificial division of the larger Arab nation. Unlike the Arab critics of the Jordanian "annexation" of the West Bank, many Arabists active in the Jordanian public sphere celebrate the Jordanian "union" with the West Bank as an outstanding example of real Arab unity (Tal 1986, 1993). They call for an inclusivist identity incorporating the West Bank, and denounced the severing of ties as "separatism [*infisaliyya*]." Fahd al-Rimawi, editor of a major Arabist weekly, argues that the process of intermingling of populations has progressed to the point where it is impossible to really speak of two peoples. For political purposes, he recognizes the utility of the assertion of such separate identities but, he contends, the vast majority of "Jordastinians" have little use for these formulations. The primary use of the identity differentiation is to prevent the consolidation of a united opposition front and to further the agenda of prioritizing Jordanian state interests over Arab nationalist interests. Rimawi remained unfazed by rancorous identity debates, dismissing them as futile attempts by self-interested chauvinists to invoke a nonexistent reality: "I don't feel any danger from chauvinist attempts at division. . . . our unity is just fine despite the efforts of some saboteurs who try and create chauvinism."[23] Despite the strong Arabist convictions of most Jordanians, however, Arabist parties have become marginalized. The identification of Arabist parties with Syria or Iraq, in particular, has been a target of the articulation of specifically Jordanian identity and interests.

Finally, a liberal position, heavily represented in the semi-official daily press, relies upon the concept of citizenship to overcome identity-based differences.[24] This position accepts the consensus on the revision of state borders, while opposing the exclusivist vision of identity for domestic politics. This position most accords with the public position of King Hussein, and its supporters often invoke his prestige and his public statements. Both the Constitution and the 1991 National Charter explicitly guarantee full rights to all citizens regardless of roots or origins. The liberals place their hopes in the power of open debate to overcome discrimination and the rise of exclusivist identity positions, and are the most dedicated in their defense of the public sphere, although they occasionally call for an end to destructive, irresponsible identity discourse. While their position relies on identity-blind citizenship and public sphere debate, the liberals frequently are on the defensive.

Many opposition figures decried the emphasis on identity politics, which divided the opposition, and blamed the regime for their appearance. In February 1997, Layth Shubaylat released a provocative open letter warning that "the state is collapsing and society is dividing"; his trenchant critiques of regime policy have landed him in jail repeatedly.[25] Toujan Faisal, Shubaylat's ideological opposite in most regards, similarly accused the Palace of manipulating identity tensions in order to prevent society from unifying. She, like many more moderate serious political observers, warned that the manipulation of communal tensions could spin out of control and cause Jordanian society to splinter. In February 1997, the coalition of opposition parties denounced identity extremism: "We reject allowing parochialism and sectarianism to emerge with their evil manifestations.. We should unite the people and not divide them. . . . The Jordanian national opposition parties call on everybody to halt this harmful debate."[26] The outlines of an elite, establishment opposition emerged in 1997, although it failed to establish a political party to contest the elections. This coalition, revolving around the unlikely combination of the Palestinian-origin Taher al-Masri and the Transjordanian-origin Ahmed Obaydat, articulated an inclusivist internal order along with a clear acceptance of the East Bank borders. As the opposition formulated plans for a comprehensive National Conference in the summer of 1998, defense of national unity and rejection of Jordanian-Palestinian conflict, combined with acceptance of the severing of ties and the need for a Palestinian state, were prominent components of its alternative national agenda.

Jordanian Institutions: Consolidating Change

Unlike earlier Jordanian strategies toward the West Bank after 1967, the revision of Jordan's borders after 1988 became embedded in domestic institutions. The institutionalization of the new consensus on the borders of the state, embedded in state and civil societal institutions, stabilized the new foreign policy preferences (Katzenstein 1996a; Lustick 1997). The new norms moved from the state and Parliament into societal institutions, including the press, political parties, and the Professional Associations. Not everything changed; in particular, the failure to revise the Constitution, which enshrined the principle of unity, left a window for opponents of the decision to criticize its legality or reality. Nevertheless, by the early 1990s, institutional change had progressed to a point that made any return unlikely. A return to the West Bank by the late 1990s would involve institutional and discursive transformation as dramatic as the unification in 1950 or the severing of ties itself.

State Institutions

Institutional change began within the state apparatus. Every state agency underwent a comprehensive review of its policies in order to conform with the new concept of Jordan, changing regulations on everything from drivers licenses to marriage regulations. Jordanian employees in the West Bank were pensioned off based on their years of service and their activities discontinued. New sets of regulations were drafted governing travel permits, green cards, applications to public universities. A Palestinian office in the Foreign Ministry replaced the Ministry for Occupied Territory Affairs, dramatically symbolizing the new conception of the West Bank. Officials emphasized that the measures applied only to those Palestinians resident on the West Bank, not to Jordanian citizens of Palestinian origin resident on the East Bank. In other words, the severing of ties was initially intended to affect borders without affecting domestic order or state identity.

Since the severing of ties, observers have noted an unpublicized but widespread "Jordanization" of the state apparatus. While the state has always been the primary employer of the Transjordanian community, since 1988 it is perceived to have become much more "ethnically pure." A widespread belief exists that there is an ethnic division of labor in society: Transjordanians control the public sector, Palestinians control the private sector (Center for

Strategic Studies [hereafter CSS] 1995; Hourani and Abd al-Rahman 1995;
T. Tal 1996). Successive Prime Ministers (Abd al-Salam al-Majali, Zayd bin
Shakir, Abd al-Karim Kabariti) have been perceived as sympathetic to the
conservative Jordanian nationalist trend and hostile to Palestinians. This
"hostility," interestingly, has not interfered with their ability to build good
relations with Arafat and the PNA; the severing of ties consensus reconciles
precisely these two positions.

Parliament

The dissolution of Parliament, with its West Bank representation from
pre-1967 days, marked a particularly significant step in the institutionalization of the new borders. The justification for the freezing of Parliamentary
life had long been that new elections could not be called as long as half the
Kingdom was under occupation. Dissolving Parliament delivered a deeply
symbolic political statement that the West Bank no longer constituted part
of the state. The election of a new Parliament from the East Bank had long
been considered a point of no return in discussions about Jordan-West Bank
relations. Once taken, this step strengthened the interpretation that a substantively new era had begun: "the elections deepened the legality of the
severing of ties . . . [because] the postponing of Parliamentary life had been
deeply tied to the situation of the West Bank" (Abu Roman 1989: 26). The
drafting of an electoral law specific to the East Bank powerfully symbolized
the new conception of the Jordanian political community.

Despite its lack of real power, the Parliament represented an important
locus of Jordanian national identity. The 1989 elections produced a major
victory for the Islamist movement, brought in numerous independent and
opposition figures, and almost completely defeated regime-identified candidates. This independent, popular Parliament became a central site for
national political commentary and an active forum for debate, and would
eventually produce a series of important, relatively liberal laws governing
the press and political parties, and revoking martial law. The ardor for the
Parliament cooled over the years, in the face of its impotence before the
executive branch. Nevertheless, Parliament continued to play an important
symbolic and practical role in the political process, and its election from
East Bank districts affirmed the borders and identity of the state. In 1993, in
the wake of the Oslo accords, many voices called for the postponing of
elections until the status of Jordanians of Palestinian origin could be made
clear (Riedel 1994; Hourani 1995). Nevertheless, elections went ahead as

scheduled, as the King and most Jordanians came to agree that Jordan should not allow its political life to be held hostage to Palestinian developments. Changes to the election law and gerrymandering produced a much less independent and effective Parliament than in 1989, to the dismay of political society. Palestinian representation was low, not least because of the conflicting official statements about the relationship between voting in these elections and possible forfeiture of the right of return (Riedel 1994). In 1997, despite a popular consensus against the electoral law, elections went ahead in the face of a boycott by the Islamic opposition and significant state repression. Palestinian representation in the 1997 Parliament was exceptionally low, as tribal candidates dominated the voting and most politically active Palestinians honored the opposition boycott.[27]

Citizenship and Passports

Prior to the severing of ties, Jordanian law considered all West Bank residents, as well as West Bank refugees on the East Bank, to be Jordanians, carrying standard Jordanian passports (al-Hadawi 1993). After the disengagement, the citizenship laws developed new criteria based on place of residence. Those whose normal place of residence was the West Bank were to be considered Palestinian while those who normally resided on the East Bank were to be considered Jordanian. As the Minister of the Interior explained, "who is Jordanian and who is Palestinian is determined by his natural, regular place of residence"—not by blood, political preference, or outside attribution.[28] Those classified as Palestinian under the new system were to receive temporary two-year passports for convenience, but without citizenship. The government emphasized that participating in the Jordanian system would in no way prejudice the citizen of Palestinian origin's right to choose to become a citizen of any independent Palestinian state which some day might be created.

Reports of the confiscation of the passports of citizens of Palestinian origin entered the public sphere in the mid-1990s, raising new questions about state policy.[29] The government downplayed the issue as isolated, individual cases, but the Parliamentary Committee on Public Freedoms continued to pressure the government to explain its policies. In the state of confusion, uncertainty and state-society distrust which characterized the period after the peace treaty, the combination of persistent reports of such actions and of government denial fueled popular concern. In late 1995, the issue would be blurred again after the government offered five-year passports to residents of the West Bank. The passport would not be compulsory, and would not connote Jordanian citizenship. Jordanian exclusivists, infuriated by an apparent step back from the severing of ties, complained bitterly. Regime spokesmen countered that "granting Palestinians five year passports does not mean that they are Jordanians, because a passport does not mean nationality" or give their carriers the right to take residence in Jordan, to vote in elections or to run for office.[30] This effort to sever the administrative dimensions of the passport from the politics of identity found few takers. Prime Minister Zayd bin Shakir's warning that "the issue of citizenship is a very sensitive one and we reject that it becomes an issue of debate" did little to stem the debate.[31]

It is important to remember that the 1967 refugees from the West Bank had been full Jordanian citizens at the time of their exodus from West to East Bank, giving them a very different status both in international law and in Jordanian law from the 1948 refugees.[32] This legal difference did not always translate into political differentiation. Referring to the election activities of the Palestinian-origin Islamist Mohammed Awida, a Jordanian exclusivist wrote: "I advise him to pack his bags and nominate himself in the appropriate place, for the elections in Palestine are near and his discourse will succeed there better than in Amman." Al-Sabil responded that "these words are not new and not surprising, considering their source which is full of hatred and evil, but what is new is that these words were published." This point refers back to the structural shift in the public sphere, as issues of identity previously beyond the pale moved to center stage. "When Mohammed Awida and Taher Masri and others [from the West Bank] came to Jordan they carried Jordanian nationality, and had been resident on land under Jordanian sovereignty and they left it under the force of occupation.. if the Jews occupied Kerak [the southern, tribal stronghold of Jordanian nationalism] and its residents fled to Amman, would we say to them, you are no longer citizens?!" The struggle to frame the relationship between citizenship and identity could hardly be more forcefully presented: why should the citizenship of former residents of the West Bank be implicated in the debates over Jordanian identity? Was the severing of ties retroactive? Furthermore, as Taher al-Masri asked Abd al-Hadi al-Majali in a public exchange, what criteria could possibly be used to conclusively identify every citizen as Jordanian or Palestinian, given intermarriage, long residency, and overlapping identities?

The clearest flaw in any strict correspondence between passport and identity lay with the population of the refugee camps. Controversies over the camps regularly exploded, over the suspected intentions of Jordan to expel the refugees, to resettle them permanently in Jordan, or even to maintain the status quo. In 1997, a project funded by international agencies to improve living conditions in the camps was framed as evidence of regime intentions to resettle the refugees in Jordan. Despite regime claims that "there is no political goal" and that "this and every government has been consistent in rejecting resettlement," the *tawtin* frame remained active.[33] Jordanian officials consistently denied any intention of accepting the resettlement of Palestinian refugees in Jordan. Rejection of *tawtin* represented a fundamental point of consensus across the entire Jordanian political spectrum, similar to the consensus found in Palestinian, Lebanese, and general Arab political opinion. Of course, there were sharply conflicting interpretations within the *tawtin* frame about what constituted resettlement. Considerable evidence suggests that regime officials do not share the popular consensus rejecting any resettlement of Palestinian refugees, but rather are taking a more flexible approach.[34] The process of Jordanization mingled uneasily with Palestinian and Jordanian peace treaties, which seemed to surrender any real hope of the return of Palestinian refugees to Palestine. The consensus against *tawtin* both constrained state behavior and, I would argue, constituted Jordan's conception of its interests in the refugee negotiations. Certainly, Jordan had complicated and crosscutting interests, in terms of retaining access to UNRWA funding and achieving a final status settlement with Israel, but the underlying consensus against resettlement was consistently expressed in Jordanian discourse and practice.

Jordanian exclusivists relentlessly pursued the idea that the Jordanian state had accepted the principle of resettling the Palestinian refugees and were no longer committed to the Jordanian consensus. Radicals searched every government statement and every government policy for evidence of a resettlement decision.[35] Everything from improvements of the camps to administrative redistricting "proved" that resettlement was nigh. For the radicals, resettlement of the refugees represented the worst possible outcome, since it would permanently ratify a demographic situation unfavorable to Transjordanians and prevent the consolidation of the Jordanian identity and state. The fear that Jordanians would "lack sovereignty in their own country" permeated radical discourse. Radical exclusivists opposed the peace process, unlike the conservative exclusivists, because they saw it as inevitably leading to the resettlement of the Palestinians in Jordan. The issue of resettlement divided the radical and conservative Jordanian exclusivists in interesting ways. The radicals accused the conservatives of secretly supporting resettlement, because their support for the peace process could not have any other implication. Conservative exclusivists thus had to respond to attacks from Palestinians and liberals, who accused them of working against the interests of the Palestinian community, and the radical Transjordanians, who accused them of working too much for the interests of the Palestinian elite. The ability of the exclusivists to raise havoc in the public sphere over anything that looked like resettlement did constrain the Jordanian government. Their extreme distaste for the protagonists probably meant that this particular stream of argument did not shape state understandings of Jordanian interests, however.

Civil Society

While the state could be restructured by fiat, societal institutions resisted what could be viewed as state encroachment on civil society. The institutional restructuring could succeed only by brute state force—power—or by successfully establishing new norms about Jordanian identity—argumentation. Advocates of the new Jordan repeated the mantra that "the severing of ties must be implemented comprehensively." This implementation was expected to extend deep into civil society and not be restricted to state and official institutions. In general, the more deeply embedded and autonomous the civil society institution, the more it resisted the demand for change— the professional associations and the Islamic movement being the key examples. Less well-entrenched or autonomous institutions, such as the press and the newly legalized political parties, proved more responsive. Within a few years, however, virtually all Jordanian institutions had at least begun to restructure around the new state identity.

Professional Associations

The Professional Associations proved most resistant to the attempt to impose change in identity norms from above. These Associations had long been a center of opposition political activity in Jordan, given the illegality of political parties and the constraints upon political and societal organization (Hamarneh 1995; Abu Bandura 1993). Since the early 1970s, the professional associations had represented the primary site of open political contestation for the Jordanian elite, and had succeeded in carving out relative autonomy from the state. In October 1988, the editor of the leading daily newspaper unleashed a fierce assault on the political role of the Professional

Associations.[36] There had always been a Jordanian-Palestinian dimension in the political role of the Associations, because of the Palestinian domination of the private sector and the prominence of Palestinian factions in their elections (Hamarneh 1995; Brand 1988; Sha'ir 1987). After the severing of ties, this dimension became explicit.[37] Majali called to solve the "problem of Palestinian representation" in the Associations by dissolving the organizational links between their West Bank and East Bank memberships. The Associations, he concluded, must implement the separation between Jordan and Palestine, or else they must surrender their political role. In either case, defenders of the Associations saw a direct strike against their independence, and reacted by tenaciously defending their West Bank branches.

The liberal transition in 1989 temporarily eased the pressure on the Associations, but the linkage between identity politics and political opposition in the Associations carried forward. The battle over the Associations wove together themes of political opposition, identity, and the boundaries of Jordanian political action. In late 1992, the participation of West Bank lawyers in the Association elections drew fire in press articles such as the bluntly titled "Sever your ties, oh lawyers!!"[38] One exclusivist complained that the Association had "surrendered its right to represent itself . . . despite the severing of ties . . . Jordan's Associations remain only a waiting station for our West Bank brothers."[39] In June 1994, exclusivists charged the Associations with failing to adapt to the new Jordanian realities: "It was assumed that the Associations would change their situation in line with the severing of ties, but they . . . consider themselves outside the Jordanian framework."[40] Engineer Association President Layth Shubaylat's response rejected the attempt to impose a narrow interpretation of Jordanian identity and interests: "These are injurious words which divide the nation. . . . while he claims that it is a 'patriotic duty' to expel these [Palestinian] members . . . we say that it is a patriotic duty to silence this pen which aims at destroying the unity of society."[41] The resistance to the demand to sever organizational ties in the Associations generally framed its opposition in terms of resistance to state encroachment on civil society—a democracy frame—rather than in terms of an identity frame.

By February 1995, the Associations had emerged as a center of opposition to the peace process and normalization with Israel. The elected leaderships of most Associations opposed normalization, which undermined regime claims to represent the will of the Jordanian majority. The elected councils of the Associations adopted binding resolutions forbidding their members from dealing with Israelis. In February and March, the government challenged the results of Lawyers and Doctors Association elections by invoking an identity, rather than a democracy, frame. The Minister of Justice challenged the West Bank lawyers' participation as "an issue of state sovereignty," citing the incompatibility of the West Bank participation with Jordanian identity and legislation. The bitterness of the campaign, the depth of the ensuing debate, and the participation in that debate of a wide range of personalities demonstrate that the public recognized the importance of the Associations as the testing ground of competing visions of Jordanian identity and norms.

In November 1995, the government struck at the Associations again, proposing fundamental revisions of the Association laws which would eviscerate their political and professional role. Despite a show of concern over the Associations' failure to provide professional services, the regime made little effort to conceal that its actions were intended to break societal opposition to the peace treaty. It claimed that the elected leadership did not really represent the silent majority in the Associations and threatened to appoint new, truly representative, leadership. At the height of the campaign against the Associations and their "unrepresentative" political positions, the Islamist ticket embarrassingly swept 40 of 49 seats in the Engineer elections, which re-elected the imprisoned opposition leader Layth Shubaylat as President with over 90 percent of the vote. After boycotting the 1997 national elections, Islamist candidates swept almost all civil society elections, pointedly demonstrating the unrepresentative character of a Parliament devoid of opposition. A leading Islamist commentator pointed out that "the election of the opposition in the Associations destroys the government claim, both at home and abroad, that its actions enjoy popular support."[42] The government implied that "the opposition has a Palestinian face," while opposition leaders insisted that they represented a popular front which crossed communal lines. If positions expressed by civil society could be labeled Palestinian, they could be dismissed as outside the Jordanian national consensus; if they represented the voice of a democratically elected leadership, they could not be so dismissed.

In terms of an identity frame, based on the logic of the severing of ties, it was hard to dispute the need to separate the Jordanian and Palestinian branches of the Associations; however, in a democracy frame, the autonomy of civil society demanded the defense of their institutional integrity. The public sphere rallied behind the Associations, primarily on the grounds of protecting democracy against state repression. The frustration of one regime supporter is extremely telling: "How do these people want to play a role in two states? [the Government] was right both legally and politically. . . . only the political salons and the press don't seem to understand this political era."[43] Through this public deliberation over the Associations, the broader consensus on the East Bank conception of Jordan was strengthened, even as the Associations resisted the separation. Justifications and arguments were presented on both sides in terms that accepted the boundaries between the two entities; even the most ardent defenders of institutional unity argued their case in terms of helping Palestinians achieve their independent state, not in terms of maintaining a Jordanian role in the West Bank.

Political Parties

Other civil society institutions lacked the Associations' entrenched position and adapted more readily to the new borders. The new identity norms played a major role in the formation of political parties. The public deliberation over the adoption of a new Political Parties Law emphasized the goal of establishing the Jordanian identity of political parties. The first parties to be formed and recognized were Jordanian exclusivist parties with close ties to the state, such as al-Ahd (Haddad 1994; Hourani 1995). The Muslim Brotherhood formed a political party, the Islamic Action Front, to contest elections, after a heated internal debate over the legitimacy of democratic participation (Robinson 1997a; Abu Roman 1991). Underground ideological parties, such as the various branches of the Ba'th and the Jordanian Communist Party, hastened to emerge as legal Jordanian parties by demonstrating their financial and operational independence. Palestinian factions, as discussed below, had the most turbulent road to legality. Unlike the Associations, these political parties were new creations without deeply embedded institutional structures or constituencies. The older parties often had difficulty making the transition from underground activity to legal activity. Constant government inspection of party finances, complaints of internal authoritarianism, and the difficulties of attracting a mass membership left most parties weak and ineffective.

The Political Parties Law ratified in 1993 mandated that parties must not have any outside organizational or political ties. While Arabist parties tied to Syria and Iraq and smaller Islamist parties were targeted by the "Jordanian character" dimension of the law, the primary intent was to establish Jordanian parties independent of the Palestinian arena. Palestinian factions did obtain licenses, but they did so only by accepting and validating the normative principle of a sharp distinction between Jordanian and Palestinian.

Few of these parties proved successful in the electoral arena, and none explicitly claimed to represent the Palestinian community. The generally low rates of participation in Jordanian elections by the Palestinian communities partially explains the weakness of these parties, but their problems go deeper. Electoral districting ensured that Palestinian population centers would be underrepresented (Hourani 1995; Riedel 1994). More fundamentally, the identity structure of the new Jordanian political arena discouraged Palestinian political participation and prevented the articulation of a legitimate generalizable interest in their name.

Fateh, the largest Palestinian faction in Jordan, chose not to organize a party. Jordanian officials recognized that Fateh would be able to exert a powerful influence over Jordanian politics if it so chose. The power of the "Jordan is Jordan, Palestine is Palestine" formula lay in this implicit bargain. For *Fateh*, Jordanian support for a Palestinian state far outweighed the advantages of playing an active role in Jordanian electoral politics. As the PLO splintered over the Oslo process, and the establishment of the PNA created tremendous organizational problems on the ground, Arafat badly needed the support that Hussein could provide.

Other Palestinian factions did organize into Jordanian parties. As discussed above, *Hashd* generated the most public debate. In the early 1990s, the Jordanian wing of the DFLP reconstituted itself as an independent Jordanian party, arguing that "after the severing of ties we felt that something had really changed."[44] *Hashd* became a test case for the broader questions of political parties and identity. As early as April 1991, Jordanian exclusivists attacked the newly reconstituted party: "is it logical that there be a Jordanian party with the goal of guaranteeing the right of part of the Jordanian people to preserve a non-Jordanian identity and to express it in a framework that is not the Jordanian state?"[45] In early 1992 the question resurfaced.[46] Parliamentary debates over the Political Parties Law in 1992 and 1993 were obsessed with "Palestinian factions pretending to be Jordanian parties."[47] As parties began to apply for licenses in late 1992, the debate escalated: "In this new era . . . with a National Charter aimed at eliminating the phenomenon of dual loyalty and dual nationality . . . is it rational to license a party that has a non-Jordanian nationality and has loyalty to something other than Jordan?"[48] After the Interior Ministry rejected its first application, public opinion leaned toward granting the license on democratic grounds despite deep unease on identity grounds. Public opinion could be mobilized behind the right to form opposition parties—the democracy frame—but not around the right of Jordanians of Palestinian origin to be represented by Palestinian parties. Despite complaints of "hired pens in the service of a coordinated campaign . . . about the necessity of licensing certain parties that have non-Jordanian foundations and financing and affiliation and loyalty," the Interior Ministry eventually granted the license.[49] In February, Fahd al-Fanik offered an eloquent statement of the logic of identity in the public sphere, writing that "the democratic process of Jordan will influence *Hashd* more than *Hashd* will influence it, and the result will be the focus of *Hashd* on Jordanian national issues . . . from a Jordanian perspective."[50]

Despite its attempts to develop a Jordanian Palestinian identity, *Hashd* suffered defections and a power struggle between its "Jordanian" and "Palestinian" factions. A party conference in September 1994 affirmed close control by the DFLP over the nominally independent party, igniting a firestorm of criticism within the Jordanian public sphere. Most of the party's public figures left the party, expressing their anger that the party had failed to live up to its ambition of becoming a truly Jordanian party. In July 1995 the Interior Ministry took the smaller and more "Palestinian-ized" *Hashd* to court over its "foreign connections."[51] Politically moderate Palestinian-origin defectors formed smaller liberal or leftist parties, but struggled to mobilize support absent a clear identity.

More important than the details of *Hashd*'s struggle for legal recognition is what this case reveals about identity politics in the new Jordan. First, the primary arena for contesting interpretations was the Jordanian press, which allowed a wide range of positions to be articulated in the search for consensus. The strongly felt need to establish consensus on political identity drove participation in this debate, and the fear of the consolidation of unacceptable norms prevented concerned writers from abstaining from comment. The party did change in the course of this debate, as it sought a publicly acceptable formula for combining a Palestinian and a Jordanian identity. Third, the debate was primarily driven by the Jordanian exclusivists. Centrists, liberals, and Palestinians were almost always on the defensive when identity politics came to define the political situation. Only when conflict could be framed in terms of an issue like normalization or democracy, which could unite Jordanians of all origins, could these actors reclaim the offensive.

The contrast between the experience of a primarily Palestinian party like *Hashd* and the experience of the Jordanian-identified National Constitutional Party is instructive. The NCP received tremendous coverage in the media, mostly positive in the semi-official dailies, with more criticism from the opposition weeklies. The NCP leadership was composed mainly of former government ministers and regime figures, lending it an air of power.

Despite all these advantages, however, the NCP failed to be much more successful than other political parties in the 1997 elections, demonstrating the general weakness of political parties in the new Jordan.

The Press

The press, as the primary media for public sphere debate, played an important role in shaping identity discourse. Before the passage of a new Press and Publications Law, some new independent weeklies began to publish abroad. After the passage of the new law, Jordanian streets were filled with dozens of new political weeklies, all seeking market share and aggressively pushing the bounds of public discourse. This weekly press significantly transformed the Jordanian public sphere. Identity politics sold newspapers, and the weekly press pushed every red line in pursuit of market share. Political entrepreneurs took advantage of this willingness to publish a wide range of views and used the weekly press as a forum for advancing their competing identity projects.

The 1993 Press and Publications Law was a fundamental part of the attempt to institutionalize a liberalized political system. Along with concern for "responsible" freedoms, a major theme in public debates about the new Press Law was the need for all publications to be Jordanian, with no external ties or support. Palestinians were again the major target of the debate, although ties to Syria, Iraq and Iran also aroused significant attention. Like the state, the Parliament, the Professional Associations, and political parties, the press became a site for situating the distinct Jordanian identity. Harming national unity was one of the specified red lines in the Law. The ownership provisions in the new Press Law favored Jordanians, which helps to account for the prominent position of Jordanian exclusivists in many weeklies. *Shihan*, the one well-established weekly, was owned by the Transjordanian-origin Riyad al-Haroub, and highlighted Jordanian-Palestinian tensions and published leading exclusivist writers. Proposed revisions to the 1993 law tightened these ownership provisions.[52] The 1997 temporary press law, which closed down most of the weekly press, did not focus specifically upon the identity issue, but did target all manifestations of societal criticism of regime policies. The 1998 revised Press and Publications Law aimed to control the public sphere even more tightly, and the alleged harms to national unity and attacks on Arafat's PNA played a key role in the framing of the new legislation.[53]

It is difficult to exaggerate the extent to which Jordanian-Palestinian identity issues came to dominate press debate. Discussion of identity politics, long banned, became commonplace. Among the many issues framed in communal terms were the privatization of the state; administrative reform; electoral districts and the election law; press reporting; the professional associations; economic reform; university admissions; military spending; public spending on refugee camps; the allocation of water; subsidies for agriculture. Deliberation about the relationship between identity and politics appeared regularly. Identity extremists were the first to take advantage of the new freedoms. As early as September 1989, two prominent liberals warned that "for the first time in the history of the Jordanian press there appear hateful essays trying to arouse hatred and envy" (Masri and Arar 1989). The implications of these public debates were not universally negative, however. Given the absence of consensus identity norms, public debate was essential for the production of a new consensus. The real sense of grievance and discrimination felt by both Palestinians and Transjordanians deserved a public hearing (CSS 1995; Hourani and Abd al-Rahman 1995). Liberals, particularly those of Palestinian origin, felt that debate had not gone far enough, and that fundamental issues of discrimination and inequality remained untouched. Jordanian exclusivists, for their part, vented the "fear of being charged with chauvinism [iqlimiya], which has become a terrorist weapon easily waved in the face of anyone to prevent him from thinking aloud about the future of Jordan."[54]

Opinion was sharply divided about the benefit of public discussion of identity. Participants and readers alike began to question the liberal premise that debate would secure a more stable consensus. Mohammed al-Subayhi, for example, observed in October 1995 that "the only result . . . has been the forming of two trenches inside the Jordanian state."[55] Rather than producing a new consensus on identity, debate seemed to be polarizing positions and exacerbating problems. As opposed to the consolidation of a consensus on the external dimension of state borders, the Jordanian public sphere seemed unable to produce a consensus about the internal questions of national identity. Fahd al-Fanik bemoaned this failure, noting that "we are the country in the world which talks the most about national unity, but we have not yet answered the most basic question: who are we?"[56]

The Islamist Movement

Islamic organizations resisted the new Jordanian discourse, combining a principled rejection of the severing of ties with opposition to the reinterpre-

tation of Jordanian interests in the peace process. The one institutional clus-
ter in the West Bank unaffected by the disengagement remained the Islamic
waqf, over which Jordan retained custody until late 1994. Islamist discourse
framed the severing of ties as an illegitimate division of the Islamic *umma*:
"The Islamist movement stands clearly and doctrinally against the disease
of division . . . which infects the Jordanian-Palestinian body."[57] However,
even the Islamist movement accepted the severing of ties as a change of
strategy which best protected the interests of both Jordan and Palestine, even
if it (unlike most other actors) did not change its underlying preferences. In
late 1995, the leader of the Muslim Brotherhood, Abd al-Majid Thunaybat,
noted that "we were the loudest voice in rejecting the severing of ties and
in considering unity to be the basis of relations . . . but today confederation
[between Jordan and the West Bank] is nothing more than an invitation to
the Alternative Homeland."[58] In other words, despite their commitment to
unity as an outcome, the Muslim Brotherhood accepted the severing of ties
as a necessary strategy.

The debate over the Islamists and the severing of ties revolved around
the relationship between the Jordanian Muslim Brotherhood and the Palestinian Islamist resistance movement (Hamas). This relationship would become a subject of public controversy, as Israel and Arafat pressured Jordan
to curtail Hamas activities in Jordan. For Arafat, the Hamas presence implied
that Jordan viewed the Islamic movement as a potential alternative to the
PLO, despite Hussein's repeated reassurances.[59] In April 1996, Arafat accused Jordan of supporting Hamas political and military activities, and of
using Hamas to destabilize the PNA. The fact that many Hamas representatives in Amman were Jordanian citizens demonstrates the difficulties of
neatly separating the Jordanian and the Palestinian identities. When the
Jordanian government did try to crack down on Hamas activities, its actions
became part of the broader state-society confrontation. Jordan's acceptance
of Musa Abu Marzouq from an American jail; its securing of the release of
Hamas spiritual leader Ahmed Yassin from an Israeli prison after a failed
Mossad assassination attempt on Khalid Misha'al in Amman; all seemed to
signal Jordanian support for Hamas, despite Hussein's constant declaration
that Jordan would not recognize anyone other than the PLO (and then the
PNA) as the representative of the Palestinian people. Indeed, one Jordanian
columnist speculated that "this represents an attempt to form a Jordanian
lobby in Palestine as a balance to *Fateh*'s extensions into Jordan."[60]

The Islamist defense of unity was reflected in strong organizational ties:
the severing of ties made an exception of Islamic *waqf* institutions; Hamas

maintained offices in the Muslim Brotherhood's building; and Jordanian Islamists consistently placed Palestinian issues at the forefront of their political agenda. In November 1994, the Islamist weekly *al-Sabil* emphasized that "the physical unity of the two banks can not be ended." Ibrahim Ghousha, Hamas representative in Jordan, summed up the dominant Islamist position: "We are in favor of unity . . . the severing of ties was a temporary measure. . . . It is the right of the Palestinian identity to make itself prominent and the right of the Jordanian identity to make itself prominent, but we search for a wider Islamic identity."[61] Despite these strong words in favor of unity, identity tensions did emerge in the Muslim Brotherhood and the Islamic Action Front (Robinson 1997b). Calls by Islamist doves, such as Bisam al-Amoush's for a focus on Jordanian identity and Jordanian interests, and Abdullah al-Akaylah's for participation in the government, set in motion significant dissension within the Islamist organizations.[62] Abd al-Mana'm Abu Zant, a prominent Islamist hawk, blasted the reformers who wanted to focus on the Jordanian arena, warning "God save he who would Jordanize the Muslim Brotherhood!"[63] As Jawad al-Anani notes, the Islamists were not immune to the identity debates: "the dialogue going on in the nation about the divisions between Jordanians of different origins has influenced the position of the Islamist movement . . . which fears division along geographic lines."[64]

"Jordanian-Palestinian Relations" Opinion Surveys

The Center for Strategic Studies carried out an unprecedented public opinion survey in 1995 and a follow-up survey in 1997 on the subject of Jordanian-Palestinian relations (CSS 1995b; 1998a).[65] Both surveys found a sharp distinction between elite opinion leaders and the general public. In each case, the elite sample proved far more inclined to Jordanian or Palestinian exclusivism, to total separation between the two entities, and to the promotion of distinct national identities and interests. The popular sample, on the other hand, was more sympathetic to close relations between the two identities and entities and generally rejected Jordanian chauvinism. In 1995, when asked about the degree to which the groups had merged into a single identity, 69 percent of the popular sample replied that there had been a great deal of integration, while only 49 percent of Jordanian-origin elites thought so. Only 30 percent of the popular sample suspected Jordanians of Palestinian origin of dual loyalties, compared to 54 percent of Jordanian-origin elites who harbored such suspicions. In 1997, 63 percent of the national sample supported Jordanian-Palestinian unity, compared to only 37 percent of the elite sample. Such differences suggest that the changes in identity wrought by participation in the public sphere affect participants more than they do readers, who perhaps draw their ideas about identity more from the face to face public interaction in which they actively participate. The high level of intermarriage, interaction, and shared lives of Jordanians and Palestinians, especially in Amman, undermines the clarity with which political commentators define Jordanian and Palestinian identities and interests. Above all, the discrepancy suggests the extent to which Jordanian-Palestinian controversies inside of Jordan are driven by political entrepreneurs with access to the media, whose attempts to inflame identity issues are driven by other interests. These findings give considerable support to theories of ethnic conflict which highlight the role of intra-elite competition in driving identity politics (Lake and Rothschild 1998; Gagnon 1994.95).

International Behavior: Jordanian Interests in the West Bank

The final step for the constructivist public sphere argument is to demonstrate that the reconfiguration of Jordanian identity had significant implications for international behavior. While the discussion in the chapter to this point reconstructs and evaluates the process of public deliberation in Jordan (c.f. Bohman 1996; Chambers 1996), for the purposes of International Relations theory it is necessary to link these public deliberations to state behavior. One dimension where this linkage will be explored (in chapters 6 and 7) is Jordanian behavior in the Jordanian-Israeli peace negotiations, which directly followed from the redefinition of Jordanian identity and interests. The drive to center Jordanian state interests involved the explicit renunciation of Palestinian interests as a Jordanian state concern. Only by eliminating the Palestinian dimension of Jordanian identity could Jordanian interests be defined in such a way as to permit the conceptions of interest involved in the peace treaty. In the remainder of this chapter, I focus on Jordanian behavior toward the West Bank after the disengagement and the Jordanian position on Palestinian-Israeli final status issues as the most important indicators. Above all, Jordan's shift from opposition to support of a Palestinian state manifests the change.

King Hussein has, on a number of occasions, explicitly explained Jordanian preferences on Palestinian-Israeli final status issues. He has found it necessary to directly respond to the assertions by Israeli leaders, who invoke assumptions about Jordanian preferences based on Jordanian fears of a Palestinian state, by asserting Jordan's right to define its own interests rather than accept the attribution of its interests by outside observers. In the mid 1990s, Hussein has defined a set of clearly defined Jordanian state preferences, which sharply diverge from Jordanian preferences as articulated as recently as 1987. First, Jordan prefers to see an independent Palestinian state on the West Bank and Gaza. Second, Jordan wants close economic ties with the Palestinian state, and with Israel, to allow the development of the region. Third, Jordan will entertain the possibility of political confederation (not federal unity) only on the condition that Palestine has achieved its full sovereign independence and freely chooses this confederation. Fourth, Jordan considers the PLO, and now the PNA, the legitimate representative of the Palestinians, and refuses categorically to negotiate or substitute for the PLO in any negotiations. Jordan will not be the alternative spokesman for the Palestinians any more than it will be their Alternative Homeland. Finally, Jordan's national unity is not subject to discussion, and all citizens enjoy full rights and responsibilities until the opportunity comes for them to choose otherwise. These avowed preferences might be challenged as "only" public positions, not indicative of Jordan's "real" concerns. The fact that Jordan has consistently and publicly articulated these preferences over a period of years, and behaved in a manner consistent with them, belies such an interpretation, however.

The most direct behavioral indicators of the significance of the severing ties are Jordan's subsequent positions on the West Bank: did Jordan reassert its claim? As an operational indicator of opportunity, I use the proposal of Jordanian-Palestinian confederation. It is significant that confederation represented the farthest feasible compromise, because confederation implies the existence of two sovereign states rather than Jordanian sovereignty over the West Bank. At no time did any Jordanian official so much as hint at reversing the disengagement and restoring full unity.

The Jordanian position on confederation has remained consistent since the achievement of the "severing of ties consensus": any talk of confederation is before its time until the Palestinians possess a sovereign state. Confederation was not a new idea (N. Tal 1993; Hassan 1985; Gresh 1989). It had been adopted as the official goal of the PLO at the 1983 Palestinian National Council session, and had been the basis for the February 1985 Jordanian-Palestinian agreement. In the 1990s, confederation carried new significance. The severing of ties penetrated deep into Jordanian society and the new conception of Jordan came to structure virtually all public discourse.

In the West Bank, the Intifada had clearly expressed Palestinian rejection of renewed Jordanian rule. By the early 1990s, a Jordanian consensus had consolidated on the revision of its borders to exclude the West Bank, matching the long-established Palestinian consensus. Virtually all of Jordanian political society accepted the redefinition of Jordanian interests such that ties to the West Bank represented a threat rather than an opportunity, and that a Palestinian state now protected, rather than threatened, Jordanian security.

Confederation came up during the negotiations over the framework for the Madrid peace talks in April 1991, with the United States and the Labor Party preferring confederation between the West Bank/Gaza and Jordan as a final status arrangement. Israel insisted that Palestinian representatives (not from the PLO) participate only within a Jordanian delegation, in order to structurally link Jordan and the West Bank in the negotiating process (Quandt 1993; Shamir 1994; Arens 1995). Jordan had the opportunity, and considerable American and Israeli encouragement, to assert a claim to negotiate on behalf of the West Bank. In the aftermath of the Gulf war, the PLO was extremely weak and even more of a pariah to the American and Israeli leaderships than before, while Hussein's popularity in the West Bank had rebounded noticeably. Rather than take advantage of this situation, Jordan insisted on maintaining a distinct Palestinian delegation within the joint Jordanian-Palestinian delegation, and rejected every attempt to treat them as a single delegation (Abass 1995; Ashrawi 1995). Jordanians complained about even the joint delegation that emerged, arguing that because of the severing of ties Jordan had nothing to do with representing the Palestinians.[66] They feared that Jordanian interests would get buried beneath the more controversial Palestinian demands. Even more, they feared that a joint delegation would undermine the new distinction between Jordan and Palestine driving the new conception of Jordanian identity and interests. Support for the joint delegation format depended on maintaining absolute clarity about the distinction between the two delegations.[67] Nobody expressed the desire to exploit the opportunity to assert Jordanian power over the Palestinians to reclaim the West Bank.

In March 1992, a proposal of confederation emerged as a way out of the blocked Washington negotiations. The return of some form of the Jordan option was a real possibility, as both Israeli and PLO figures publicly speculated about a Jordanian role to break the impasse. The loud Jordanian public outcry startled most observers and almost certainly played a decisive role in killing the idea.[68] For several weeks, discussion of confederation dominated the Jordanian public sphere, with opinion running strongly against.

The emergent consensus did not reject popular Jordanian-Palestinian unity, but rather rejected the institutional form and timing of the proposal. The majority of writers saw the confederation under existing circumstances as serving Israeli interests by preventing the creation of a Palestinian state. The plan was also seen as a threat to Jordan, in that it would facilitate turning Jordan into Palestine.[69] Where the pre-1988 consensus had assumed the political and economic benefits of a prominent role in the West Bank, this deliberation revealed a conviction that any ties to the West Bank could prove an existential threat to Jordan. Jordanian interests were thus sharply distinct from — and compatible with — Palestinian interests.

In August 1993, just before the revelation of Oslo, a confederation proposal again ignited fierce denunciations in the Jordanian public sphere. Americans, Israelis, and Palestinians all vetted confederation, with Jordan the only party to express strong reservations. Jordan refused to be taken for granted in a confederation agreement, and refused to be party to such an agreement unless a sovereign Palestinian state were achieved first. Nevertheless, public opinion reacted strongly to the appearance of the idea in the international public sphere: "Has Jordan withdrawn from its decision to sever ties after King Hussein vowed Jordan would never do so?"[70] Commentators again stressed the danger to Jordan inherent in any role in the West Bank: "it is well-known that both Jordanian and Palestinian political circles reject confederation as a conspiracy on Jordan."[71] Why should Jordan, a sovereign state, unite as an equal partner with an unformed Palestinian entity under effective Israeli control? This consensus constrained any movement toward restoring ties even under propitious circumstances; it also constituted a new conceptions of Jordanian interests. Beyond constraining state behavior, this consensus informed the state's articulation of its preferences: Jordanian leaders and the public alike came to believe in this definition of threat and of interests, and interpreted political interaction accordingly.

Oslo shocked and angered the Jordanians, and sparked serious concerns about the future of Jordan, but in fact the Oslo process fit well with and reinforced the East Bank conception of Jordan (L. Tal 1993). The Palestinian defection from coordination removed the normative and practical barriers to the Jordanian pursuit of self-interest. When challenged on its exclusion of "Palestinian" interests from its negotiating agenda, Jordan could now respond by referring such questions to the Palestinian negotiators or to the multilateral talks. The establishment of the PNA began the construction of a Palestinian institutional structure on the West Bank, replacing vestigial Jordanian institutions.

The Jordan-Israel Washington Declaration of July 1994 recognized Jordan's special status in the Jerusalem holy sites, which brought the sensitive issue of Jerusalem into the spotlight. Interpreted by Arafat as an unacceptable encroachment on Palestinian rights, this led to sharp exchanges in the Arabist public sphere and another explosion of resistance to involvement in the West Bank in the Jordanian public sphere. While Jordanian officials claimed that the Article only recognized longstanding reality and that the recognition of some Arab claim in Jerusalem was an Arab victory, their arguments failed to convince either the PNA or the Jordanian critics. Most observers saw this controversy as an Israeli attempt to drive a wedge between Jordan and the PNA. This controversy ended with Jordan's extension of the severing of ties to the West Bank religious courts and institutions which it had maintained after 1988, demonstrating the power of the new borders for guiding behavior.

The November 1995 decision to issue five-year passports to West Bank residents to facilitate travel ignited unusually loud criticism, as it came in the context of Jordanian-Israeli peace and increasing belief that the Palestinian-Israeli process would not allow the Palestinian refugees to return.[72] The radical exclusivists were most outspoken in their criticism: "When the Jordanian Nationalist Movement agreed to the peace treaty, this was because of our belief that it had destroyed the Alternative Homeland threat . . . and now, the Jordanian people are shocked to find that the peace treaty will lead to establishing the Alternative Homeland."[73] From this perspective, the focus on the Jordanian identity and interests had been the primary fruit of the treaty, and they were appalled to find their increasingly consolidated position suddenly contestable. The fierce public reaction compelled the state to alter its behavior, by forcing it to live up to its publicly avowed principles. King Hussein's reported anger at this domestic pressure suggests that he perceived this particular dimension of the consensus as a constraint. The regime and public opinion continued to hold very different interpretations, even within the shared consensus on East Bank borders. Even if the regime had intentions of reversing the severing of ties, which is unlikely, they could no longer be publicly avowed. A return to the West Bank had acquired such negative normative connotations that it no longer represented a legitimate option for state policy. The question of the place of Palestinians inside of Jordan had no such normative consensus, however, as the recurring controversies over the future of the refugees indicate.

In November 1997, King Hussein reacted angrily to an Israeli suggestion that Jordan shared Israel's interests in preventing the emergence of a Palestinian state. Israeli officials, in an attempt to reduce international pressure for progress on negotiations with the PNA, argued that the Jordanians shared their fear of a Palestinian state. This Israeli claim implied that Jordan's public discourse since the severing of ties misrepresented true Jordanian preferences. Hussein responded with a furious open letter to Prime Minister Majali, clearly directed at Israel and the international public sphere as well as the Jordanian public sphere, in which he acidly asserted that Jordan was fully capable of defining its own interests.[74] In the course of this letter, Hussein provided one of the most explicit statements yet of Jordan's vision of a final status agreement. Most crucially, Hussein forcefully restated Jordan's support for a Palestinian state and denied any Jordanian fears of sharing a border with that state. Jordan's refusal to return to the West Bank had become so manifest, to Jordanians, Palestinians, and Israelis, that it did not even need to be stated.

Several common themes emerge from these instances. First, Jordan rarely initiated controversies over confederation, more often reacting to PLO or Israeli statements. Hussein called for "confederation to be struck from the Jordanian political vocabulary" and warned against other parties "taking Jordan for granted." The opportunity to reverse positions presented itself on numerous occasions, but Jordan neither instigated such discussions nor took advantage of them. Second, every action framed in such terms drew immediate, harsh criticism in the Jordanian public sphere. Opposition to a return to a Jordanian role in the West Bank spanned the political and identity spectrum, from Jordanian exclusivists to Palestinian leftists. Even Islamists, who rejected the severing of ties on principle, opposed confederation under 1990s conditions. A clear, powerful societal constraint stood against any reversal of the disengagement. Framing any issue in such terms, even if it had not been intended in that way, served to delegitimize the policy, whether redistricting, the extension of municipal boundaries, water distribution, or the improvement of living standards in the camps. Third, Jordanian debates inevitably interpreted such proposals as serving Israeli or PLO interests, never as serving Jordanian interests.

Four possibilities present themselves as to why Jordan did not reengage: the opportunity never arose; the regime tried but failed; threat remained overwhelming; or Jordanian identity and interests changed. The first does not hold: the above instances show several opportunities. The second explanation has some adherents. The appearance of the issue could be seen as a trial balloon, a testing of political currents to see if public opinion would bear an act. The evidence suggests, however, that state policymakers did share the public conceptions of the identity and interests of the new Jordan and the nature of the threats it faced with regard to the West Bank, but not necessarily with regard to the future of the refugees. The proposals tended to originate among Palestinian or Israeli actors, not from Jordanians, as the "regime trial balloon" argument would suggest.

It is harder to differentiate between changing identity and interests and continuing reaction to threat. Arguments against confederation constantly warned of the dangers to Jordan. It is necessary to look carefully at the specific threat invoked, however: the fear that confederation would serve to transform Jordan into Palestine, and that links with the West Bank could destabilize Jordan. This perception of threat is clearly the product of the change in identity and the understanding of interests. The idea that close ties to the West Bank represented a threat to Jordan represents a fundamental change from the longstanding conviction that Jordan had a deep interest in control over the West Bank, and does not follow directly from objective realities. Only given the new identity frame did such contacts appear threatening. In other words, perception of threat is as much the outcome of the transformation of identity as it is the cause of Jordanian behavior.

Since the severing of ties, Jordan has established close working relations with the PNA. The two sides have signed an impressive array of functional agreements, even if many remain unimplemented. King Hussein and Arafat meet regularly to coordinate positions, and a steady stream of top government officials travels between Gaza and Amman. In a 1997 opinion poll, 86.5 percent of Jordanians considered relations with the PNA to be "good" or "very good," and only 1.8 percent said "bad" or "very bad."[75] Hussein has intervened repeatedly on behalf of Arafat with Israeli leaders, most dramatically in the endgame of the negotiation of the Hebron Agreement in January 1997. The consistency of Hussein's declarations in support of a Palestinian state and rejecting any alternative to the PNA represent real Jordanian convictions about Jordan's interests.

One of the most contentious issues in Jordanian-Israeli relations has been Israel's continued obstruction of trade between Jordan and the West Bank, blocking one of the major presumed economic benefits of peace. Crucially, such trade relations would differentially benefit the Palestinian elite, strengthening those sectors with material and identity based interests in closer Jordanian-Palestinian relations. As the West Bank market became more important to the Jordanian political economy, these trade networks would work to reconstruct Jordanian identity and interests in much the same way that Jordan's trade relations with Iraq reconstructed Jordan's Arab relations in the 1980s (see chapter 5).

This should not be misunderstood as a claim that relations between Jordan and the PNA have become conflict-free. Serious conflicts over economic relations, Jerusalem, Hamas, and the like have generated friction and revealed continuing suspicions and hostility between the two leaderships. These conflicts differ in kind from conflicts before 1988, however. Disputes revolve around distributive rather than representation issues.[76] The dominant questions have become the extent of sovereignty exercised by each side over matters of mutual concern, such as the use of the Jordanian Dinar as a Palestinian currency or control over bridge crossings. Only Jerusalem partially contradicts this analysis, but even there Jordan has conceded, albeit under pressure, the priority of Palestinian political rights. While the PNA and Jordan continue to compete for power, and over the distribution of benefits in final status arrangements, they no longer compete for the right to represent the Palestinian people. Suspicions remain, particularly on the part of Arafat, that Hussein is conspiring with Israel and Hamas against the PNA, but these primarily reflect frustration and political gamesmanship. By severing ties with the West Bank and constantly recognizing the PLO throughout the 1990s, Jordan has qualitatively changed the nature of conflict and cooperation. This constructivist analysis has important policy implications: the persistent assertion that Jordan is only biding its time before renewing its bid, which reflects the rationalist assumption of fixed preferences and strategic response to changing power relations, is fundamentally mistaken.[77]

Nor does this imply that Jordan wants a complete separation from the West Bank. Most Jordanian scenarios involve close functional cooperation with a Palestinian state, including significant economic interdependencies. Total separation is not seen as a viable alternative, any more than is a return to Jordanian rule over the West Bank. The construction of economic and functional cooperation depends upon the ability of each side to convince the other of the sincerity of its political positions. Building trust depends on convincingly demonstrating that Jordan's renunciation of the West Bank is final. The renunciation, and the redefinition of Jordan's identity and interests, therefore should increase, rather than decrease, the prospects for cooperative interaction.

The national identity of Jordanians of Palestinian origin remains the most unsettled and disruptive question in Jordanian politics. Full participation of Palestinians in the Jordanian political system could have important foreign policy implications. This is not impossible; indeed, the peace process, the structural economic adjustments taking place in the 1990s, and the move to a post-Hussein regime suggest a possible shift in the ruling coalition.

Privatization and the slashing of state subsidies has hurt the Transjordanian tribes more than any other social group, while strengthening the hand of the Palestinian private sector; the eruption of riots in the southern cities in 1996 and 1998 serve notice of the growing discontent among the tribes. The economic orientation of the peace process is toward trade with Israel and the West Bank, which favors the Palestinian elite over the Transjordanians, whose trade networks are with Iraq and the Gulf. The peace process seems to almost certainly imply the large-scale resettlement of Palestinian refugees in Jordan. All of these factors point to an increased role for the Palestinian elite in the ruling coalition and a decreasing reliance upon the Transjordanian tribes. Hashemite discourse on identity in the 1990s has repeatedly called for full citizenship and participation for all citizens, which would imply a greater role for the Palestinian elite. King Hussein enjoyed great personal popularity in the tribes. Hussein's successors may have less support among the tribes, however, and see opportunities to align with the Palestinian elite. Hence, it is feasible to imagine a shift in the ruling coalition toward the Palestinian elite—a trend that Jordanian nationalist political entrepreneurs have been vocally denouncing as "a creeping transformation of Jordan into Palestine."[78] Even with such a shift, a return to the physical unity of the two entities seems unlikely, given the transformations in Jordanian identity and interests.

While the East Bank consensus has been firmly institutionalized, it is not beyond all debate or question. Opponents note that the Constitution, which specifies Jordan's borders as including both Banks, has never been amended. Therefore, the severing of ties remained unconstitutional. Arabist and Islamist deputies based one strand of criticism of the peace treaty with Israel during the Parliamentary ratification debate on the premise that the treaty accepted the severing of ties, which was contrary to the Constitution and to Jordanian and Arab identity.[79] These challenges failed to undermine the strong consensus, however. Whenever political unity with the West Bank is introduced in the public sphere, it is immediately challenged, condemned, and dismissed as contrary to both Jordanian and Palestinian interests. Confederation remained a principled goal, but only after the achievement of a fully sovereign Palestinian state able to exercise its free will to choose political unity.

The formation of a Likud government in June 1996, and the subsequent deterioration of the Palestinian-Israeli relationship, posed new opportunities for a Jordanian reassertion. As press reports immediately indicated, "Palestinians were concerned that Jordan and Netanyahu may find a common interest in preventing the creation of a Palestinian state."[80] While I return to the impact of Netanyahu's election and peace policies in chapter 7 and the Conclusion, the important point to close with here is the significance of the change in Jordanian preferences. Many Israelis assume the consistency of Jordanian preferences and will not believe that King Hussein has changed his basic interest in competing with Arafat and regaining the West Bank. If my argument is correct, then policies based on this belief are profoundly mistaken. Jordanian response to Netanyahu's initiatives offer a crucial test; to this point, Jordanian support for the PNA and for a Palestinian state supports my conclusions.

The theoretical implications of the transformation of Jordanian identity and interests are threefold. First, the empirical change after 1988 is important. Given the centrality of the assumption of the stability of identity and interests, demonstrating such a major change in preferences in an issue area of fundamental importance to the Jordanian state should help to establish the empirical plausibility of this research agenda. Second, the wider discussion offers little support for those constructivists who contend that identity and interests are constantly in flux, that they change regularly and fluidly. Jordan clung to its West Bank-inclusive identity and interests in the face of Arabist consensus, public denunciation, Palestinian diplomatic efforts, civil war, and the growing realities on the ground. Only the conjunction of the Intifada, the severing of ties, and the unprecedented liberalization of 1989 produced the necessary conditions for the production of a new identity consensus. Therefore, the findings on Jordanian-Palestinian relations offer support for both rationalists and constructivists, and demonstrate the need for synthesis. Third, the empirical discussion helps to develop the positive theoretical argument for the role of public deliberation in producing a new consensus on identity and state interests.

5   Jordan in the Gulf Crisis: The Construction of Public Opinion

During the Gulf crisis, Jordan faced a set of excruciating choices, all of which potentially threatened the security and even survival of the state and the regime. With the exception of Iraq and Kuwait, no state in the region was more directly threatened in the crisis; and no state was more deeply affected by the course of events. Jordan's decisions placed it outside the mainstream of the Arab order and outside the Western coalition. Despite its close relations with Iraq, Iraqi behavior placed Jordan in grave danger. Despite Jordan's long covert relations and tacit cooperation with Israel, the crisis almost led to an Israeli-Jordanian confrontation. Why did Jordan decide to remain outside the American coalition, in the face of all these threats and dangers? What role did deliberation, whether at the Arab, international, or domestic levels, play in formulating Jordan's sense of its interests in the crisis?

The Gulf war case is important both for Jordan and for broader trends in the Arab system. Like the Suez crisis and the 1967 war, the Gulf War profoundly changed the Arab order: ending Arab summitry; placing Iraq outside the bounds of Arab alliances and under a seemingly permanent sanctions regime; beginning the Madrid peace process and the articulation of a "Middle Eastern" regional identity; and initiating new regional alliances.

My object here is not to provide a detailed history of the Gulf crisis, but rather to compare competing explanations for Jordan's behavior and to examine the implications for Jordanian identity and interests (see Hiro 1992; Haykal 1992; Freedman and Karsh 1993; Khadduri and Ghareeb 1997).

Jordan's refusal to join the coalition against Iraq in 1990–91 set it against Egypt and Syria, its traditional allies in the Gulf, the United States and Israel. From a rationalist perspective, Jordanian behavior would have to be considered surprising, despite post facto explanations. Power balancing, threat balancing, and political economy explanations all underdetermine outcomes. A constructivist public sphere approach can better explain Jordanian decisions. The framing of the crisis, public sphere structure, and the linking of Jordanian Arabist identity and interests to Iraq drove behavior under conditions of profound uncertainty. Jordan's isolation from the Arabist public sphere during and after the Gulf crisis, combined with an Arabist public consensus produced within a specifically Jordanian public sphere, created a distinctive conception of identity and interests. Over the 1980s, Jordan developed a powerful positive identification with Iraq, based upon trade networks, political cooperation, and a carefully cultivated public friendship. The Gulf crisis placed central norms of Jordanian policy into conflict: opposition to the acquisition of land by force, to inter-Arab warfare, and to forceful Arab unity; support for Arab solutions, for Arabist dialogue, and for outcomes within the Arab consensus over those outside them. Jordan's behavior in the Gulf crisis involved a concerted attempt to maintain an autonomous Arabist order while consolidating the domestic public consensus about Jordanian identity, interests, and regime legitimacy. The failure of the Arab order to produce a legitimate consensus, combined with the unprecedented openness of the Jordanian public sphere, shifted the terrain of the interpretive struggle.

Background

Relations between Jordan and Iraq in the decade prior to the Gulf Crisis had developed to the point of a close alignment, after a long period of suspicion and hostility beginning with the Iraqi revolution of 1958 overthrowing King Hussein's Hashemite kinsmen (Baram 1991). In the late 1970s, Jordan turned toward Iraq as the state most likely to provide both strategic depth and economic benefits (Brand 1994, 1994b). The war between Iran and Iraq (1980–1988) facilitated the consolidation of Jordanian-Iraqi relations. The active construction of positive identification can be seen in that the reaction to the embrace of Iraq in 1980 was far from positive. As one political activist remembers, "most Jordanian politicians were against the war, many going to the point of hoping the Iraqis would fail militarily. . . . the popular sentiments were similarly against Iraq . . . all despite the official position of the King" (Sha'ir 1987: 270–272). The negative public response, only a decade before the Gulf crisis, belies any assertion of organic, essential, or eternal pro-Iraqi public opinion. The closed and underdeveloped Jordanian public sphere had little impact on state policy, however. Opinion changed in Iraqi favor in the early 1980s, with official media encouragement, growing economic interaction, and popular anger inflamed by Syria's threatening behavior. By the late 1980s, official relations had grown unusually close. The formation of the Arab Cooperation Council in 1989 represented a major—albeit short-lived—institutional formalization of the relationship (Ryan 1998). The development of Jordanian-Iraqi relations involved growing positive identification and a sense among Jordanians of a common destiny and shared interests which went beyond a temporary convergence of interests. Positive identification with Iraq developed over the course of a decade of close interaction and active construction of such identification.

Despite these close relations with Iraq, Jordan's refusal to join the American coalition surprised most observers. Jordan was viewed as among the closest and most reliable American allies in the region, likely to be persuaded by an Arab consensus, likely to respond to economic incentives, and likely to perceive a serious threat from an aggressive Iraq. Jordanian behavior in this period is often misunderstood, both by its supporters and its critics. Popular perceptions of a Jordan enthusiastically supporting Iraqi aggression against Kuwait are as misleading as are revisionist arguments that Jordanian policymakers reluctantly sided with Iraq only because of irresistible popular or economic pressure. From the outset of the crisis, King Hussein condemned the Iraqi invasion of Kuwait. Shuttling among world and Arab capitals, Hussein sought to find an acceptable solution within an Arab framework that would avoid war. After the failure of diplomatic efforts and the growing deployment of coalition troops, Jordan campaigned desperately for a peaceful solution within the Arab framework. The American deployment shifted the nature of the crisis from a controversial aggression by one Arab state against another to a face-off between an Arab power and the United States. From this shift emerged a position seen across the Arab world: against the Iraqi invasion, but even more against the Western intervention (Sayigh 1991; Joffe 1993; Ebert 1992; Khadduri and Ghareeb 1997).

This interpretation, despite its resonance at the popular level, failed to command a consensus at the official Arab level. On August 11, 1990, the Cairo Arab Summit issued a Resolution authorizing United Nations intervention, in effect absolving the Arab order of responsibility. Jordan strongly opposed this decision, for reasons discussed below. The buck-passing by the Arab League, the refusal to initiate inter-Arab dialogue toward a consensus solution, had as deep an impact on the Arab order as did Iraq's violation of the norm prohibiting direct military action between Arab states. The remarkable admission of the failure of the regional framework effectively shattered the normative centrality of the Arabist order. That deliberation had failed would have been damaging but understandable; that deliberation was rejected violated the basic principles of the Arab public sphere. Deep rifts erupted between Arab states which have not healed, preventing the resumption of Arab summitry and profoundly undermining the institutional and normative foundations of the Arab order. The Cairo Summit, therefore, revealed the loss of the "will to consensus."

After the failure of initial diplomatic efforts, the American-led coalition escalated its deployment in Saudi Arabia. The Americans and their Arab allies fashioned a sharply bipolar construction of the crisis in which neutrality equaled hostility. Jordan's nuanced interpretation of its position fell on deaf ears.[1] Jordan adhered to the letter of UN resolutions, even as it came under punitive inspection regimes and accusations of sanctions-busting, and consistently maintained its neutrality as it argued for a diplomatic solution and rejected demands for active participation in the coalition efforts. Jordanian appeals for an Arab solution were interpreted as nothing but appeasement and Iraqi propaganda. Combined with the influx of hundreds of thousands of returnees from Kuwait, sanctions helped make Jordan the country that suffered the most after Kuwait and Iraq from the crisis. Jordanian society was extraordinarily mobilized during the crisis, with enormous pro-Iraqi rallies throughout the Kingdom. Jordanian officials point out that the "radicalism" of the Jordanian public often obscured the pragmatism and caution of Jordan's actual behavior (Sharaf 1991).

Rationalist Explanations

Jordan's behavior during the crisis reflected the extreme pressure, conflicting demands, and profound uncertainty it faced. Under such conditions of crisis and uncertainty, with major norms violated with impunity, public deliberation played an unusually important role in shaping state behavior. It is precisely when norms and expectations break down that public sphere theory expects deliberation to produce new collective understandings. I argue that each major rationalist explanation for Jordan's Gulf crisis behavior underdetermines outcomes. While all of these explanations point to important dimensions of Jordanian considerations, they slight the centrality of public sphere deliberation for articulating Jordan's interests and identifying appropriate strategies.

Threat Balancing

As has been noted by those attempting to apply rationalist models of alliance behavior, the wide range of threats facing Jordan during the Gulf crisis renders threat-based explanations problematic (Brand 1994; Harknett and VanDenBerg 1997). Threat-balancing explanations, even "omnibalancing" approaches which consider domestic threats to regime survival, assume the existence of a primary overriding threat. In 1990, Israel, Iraq, and domestic turbulence each posed some serious threat to Jordanian external security or regime survival. Which threat motivated Jordanian behavior?

My argument is not that threat was irrelevant for Jordanian behavior, but that public framing, interpretation, and identity drove the perception of threat. Threat clearly mattered for Jordan, given the intensity, scope, and militarization of the Gulf crisis. I argue that the construction of threat was the product of public interaction rather than an independent rational calculation. Because of uncertainty and the perception of threats emanating from every direction, interpretation necessarily played a major role. The most dangerous threat could quite plausibly have been constructed differently, and the appropriate response articulated differently. Analysis should be directed at the process of construction of national interests and threats which produces the articulation of relative threat, rather than at the independent causal power of threat perception (Campbell 1992).

Among the threats that could have plausibly driven Jordanian alignments in the crisis are Israel, Iraq, domestic upheaval, and a generalized fear of war. First, Jordan faced a potential threat of Israeli intervention. Even prior to the crisis, Jordanian leaders expressed fears of an Israeli mass expulsion of West Bank Palestinians into Jordan in order to create a Palestinian state on the East Bank (Telhami 1992a). Since the departure of Labor from the Israeli coalition, King Hussein enjoyed far less personal relations with Israeli decisionmakers. After Iraq invaded Kuwait, many Jordanians feared that Israel would use the pretext of Iraqi hostility to occupy Jordan on route to an invasion of Iraq. Public discussions of the diminishing value of Jordan for Israeli interests fed these fears (Sharara 1990; Lukacs 1997). In an October 1990 Knesset session, Shamir warned that "any destabilization [in Jordan] or intervention in its territory.. could increase the tensions to dimensions we will be unable to accept."[2] Even the deployment of the Jordanian army in defensive positions along the Jordan River sparked bellicose Israeli comments and public threats. Jordan's tilt to Iraq was interpreted by influential Israelis as evidence that Hussein had "lost control of his country," that Jordan had become "an Iraqi satellite" and "thoroughly Palestinianized."[3] While these sentiments were most expressed on the right, even Shimon Peres remarked that "as for its political life, Jordan has reached a dead end."[4] Liberalization, when it gave voice to anti-Israeli opinion, compromised Hussein's value as a guarantor of Israeli interests, the primary source of his legitimacy in their eyes. His "loss of control," however much it accorded with Jordanian public opinion or interests, demonstrated Hussein's failure as a leader. These arguments were prominent in the Israeli public sphere, and contained a barely veiled threat of military intervention.

While Israel certainly represented a threat, there are strong reasons to believe that such threats did not drive Jordanian behavior. Israel very clearly specified the conditions for intervention, allowing Jordan room for maneuver without bringing on retaliation. Furthermore, Israeli realization that a Palestinian state in Jordan would very likely have been even more pro-Iraq drove many previously ambivalent Israeli figures to publicly affirm Israel's strategic interest in retaining the Hashemite regime (Klieman 1998). Finally, since the United States promised to achieve Israel's strategic interest in destroying Iraqi military power, and desperately wanted Israel to stay out of the war in order to keep the Arab members in the coalition, there was little rational reason for Israeli military action. Indeed, American policymakers viewed Israel's entry into the war as a worst-case scenario (Baker 1995). For obvious geographic reasons, any combat between Israel and Iraq would take place through Jordanian territory or airspace, while also resisting any Iraqi use of Jordanian territory. King Hussein warned Israel that Jordan would attempt to intercept any Israeli aircraft entering its airspace. While the Israeli military was confident of its ability to defeat Jordan militarily, the political consequences would have been shattering. Even when Iraq tried to provoke Israel by firing SCUD missiles—through Jordanian airspace—Israel did not respond.[5] Under these circumstances, the actual threat of an Israeli intervention would have to be seen as low. On the other hand, Israeli strategic policy had long been certain, massive retaliation for any attack, so even such strong disincentives could not be taken as a guarantee. And can leaders rely on the rationality of other leaders in such tense moments (Lebow 1981)?

Direct and indirect Jordanian-Israeli communications during the crisis were therefore of primary importance in moderating Jordanian threat perception (Baker 1995: 386; Susser 1994: 21; Arens 1995). Moshe Zak, one of the most informed sources on covert Jordanian-Israeli contacts, writes that King Hussein and Yitzhak Shamir met in London on January 4, 1991 to exchange views on the crisis and to find ways to avoid conflict.[6] Israeli officials made a series of public statements clearly signaling the red lines for Jordanian behavior: Israel would intervene if and only if Iraqi troops entered Jordan and "Israel's eastern border became hostile." In these statements, Israel specified which behavior would be seen as unacceptably threatening. Foreign Minister David Levy stated that "any threat coming from Jordan into Israel . . . or movement of troops from outside Jordan into Jordan will be a warning signal to Israel."[7] Levy also claims to have privately reassured King Hussein through an intermediary and to have received a satisfactory response.[8] Defense Minister Moshe Arens credits his August 7 speech in the Knesset warning that "the moment we see.. the entry of the Iraqi army into Jordan, we shall act" with deterring both Jordan and Iraq from such an action (Arens 1995: 153). Hussein's August 8 statement that "Jordan is not a passageway for anyone in either direction" satisfied the Israelis of his understanding of the signal, while also conveying a warning against Israeli attacks on Iraq over Jordanian airspace.[9] Prime Minister Mudar Badran also declared that Iraqi troops would not enter Jordan except in response to an Israeli incursion.[10] These communications, combined with the strategic factors discussed above, alleviated Jordanian concern with this threat. However, the difficulties of public signaling, as opposed to direct communications, can be seen in Arens's recollection of his reaction to Jordan's August 17 decision to raise the level of alert of the Jordanian Army: "I do not know if this was in expectation of an attack by us, in anticipation of the entry of Iraqi forces into Jordan, or maybe just King Hussein's way of gaining support for himself from the mobs demonstrating in Amman" (Arens 1995: 154). Because of the strategic situation and the private communications, Jordanian state decisionmakers placed less weight on the Israeli threat than did the wider public, which demanded preparations for self-defense and regularly warned of immanent Israeli invasion. Jordanian officials stressed the Israeli threat in public more as a justification and demonstration of the regime's valor, and as a signal to the Israelis, than as an indication of their true concerns.

Second, Jordan could be seen as bandwagoning with Iraq in order to protect itself against an Iraqi threat. Some analysts have suggested that Hussein's real fear was that Iraq, surrounded on all sides, would decide to break out by invading Jordan en route to Israel in order to spark a general Arab-

Israeli war and break up the coalition. By maintaining friendly relations with Iraq, Jordan could presumably forestall Iraqi aggression, by making itself too valuable to risk. In this case, aligning with Israel, openly or through participation in the U.S. coalition, in order to secure a credible balance against an Iraqi threat would be a more effective response. While Arabist norms in the past would have prohibited such an alliance choice, the participation of Egypt, Syria, and Saudi Arabia in the coalition certainly provided sufficient cover in the Arabist public sphere.[11] Bandwagoning with Iraq to meet an Iraqi threat does not seem like a plausible explanation; Brand notes that "Jordanian decision makers did not understand their behavior as bandwagoning with Iraq" (1994: 294), and King Hussein regularly rejected any suggestion that this was Jordan's policy. Israeli statements signaling their red lines to Jordan were also a clearly stated exercise in deterrence against Iraq. Since Iraqi movement into Jordan would have immediately brought on an Israeli retaliation, aligning with Iraq in order to forestall an Iraqi attack would have been somewhat superfluous. Finally, no evidence exists that Iraq conveyed a threat, explicit or implicit, to Jordan that it would attack if Jordan did not take its side.

Third, King Hussein could be seen less as bandwagoning with Iraq than as bandwagoning with domestic pro-Iraqi political actors in order to protect his regime from domestic upheaval. This has become the explanation of choice for analysts despairing of assigning causal weights to external threats to Jordan. In their analysis of Jordan's behavior, for example, Harknett and VanDenBerg conclude that "joining the Arab-American coalition [sic] would have inflamed his [King Hussein's] population and placed the monarchy in jeopardy of overthrow" (1997: 144). Brand similarly argues that "the clear and vociferous anti-American/pro-Iraqi message of a largely united Jordanian people during a period of transition from authoritarianism meant that a Gulf policy even remotely pro-coalition might well have led to severe instability, if not the end of the monarchy" (1993: 2–3). This threat to regime survival tends to be assumed rather than proved, however. While the atmosphere of late 1990 was certainly charged, no observers have produced convincing evidence that the army, the security services, or even major political groupings would have acted to overthrow the king had he sided with the U.S. coalition. Jordanian diplomatic history is a recitation of instances of Hussein's decisions taken against the express desires of the majority of the Jordanian political public, none of which have cost the king his throne. The regime could certainly have explained the tremendous pressures Jordan faced, accused Iraq of violating Arab norms by invading Kuwait, and repressed the popular expression of anger. The regime's ability to sign a peace treaty with Israel in 1994, and to turn against Iraq in 1995, without any serious threat of revolution suggests its relative stability in the face of popular anger. The causal argument for domestic threat rests on a counterfactual that seems implausible based on historical experience and contemporary evidence.

Fourth, perhaps Jordan felt that the outbreak of war under any conditions represented a fundamental threat to its interests and even to its survival. Should war break out, Jordan could become a battleground, its economy ruined, and its territory flooded with refugees. Hussein repeatedly, in every forum, warned that war would be a holocaust [*karitha*] for his country, the region, and the world. The search for a diplomatic resolution of the crisis, no matter what its conditions, was preferable to war. Therefore, Jordan balanced against a generalized threat of war by remaining neutral and trying to broker a diplomatic solution. This strains the threat-balancing concept, which assumes that states balance against each other, not against processes or generalized fears. However, Hussein and other Jordanian policymakers consistently explained their fears in this way: responding to the generalized threat of war in the region. In each of the crises between the United States and Iraq in the mid-1990s, Jordan expressed identical concerns about the catastrophic impact of any war in the area. The consistency of Jordanian mediation efforts and appeals for a peaceful solution, with no international support, reflects this perception.

Each of the threat-based explanations seems plausible. The very plausibility of such different causal paths, however, suggests that threat is not alone sufficient to explain Jordanian behavior. Some other process seems to be at work which made some behavior seem more threatening than others. The process of interpretation thus moves to the forefront in any threat-based explanation. I argue that the threat motivating policy emerges from the process of public sphere debate rather than following directly from any objective indicators. It was the interpretive process of framing the crisis, both inside of Jordan and within the Arabist and international public spheres, that produced the sense of the greater threat.

Political Economy

If threat balancing explanations fail to adequately explain Jordanian behavior, then what about material economic interests? Jordan's economic dependence on Iraq has often been highlighted by rationalists frustrated by the shortcomings of power and threat theories. By focusing on the financial, oil, and trade relationships binding Jordan to Iraq, rationalists hold on to the primacy of objective, material interests. For example, Stanley Reed explained Hussein's decisions in economic terms: "Behind his positions lies a Jordanian-Iraqi interdependence that has grown deep in recent years. Jordan has grown so dependent on Iraq as a market for its exports and as a source of cheap oil that destruction of the Iraqi economy threatens to destroy Jordan's economy as well." (Reed 1990/1991: 22; Ebert 1992) Statistics convincingly demonstrate this Jordanian dependence on Iraqi markets and oil. More problematic is the assumption of a direct, unmediated causal relationship between these material interests and political positions.

Like threat-based explanations, the economic argument underdetermines outcomes. For all Jordan's trade dependence on Iraq, it also received huge and vital direct budget subsidies from many of the actors arrayed against Iraq. Brand's (1994) budget security explanation of Jordanian foreign policy, emphasizing the importance of these direct subsidies for the maintenance of the neopatrimonial rentier state, argues that the state should give higher priority to such subsidies than to markets. Besides direct budget support, the remittances of Jordanians and Palestinians employed in the Gulf to Jordanian banks represented an essential pillar of Jordan's political economy. The state also relied heavily upon international aid, from the U.S. and from international lending agencies such as the IMF and the World Bank. Support for Iraq clearly and unambiguously threatened all of these sources of budget support. Why were trade relations with Iraq valued more highly than the massive budget supports from the states ranged on the other side of the confrontation?

One explanation is that even prior to the crisis, Gulf states had been substantially cutting back on budget support to Jordan. By 1989, "it became apparent that none of Jordan's traditional financial backers was prepared to be committed to an extended period of assistance . . . future aid would only be proffered on an ad hoc basis, often only after considerable Jordanian pleading" (Brynen 1992: 92). American and Gulf promises of aid in exchange for participation would have solved precisely this problem, however, making this explanation difficult to sustain.

The Jordanian decision also is not adequately explained in terms of poor information or incorrect beliefs about the economic consequences of alignment decisions. Decisionmakers and the public were painfully aware of the likely impact of the crisis on the Jordanian economy. The press published frank evaluations of the probable economic implications of the loss of Gulf support, of the blockade of the Port of Aqaba, of the mass return of Jordanians and Palestinians from jobs in the Gulf. There was very little in the public discourse to suggest any expectation that support for Iraq would prove financially rewarding in the short or medium term. The public exulted in the regime's independence from budget imperatives in this crisis: "All Jordanians know that this position will cost Jordan dearly financially . . . but Jordan is governed by considerations deeper than money."[12] Jordanians knew of the American inducements to its Arab coalition partners, such as forgiving billions of dollars in Egyptian military debt: "Jordan is fully aware of the size of the bribe it would have received had it agreed [to join the coalition]. We know that our foreign debts would have been canceled with a stroke of a pen, that the siege [of Aqaba] would have been lifted, . . . and that aid and money would have poured into Jordan from all directions. . . . The reason [Jordan refuses] can be summed up in one word: honor."[13] King Hussein, in a press conference in mid-August 1990, explicitly declared that "money is the least of my concerns right now."[14] When directly asked whether Jordanian economic ties to Iraq drove his policy, he responded, "this is not the truth."[15] And when an American journalist asked King Hussein what one thing he would most like to say to President Bush, Hussein responded: "Our relations are not based on material considerations. . . . we have borne great hardships, but we are not cheap, believe me, we are proud."[16] The express denial that financial considerations were driving policy should be taken seriously, given Hussein's consistent expression of other justifications, as well as the demands of public consistency: if he had really been waiting for a better financial deal, then publicly disavowing the legitimacy of such incentives would have bound his hands in dangerous ways.

A more powerful explanation is that whatever the short-term losses, "Jordan's long-run economic interests are in Iraq."[17] Trade with Iraq involved the development of infrastructure, supply networks, regularized patterns of exchange, and product specialization which could not simply be redirected in the way that direct budget subsidies theoretically could be. While a French check for $200 million could completely and frictionlessly replace a Saudi check for that amount, the Iraqi market and the capital, transportation, and information investments underlying it could not be replaced with similar ease. No comparable markets existed in the area to replace the Iraqi market. Trade with the Iraqi market formed human networks of partnership and contacts. Amman Chamber of Commerce statistics indicate that some 250 Jordanian companies were established specifically for the Iraqi market, with 40 percent of manufactured exports going to Iraq immediately prior to the war.[18] As one Jordanian political scientist explains, "Iraq was the only Arab state that could solve Jordan's long-term economic problems" (Naqrash 1994: 330–332).

The celebration of Jordan's rejection of Western and Gulf financial incentives suggests that public framing produced a political reading of economic relations. The Jordanian public interpreted economic ties to Iraq as holding normative value deeper than their economic value. Ties to Iraq took on a heroic quality as an expression of Arab solidarity. Economic relations were interpreted, and became politically relevant, through the lens of identity. The constructivist argument that trade relations between Jordanians and Iraqis had built networks of community of identity and interests is thus more satisfying than a straightforward equation of economic interdependence and political interests, and better explains why Jordanian society placed higher value on Iraqi rather than Gulf economic relations.

Public Opinion and the Public Sphere

Rationalist explanations of Jordanian Gulf crisis behavior regularly import public opinion into ostensibly state-centric, materialist, and interest-based accounts (Anderson 1996). Brand, for example, modifies her rent-seeking theory in the Gulf war case by proposing that above all "King Hussein was responding to . . . popular opinion in the Jordanian street" (Brand 1994: 228). Virtually every account of Jordanian policy stresses the importance of public opinion, without allowing this recognition to infiltrate the broader theoretical reliance on variables such as power, economics, or threat. Many analysts admit that their theories underdetermine Jordanian behavior and then introduce a stylized reading of public opinion on an ad hoc basis to fill in the gap. The conventional version of this argument portrays a unified, mobilized Jordanian political society putting irresistible pressure on a beleaguered king who knew better but could not stand against the public trend. Support for Iraq welled up from the deep Arabist convictions of the people, who were emotionally swept away by the appearance of a "new Saladin" [or at least a new Nasser] bidding to unite the Arab world and confront the West. Because of the liberalization of 1989, the public had the means through which to declare and act upon its convictions. Since the democratization had become essential for regime legitimacy, the regime could not afford repression and could not oppose the will of the aroused public.

As the discussion in chapter 2 made clear, the public opinion introduced in these accounts should not be mistaken for the public sphere. The rationalist use of public opinion posits a sharp distinction between state interests and public opinion, where policy is potentially constrained by fear of "the street." Public opinion represents a constraint upon the rational action of states. A public sphere account, in contrast, views public deliberation as constitutive of interests. In the Gulf crisis, the international public sphere demanded a binary choice which Jordan could not make, forcing Jordan out of the international consensus. The Arabist arena produced an official consensus through a process perceived as illegitimate, again forcing Jordan to stand outside the consensus. The Jordanian public sphere, opened by the 1989 liberalization, emerged as the primary location for debate about Jordanian identity and interests. This public deliberation produced an effective frame in support of Iraq which drove conceptions of Jordan's Arabist identity and state interests. This consensus had a powerful effect on state behavior, not by compelling or constraining policy, but by framing the meaning and consequences of choices.

International Public Spheres

Despite Jordanian efforts to find an Arab solution, the international dimensions of the crisis almost immediately overwhelmed the Arab. In the eyes of Jordanians, the appeal for Arab dialogue and an Arab solution represented a vain effort to maintain the integrity and autonomy of the Arabist public sphere. When Iraq invaded Kuwait, it became almost inevitable that the United States would intervene and the crisis would become "internationalized" (Telhami 1992a). As the United States built its international coalition, it framed the crisis in a sharply dichotomous way: either with the coalition or against it. Within such a frame, Jordan's attempts to remain neutral became nothing less than an alliance with Iraq and open hostility to the United States. King Hussein complained often about the failure of the West to understand Jordan's position, objecting to the characterization of Jordan as supporting or defending Iraq. Jordanian officials referred to "an organized media campaign aimed at distorting Jordan's position."[19] Hussein's attempts to address American public opinion failed to make any headway in convincing the United States of Jordan's neutrality. Even King Hussein's personal friendship with George Bush, and the general understanding in the Bush Administration of Jordan's difficult strategic and political situation, could not overcome the power of this interpretive frame.

Bush regarded Hussein as "one of the worst offenders.. almost a spokesman for his neighbor Iraq" (Bush and Scowcroft 1998: 331). While the Bush

Administration recognized that Jordan had not "backed Iraq," in that it had refused to recognize the new Kuwaiti regime, rejected the acquisition of territory by force, and cooperated with sanctions, it nevertheless was infuriated by Jordan's voicing of Iraqi "propaganda" (Bush and Scowcroft 1998: 347–48). Congress voted harsh penalties on Jordan as an "Iraqi ally."[20] American and international media ridiculed King Hussein, usually portrayed as a dignified and moderate monarch, as an irresponsible Iraqi puppet.

Hussein's greatest frustration in the international public sphere, besides the seemingly willful misrepresentation of Jordanian positions, came from the evident lack of American interest in finding a peaceful solution. Because of the strong Jordanian preference to avoid war, the American unwillingness to seriously engage in negotiations infuriated the King. Jordanian officials often expressed the belief that the United States, like the Arab order before it, had not given diplomacy a chance. Once the decision had been made for military action, the United States had no interest in allowing the initiative of real dialogue oriented toward finding a diplomatic compromise. The United States therefore drew a firm, uncompromisable line: full, unconditional Iraqi withdrawal. The exchange of argument and dialogue in the international public sphere, which might lead toward a compromise in which the interests of both sides were represented, would signify failure for American policy and a disaster for American interests as articulated by the Bush Administration.

The Americans objected to the Jordanian media, which provided one of the only outlets by which Iraqi positions and justifications, as well as undesirable information, might reach the international public sphere (Bush and Scowcroft 1998: 347–48). From the American perspective, the Jordanian media served Iraqi propaganda and, worse, willfully rejected the coalition's imposed interpretative frame. The United States placed great importance on controlling information during the crisis, both to ward off uprisings in Arab members of the coalition and to prevent the Iraqi case from being expressed in any international public sphere (Telhami 1992a; Taylor 1992). At several points, Bush publicly vented his anger with the Jordanian media, alternately amusing and infuriating Jordanians, who wondered cynically how the leader of the democratic world found it in himself to criticize their free expression of opinion. As a Professional Associations committee declared, "they deny the Jordanian people their right to express their opinions freely and deny the leadership of the country the democratic approach, as if democracy were the monopoly of the West."[21] Jordanians felt themselves to be the object of American psychological warfare, and tended to dismiss news in Western media as disinformation—a perspective which was used as evidence of their irrationality and susceptibility to conspiracy theories at that time, but which seems rather reasonable in light of later self-criticism by the American media.

The most important practical manifestation of Jordan's behavior from the viewpoint of the international community was its compliance with the sanctions regime. Jordan agreed to comply with all sanctions authorized by the UN, though it questioned their motives, scope, and legitimacy. The UN, for its part, recognized the severe consequences of the sanctions for the Jordanian economy and provided special waivers and compensation for Jordanian compliance. The intrusive inspection regime at the Port of Aqaba often seemed, at least to Jordanians, to be aimed more at punishing Jordan than at isolating Iraq. Aid to Jordan was tied to compliance with the sanctions, much as it had in the past been tied to participation in the peace process.

Israel provided the context for the other major international public sphere concern. Above I discussed Israeli-Jordanian communications over the conditions for Israeli intervention in Jordan. Despite the basic strategic understanding between the two leaderships, Israeli public interpretations of the "radicalization" and "Palestinianization" of Jordan powerfully influenced international perceptions of Jordan during the crisis. One of the major justifications for Israeli support of a Hashemite regime in Jordan had long been that the Hashemites were superior to any alternative regime, whether PLO, Islamist, Transjordanian nationalist. If King Hussein could not control the expression of radical public opinion, and allowed this public opinion to guide Jordanian foreign policy, then some Israelis suggested that perhaps Hussein's regime was no better than an alternative regime after all. Perhaps even more crucially, Jordan blasted the double standard in the enforcement of international law, the disjuncture between the emphasis on the need to enforce UN resolutions on Kuwait and the failure to enforce UN resolutions on Palestine, which raised the question of "linkage" the United States and Israel wanted to avoid.

Arabist Public Sphere

Throughout the crisis, Hussein pleaded for a peaceful Arab solution through dialogue, searching for a way to maintain the integrity of regional institutions against the demand for international intervention. Jordan consistently justified its behavior in terms of the norms of an autonomous Arabist order, the inadmissibility of acquiring land by force, and peaceful conflict resolution through dialogue (Naqrash 1994; Nahar 1993; White Book 1991). The consistency of Jordanian discourse, over time, over different issue areas, and across public spheres with widely varying interpretive demands, should be taken seriously as an indicator of the weight of the Jordanian interpretation on its behavior. The norms emphasized in Jordan's framing of the crisis were consistent across domestic and foreign policy, deeply institutionalized in Jordanian discourse and practice, and actively invoked to explain Jordan's behavior.

Brand objects to a norms-based account, which might claim that "the King's sense of Arabism—by all accounts quite strong—motivated him to seek an inter-Arab solution," because "then one would have to argue why such a sense of Arabism . . . led him to stand more firmly by Arab Iraq than by Arab Kuwait." (Brand 1994: 287). An important theoretical point common to rationalist theories lies concealed within this formulation. Arabism here seems to be a conviction located within Hussein's subjectivity: "the King's sense of Arabism." This construction slights the intersubjective dimension of norms. Arabism should be conceptualized as a set of publicly contestable norms to which Jordanian politicians and publics respond, and on which they rely to interpret reality and to construct meaningful action.

Brand's objection nevertheless poses a core rationalist challenge to constructivism: why does one interpretation of Arabism defeat another? After all, Iraq clearly violated a central Arabist norm by occupying another Arab state. The answer to this important question lies in the process of strategic framing and the structure of the relevant public spheres. Jordan's interpretive frame clearly integrated these norms. Jordan rejected the Iraqi annexation of Kuwait, continued to recognize the Kuwaiti ruling family, and endorsed the principle of the inadmissibility of acquiring land by force. On the other hand, Jordan objected to the internationalization of the crisis, the rejection of dialogue and diplomacy, and the rush to war. In the Jordanian view, Iraq had legitimate complaints against Kuwait with regard to oil and finance. Such complaints must not be resolved by force—hence, the condemnation of the invasion. Instead, they should be resolved through dialogue within Arab institutions aimed at establishing mutually acceptable norms of justice with regard to the distribution of Arab oil wealth. The normative centrality of dialogue emerged with unusual clarity throughout the crisis, as Jordan elevated the principle of *hiwar* to the defining feature of the Arabist order. By calling on American intervention, Kuwait and other Arab states implicitly abandoned the principle of an Arab order. King Hussein charged that "certain Arab actors chose from the beginning to reject any Arab political dialogue with Iraq," and blamed them for the failure of the Arab solution.[22]

The theme of the primacy of maintaining an Arab framework for resolving inter-Arab disputes took precedence over all other Jordanian arguments. The existence of the Arab order depended upon the autonomy of Arabist institutions and the primacy of the Arab will to consensus. Maintaining an Arab framework for conflict resolution represented a cornerstone of the institutional identity of the Arab order. This interpretation of Arabism, centering on cooperation within Arab institutions between sovereign Arab states, resonated with the sovereignty-based interpretation of Arabism championed by Hussein since the 1960s. Jordan's representative to the Arab League forcefully argued this position: "Jordan sees this situation as an Arab affair in the first degree which must be settled within an Arab framework without being turned into an opportunity for foreign intervention."[23]

The principle of the inadmissibility of acquiring land by force represented a second deeply embedded constitutive norm of Jordanian foreign policy. Since the emergence of the Arab order Jordan had advocated a form of Arabism that recognized state sovereignty and that rejected intervention in the affairs of other Arab states. This position follows from Jordanian interest in state survival amidst more powerful neighbors, as Jordan regularly appealed to norms of sovereignty and nonintervention in the face of Arabist challenges. This defense of sovereignty surpassed the simple expression of interest, becoming a focal point for Jordanian discourse in the Arabist public sphere. Like its defense of the autonomy of the Arab order, the Jordanian interpretation of the norm of sovereignty has been expressed consistently over a long period of time in its Arabist argumentation.

After Jordan lost the West Bank in 1967, the principle of the inadmissibility of acquiring land by force assumed particular importance in Jordanian discourse in the international public sphere. In its struggles with Israel over the eventual disposition of the West Bank, Jordan built its case on this principle and argued it so consistently that it surpassed an expression of interest. The principle became a central norm, not only for Jordanian diplomacy but also for the internal construction of Jordanian identity. Regardless of any sympathy with Iraqi claims against Kuwait, Jordanian policymakers insisted on applying this norm to that situation as well. Of course, norms and interest were not exclusive, actively reinforcing one another. Jordanians feared that any recognition of the Iraqi right to occupy Kuwait would fatally undermine the objection to Israeli occupation of Palestine. In a letter to Saddam Hussein in September 1990, King Hussein made this fear explicit: "You know that we are committed to the principle of not permitting the acquisition of land by force.. not only because of international principles but also because of our situation in confronting Zionist ambitions.. Violating the principle sets a dangerous precedent which will benefit Israel and will threaten the security and the existence of Jordan."[24]

Jordanian diplomatic initiatives based on these principles—the autonomy of the Arabist order, peaceful conflict resolution, and the inadmissibility of acquiring land by force—foundered upon the American determination to prevent a regional solution, Iraqi intransigence, and the submission of key Arab actors to American policy. The Cairo Summit on August 11, 1990 condemned the Iraqi occupation and authorized UN intervention. Despite its principled appeal to Arab consensus, Jordan in practice rejected the consensus produced at the Cairo Summit. This rejection is puzzling: why should a state desperately campaigning for an Arab solution and committed to achieving Arab consensus reject the summit decision? The simple answer that the summit produced the "wrong" result is unconvincing. Jordan has frequently accepted an Arab consensus against its strong and impassioned objections, most notably at the 1974 Rabat summit recognizing the PLO as the sole Palestinian representative. Jordan has consistently preferred outcomes within an Arab consensus to an objectively better outcome outside the Arab consensus.

One major reason for Jordan's rejection of the Cairo resolutions relates to the procedures governing consensus formation: by violating the norms of Arab consensus formation, the Cairo Summit forfeited legitimacy as a statement of an authentic Arab consensus (Khalidi 1991; Haykal 1992). This argument draws on Habermas's discourse ethics, in which the legitimacy of a consensus depends upon its having been achieved in accordance with certain procedural rules (Habermas 1996; Bohman 1996; Chambers 1996). For the Arabist public sphere, the minimal requirements might be characterized as the participants representing Arab positions independent of foreign influences and exerting a genuine effort to achieve consensus in defense of collective Arab interests and norms. The Jordanians, like many others, believed that these minimal conditions had not been met in Cairo (Mattar 1995; Khalidi 1991). Argumentation between Arab leaders was palpably irrelevant to the summit resolution. Jordanian and other dissenting participants were not persuaded of the value of the adopted position, which they perceived as compelled by power. According to Jordanian and Palestinian commentators, as well as the towering Egyptian journalist Mohammed Hassanein Haykal (1992), Egyptian President Mubarak tightly controlled the summit, to the outrage of dissenters: "After the [Egyptian-Saudi] resolution

was introduced, Mubarak asked only for the votes in favor—there were
twelve [a simple majority]—and then concluded the session refusing to allow
amendments, discussion, votes against, or abstentions. Three heads of state
later claimed that Mubarak had prevented them from speaking at the summit, and alternatives . . . were not presented for a vote" (Khalidi 1991).
Egyptian government sympathizers contest this description of the Summit
proceedings, providing a counter-narrative in which all participants spoke at
great length; in which King Hussein and Yasir Arafat were among those
eager to end debate; and in which the final resolution commanded wide
support. The vehemence of the presentation of this frame, particularly the
furious responses to the Jordanian White Book and to Haykal, demonstrates
the importance placed on the legitimacy of these procedures. Were these
allegations true, the consensus could not claim to be the product of open,
rational debate.

Besides the absence of deliberation, the Cairo Resolutions came under
attack as not authentically Arab. The Egyptian position, according to the
Jordanians, changed under American pressure. Hussein claimed that in early
August he had secured, with Egyptian backing, an Iraqi commitment to
withdraw from Kuwait, only to have Mubarak dramatically reverse his position and wreck the deal. Egypt furiously denied the allegation, but the
argument is important for understanding Jordanian framing of the crisis.
The intrusion of external power doubly corrupted the process of consensus
formation. First, by compelling the Egyptian position, the American exertion
of power prevented the operation of rational debate. Second, since the Egyptian position came from the Americans, it did not represent an authentic
Arab position. Rather than a consensus expressing true Arab preferences, the
Resolution represented the forceful imposition of American preferences. Because of the intrusion of power and the role of external actors, the Cairo
Summit forfeited legitimacy as a carrier of an Arab consensus. For Jordanians, this corrupted summit represented not the freely determined consensus
of Arab states but "Arab cover for American decisions."[25] The Arab coalition
members were "mortgaged to the aggressive desires and will of the United
States," not representing authentic, free Arab will.[26] Wherever Arab states
permitted some degree of free expression, public opinion generally supported Iraq and criticized the performance of the Arab regimes. The sharp
divergence between the interpretation of the situation held by most Arab
publics and the interpretation advanced to justify the summit resolution
further undermined the validity and authenticity of the Arab consensus.

After the Cairo Summit, Jordan continued to campaign for a diplomatic solution. Hussein's itinerary during the months of the crisis indicates the extent of his efforts to find such a solution. Jordanian spokesmen complained bitterly about the misrepresentation of Jordanian positions: "There have been persistent attempts to do violence to Jordan's reputation and credibility, when we are making every effort to bring back stability to the region through dialogue."[27] The Arab coalition members engaged in fierce political campaigns against Jordan, rejecting any dialogue and damning Jordan as an Iraqi apologist. Jordan threatened these states by contesting the interpretive frame installed at the Cairo summit and exposing its failure to meet Arab norms and to defend Arab interests. The coalition regimes, afraid of popular unrest as well as uneasy with the implications for Arab norms, feared the impact of Jordanian discourse on their public opinion and worked to misrepresent it and silence it, rather than responding to the arguments in a reasoned way. Events such as the massacre of Palestinian worshipers at the al-Aqsa mosque in Jerusalem and the Israeli deportation of Palestinians from the West Bank exacerbated the situation, forcing Arab publics and leaders to confront the de facto alliance with Israel which the Cairo frame obscured and the Jordanian discourse exposed.

Because of the divergence between the Jordanian frame and the "official" Arab position, Jordan found itself largely excluded from the Arabist public sphere. This exclusion meant that the Arabism of Jordanian behavior would primarily be determined in the Jordanian public sphere. Jordanian policy was framed in Arabist terms, despite its exclusion from the Arab consensus. For perhaps the first time in Jordanian history, the Hashemite isolation from the Arab consensus was viewed by the Jordanian—and Palestinian—publics as the result of the superior Arabism of the Jordanian position. This provided great normative value for the regime, while largely insulating it from Arab criticism: for once it was the Syrian and the Gulf positions which were seen by public opinion to be corrupt, inauthentic, and anti-Arabist.

The Jordanian Public Sphere

While Jordan's interpretation of international norms can explain a great deal of its behavior, the analysis is critically incomplete without taking into account the domestic articulation of Jordanian identity and interests. The public sphere argument developed here should be distinguished from the common interpretation that Jordanian policy simply responded to the constraints imposed by mass public opinion. By this argument, unified public opinion in the newly liberalized Jordanian political system shaped state behavior. A characteristic statement comes from Dilip Hiro's history of the war: "32 out of 80 elected deputies were Islamic fundamentalists, and three-fifths of the citizens were of Palestinian origin who regarded Saddam Hussein as a modern-day Saladin. . . . King Hussein had little choice but to tilt to the Iraqi regime" (Hiro: 123). Faced with intense public pressure and unable to crack down, King Hussein followed the mob (Brand 1991a).

This account, while persuasive in its broad outline, misrepresents the nature of Jordanian public opinion formation. It tends to assume a prior and constant degree of support for Iraq among all sectors of political society, which was then revealed by liberalization and the Gulf crisis rather than formed in the political process. It reads political behavior directly off of essentialized, ascribed identities: Jordanians supported Saddam because of their nature as "Islamic fundamentalists" and "Palestinians." I would argue, by contrast, that the commitment of Jordanian society to Iraq emerged through the process of public deliberation. Noting that many Jordanians are Islamists, Palestinian in origin, or economically dependent on Iraq is not a sufficient explanation for their political behavior. Where Palestinians or Islamists rallied to Iraq, it was because of the successful articulation of an identity frame which asserted a shared Jordanian-Iraqi identity and interests. For the emergent Jordanian consensus, "the unjust war did not only target Iraq but also all who stand beside Iraq and its Arab nationalist message."[28] This collective identity frame, in which Jordan's Arab identity was articulated as directly linked to Iraq, was both the cause of Jordanian behavior and the outcome of public debate.

Highly contested questions continue about the origin of the 1990 Jordanian consensus. Some observers saw the press commentary as led directly by the regime: "when al-Ra'i writes that the war in Iraq is a holy war . . . this is not evidence of a free press in Jordan giving vent to its unfettered views. . . . it is an expression of the opinions prevailing today in the royal court."[29] Others saw public opinion driving state behavior, arguing that King Hussein had "lost control" and was "at the mercy of radical trends." Participants also disagreed about the precise relationship between opinion leaders and public opinion. Nabil Sharif, editor of a major daily, contends that "during the Gulf war, the press was primarily responsible for the mass mobilization on the side of Iraq. . . . there was already predisposition in that direction, but the press crystallized and focused popular sentiment."[30] Rather than public opinion existing fully formed and waiting for an opportunity to express itself, opinion leaders played an important role in interpreting the crisis and influencing the direction of public mobilization. The only book-length treatment of the performance of the Jordanian press in the crisis documents the ways in which the press guided public behavior: enforcing unanimity of interpretation, publishing prominently the statements of political parties and activists, publicizing rallies and meetings, printing analysis and debate, contesting Western news reports, and spreading hope of victory (Barakat 1992).

Still, not all participants accept the proposition that the press created or even led public opinion. Some writers tend to be more struck by the power exerted by popular consensus on the press than on the role of the press in creating consensus. In the midst of the crisis, Fahd al-Rimawi located the real force of the consensus in the public: "Most of the time I feel that the writer follows public opinion and does not create it. . . . he represents the dictatorship of mass frenzy and does not oppose it."[31] Muna Shaqir, a formidable political analyst, similarly observed that "writers said what the people wanted to hear . . . we reflected the convictions of the masses rather than producing new convictions . . . we swam with the tide rather than try to redirect it."[32] This interpretation seems to remove all agency from the explanation, portraying an authoritative consensus that emerged on its own. While this analysis certainly captures the sense of helplessness felt by many Jordanians in the face of the relentless slide to war, it unnecessarily and incorrectly slights the importance of the public sphere in shaping the political consensus. The existence of a public sphere in which collective interpretations were shaped, rather than the specific agency of individual writers, explains the impact of public deliberation. The press established the interpretive frame by which the public understood the crisis.

The argument that public deliberation produced the consensus begins from the important but overlooked fact that the initial reaction was far from unanimous. In the first few days after the Iraqi invasion, a wide array of reactions appeared in the press and throughout public discourse. Many Jordanians initially condemned the invasion as an impermissible Arab-Arab bloodletting. Analysts weighed, with varying results, the norms of sovereignty and peaceful resolution of conflicts against the merit of Iraqi claims against Kuwait and Kuwaiti intransigence. Most were impressed by Iraqi arguments but profoundly uneasy about the precedent of the military annexation of one Arab country by another. The initial reaction, hesitant and frightened for regional security, belies the post-facto reconstruction of Jordanian opinion as fervently pro-Iraqi from the beginning. An alternative frame was readily available which would have convincingly justified Jordanian participation in an anti-Iraq coalition. A number of influential writers argued the Iraqi case immediately, but this should not conceal the real pluralism of opinion: their arguments were hotly contested, rather than accepted blindly, and both frames could have reasonably emerged as dominant.

This intense public sphere contestation did not last long. Consensus followed closely upon the shifting of the terms of debate from "Iraq vs. Kuwait" to "Iraq vs. United States" in the first weeks of the crisis. The rise of this frame is essential to understanding the process of consensus formation in the Jordanian public sphere. Once the conflict left the inter-Arab framework, many of the ambiguities of the interpretive process disappeared: "We don't incline toward Iraq or toward Kuwait. . . . the choice is between Arabs and the forces of foreign imperialism . . . and so we incline to ourselves and to all Arabs."[33] Rather than weighing the violation of Kuwaiti sovereignty against the manifest injustice of the distribution of Arab wealth, observers now saw an intervention by the imperial powers against an Arab challenger. The frame made sense of all that had taken place and offered a clear normative prescription. Obviously, the coalition's primary concern was to restore control of Arab oil to the compliant hands of the Kuwaitis. Obviously, the U.S. sought to serve Israel by destroying its rising Iraqi challenger. Obviously, the coalition represented naked self-interest, power against principle. Obviously, the Arab states had abandoned their norms and identity in return for selfish interests. In such an interpretive frame, Arab identity and Arab interests seemed to demand resistance to foreign power, meaning support for Iraq. In the absence of this frame, it is not at all clear that the Jordanian public would have settled upon consensus support of Iraq: "if the differences had remained between Iraq and Kuwait only, there could have been division on the method of tackling the issue."[34] The equation of Arab identity and the Iraqi position emerged from the frame, then, rather than from pre-existing or objective factors.

Once this frame crystallized, it translated quickly into an articulation of Jordanian interests and prescriptions for behavior. The Jordanian public asserted a conception of Jordanian interests based on identification with Iraq and with Arabism. Barakat points out that "quickly there came to be only one opinion . . . to the extent that some writers totally changed their positions with astonishing speed" (1992: 17). Once this popular consensus formed "there was almost a complete consensus among the writers, and in fact it was virtually impossible for anyone to write anything on the other side of the issue.. popular pressure prevented anyone from taking other positions than support for Iraq against Kuwait and the US."[35]

A controversial explanation of the Jordanian consensus has been Iraqi penetration of the Jordanian public sphere. In October 1995, the Arab daily *al-Hayat* alleged wide scale Iraqi penetration of Jordanian political and media circles. According to this report, based on leaks from official sources then looking to break Jordanian-Iraqi relations, Iraq had for decades paid a large number of prominent writers substantial amounts to push the Iraqi line in the Jordanian public sphere. While the government declined to prosecute the alleged Iraqi agents, citing the difficulty of proving such clandestine ties, few Jordanians find it implausible.[36] The pro-Iraq position of many opinion leaders, as well as their furious reaction, could well be explained by such payoffs. Such subsidies to writers are a well-established practice in the Arab press and a well-known Iraqi policy.[37] Egyptian President Mubarak explained the position of the Jordanian press as directly attributable to Iraqi bribes: "You go to Amman and you'll see all the new Mercedes" (Baker 1995: 291). The close Jordanian-Iraqi alliance of the 1980s meant that many of those allegedly on the Iraqi payroll were regime loyalists, not opposition figures who could be easily dismissed. Prior to the crisis, however, there were wide sectors of the political public who did not express any particular sympathy with Iraq. The Arabist frame brought together Arabists, Islamists, Palestinians, and Jordanian nationalists, all of whom felt that support for Iraq best served both their identity and their interests. The support of Iraq emerged during the crisis rather than preceding it, and developed out of the interpretive frame of identity and interests, not out of an Iraqi checkbook.

Whatever the extent of Iraqi influence in producing a consensus among writers, it is insufficient to explain the political efficacy of the consensus. The consensus emerged from the dynamics of the public sphere debates, in which the public responded to and shaped the press response. The process of consensus formation in the early days of the crisis involved a real exchange of interpretations and arguments. Consensus quickly coalesced behind general agreement at the level of opinion leaders and the enthusiastic mobilization of the mass public. Enormous public rallies in support of Iraq, collections of funds to support the Iraqi people, volunteering to defend Iraq, and the issuing of declarations for the international media were some of the forms of action taken. In September, King Hussein even allowed a controversial conference of Arab popular opposition forces, which included some of Hussein's bitterest political enemies, including George Habash and Nayif Hawatmeh. Once formed, the consensus proved extremely effective at uniting opinion, guiding behavior, and framing the interpretation of subsequent events.

The consensus in many ways became a barrier to rational public debate.

Rimawi argued that "the mechanisms of repression are still present but have changed positions . . . before it came from official quarters, but now it comes from popular quarters."[38] Fanik pointed out the interaction between the press and the public in the enforcement of consensus: "Had there been a Jordanian writer who wanted to argue against the popular consensus, he probably could not have found a paper to publish him, because no editor was ready to face the popular abuse."[39] Other observers noted the divergence between public consensus and privately held opinion: "One did not read or even notice the existence of the other opinion despite the existence of a large number of writers who held other opinions and who presented them in studies, statements and analyses without their being published" (Suess and Tal 1991). Yaqoub Ziyadin, a veteran Communist Party leader, experienced harsh denunciations and personal attacks after publicly rejecting the Iraqi annexation of Kuwait and warning that no good could come of such behavior (Suess and Tal 1991). The force of this consensus reflects the concerns of some liberal theorists about the implications of Habermas's ideal of consensus (Benhabib 1996; Rescher 1993).

This account of a suffocating consensus growing out of a constitutive moment of rational debate perhaps leaves an incorrect impression that most Jordanians were compelled into their pro-Iraq position by a combination of the media and the popular pressure of ideological groups (MacLeod 1991). This does not capture the reality of public sphere dynamics in Jordan during the crisis. Certainly, there was some degree of conformism enforced by public pressures. After the war, fashionable self-criticism admitted that "some of us take one position in our columns in daily newspapers and another position in private meetings."[40] Publicly expressed convictions deepened palpably as time went by, as the course of international events reinforced the dichotomous structure of positions and the public response rewarded writers who argued the Iraqi case with praise, esteem, and popularity. This pressure to conformity with the consensus should not obscure the initial process of opinion formation, however, and the reality of competing frames within a relatively open public sphere.

An important point in support of the argument that the regime shared the public sphere articulation of state interests, rather than being compelled by its fear of public rebellion, is that the state did not respond to all popular demands. First, many of the more radical political parties and figures called on the government to arm and train the population to allow all Jordanians to participate in the national defense should Israel invade. Layth Shubaylat threatened a no-confidence vote in Parliament against Prime Minister Badran if he did not immediately begin a meaningful civil defense program.[41] The regime did not see that arming the population would contribute to its long-term security, and declined to take more than symbolic steps.

Second, the public demanded that Jordan defy the economic blockade of Iraq. The government could not afford to alienate the country from international society, however, and acceded to the sanctions decreed by the UN. In each case, the government easily deflected public demands which it deemed detrimental to Jordanian interests. The ability of the government to resist the more radical demands lends weight to the argument that the government acted as it did not out of fear of public uprisings but because it shared the conception of Jordanian interests articulated in the public sphere.

As should be clear, I am not arguing that the public commitment to Arabism led Jordan to act against its state interests. On the contrary, my argument is that the interpretations of Arabism in the Jordanian public sphere led Jordanians to articulate their state interests as best served by not joining the anti-Iraq coalition. Writers and officials alike argued that this policy served Jordanian interests, which coincided with generalized Arab interests. The Arabist frame, combined with Jordan's exclusion from the official Arab consensus, largely determined the formulation of interests and behavior. The understanding of state interests which guided state behavior developed through positive engagement with the Jordanian public sphere and the harsh rejection in the Arabist and international public spheres. Jordan's international and Arab isolation after the crisis, combined with the great domestic support for these positions, form the context for the three chapters to follow: the peace treaty with Israel, the struggles over normalization with Israel and new conceptions of regional order, and the turn against Iraq in 1995.

The Jordanian-Israeli Peace Process: Publicity, Interests, and Bargaining

Few relationships more clearly demonstrate the importance of public sphere considerations than the Jordanian-Israeli relationship. Israel has been the constitutively excluded Other in Arabist discourse, and the longstanding covert (but widely recognized) Jordanian-Israeli relations have complicated Jordan's identity and for its security. Indeed, the sharp contradiction between the demands of identity (Israel as enemy) and of interest (Israel as necessary partner) has long been of central concern. In the 1930s and 1940s, Abdullah pursued his personal and political interests in cooperation with the Jewish leadership in Palestine, but within the bounds of Jordanian and Arab public opinion and against the reservations of senior Transjordanian political figures (Shlaim 1987). Since at least the late 1950s, Israeli leaders accepted that the independent existence of Jordan under a Hashemite regime best served Israeli interests. Openly relying on Israeli support, however, would have fatally undermined regime survival, casting Jordan outside of the Arab order. Jordan and Israel engaged in "functional cooperation" on a wide range of technical and practical issues. The two states recognize a shared interest in maintaining quiet along their border, a Jordanian "interest" reinforced by the Israeli policy of massive retaliation in the 1950s-60s, and manifested by the Jordanian army's prevention of cross-border *fida'yin* activity. The two sides are assumed to share a preference for preventing the emergence of a Palestinian state. Because of the covert ties and mutual strategic value, outside observers often *assume* these "shared interests" between the two states (Lukacs 1997; Garfinkle 1992; Satloff

1995b). Public Jordanian commitment to Arabism or to Palestinian rights, or public concerns about an Israeli threat, are assumed to represent empty words for Arab consumption rather than real beliefs. For this paradigm, the primary significance of the Jordanian-Israeli peace treaty has been to "make public" relations which had been private, rather than to introduce qualitatively new kinds of relations.

While this paradigm correctly identifies certain dimensions of Jordanian interests, it ignores the importance of identity and public deliberation in producing state interests. Like rationalist approaches to state interests, it assumes that these Jordanian interests are fixed, exogenous, and unaffected by identity or norms. "Real" interests can be exogenously identified and behavior modeled accordingly, regardless of what actors actually say or do. Because it assumes constant, objective interests independent of public discourse, the paradigm captures only one dimension of Jordan's interests. While shared interests between Jordan and Israel do exist, they must be articulated as such; they do not objectively appear. A different Jordanian regime might well conceptualize its relationship with Israel differently, and certainly wide segments of Jordanian political society have not accepted the notion of shared interests with Israel which trump all other interests. Shared interests with Israel could not be publicly avowed, since such a public admission would have clashed with Arabist norms and Jordan's publicly constituted identity. Jordanian interests have often included those prioritized by the "shared interests" paradigm, but have never been reducible to them; only since the peace treaty could they even begin to be publicly justified.

Despite ascribed shared interests and the reality of functional cooperation, Jordanian-Israeli relations remained tacit until 1994. King Hussein met with Israeli leaders dozens of times, but always in secret (Zak 1985, 1997). The need for secrecy follows from the norms of the Arabist public sphere, which identifies Israel as the enemy and as a threat to Arab security, identity, and interests. Privacy was the necessary condition of the possibility of functional cooperation (Lukacs 1997). From the "shared interests" paradigm, these norms represent an externally imposed sanction rather than a constitutive dimension of Jordan's interests; a constructivist perspective suggests that normative commitments to Arab identity and comprehensive peace did inform Jordan's understanding of its interests. The Jordanian-Israeli "partnership" remained an "adversarial" one (Lustick 1977). Public alignment with Israel would have exposed Hussein to denunciation, subversion, and expulsion from the Arab order, but would also have meant compromising Jordan's Arab identity and the pursuit of Arab interests. Hussein went to the brink several times, most notably in his London meetings with Shimon Peres in 1987, but never made the final leap into publicity. While external constraints explain his hesitation to meet publicly with Israeli leaders, the broader unwillingness to conclude an independent peace treaty in the absence of Arab and Palestinian support transcended constraint.

The "shared interests" paradigm misrepresents the very real conflict between the functional demands of coexistence and the sense of state interests derived from state identity. Israeli leaders invariably describe King Hussein as not only sympathetic to Israel, and hostile to the PLO, but also sincerely committed to Jordanian, Palestinian, and Arab interests, and sensitive to what Arab public opinion would bear (Peres 1995; Rabin 1994; Shamir 1994). Arabist norms ruled out Israel as a viable alliance partner, even when such an alliance might be the most rational dictated by either power or threat. For the vast majority of Jordanians, Israel represented the enemy described in Arabist discourse, not a partner for functional cooperation or coordination against the PLO. Israeli arguments that the Israeli deterrent would protect Jordan against threats from its Arab neighbors might reflect private discussions with Jordanian state officials, but were met with harsh denunciation by all Jordanian public discourse: Jordanian identity discourse would not accept the substitution of Israeli for Arab "friends." Even where Israeli action manifestly supported the Jordanian regime, such as its "deterrence" of Syria during the 1970 crisis, Jordan could not acknowledge or admit publicly such assistance (Quandt 1978). Jordanian elites would tolerate relations with Israel to the extent to which they were not made public, and did not challenge Jordan's normative position in the Arab order. Open collaboration with Israel would expose Jordan as outside the Arab consensus, while in violation of its own norms and identity. As long as the public facade was maintained, Jordanians could reconcile their strategic needs with their normative beliefs. This should not be dismissed as hypocrisy, or as evidence for the irrelevance of norms and identity. All policies had to be justified in terms congruent with Arab identity and interests. Regime autonomy was circumscribed by the rejection of public relations with Israel and the public acceptance of the "Arab Self/Israeli Other" identity frame, ruling out a number of policy options and severely restricting the extent of open cooperation and alignment. Most Arab states accepted Jordanian-Israeli tacit relations, out of recognition of Jordan's security and functional needs, and the utility of Jordan's moderate position for dealing with the United States, as long as Jordan did not openly defect from the Arab order and openly align with

Israel. Making public the relations that had been private forced a direct engagement with the contradictions inherent in discourse and practice.

Jordan's decision to "go public" in its relations with Israel took place only after major regional and domestic changes. Both Arab and domestic identity were at stake in the debates over the peace process. The severing of ties and Oslo allowed Jordan to dissociate its interests from Palestinian issues, while the wider peace process placed Jordan in line with an Arab consensus on a comprehensive peace. As long as the peace process moved forward on other tracks, Jordan's policy coincided with changes in the regional order: Jordan's peace was part of a broader regional transformation. While Syria might complain about Jordanian "individual" behavior, this criticism was tactical rather than existential and could be rebutted in tactical terms. The Gulf War, Madrid, and Oslo produced regional momentum toward a seemingly inevitable conclusion of the peace process. Jordan's peace was a "strategic choice," as King Hussein and regime officials consistently emphasized, made in order to align Jordan with the expected new regional order. Only with the transformation of regional order could Jordan's state interests be brought in line with the demands of Arab and Jordanian state identity.

The interpretation of the Jordanian-Israeli peace treaty, like the severing of ties, depended upon competitive framing in the international, Arabist, and Jordanian public spheres. Comparing the peace treaty deliberation to the deliberation over the severing of ties reveals dramatically different processes. The severing of ties produced a negative response in the international arenas, a strongly positive reception in the Arabist arena, and an ambivalent Jordanian response, which eventually transformed into a positive consensus. The peace treaty, on the other hand, generated an extremely positive consensus in the international public sphere, an ambivalent and muted response in the Arabist arena, and an ambivalent Jordanian response, which became increasingly negative over time. Where the severing of ties was institutionalized at the levels of state and civil society and secured by a strong consensus on identity and interests, the peace treaty was institutionalized only at the state level. Even as Jordan and Israel developed increasingly normal, and even closer than normal, official relations, the opposition prevented the institutionalization of the peace in civil society by resisting all forms of normalization with Israel. Despite frequent claims that the vast majority of Jordanians—and even that all "true" Jordanians—supported the peace, the wide opposition in the public sphere effectively refuted this appeal to consensus.

Above all, the regime justified the peace treaty with Israel on the basis of specifically Jordanian interests, not with reference to Arab or Palestinian interests. The decision to emphasize, while reinterpreting, state interests represents the single most significant dimension of the public discourse over the treaty. Jordan, "like all states" (and implicitly therefore like Syria and its other Arab critics), must look out for its own survival and prosperity first. Second, Jordanian interests were disaggregated from "Arab interests," with the major argument being that anything which benefited Jordan by definition was good for Arab interests. Finally, and most controversially, Jordanian interests were distinguished from Palestinian interests. Invoking the 1974 Rabat Summit, the Arab demands that the PLO be the sole legitimate representative of the Palestinians, and the severing of ties, Jordan argued that its pursuit of narrowly defined state interests followed the Arab consensus in every sense. This meant that the central issue of refugees disappeared from Jordanian preferences, instead being deferred to the multilateral and quadrilateral talks as "regional" issues beyond the competence of Jordan to decide alone.

This chapter considers explanations for the Jordanian-Israeli peace treaty, while chapter 7 discusses the effect of the treaty on both the Jordanian polity and its international behavior. Like the severing of ties, the peace treaty represents a critical case for rationalist and constructivist theories. Rationalist approaches offer powerful explanations for the Jordanian decision to sign the treaty and for the distribution of benefits within the treaty but depend upon constructivist public sphere theory to explain the changes in Jordanian preferences which account for its bargaining behavior. A public sphere explanation accepts the importance of shifts in the balance of power, but places them within the perspective of the collapse of the Arabist public sphere in the Gulf War, and the transformation of Jordanian preferences toward the West Bank after the severing of ties. The strategic bargaining in the peace negotiations depends upon prior changes in Jordanian identity and interests, which need to be explained, not assumed. The peace treaty involved Arab and domestic deliberation over the meaning of such a peace for Jordanian and Arab identity and interests, which structured and gave meaning to the strategic interaction.

Jordan, Israel, and the Peace Process

While I do not discuss earlier Jordanian-Israeli negotiations in any length (see Madfai 1993; Tahboub 1994; and Quandt 1993 for such discussions), earlier moments in the Arab-Israeli peace process provide context for the discussion of the Wadi Araba negotiations. King Hussein met frequently with American and Israeli leaders in pursuit of a peace agreement, and Jordan had numerous opportunities to seek a formal agreement. In 1987, Shimon Peres and King Hussein initialed a draft of a peace settlement which collapsed only when Prime Minister Shamir refused to endorse his Foreign Minister's initiative (Peres 1995). Prior to the severing of ties, Jordan's preference was for a comprehensive peace within an Arab consensus in which it recovered the West Bank. Jordan's interests in peace negotiations fundamentally changed with the severing of ties. After the reconstruction of Jordan's identity and institutions, it no longer sought to reclaim the West Bank; this change in Jordanian preferences made the Wadi Araba negotiations possible. After Oslo, in which the PLO sought its own separate peace, Jordan no longer felt constrained by the demands of Arab consensus, although it still identified its interests in terms of achieving a comprehensive peace at the regional level.

Camp David represents a particularly important case demonstrating Jordan's conflicting interests in the peace process. When Sadat reached agreement with Israel, he hoped for a comprehensive peace, even though he was willing to settle for a separate peace (Telhami 1990). To that end, the Camp David Framework included a Jordanian role in a transitional Palestinian autonomy in the West Bank. Jordan did not reject participation out of hand; Jordan sent the United States a set of questions on the Accords, seeking to get clarifications of their true meaning (Quandt 1993; Madfai 1993). Joining the Camp David process would have provided a leading Jordanian role in the West Bank; formalized Jordan's relations with Israel; solidified political, economic, and security relations with the United States; and provided an important push toward regional transformation around the Egyptian initiative. All of these outcomes accord well with Jordanian preferences; Jordan's rejection therefore seems rather surprising.

Jordan's decision to reject Camp David has been explained in terms of the economic incentives provided by Gulf states, Hussein's distrust of Sadat's intentions, the fear of domestic unrest, and other such variables. Some analysts have focused narrowly on King Hussein's personal pique at Jordan's being included in the Accords without being included in the negotiations. This explanation neglects the broader context of the construction of Jordan's interests. I would argue that Jordan's refusal to participate in Camp David follows directly from the formation of an Arab consensus, articulated in the Baghdad Summit, against the Egyptian gambit. When it became clear that

Jordan's participation would place Jordan outside the Arab consensus, rather than pushing the consensus toward accepting the Camp David framework, Jordan chose to stay with the Arab consensus.

Wadi Araba

The Jordan-Israel peace treaty came as the culmination of Jordanian participation in the Madrid peace process, which brought all the Arab "Confrontation States" into the process of negotiations. This changed the central Arabist issue from an existential debate—should there be negotiations?—into a distributional debate—under what conditions should a treaty be signed? The avowed goal of the Madrid Process around which an Arab consensus had converged was a comprehensive peace, in which the Syrian, Lebanese, Jordanian, and Palestinian tracks would be linked. Despite efforts to secure coordination around common positions, the Arab states largely failed to maintain coordination, instead moving directly to bilateral talks. Jordan attended the Madrid Conference and the Washington negotiations both on its own behalf and as an "umbrella" for the PLO. After months of fruitless negotiations, this process seemed stalled, until the surprise announcement of the PLO-Israel Declaration of Principles in August 1993. This unilateral Palestinian defection opened the door to Jordanian movement. The day after the PLO-Israel signing ceremony in Washington, Jordan and Israel signed a working agenda. In July 1994, the two states issued a joint declaration ending the state of war, and after several months of public negotiations announced a treaty. On October 26, 1994 Jordan and Israel signed the treaty in the Jordanian desert to much international fanfare, and soon thereafter moved toward implementation of its key provisions.

The major articles of the treaty involved land, water, and security guarantees; in addition, wide ranging provisions for normalization, good relations, and joint development led many observers to label it a "remarkable document" and a blueprint for true regional peace (Satloff 1995b). Based on its negotiating positions, Jordan received some benefits. A small portion of Jordanian territory under Israeli occupation returned to Jordanian sovereignty. While few Jordanians had been aware of the existence of this occupied territory, and it had never ranked as an important Jordanian interest, the negotiators could claim the return of land for peace. Border demarcation generated some controversy, as the two sides took recourse to maps from the days of the British Mandate and bargained hard over the precise boundaries. Overall, however, these were minor disputes, and the more difficult questions of the territorial dispensation of the West Bank were left to the Palestinian track. Several areas in which Israel had established agricultural settlements were leased back for 25 years, renewable. This annex to the treaty generated considerable controversy, as Jordanians wondered about its implications for Jordanian sovereignty over the land, and Syria attacked the agreement as a precedent for Israeli demands on the Golan. Jordan regained some water rights, without compensation for past Israeli water appropriations, with the emphasis upon joint ventures to develop new water sources. Politically, each side recognized the other's borders and legitimacy as a sovereign entity and committed itself to avoiding hostile alliances and to not causing threatening population movements. This represented perhaps the most important provision, since it granted Israel unconditional Arab recognition, while establishing a legal barrier against the Israeli "Jordan is Palestine" threat. Each side promised to normalize relations and to prevent any cross-border hostile activity and propaganda. The treaty called for extensive economic cooperation and joint development programs.

One of the most important dimensions of the treaty lay in what was not discussed: the key issue of refugees, which was deferred to the quadrilateral (Jordanian-Palestinian-Egyptian-Israeli) negotiations. The refugees formed the most serious issue between Jordan and Israel in the Arabist public sphere and had always been on the Jordanian short list of interests. The removal of the refugees from the list of Jordanian priorities was necessary for the achievement of the treaty, and signaled a major change in Jordanian positions. I argue that the acceptance of a peace treaty that did not deal with the refugee issue could have been accomplished only as a result of the transformation and redefinition of Jordanian identity after the severing of ties. Jordanian issues could be advanced, distinct from Palestinian issues, in radically new ways. Even though the opposition denounced the exclusion of the refugee issue, the new consensus on the external identity of the state bound their hands: only "Jordanian" issues could be the terms of legitimate debate. Official discourse framed the clauses on refugees as allowing for coordination with the Palestinians and the Egyptians on this sensitive issue, rather than as Jordanian abandonment of the issue.

Overall, the treaty represented Israeli rather than Arab, Jordanian, or Palestinian discourse, assumptions, and interests. For example, the question of refugees was not only deferred to future negotiations, but also defined from the Israeli point of view as a humanitarian rather than as a national issue. Extensive provisions dealt with security and terrorism, but with little regard for potential threats from Israel to Jordan. Article 4.4 prohibits either party from participating in any alliance with security implications for the other, a provision interpreted primarily as governing Jordanian alliances with Arab states rather than Israeli alliances. Article 11 demands the revision of all legislation deemed prejudicial against the other party. But once again, this meant Jordanian revision of its laws against selling land to Israelis, not revision of Israeli laws against selling land to non-Jews. Whether this distinctive feature of the treaty is explained by the extreme imbalance of power or by some version of constructivism, it must be recognized.

Jordanian officials, of course, rejected this characterization of the treaty, justifying the Jordanian moves both in terms of the details of the treaty and in terms of a broader agenda of regional transformation. Where Israelis, and most outside observers, generally observed that the differences between the two sides were minor, Jordan emphasized the depths of difference in order to claim that they had won substantial concessions.[1] Jordanian spokesman emphasized that they had won full sovereignty over all occupied land, and that the leasing of land back to Israel was both a creative solution to a difficult problem and a sovereign decision on Jordan's part. The agreements on water rights were portrayed as fair and as the best possible outcome given the crushing water needs of both sides. As for the abandonment of the refugee issue, Jordan argued that it could not negotiate over the refugees without Palestinian participation, effectively turning Arabist arguments on their head. In addition, Jordanians argued that the treaty's discussion of economic development and cooperation offered the foundations for a new conception of regional order, and represented a victory rather than a loss. Jordanian discourse called for rapid movement to normalize relations and to lay the foundations for the joint pursuit of absolute gains.

For the "shared interests" paradigm, the changes involved in the formalization of peaceful relations between Jordan and Israel had less to do with strategic realities than with public discourse. At Madrid, Israeli Prime Minister Shamir referred casually to "a situation of de facto nonbelligerency with the Kingdom of Jordan" and expressed confidence that "a peace treaty with Jordan is achievable."[2] In terms of the threat of war, the need to deploy military forces, and other such Realist concerns, very little changed because of the peace treaty. Nevertheless, it should be taken seriously that virtually everyone viewed the treaty as a major change. That this change lies primarily in the realm of the public sphere does not diminish its reality. By signing treaties with Israel, Hussein transformed Israel into a legitimate partner for political, economic, and security cooperation. The treaty made public what had been private. Publicity, however, places new demands on relations, forcing both sides to justify them before the public sphere. Jordanians could now publicly question and challenge the value and nature of relations with Israel, and the government had to publicly explain and defend its policies.[3] King Hussein attempted to transform the demands of publicity into an advantage, demonstrating a depth of positive relations in order to set an example for others. By cultivating close relations with Israel, pushing for normalization, speaking eloquently at the funeral of Yitzhak Rabin, and speaking often in favor of an historic reconciliation, Hussein framed the Jordanian-Israeli peace as a step toward the construction of a new cooperative regional order. This official Jordanian frame perplexed many observers who approached the treaty from a Realist framework. How could the justifications for the treaty, as a pragmatic response to external pressures and the hard-headed pursuit of the national interest in the face of an untenable balance of power, be reconciled with the push to rapid normalization and close political, economic, social, and cultural ties?

Regional transformation plays an important role in the reconfiguration of state preferences. Such a transformation depends upon communicative action, the negotiation of a new consensus within the relevant public spheres. The shift in Jordanian policy extended to a comprehensive embrace of an American-Israeli alliance, a repudiation of Iraq, and an escalating campaign against the Islamist opposition. Hussein took a leading role in the "Peace Camp," urging Arabs to embrace normalization with Israel, join in economic projects, and to repudiate Islamist movements. This vision of regional politics shifted the fundamental regional fault line from Arab/Israeli to Peace Camp/Enemies of Peace. Such an identity frame would transform Jordan's relations with Israel from a liability, to be carefully concealed from public scrutiny, into an advantage, making Jordan a preferred intermediary between the Arab world and Israel. The debates about Jordanian interests therefore involved a wider debate over regional identity and regional order. Normalization was not a byproduct of the peace, or an Israeli demand grudgingly accepted, but an essential component to the regime's framing of the political meaning of the treaty.

Rationalist Explanations: The Peace Treaty as Strategic Bargaining

American political scientists, perhaps grown callous to major regional change in the wake of the Israeli-PLO breakthrough and the end of the Cold War, have seen little that is problematic in the case. The balance of power explained the Jordanian decision to seek a peace treaty, and determined rather accurately the distribution of benefits in the peace treaty. Because of the presumed absence of serious Jordanian-Israeli differences and the existing relationship between the leaders, political scientists found little of interest in the treaty beyond its implications for other peace negotiation tracks.

Given the distribution of power and of preferences, a simple two-level game model can account for the distribution of goods in the negotiated outcome (Telhami 1990). Changes in the international and regional balance of power made the Jordanian decision to seek a peace treaty necessary. At the international level, the collapse of the Soviet Union profoundly affected the calculus of all regional states. The Arab confrontation states, especially Syria, lost strategic support, economic support and political backing. In the new unipolar world, international economic and military assistance ran through Washington, and the price for American aid would presumably be peace. At the regional level, the destruction of Iraq represented a major setback in an Arab bid for any balance of power with Israel. Prior to the invasion of Kuwait, Iraq's powerful military seemed to offer the first possibility of parity with Israel since the 1967 disaster. The destruction of Iraqi power after its invasion of Kuwait and the imposition of a semi-permanent sanctions regime destroyed this option, reinforcing Arab and Jordanian dependence upon the United States. The participation of Syria, Egypt, Saudi Arabia and other Arab states in the coalition against Iraq shattered whatever norms of Arab solidarity against outside intervention remained, and placed all of them within the American sphere of influence. The American need to maintain sanctions on Iraq, its temporary position of unchallenged hegemony in the region, and the promises made to these coalition partners in the Gulf war all led the United States to view 1991 as a window of opportunity to achieve a satisfactory resolution to the Arab-Israeli conflict.

These changes in the balance of power and the preferences of major actors left Jordan little choice but to come to terms with Israel in the time and manner it did. The timing of the treaty follows from the assumption of the inevitability of peace. If Jordan waited for Syria to sign, then it would be seen as irrelevant and would gain nothing in negotiations. Jordanian leaders saw a brief window of opportunity between the PLO settlement and an anticipated Syrian settlement in which they might be able to cash in the peace card for major economic and political payoffs.[4] Rabin reportedly reinforced this interpretation in May 1994, urging the King to "get off the fence" before the opportunity passed (Susser 1994; Makovsky 1995: 154–60).

While the sharply skewed balance of power established the potential range of outcomes, the structure of domestic constraints also contributes to the possible win-sets (Putnam 1987). Negotiators on both sides assumed that the near-even division in the Israeli democratic public greatly exceeded the popular constraints on the Jordanian monarch. Rabin's thin majority in the Knesset prevented the Israeli side from offering concessions beyond the absolute minimum dictated by the balance of power. The fact that the final treaty passed the usually sharply divided Knesset by a vote of 105–3 (with 6 abstentions) indicates how successfully the Israeli negotiators produced a document within the bounds of the Israeli domestic consensus. Likud opposition leader Netanyahu endorsed the treaty, and even Ariel Sharon, the most prominent advocate of the "Jordan is Palestine" thesis, only abstained. At the same time, the surge of opposition in Jordan and the defection of key regime figures to the opposition shows how far outside the acceptable winset of the Jordanian public the final document lay. Prior to the beginning of the direct negotiations (November 1993), elections held under a controversial new election law produced a more compliant Parliament, which made ratification of a treaty inevitable. The presumption that the Israeli delegation operated under tighter boundaries than did the Jordanian mattered as much as any empirical comparison of the efficacy and extent of opposition. While the Jordanian negotiators tried to use public opinion for bargaining leverage, it could not credibly portray itself as bound by an effective opposition. Israelis continued to believe, correctly in the event, that Jordan's authoritarian system could force through an unpopular agreement more efficiently than could Israel's contentious democracy.

Finally, Telhami points to the composition of negotiating teams, specifically the centralization of decisionmaking. The Jordanian need for a fast resolution of negotiations further strengthened an already overwhelming Israeli position. On numerous occasions, Hussein stepped in to overrule the tough bargaining strategy of his chief negotiator, Fayz Tarawneh, in order to speed up the process. Hussein's strategic vision of the need for a peace treaty outweighed his concern with the details of the treaty, to Jordan's detriment in the final disbursement of benefits. In short, the combination of the balance of power, the relative domestic constraints, and the structure of the negotiating teams all combined to produce a peace treaty sharply skewed toward Israeli interests.

Rationalist Explanations

Each of the competing rationalist hypotheses elaborated above has been applied to Jordanian decisionmaking in the peace process. In each case,

Jordanian foreign policy is seen as rational pursuit of some stable interest which is identified as consistently dominating Jordanian priorities. The peace treaty reflects continuity in the pursuit of this fundamental, basic interest, rather than change. Three major rationalist explanations have been advanced: strategic interaction based on Jordanian-PLO (rather than Jordanian-Israeli) rivalry; political economy/rent-seeking; and regime survival. As before, I do not argue that any of these explanations is necessarily wrong, but that each is incomplete or misleading in important ways.

The first rationalist alternative assumes that Jordan-PLO rivalry is the single overriding consideration driving Jordanian foreign policy. From this perspective, neither the disengagement nor the various developments in the peace process fundamentally affected Jordan-PLO rivalry, and the revival of the Jordanian claim to the West Bank awaited only a propitious balance of power. Jordan and the PLO adopted new strategies without fundamental change in their preferences. The Oslo agreement reversed PLO fortunes, with huge implications for Jordan (L. Tal 1993). The PLO's position on the Gulf war had left it bereft of Gulf financial support and with tattered international legitimacy. As the Madrid process stalled, the Intifada sputtered and Hamas mounted a serious challenge to the PLO's claim to be the sole legitimate representative of the Palestinian people. With the Oslo Accords, Arafat made a powerful bid against his rivals. American and Israeli recognition of the PLO as a legitimate partner for negotiations seriously eroded one of Jordan's principal international resources, that it was the only acceptable partner for any settlement. On the other hand, the PLO lost power at the level of its own constituency. Its betrayal, in the eyes of many Palestinians, of the most basic political norms upon which the imagined Palestinian entity had been constructed led to massive defections (Said 1995; Dajani 1994). In short, the moment of the PLO's international triumph marked a moment of crisis for its representative legitimacy. The PLO position after Oslo thus created both threats and opportunities for Jordan. The Jordanian treaty with Israel can be read as an attempt to minimize the dangers of Oslo while positioning Jordan to take advantage of its possibilities. By signing a peace treaty with Israel, "Hussein is now clawing back ground he lost to the PLO" (Susser 1994).

While this strategic interaction argument accurately captures the interdependence of the Palestinian and Jordanian tracks, it fails to take into account the fundamental changes in Jordanian identity and interests after the severing of ties. Quite simply, the evidence does not support this widely repeated argument. Jordan's refusal to take advantage of opportunities to challenge PLO or PNA representation and its support for the PNA in its interaction with Israel belie any assumption that Jordanian behavior is driven by its strategic conflict with the Palestinian leadership. As documented in chapters 3 and 4, Jordan in the mid-1990s continued to have conflictual relations with the PLO, and later the PNA, but it no longer sought a return to the West Bank. Since 1994, Jordan has consistently and emphatically declared its support for the creation of a Palestinian state in the West Bank and Gaza and pushed for progress on the Palestinian-Israeli track. The Jordanian conception of its state interests is now built upon the conviction that Jordanian security and interests depend upon a successful peace process and regional transformation. In this vision of Jordanian identity, a Palestinian state serves, rather than threatens, Jordanian security and vital interests.

A second rationalist reading of the Jordanian decision, most cogently advanced by Brand (1994), suggests that Jordan's primary concern in foreign policy is budget security and rent-seeking. Because of the Gulf War, Jordan lost Gulf financial support, American aid, the Iraqi market, and the huge volume of remittances from expatriates in Kuwait. Facing serious economic problems, with no evident alternative sources of support, Jordan turned to the United States. The price of this support was obvious: a peace treaty with Israel. James Baker, for example, asserts that "simply stated, the King was broke and needed America's help to persuade his longtime benefactors in Riyadh to help him out" (Baker 1995: 450). The American failure to deliver on many of these promises, both in direct American financial aid and in repairing Jordanian relations with the Gulf states, undermined support for the treaty among Establishment figures. As the economy continued to deteriorate, support for the treaty dwindled. Increasing evidence suggested that Jordanian decisionmakers had few expectations of immediate economic benefit from the peace treaty. Thouqan Hindawi, a major figure in the government that shepherded the peace process to its conclusion, resigned in a very public outburst in December 1994. He explained that contrary to the government promises of a coming economic boom because of the treaty, Jordan in fact had received no concrete commitments on debt reduction, new investment, or loans.[5] A World Bank report (1994) made available prior to the peace treaty's conclusion found that peace would have few short-term economic benefits, and that the long-term prognosis included serious threats. This suggests that the economic rewards were more of a public sphere justificatory strategy than a major cause. Even leading advocates of the treaty such as the economist Fahd al-Fanik criticized the government for overselling the economic dimension of the treaty.

This is not to say that the economic dimension was unimportant. As in Camp David, the provision of financial incentives such as debt relief and investment helped to make the decision easier, even if it did not cause the decision. More significant, however, was the powerful idea of a transformed regional order in which Jordan's close ties to Israel, relatively developed banking and technology, and high levels of education might allow the Jordanian economy to find a profitable niche. The peace had more to do with the principle of a substantive change in norms and institutions than with specific budgetary considerations. The idea of a New Middle East based on regional economic integration was part of the broader issue at stake. As Prince Hassan often explained, a Middle East Market could allow Jordan to break its dependence upon foreign aid and turn its particular combination of human capital, close ties to Israel, and poor natural endowments to its long-term economic advantage. A political economy explanation for the Jordanian-Israeli treaty goes deeper than "peace for cash," and can be usefully combined with the constructivist, public sphere approach developed here.

A third common rationalist explanation is regime survival: Hussein signed the peace treaty in order to best guarantee personal and dynastic survival. On this argument, economic hardships and Oslo threatened the very survival of the Hashemite regime and perhaps of Jordan itself (L. Tal 1993). The peace treaty, above all, offered an American and Israeli guarantee of the Hashemite regime. Since the treaty, Israeli figures have regularly spoken of the Hashemite regime as a vital Israeli interest, and an Israeli deterrent guarantee is widely recognized in the region. On the other hand, such an Israeli preference for Hashemite rule in Jordan over either a Palestinian or a Jordanian nationalist government was widely held before the treaty. The peace treaty placed extreme stress on the Jordanian political order, and Jordanian behavior (see below) seems to transcend any conception of a peace treaty based on compulsion or threat. The polarization of society, the loss of public confidence, the need to restrict democratic participation, and being outside the Arab consensus all put the regime in danger. The treaty inflamed Syrian anger, increasing the risks of Syrian, Palestinian, or Islamist subversion. The impetus given by the treaty to sever ties with Iraq further destabilized Jordanian society and increased the risks of Iraqi subversion. While it could be argued that Hussein concluded he had no choice, the peace treaty still represented a risky decision. In other words, the treaty created both new guarantees and more dangers. A long-term American and Israeli guarantee for the Hashemite regime may have played some role in the decision to pursue peace, but there are few short-term threats to regime survival that could explain such a dramatic departure.

Jordanian Identity and the Peace Bargaining

These rationalist perspectives depend upon the prior specification of preferences. They ignore the central problem of how the situation came to be defined such that Jordan negotiated alone for narrowly defined interests and why the situation was not so defined in the past. The benefits Jordan won in the treaty—border revisions, water sharing—had not been high-priority Jordanian interests prior to 1994. Assuming the decision to begin negotiations toward a serious settlement on these bases, bargaining theory correctly explains the distribution of benefits in the outcome. The bargaining seems to reflect significant change in Jordanian preferences over outcomes, however. The question should be: "Why did Jordan negotiate for these narrow state interests and ignore its own long-asserted interests in refugees and a comprehensive Arab-Israeli peace?" Explaining the redefinition of interests is essential. I argue that the severing of ties brought on the reconception of Jordanian identity on which the narrow specification of Jordan's interests was based, while the Gulf War, Oslo, and the Jordanian liberalization dramatically changed the public sphere structure in which these interests were articulated, justified, interpreted, and pursued.

The removal of the issues of refugees from the top of Jordanian preferences represents the single most important point of departure. At the beginning of the talks, during the explanations for Jordan's decision to go to Madrid and in the Washington talks, the refugee issue occupied a very high place in Jordanian concerns. The 1993 Working Agenda placed the refugee issue near the top of the issues to be negotiated. After Oslo, it dropped down the list, and the July 1994 Washington Declaration hardly mentions it. The peace treaty itself refers only to the humanitarian problem of refugees, and leaves the solution to the multilateral and quadrilateral negotiations.

This particular articulation of Jordanian preferences depended upon the disaggregation of Jordanian and Palestinian identities and interests. The relationship between the Jordanian and Palestinian delegations emerged as a contentious issue, as many Jordanian nationalists believed that the Joint Delegation hindered the pursuit of particular Jordanian interests.[6] Because Israel refused to negotiate directly with the PLO, Jordan offered the only formula by which the Palestinians could participate. The changes wrought by the severing of ties were taken seriously, however, and Jordan refused to negotiate for the Palestinians or take their place. The formula of a joint delegation emerged, in which the Palestinians formed a distinct and autonomous delegation under a Jordanian umbrella. As Israel had no intention of making progress at these talks, while the PLO preferred the Oslo back channel by mid-1993, the progress of the Washington negotiations was impeded. Jordanian negotiators refused to move ahead while the Palestinian track was blocked, despite considerable American and Israeli pressure and incentives.

The revelation of the secret talks at Oslo in August 1993 exploded in Jordan. Despite the sometimes tense relations in the Joint Delegation, Jordan had maintained cooperation in the face of powerful incentives to defect (Ashawi 1995; M. Abass 1994). The Joint Delegation had facilitated an effective justification frame in Jordan of coordination [tansiq] with the PLO. This coordination, like the support of Iraq in the war, put the regime on the side of major forces in the political public which had traditionally been hostile or suspicious. By working closely with the PLO, Jordan showed itself to be supporting the Palestinian cause in practice and foregoing its own ambitions in the West Bank. The revelation of the Oslo negotiations, not only outside the framework of the joint delegation but also unknown to most Jordanian decisionmakers, could be interpreted only as a premeditated deception. King Hussein has consistently maintained that he was not informed of the Oslo talks and was completely surprised by their announcement; his anger and concern at their implications for Jordan are well documented. Abd al-Salam al-Majali, the head of the Jordanian delegation, claims that he heard about Oslo on the radio.[7] In his memoirs, Mahmoud Abass (Abu Mazen) (1994) provides an elaborate story of his failed effort to tell Hussein about Oslo. The fact that Jordan had only been waiting on the Palestinians was demonstrated by the rapid Jordanian-Israeli progress after Oslo.

Like the Gulf war, Oslo had a dramatic impact on the foundations of the Arabist public sphere. Oslo fragmented what remained of a Palestinian consensus and destroyed the institutions of the Palestinian public sphere. After Oslo, Arafat could no longer convene the Palestinian National Council, which had been the ultimate site of Palestinian participation. Hamas emerged as the leading opposition force to the emergent PNA, arousing Arafat's fears of Jordanian-Hamas collaboration against him. The organizational and doctrinal ties between Hamas and the Jordanian Muslim Brotherhood fed Arafat's suspicions, particularly given the traditionally close relations between King Hussein and the Muslim Brotherhood. Hamas leaders based in Amman had offices in the Muslim Brotherhood buildings, and were generally allowed to operate without official harassment. As Jordanian-PNA and Jordanian-Israeli relations improved, the government grew less tolerant of Hamas activity, though it still refrained from a full crackdown that would have provoked a full, direct confrontation with the Muslim Brotherhood. The fragmentation of the Palestinian consensus resonated among Jordanians of Palestinian origin, generating tremendous uncertainty about their future in Jordan and their status in the Palestinian national identity. Could the Oslo process ever lead to a Palestinian state? Would the refugees ever be allowed to return, even if such a state emerged?

From the official Jordanian perspective, the Palestinian defection from coordination removed any justification for restraint. With Arafat moving unilaterally in pursuit of Palestinian interests, and Syria negotiating for the Golan Heights, Jordan could convincingly articulate specifically Jordanian interests irreducible to Palestinian concerns. If the Palestinians acted without Jordan, why should Jordan not now look to its own interests?

Identity represented a crucial dimension in the treaty outcome. Among all the justifications for the treaty, the trump card clearly was seen as the guarantee the existence of Jordan as an entity. The treaty "defined Israel's eastern border for the first time in history," ending the discursive struggle in the international public sphere: Jordan is not Palestine. In other words, the treaty offered a formal Israeli endorsement of the identity consensus secured between Jordanians and Palestinians after the severing of ties. *Al-Rai's* lead editorial prior to the signing ceremony, entitled, "Jordan is not Palestine!," claimed that the treaty "silences the Israeli idea . . . that Jordan is the eastern extension of the Hebrew state, which was a source of Israeli aggression and threat. . . . this treaty means that Jordan is Jordan and Palestine is Palestine."[8] Fahd al-Fanik emblematically asserted that "the main reason for the peace treaty was, in fact, to end the threat of the Alternative Homeland."[9] Information Minister Jawad al-Anani explained that "Jordan's basic concern is to achieve Jordanian rights and to confirm its self and its independent entity."[10] At the signing of the Washington Declaration in July 1994, Shimon Peres declared adamantly that "I affirm here that Jordan is Jordan and Jordan is not Palestine."[11] As various dimensions of the treaty came under fire, this occupied an ever more central position in the regime's justifications: "From every official platform . . . we hear the cry that the Alternative Homeland has been ended with a stroke of the pen . . . and this is the most important achievement of the agreement."[12] The consistent, determined focus on the confirmation of Jordan's state identity in the framing of the treaty indicates the centrality of identity concerns.

Since Jordanians and Palestinians were already convinced that Jordan was not Palestine, the change involved in this affirmation of Jordan's state identity was on the part of Israel. To what extent did this signal a change in Israeli preferences? The Jordan Option, whether in the form of a Jordanian-Israeli condominium over the West Bank, a confederation under Jordanian domination, or an imposed Alternative Homeland in the East Bank, had been a part of almost every Israeli final status proposal for decades; it essentially disappeared from official discourse after Oslo and Wadi Araba. Even before the peace process, the Gulf War seems to have made many Likud thinkers re-evaluate their support for the Jordan is Palestine idea: as unfriendly as King Hussein had been during the war, all agreed that a Palestinian or nationalist regime in Jordan might well have allowed the entry of Iraqi troops and thereby brought Israel into the war (Schiff 1991). Rabin and Peres both preferred dealing with Jordan, but recognized that a workable peace agreement could now be made only with the PLO; both envisioned a final status agreement involving a confederation between the Palestinian areas and Jordan. In general, however, the severing of ties, the consistent Jordanian refusal to negotiate for the Palestinians, and the creation of the PNA as a reality on the ground, removed the Jordan option from Israeli strategy. Many Israelis were reluctant to acknowledge that the treaty had changed reality. The fact that Ariel Sharon, the most prominent advocate of the idea, abstained from voting rather than rejecting the treaty, indicates that Israelis did not necessarily regard the treaty as marking the definitive end of the "Jordan is Palestine" idea. However, after the ratification and institutionalization of the treaty, the idea faded from mainstream Israeli discourse (even for Klieman 1998). The return of the Likud in 1996 brought no significant return to the "Jordan is Palestine" argument. Netanyahu had long expressed support for the idea (Netanyahu 1993), and Sharon held a prominent place in Netanyahu's narrow, right wing coalition. Despite all of these reasons to expect a resurgence of the argument, particularly as the Oslo process collapsed, it did not return. The treaty with Jordan offered important benefits to Israel and was widely popular. The treaty changed Israeli strategies, if not preferences, making the maintenance of the Jordanian peace treaty preferable to the pursuit of the Alternative Homeland, and creating an increasingly institutionalized Israeli interest in maintaining the treaty. The change in Israeli preferences, generally recognizing that Jordan would neither be Palestine nor rule Palestine, brought all three major actors in the peace negotiations (Jordan, the PLO, and Israel) into accord on this basic and crucial point.

The various responses to "Jordan is Palestine" are central to the reconceptualization of Jordanian identity. The Israeli threat served as the justification for the need to emphasize and develop the Jordanian identity, a valorization of state identity frowned upon from the perspective of Arabist norms. From this perspective, the consolidation of the Jordanian identity helped the Palestinian cause by confirming the distinctive Palestinian identity and thereby forcing Israel to come to terms with the Palestinians rather than continue to hold out hope for a Jordanian intermediary. Prior to Oslo, this ability to justify the public assertion of Jordanian identity in terms of Palestinian—not Jordanian—interests was extremely important. After Oslo, the justification of Jordanian identity in terms of Jordanian interests assumed an increasingly prominent place. For example, compare characteristic justifications put forward by centrist commentators. In early 1992, a typical formulation reads: "to confirm the Jordanian national identity is also to confirm the Palestinian national identity . . . to confront together the Zionist expansionist project which aims to erase both identities."[13] After Oslo, Jordanian identity became an acceptable end unto itself, not merely a means toward advancing the Palestinian cause: "Jordan has nothing to apologize for as a nation or as a nationalism."[14]

Official discourse defended the reliance on narrowly defined interests partly in terms of the identity claim discussed above, and partly in light of Arab-level developments. The distinction from Arab interests was defended by the claim that all the Arabs had chosen the peace process at Madrid. The Arab consensus that the PLO must negotiate for Palestinian interests was an integral part of the official frame. Official discourse regularly invoked the Rabat consensus and the severing of ties, justifying the pursuit of narrowly defined Jordanian interests in terms of an Arabist frame.[15]

The change in conceptions of Jordan's state identity and its implications for its preferences in the peace negotiations represents a major dimension which is not captured by rationalist bargaining theory. The removal of the refugee issue from the top of Jordanian preferences depended upon the reconstruction of Jordanian identity. First, Jordan's identity changed, with the severing of ties. Second, Jordan's preferences changed, with the refugee issue dropping out, making the final status outcome possible. Third, this change in preferences over outcomes in the West Bank defined Jordanian strategies in the bargaining, making this Jordan a different actor, in many respects, from the Jordan that discussed possible settlements with Israel in the 1970s and 1980s. Fourth, Israel's negotiations with the PLO, combined with the growing recognition that Jordan's preferences and identity had changed, led it to abandon the Jordan option as a viable final settlement. The recognition that "Jordan is Jordan" represented the achievement of a powerful and critically important acceptance in the international public sphere of this "reality." This acceptance of Jordan's identity allowed its interests to be recognized as legitimate and to be publicly avowed. Finally, the centering of a Jordanian identity within a Jordanian public sphere made the articulation and justification of specifically Jordanian interests more normatively defensible.

Arabist Debates Over the Peace Treaty

While bargaining alone for narrow state interests fits the rationalist model of state behavior, it should hardly be considered collectively rational. The best solution for all Arab actors in a final settlement with Israel could be achieved only by bargaining as a single, powerful actor rather than as individual, weak states. Arab unity represented a textbook collective action problem. Each individual state could arrive at substantial benefits through an individual settlement, defecting from the collective position. Those states that stood fast while others defected would receive substantially less in an eventual settlement, but if all held together they would receive the best payoff in the end. Thus the classic stag hunt dilemma: how to prevent the individual from grabbing for narrow self-interests at the expense of larger prospective collective benefit? Prior to the Madrid conference, for example, representatives of all the participating Arab states met in Damascus to "guarantee a unified Arab stand throughout all the phases of the conference . . . [and to give mutual] assurance that not a single Arab state would establish relations with Israel . . . before Israel gave the Palestinians and the Arabs what they demand."[16] Recognizing the importance of maintaining a united front, Arab states generally preferred collective bargaining in multilateral fora; Israel, hoping to exploit the differing interests and suspicions of the Arab states, preferred bilateral negotiating tracks. In fact, the Arabs largely failed to maintain coordination, with Israeli preferences for bilateral negotiations prevailing.

After the Gulf war, the PLO defection and the failure of the Arab actors to maintain coordination against the temptation of the individual solution, Jordan had little choice but to move quickly for whatever it could still get.

The problem in 1994, from the point of view of many Arabists, was "not individual treachery but a general Arab malaise."[17] Throughout the 1980s, most Arab states had cultivated projects of national identity formation while attempting to insulate domestic politics from the Arabist arena (Baram 1990; Brynen 1991). This long-term shift in the approach to the Arabist public sphere and national identity carries important implications for the Arab collective action problem. For the rationalist, changes occurred in the balance of power, not in the identity of the actors. The identity and interests of the state actor of the 1950s or the 1970s; only the externally imposed constraints and the balance of power had shifted. The autonomous, self-interested actor faced different expectations about the probability and expected payoffs of defection, and in the 1990s Arab states rationally decided to defect. For the constructivist, this increased individualist behavior represents a change in conceptions of self, replacing the self bound up in collective Arab norms, dialogue, and interests with a self based upon state borders and narrowly internal norms, dialogue, and interests (Barnett 1998).

The contestation of the peace treaty must be placed within the context of these changes in public sphere structure. First, the participation of many Arab states in the coalition against Iraq shattered the discourse of Arab unity prior to the initiation of peace negotiations. Jordan's position outside the coalition set Jordan outside the official Arab consensus as represented by Egypt, Syria, the Gulf, and the Arab League. Isolated from the Arab public sphere, Jordan turned inward. Second, the participation of Syria in the Madrid talks drew the teeth of any Arabist rejection of the peace negotiations. Third, inside of Jordan this period represented the high point of democratic discourse and public sphere openness. King Hussein's alignment with Iraq had placed his regime on the same side as the political public for one of the first times in Jordanian history, giving the regime considerable political capital in this early stage of the peace negotiations. Therefore, while the public sphere was relatively open, the public was not inclined to vigorously oppose the regime's foreign policy. Criticism focused upon issues of domestic policy: public freedoms, the World Bank, the sales tax, privatization, corruption, administrative reform. One wave of opposition to the peace process did bring down the "peace government" of Taher al-Masri. That Jordanian chauvinist forces played more of a role in the defeat of Masri, the first Prime Minister of Palestinian origin in the democratic era, than did the more visible anti-peace opposition is suggested by the easy confirmation of Masri's successor with a virtually identical policy statement.[18]

After the Gulf war, as the United States mounted a concerted campaign to arrive at a settlement of the Arab-Israeli conflict, Jordanian participation in the proposed peace conference was never really in doubt. Jordan had long called for the convocation of such a conference oriented toward the guidelines of the UN resolutions 242 and 338, and could hardly refuse now. Jordan badly needed the international validation implicit in an invitation to Madrid. The regime saw little reason to refuse such an invitation, and in fact treated the invitation as something of a triumph. At any rate, "Jordan is not able to swim against the tide for even one moment. . . . it is blockaded by land, air and sea, without allies or friends."[19] Under such conditions, Jordan could lose little by participating and could hope for substantial benefits.

The acceleration toward a peace treaty therefore took place within a public sphere structure dramatically changed by the Gulf war and Oslo. The Gulf War weakened the sanctioning power of Arabist norms, while the PLO defection at Oslo prevented the Palestinian leadership from criticizing the Jordanian action. Even Realists admit the centrality of the removal of Arabist and Palestinian sanctions for enabling the Jordanian move. The argument developed here goes beyond constraint, however, arguing that Jordanian preferences changed based upon the transformation of state identity within these reconfigured public spheres. A comprehensive peace would resolve Jordan's most pressing strategic problems, and allow it to finally reconcile its private needs and its public beliefs. The severing of ties meant that the return of the West Bank was not necessary within this comprehensive peace.

Jordan justified the peace treaty in the Arabist arena largely by arguing against its relevance. In a major speech to the Jordanian Parliament about the peace process, Hussein emphatically rejected Arabist criticism: "If anyone speaks of us moving alone . . . let me remind them that we have acted alone only once . . . and that was our position in the Gulf crisis . . . and we suffered the consequences. . . . Nobody may outbid us at the Arab level or at any level."[20] This frame rejecting Arab outbidding contained a number of important elements. First, all the Arab states went to Madrid in order to negotiate a peace, and it was inadmissible to now recant on that consensus. Jordan was not moving alone, since the decision to begin peace talks was a collective Arab decision. Second, Jordan argued that it had been the Arab state most devoted to coordination, but that others had failed to maintain this coordination. Hussein met several times with Syrian President Hafiz al-Asad, and kept the other Arab parties informed at every step of the negotiations. The other Arab states did not match this commitment, however, and insisted on acting alone and not coordinating moves to Jordan; how could

Jordan be expected to be the only party bound by these demands? Third, the PLO decision to seek a separate deal at Oslo meant that Jordan was certainly now free to pursue its own rights and interests. No generalizable argument could be made as to why Jordan had to be the last to sign an agreement. Fourth, in general, every Arab state had the right to pursue its interests in the negotiations, and "Syria can no more deny Jordan this right than Jordan would deny Syria its rights." Jordan retained its right to make sovereign decisions, within the context of the claimed Arab consensus. Finally, Jordan's Gulf War position demonstrated the sincerity of its Arabism, and no other Arab state, or member of the Jordanian opposition, could now criticize Jordan on these grounds.

The diminished relevance of the Arabist public sphere does not mean that the Jordanian treaty went unremarked. Shortly after the text of the treaty became public, Syria attacked the provision leasing Jordanian land with Israeli settlements back to Israel as a precedent for the Golan negotiations. King Hussein responded brusquely: "With all due respect, this is none of his business. It is Jordan's business."[21] Hussein made little effort to dispute the Syrian interpretation or to offer justifications appropriate to the Arabist public sphere. Instead, he denied the sphere's relevance, simply asserting Jordanian state interests. Syria and Jordan clashed over the treaty, with Jordan accused of abandoning Arab coordination, and Hussein denying the applicability of the concept. Syria and Jordan also clashed over the pace of normalization, and over Syrian fears that Jordan and Israel would cooperate to increase the pressure on Syria to sign its own deal. Despite Hussein's occasional accusations of Syrian support for Jordanian opposition groups, Syrian criticism seems to have been largely confined to public argumentation and not to have extended to subversion. Only in June 1996, at the Cairo Summit to discuss Netanyahu's election, did Hussein and Asad meet and agree to clear the air and end hostile media campaigns.

Palestinian opposition factions denounced the treaty vigorously, but their complaints seemed oddly irrelevant. A national strike in the West Bank and Gaza condemned the Jordanian peace, but the PNA quickly moved to contain the fallout. The Damascus-based opposition groups, including the PFLP and DFLP, as well as Hamas, denounced the Jordanian moves as repeating longstanding Jordanian treachery, putting regime interests ahead of Palestinian interests. Their opposition to Arafat's peace moves, and their dependence on Syria, helped to bind together Jordan and the PNA by linking them together in the Peace Camp: the common opposition in a sense helped to produce shared identity and interests between Jordan and the

PNA. Some PLO figures worried about Hussein's intentions with regard to the PNA, and Arafat reportedly held deep suspicions about Jordanian-Israeli coordination against Palestinian interests. Arafat did not attend the signing ceremony. The articles dealing with Jerusalem particularly enraged Palestinians, who saw Jordanian-Israeli collusion to prevent a Palestinian presence in the city. However, as Jordan did not use its treaty to undermine Arafat, some of these suspicions faded. A steady stream of high-level consultations and agreements, combined with a consensus on a common interest in the formation of a Palestinian state with good Jordanian relations, secured cooperation between the two actors. Wadi Araba ratified the conception of an East Bank Jordan, even more deeply entrenching the severing of ties. Jordan consistently affirmed that peace could only be complete and secure after the achievement of a Palestinian state, rejecting Israeli efforts to play Jordan off against the PNA.

Overall, Jordan won the deliberation in the Arabist arena. Even if it did not necessarily persuade many Arabs that the treaty was a good thing, or that rapid normalization served Arab identity or interests, it did persuade Arab states that it had not violated any norms or collective Arab demands. Unlike Egypt after Camp David, Jordan was not expelled from Arab institutions or sanctioned by the Arab order. The combined weight of the Madrid process, Oslo, the absence of compelling alternatives to the United States, and Syrian hopes for its own deal helped Jordan to achieve grudging acceptance of its new status. Other Arab states resisted Jordanian appeals for rapid normalization, and were less enthused about regional transformation, but they attended the MENA economic conferences, began relations with Israel, and refrained from overtly punishing Jordan. A certain degree of the reticence is explained by the general desire of Arab leaders to make their own deals with Israel, and some came from the lack of surprise at the treaty. More basic, however, is the general recognition that the Arab order now rested upon the pursuit of state interest, and that regional order was now defined by the American agenda. Few Arabs expressed surprise at the treaty, accepting it even if they did not enthusiastically embrace it; Egyptian hesitation derived more from concern over Jordan's contesting its role as interlocutor for Israel than from a principled rejection of the treaty.

Jordanian Debates Over the Peace Treaty

The collapse of the Arabist public sphere corresponded with the rise of the Jordanian domestic public sphere. Jordanian public opinion did pay attention to Arab positions toward Jordanian peace moves, and largely accepted Jordanian participation in the negotiations to the extent that positions were coordinated with the PLO and the other Arab participants, principally Syria. At the Jordanian level, a very active, open print public sphere had developed in which political criticism was a norm. The freedom to criticize the PLO over Oslo created expectations about the ability to criticize Jordanian peace moves. The independent weekly press had come into its own, and when Jordanian peace moves picked up in the summer of 1994 these platforms were established, popular, and open to the opposition. Unwilling, and to an important extent unable, to simply abolish the measures of freedom that had become such an important element of regime legitimation, the government was infuriated by the opposition in these independent newspapers and set out to curb it by all legal means. While the independent press acted as a platform for critical voices, and even the semi-official dailies provided some measure of diversity, the government-controlled radio and TV strictly adhered to a pro-government position—one that was intolerant of all dissent and energetically marketed peace.

The openness of the Jordanian public sphere became a public issue second only to the peace treaty itself. King Hussein and his government regularly asserted the existence of a Jordanian national consensus for peace. The public sphere had not produced such a consensus, however, and the perceived need to maintain the appearance of one drove the repression of the public sphere. The assertion of the right to political opposition often took priority over the actual exercise of such opposition, as the political public found itself compelled to defend its legitimacy as a public. A major achievement of the democratic era had been to bind the public to a Jordanian identity and norms through participation in an open Jordanian public sphere. Now the regime again strove to bind the public to a Jordanian identity while closing down the public sphere. "Loyalty" replaced "participation" as the mechanism of proving belonging [intima] to the Jordanian identity. As opposition to the Jordanian peace moves grew, the regime attempted to portray the opposition as essentially non-Jordanian. A concern for Arab interests rather than the regime's narrow definition of Jordanian interests became evidence of a non-Jordanian orientation and hence illegitimacy. In sharp contrast to the principle of public sphere participation, the regime sought to reestablish a norm of the inviolability of royal decisions: "because the King enjoys the confidence of his people, he does not have to defend his every move to them. . . . it is the right of the leader to act without needing to justify or interpret."[22] What could be farther from the norm of democratic, public sphere accountability so prominent in the early 1990s?

The regime did make considerable efforts to persuade the Jordanian political elite that Jordan's interests required the moves toward peace. The National Conference, which ratified the decision to attend the Madrid Conference, was a carefully stage-managed spectacle with none of the real dialogue that had characterized the National Charter conference on which it was modeled.[23] Hussein, Hassan, and various senior officials met with representatives of political society in various roundtables, salons, conferences, and public events in order to present their interpretations. It was only as political society converged around opposition to the peace treaty that the regime clamped down on the public sphere. While accepting the need for *hiwar*, Hussein and Hassan stressed the need for dialogue to be "responsible" and "constructive," and to avoid the competitive "outbidding" characteristic of Arab public debates.[24] The opposition divided between those who were willing to consider a settlement with Israel that met well-specified criteria and those who rejected any settlement on principle. While the regime preferred to portray all opposition as of the latter variety, the evidence does not support this contention.

During the peace negotiations, there was considerable public debate over its meaning for Jordanian identity and interests. Hussein often asserted that the opposition represented only a small minority of Jordanians, and that the vast majority supported his moves to peace. Hussein floated the idea of a national referendum over any peace treaty in July 1994, but the idea quietly faded away as the negotiations drew to a close and the outcome of such a referendum seemed less certain than a vote in the Parliament, where an absolute pro-government majority existed. Later, the opposition picked up the call for a referendum, but their calls were ignored. Hussein and Prime Minister Majali each explained that because "the vast majority of Jordanians support the peace . . . there is no need for a referendum."[25] A Center for Strategic Studies opinion poll which showed that 80 percent of Jordanians supported the Washington Declaration was often cited as evidence for this popular support; less often mentioned by government officials was the heavily conditional nature of the support in that opinion poll, which linked support to rapid economic improvement and changes in Israeli behavior.[26]

The opposition framed its objections in terms of both interests and identity. At the level of interests, the opposition made specific arguments about the text of the treaty and its implications for Jordanian security, water rights, economic development, and sovereignty. At the level of identity, the opposition argued that the treaty with Israel would cause Jordan to lose its Arab and Islamic identity. Cut off from its Arab roots, Jordan would stand alone and weak against Israeli domination. While the government emphasized the

Jordanian state interests achieved in the treaty, the opposition denied the priority of these interests in relation to the wider Arab interests and identity. Above all, the opposition insisted that because Israeli identity, interests, and behavior had not changed, it was unjustifiable to believe that the enemy had now become a friend. All Israeli actions were interpreted from a suspicious, hostile frame; until proven otherwise, Israel was assumed to remain an enemy.

The regime frame responded that Jordanian negotiators had secured all of Jordan's rights and interests. First, it argued that the treaty had returned "every centimeter" of Jordanian occupied territories and some of its rights to water, while decisively ending the threat of Israeli expansion eastward. Second, the government emphasized the economic benefits of peace in order to deflect attention from the political concessions in the treaty, and relied heavily on the premise that economic interest would trump political ideology or concerns over identity. Finally, King Hussein advanced a major innovation in identity discourse, with broad implications for domestic and regional political order. In this new frame, forces on both the Arab and the Israeli side shared an interest in peace but were challenged by extremists. With the treaty, Jordan stood not with Israel against Arabs but with the Peace Camp against Extremists. All Arab states had made a strategic decision for peace, making any criticism of Jordan's treaty hypocritical. The regime argued that Israel had changed, having made a strategic decision for peace, and that until proven otherwise it should be given the benefit of the doubt and allowed to prove its commitment to peace and positive relations with Jordan.

The Parliamentary debates over ratifying the peace treaty were highly charged, unrestrained, and tightly focused.[27] While there was never any doubt that the government's regular majority would approve the treaty, the opposition took advantage of the platform to advance powerful critiques of the treaty's text, its significance, and the justifications presented by the regime. Supportive deputies generally repeated official interpretations without extensive commentary; the Parliamentary debate was dominated by the opposition. Islamist deputies sometimes referred to religious and principled reasons to reject any form of treaty with Israel, but they and other opposition deputies offered detailed, rational critiques. Deputies contested the provisions relating to security cooperation, those forbidding hostile alliances, the definition of terrorism, and the constitutionality of the treaty. They showed particular unease over the absence of any provision for the refugees and worried that this might in fact help bring about the Alternative Homeland, despite the regime's protestations that the treaty ended this threat. They rejected the argument that the occupied land had returned to Jordanian sovereignty, asking how an arrangement in which the land continued to be farmed by Israelis, patrolled by Israeli policemen, and was not subject to Jordanian taxes or laws could be considered sovereignty. They warned against rapid normalization, especially before Israel had delivered on promised Jordanian rights. They warned that the treaty opened Jordan to Jewish settlements and exposed it to Palestine's fate; they warned that the Jordanian economy would be overwhelmed by the Israeli economy; they warned that Jordan would become a bridge for Israeli penetration into the Gulf. Deputies blasted the government for repressing debate, concealing the text of the treaty even from Parliament, so that they had to rely on the Israeli media to discover the terms of the treaty, and for surrounding the Parliament building with tanks and soldiers and excluding the public from the deliberations. In the end, the Prime Minister responded to the challenges by repeating official interpretations, and the treaty was ratified by a comfortable majority. King Hussein then called on the nation to move beyond debates over the treaty, and for the minority to accept the will of the majority.

Six months after the Wadi Araba signing ceremony, a leading Resistance voice wrote: "We understood, if not agreed with, your justifications for the agreement with the enemy . . . but what we see now leads us to believe that these justifications were not the real impetus. . . . they were nothing but sand thrown in our eyes."[28] The Resistance demonstrated a firm grasp of the international balance of power and the pressures upon Jordan: "we have said all along that it is Jordan and not Israel that will make concessions . . . because the balance of power will impose the solution."[29] Had the regime admitted it had been forced to sign the treaty to make the best of a bad situation, this would have been true, would have shown respect for the minds of the citizenry, and would have provided a shared basis for further debate about the appropriate response to this imposed situation. Instead, the official media celebrated the treaty as a victory for Jordan, in the face of both the obvious balance of power realities and the outcome that people could see in the treaty's text. The stark contrast between the official claims and reality fed the opposition's frame: "If Jordan was forced into a settlement as the least bad choice . . . how is that changed into a victory? How can one who enters negotiations weak and alone and poor leave them rich and strong and triumphant?"[30]

The course of events after the signing of the treaty cast doubt upon the claim that the Jordanian decision had been motivated by rationalist calculations of power, threat, or budget security. Behavior—the rapid move to an exceptionally close relationship between the Jordanian and Israeli leaderships—contradicted the interpretive frame of a Jordan compelled to sign by the preponderance of power: "The most important matter which contradicts the idea of pressure [as the reason for the treaty] is the great enthusiasm of the executive authority for normalization" (Mayeteh 1994b: 22). To many observers it appeared that "this is not gradual normalization between enemies who want to become friends, but closer to the embrace of brothers meeting after long separation . . . or long lost lovers finally finding the way to marriage."[31] The very warmth of the official Jordanian-Israeli relationship which led Israelis to consider the treaty successful led Jordanians to doubt the official justifications for the treaty. As Hussein argued for a transformation of regional and national identity and institutions, the dominant public image became one of Israel and the Jordanian regime allied against the Jordanian people.

In this context of shared recognition of power realities and divergent interpretations of political norms, rationalist explanations took on a distinctive role. The pro-treaty forces, unable to appeal to norms, instead fought to discredit once and for all any appeal to norms and replace them with an emphasis on national interests. As Fahd al-Fanik acidly asserted, "the reference point for the opposition is ideological or principled with sentimental slogans. . . . while the reference point for the supporters is Jordan's present and future interests, its stability and regime."[32] Only the balance of power and national interests were to be permissible in public sphere argumentation, and only Jordan could serve as the referent of this self-interest. To the extent that Jordanian national interests replace Arab or Palestinian interests, the opportunities for movement shift. And to the extent that these new norms become internalized, the way in which actors understand political reality changes. The Resistance to normalization aimed at preventing the institutionalization of these new norms, while maintaining the norms of the Arabist tradition. Crucially, the opposition accepted the centrality of Jordanian interests, defending their status as "Jordanian patriots" and denying any affiliation with non-Jordanian parties or states. The struggle over the peace treaty revealed a consensus on the priority of Jordanian state interests underlying the dissensus on the nature of those interests.

While framing arguments within the context of the national interest, the opposition strove vigorously to regain Arabist norms and identity as the locus of public claims within the context of the Jordanian public sphere. The Resistance claimed to speak for the Jordanian nation and to better represent the Jordanian national interest than the government. Naji Allush, a widely respected Palestinian Arabist intellectual, made the connection between identity and of interest most explicit: "There is a big difference between the Emirate of Transjordan . . . and the Jordan which is part of the Arab nation and bound to its norms. . . . The Jordan which signed the treaty is the former."[33] Accepting the treaty meant forfeiting Jordan, or at least the Jordanian identity defined by Arabist norms. Kamal Rashid framed the issue even more starkly: "The Jordanian Self can find some small things to celebrate . . . but if the Self of the Arab or Islamic nation speaks then his words are only pain and sorrow . . . [but] the issue is indivisible and the Jordanian Self can not speak alone."[34] The struggle thus moved inexorably from a competition to define interests to one over national identity.

Justifying the treaty rested on a bid to transform Jordanian identity. King Hussein asserted that "real peace can not result from treaties. . . . it can only emerge from a change in people's minds and hearts." The Resistance agreed: "They frankly say, "it is not enough to sign a treaty.. peace must become acceptable and a way of life for the people.' . . . they know that if you resist they will not achieve their goals. . . . they will not succeed unless you submit to the enemy's control."[35] Both regime and opposition considered the real field of struggle to be the norms of the public sphere: what norms would be seen as legitimate, which interpretive frame would be seen as best describing reality, in what kind of language would debate be conducted?

"Are you with the people or with the government?" came to be the operative question, as political position and national identity became increasingly bound together.[36] Supporters of the treaty attempted to equate support for the treaty with patriotism: "position on the peace treaty distinguishes those who see Jordan as their nation [watan] from those who do not."[37] The opposition, for its part, distinguished between "Jordan" and "the Jordanian government," asserting that the opposition rather than the government best spoke for and defended Jordanian interests. As one opposition newspaper masthead starkly claimed after the revocation of the boycott on Israeli products: "The government wins . . . the nation loses!!"[38] This discourse proved strikingly effective, as the government's reversal of long-held Jordanian positions left much of the uncommitted public deeply disconcerted. Since the opposition stood up for many of the policies and norms which until quite recently had been at the core of Jordanian policy—commitment to Iraq, resistance to Israel, support for Palestinian opposition, appeals for Arab unity—while the government advanced radically new, and dangerously unjustified, policies—support for the Iraqi opposition, rapid normalization,

condemnation of Palestinian terrorism, state interests—the opposition claim
to represent the national interest bore considerable weight. In short, a major
dimension of the political struggle over the peace treaty was over the bases
on which the struggle would—and should—be fought. Was it sufficient that
the treaty be shown to serve Jordanian interests? Or did the maintenance of
an Arab identity take precedence over any considerations of narrow state
interest?

Conclusion

The Jordanian decision to sign a peace treaty with Israel responded both
to strategic concerns and to changes in public sphere structure. The Gulf
War and Oslo changed the regional context of Jordanian policy, making an
agreement with Israel both possible and, arguably, necessary. This agreement reflected the balance of power, but also involved an ambitious project
of transformation of both Jordanian identity and interests and regional institutions and identity. The shift from privacy to publicity meant that for the
first time Jordan could publicly avow its interests in its relations with Israel.
This public avowal both made it possible to openly pursue agreements in
pursuit of these shared interests and placed the interests themselves open to
legitimate public deliberation.

7   New Jordan, New Middle East?

Peace with Israel led to a fundamental, public, and highly controversial reorientation of Jordanian foreign policy. To what extent was this change institutionalized, embedded within a consensus achieved through communicative action? I argue that a thin stratum of elites, particularly King Hussein, was fully convinced of the need for peace, based on their engagement with the international arena. The Jordanian public sphere, however, produced a consensus against rather than for the peace agreement. The Jordanian public vigorously debated the meaning of peace with Israel, the identity of the Jordanian state given its new international alliances, and the substance of Jordanian interests. Rather than blame public opposition on atavism, culture, anti-Semitism, psychological barriers, or irrational emotion, I argue that the trends in Jordanian public opinion reflect the rational evaluation of competing interpretive frames. Given a choice between two frames, one supporting and one opposing peace with Israel, the Jordanian public sphere inclined toward opposition only after an ongoing process of interpreting the costs and benefits of the treaty, the implications for identity, and changes in Israeli behavior. As the government failed to win the public debate, and eventually found itself facing a hostile popular will, it resorted to repression, shutting down the public sphere rather than engaging with it. The government remained bound to the treaty, but its enthusiasm waned. Over a series of crises between Israel and the Palestinians, and between Jordan and Israel, King Hussein began to accuse Israeli Prime Minister Netanyahu of destroying the peace process. I have argued that changes in the conception of state interests can only become a new, stable set of preferences if they are institutionalized in domestic structures. In this chapter, I consider the implications of a failure to achieve such a consensus.

I proceed as follows. First, I summarize Israeli-Jordanian relations since the peace treaty in terms of the theoretical arguments developed in this book. Second, I examine the status of the Jordanian and Arab public spheres. Third, I examine official Jordanian-Israeli relations. Fourth, I examine Jordanian public debates over the peace treaty, particularly the interpretive framing struggles, the organization of civil society into an opposition coalition, and the state turn to repression of societal resistance. Finally, I compare the public deliberation over the peace treaty with the deliberation over the severing of ties.

Overview

Viewed from the outside, the peace treaty produced a new conception of Jordanian interests that rendered cooperation with Israel not only desirable but essential. After the signing of the peace treaty, a new academic and political consensus quickly emerged about the nature of Jordanian-Israeli relations. According to this new conventional wisdom, based on the "shared interests paradigm," the treaty now allowed Jordan and Israel to openly pursue their shared overriding security interests. Israel was cast as Jordan's only defense against a set of clear, objective threats: Iraq, Syria, and a Palestinian state. Even during periods of Jordanian-Israeli tension, Israeli officials confidently asserted that "Jordan and Israel enjoy important mutual interests and a close relationship at the highest levels."[1] Did this confident assertion of shared interests and close relations match Jordanian perceptions? Does it matter that Jordanian-Israeli relations moved from secret into the public? Does it matter that the Jordanian public rejected this conception of Jordanian interests?

The Jordanian public debate viewed the stakes of the peace treaty as a comprehensive regional realignment. As opposition leader Layth Shubaylat put it, "what was Arab and Islamic in Jordan's strategic decisions is now Zionist and American . . . official Jordan has taken a strategic choice to distance itself from the Arabs and make itself their enemy."[2] The opposition mobilized within civil society, with the professional associations, the weekly press, and the Islamist movement leading the way. The major Associations passed binding resolutions forbidding their members from engaging in "normalization" with Israel. The weekly press gave full voice to the opposition frame. Leftist, Arabist, and some centrist political parties joined forces with the Islamists in a coalition opposed to normalization; accepting that they could not force the regime to abolish the treaty, they looked to deprive it of social meaning, along the Egyptian model. The Popular Conference to Resist Normalization and Protect the Nation (PCRN), organized by a coalition of opposition parties and civil society organizations, cast its discourse explicitly in terms of protecting Jordanian national interests and identity from a state action that placed the nation in danger. This form of opposition threatened the regime, forcing public engagement on normative grounds, with reference to a widely held conception of national security, identity, and interests.

Popular opposition to the treaty was not foreordained, or inherent in the Palestinian origin of much of the population, Islamic beliefs, or Arab culture. The initial response to the treaty was very much one of "wait and see"; one public opinion poll showed that 80 percent of Jordanians supported the July 1994 Washington Declaration, but that support was "soft," conditional on rapid economic improvement and progress on the Palestinian and Syrian tracks[3]. While both the regime and the opposition claimed overwhelming popular support for their positions, the truth seems to be that these two camps were competing for the support of a large, undecided public. Since the PLO had made peace, and many expected Syria to follow suit, the normative Arabist sanction did not hold; and the rise of the Jordanian public sphere after 1990 made a focus on Jordanian interests both plausible and normatively valid. During the period after the treaty, the regime, the opposition, and the undecided engaged in spirited, open debate, in which each side attempted to demonstrate the superiority of its interpretive frame. The terms of this debate were the nature of Jordanian identity and the best way to protect the entity, interests, and security. The major leading indicators in this interpretive struggle were Israeli behavior (toward Jordan, the Palestinians, and Lebanon); economic trends; and public freedoms (government tolerance of political opposition).

The shift toward the opposition frame followed from competitive interpretive framing of developments along each of these indicators. First, Israeli behavior did not justify Jordanian friendship. There was a widespread perception that Israel was failing to honor its signed agreements, especially with regard to water and access to West Bank markets. As Israel dragged its feet on negotiations with the Palestinians and Syria, attacked Lebanon, and built settlements in Jerusalem, many undecided Jordanians came to believe that Israel had not changed. With the election of Netanyahu, this belief, already established, deepened immensely. While King Hussein may well have initially welcomed Netanyahu's election, as some have claimed, this was not true of the vast majority of pro-peace and undecided Jordanians. For these Jordanians, the demands of both identity and their conception of interests could be met only by an Israeli committed to peace with Syria, creating a Palestinian state, and economic cooperation at the regional level. While many had lost confidence that Peres held these goals, nobody believed that Netanyahu did. From the narrow perspective of strategic interests, the Hashemites could perhaps see the potential for cooperation with a Likud government; from the broader perspective of Jordanian identity and interests, the Jordanian public could not. Hussein's growing anger with Netanyahu should be interpreted in light of Netanyahu's abandonment of the idea of transforming regional structures, which badly hurt the regime's domestic and Arabist framing of the peace. The attempted assassination of Hamas figure Khalid Misha'al in Amman outraged even the most enthusiastic advocates of peace.

Second, economic prosperity failed to materialize. The United States unwillingness to provide significant financial assistance, beyond the cancellation of some debt, dashed Jordanian expectations of a Camp David style financial package. The continuing deterioration of the Jordanian economy was exacerbated by IMF demands for reductions in bread subsidies. In June 1996 and again in February 1998, major riots broke out in the southern cities. Despite the expectation that the peace would bring large-scale foreign investment and joint ventures, very few such projects materialized; those that involved Israeli companies set off fierce public debates about the implications for Jordanian security, as well as whether or not such ventures were normatively appropriate. At the level of regional integration, the first MENA Economic Conferences in Dar al-Bayda and Amman held out the prospects of developing economic ties. After Netanyahu's election, however, the 1996 conference in Cairo was deeply politicized, while the 1997 conference in Doha was boycotted by almost all Arab states (Jordan attended). At Doha, Jordan and Israel agreed to create the first American-sponsored economic free zone, sparking some joint ventures and investment, but trade and investment remained low. The 1998 conference, in the context of a near-complete freeze in the Palestinian-Israeli peace process, was quietly canceled. Therefore, at both the domestic and the regional levels, the economic dimension of peace failed to materialize.

Third, increasing repression of political opposition helped to convince many Jordanians that the price of the treaty was democracy and public freedoms, which helped to consolidate the belief that the regime had pursued "state/regime" interests at the expense of "Jordanian" interests. As opposition to the peace treaty escalated, the regime responded by an increasingly harsh repression of the public sphere. The government resorted to censorship, arrests, harassment, and general hostility to public challenge. A widespread belief that "democracy is the price of peace" drove many intellectuals and activists into the opposition camp; even if they recognized the potential merits of peaceful relations with Israel, they objected to the regime's style and the rollback of the gains for liberalism since 1989.

The split between regime and opposition grew profound, with the two frames employing mutually exclusive discourse, normative positions, and interpretations. For example, a December 1997 survey revealed a striking contrast in the interpretation of a major part of the justification for the treaty: 59 percent of the members of Parliament believed that the peace treaty had ended the Israeli "Alternative Homeland" threat, while 73 percent of political party leaders and 72 percent of newspaper columnists believed that it had not.[4] The consolidation of the societal consensus could be seen in the ability of the opposition to unite a diverse coalition against normalization. In January 1997, a boycott of an Israeli Trade Fair was supported by virtually every civil society organization, political party, and political figure in the country. Nidal Mansour wrote after the boycott that "for the first time I felt real unity despite all the differences among the coalition," a unity based on the consensus that the Trade Show represented "an Israeli invasion of Jordan."[5] Opposition figures, particularly Islamists, regularly won elections in Professional Associations, university student councils, and other civil society institutions; Shubaylat was re-elected head of the Professional Associations while in prison, with more than 90 percent of the vote. In March and April 1998, after the opposition boycotted the 1997 Parliamentary elections, Islamists and opposition candidates again swept Association and student council elections. In the summer of 1998, an impressive coalition, encompassing the Islamist movement, opposition parties, civil society, independent political and cultural figures, and former regime figures such as Ahmed Obaydat and Taher al-Masri, formed a National Conference to draft a comprehensive alternative program for Jordan's future.

While repression enhanced the regime's freedom of maneuver, it also signaled the failure of its attempt to establish new norms or to transform identity. I have argued that transformation of collective identity requires public sphere interaction; by closing the public sphere, the regime implicitly accepted that Jordan's identity would not change. Netanyahu's election and the collapse of the peace process crippled the attempts to forge a "New Middle East" and sparked the tentative reconstruction of an Arab order. This regional failure of identity transformation rebounded on the Jordanian debate. Having lost the argument, the government could only use repressive power to maintain its position. Indeed, especially after Abd al-Salam al-Majali replaced Kabariti in March 1997, the government seemed perversely inclined to impose its preferences on every issue, no matter how minor, to dismiss any real dialogue, and to pointedly reject any idea advanced in the public sphere. The treaty would remain in place, and the coercive power of the state would prevent effective opposition, but the larger project of embedding a new identity into Jordanian institutions was largely abandoned.

The public rejection of the treaty, and the collapse of attempts to transform regional structures, was matched by the growing crisis in official Jordanian-Israeli relations. The convergence of interpretations of Israeli behavior did not extend to a convergence of frames. King Hussein cast every step in the deterioration in terms of Netanyahu's hostility to peace and Jordanian commitment to peace. As one well-informed American observer put it, King Hussein would not admit that his decision to ally with Israel was wrong, but would admit that Netanyahu had destroyed the foundations for cooperation.[6] While Jordanian officials consistently emphasized that Jordan's decision for peace was strategic, and not subject to change, the failure to embed this "strategic" decision in Jordanian identity or institutions made it vulnerable. The treaty provided too many substantive benefits, particularly in terms of cooperation with the United States, to be abandoned, but it did not necessarily translate into the warm peace originally advocated. As a moderate Islamist who later joined the Cabinet explained, "the peace treaty must be dealt with as an existing fact. . . . the only way to overturn the treaty now is to empty it of its meaning."[7]

The freeze in the Palestinian-Israeli and Syrian-Israeli negotiations deprived Hussein of regional support for domestic transformation. Each crisis made successful final status negotiations less likely, while also confirming the opposition's frame. In a series of increasingly bitter open letters, King Hussein asserted that Netanyahu was neither interested in nor capable of making peace with the Arabs. In other words, the Peace Camp had been abandoned by the Israeli side. Shortly after the King's first letter, a Jordanian soldier attacked a bus of Israeli tourists at Baqoura, killing several. In the following tumult, Hussein's grievances were lost as he personally traveled to Israel to apologize to the bereaved families—an authentic expression of his despair and grief, but also a pointed reminder of the contrast between himself and Netanyahu. The reception of Duqamseh as a popular hero horrified the King and much of the public, but expressed a deeply rooted hostility toward Israel that had not been changed by the peace treaty. The Misha'al Affair drove relations deeper into crisis. Indeed, a December 1997 opinion poll found that 81 percent of Jordanians thought that Jordanians still considered Israelis to be "enemies."[8] Hussein framed his attacks on Netanyahu in terms of the Jordanian desire to save the peace process, but the opposition frame rejecting the treaty on the grounds of identity and interests simply argued that they had been right all along.

Normalization, Identity and the Definition of Interests

The Jordanian public sphere did not neglect or ignore the peace process. Perhaps out of a need to discover the real preferences of the Jordanian public, the government at first allowed considerable latitude to public discussion. More crucially, the regime recognized the theoretical principle developed here, that identity and interests could be changed only through deliberation. Hiwar [dialogue] was a deeply entrenched Jordanian norm, and the government sincerely hoped to change public opinion, perceptions, and behavior through persuasion. While the government was prepared to use repressive force to guarantee the treaty if necessary, it preferred to persuade the Jordanian public of a new set of identities and interests. To this end, King Hussein became personally involved in the deliberation, linking his personal legitimacy and popularity to the treaty and rejecting all efforts to direct criticism at the Prime Minister, to the extent that the treaty came to be known as "the King's peace." In the months immediately before and after the treaty signing, the Jordanian public sphere engaged in active and contentious deliberation over the peace treaty. At this point the public sphere remained relatively open and engaged, despite loud complaints of government attempts to repress important information and dissenting opinions. The weekly press, at least, gave voice to the opposition; government officials took to distinguishing between "our" media (the daily press, television and radio) and "their" media (the weekly press).

Official tolerance of the public sphere began to wane after it became clear that the public was not sold on the benefits of the peace treaty. Harassment of journalists and weekly newspapers became increasingly common, as many opposition editors spent some time in jail and considerable time in court.[9] The passage of a temporary Press and Publications Law in 1997 sharply curtailed the public sphere, as local activists and international human rights observers alike noted; Prime Minister Majali was cited by the Committee to Protect Journalists as one of the world's ten enemies of the press for 1997. This highly restrictive law closed down most weekly newspapers and had a chilling effect upon speech in those that survived. In April 1998, the editorial board of al-Ra'i, the largest daily newspaper and the one in which the government owned the most shares, was replaced with a more politically compliant one in anger at even the muted political criticism in its staid pages.[10] As the government clamped down on the weekly press, Jordanians turned away from the public sphere. In its annual "Democracy in Jordan" opinion survey, the Center for Strategic Studies found that in May 1997 the percentage of Jordanians who claimed to read the daily press had dropped from 52.3 percent to 34.2 percent in a year, while readership of the weekly press fell from 38 percent to 16.9 percent; a rational response to the declining credibility and contentiousness of the press.[11]

It was not only government repression that corroded rational-critical discourse in the Jordanian public sphere, however. As time passed and it became clear that the government was not responsive to public opinion on this—or, increasingly, any—issue, the public began to dichotomize into camps to the detriment of real public sphere interaction. The polarization of opinion over normalization blocked real dialogue between supporters and opponents of normalization that might hold out hope for a new consensus. Some liberals—and even nonliberals—grumbled that the operative term for public sphere debate had shifted from hiwar [dialogue] to jadal [argument], with the exchange of accusations and insults replacing the circulation of arguments geared to consensus. Once it became clear both that the government could not win a popular consensus and that public opinion could not force a change in government policy, each side seemed content to reinforce the solidarity of its own bloc. The opposition boycott of the 1997 elections after the failure of a highly publicized effort at hiwar between government and opposition powerfully symbolized this retreat. In the absence of dialogue, the government drew its conceptions of identity and interests less from participation in the Jordanian public sphere and more from the international public sphere. While this made for consistency in Jordan's foreign policy in the short term, it also meant that official foreign policy alienated and antagonized most of Jordanian society; and it meant that official efforts to transform Jordan's identity and public conceptions of interest had been abandoned.

Parliament was a particularly important institutional site for contesting the peace treaty. The government had already begun to prepare the way for

ratification of the treaty, by manipulating the 1993 Parliamentary elections
to ensure a compliant legislature (Ridel 1994). Nevertheless, the heated
Parliamentary debate captured the intense differences in Jordanian political
society as well as the limitations of *hiwar* in the face of a determined government. While the opposition dominated the proceedings, the government
won its preordained majority. This "deliberation" satisfied nobody: the tolerance of Parliamentary speeches did not appease the opposition, who resented its lack of efficacy; the reasoned argument, no less than the occasional
vitriol, in the opposition speeches angered and frightened the government.

In May 1995, the opposition succeeded in preventing the revocation of
laws forbidding the sale of land to Jews and boycotting the Jewish state, but
the laws were later passed. Parliamentary deliberations forced government
officials to defend and explain Jordanian relations with Israel, although the
most sensitive dimensions of security and economic relations were discussed
only in closed session. During crises over Israeli actions in Lebanon and
Jerusalem (see below), Parliament issued nonbinding resolutions demanding the expulsion of the Israeli Ambassador and a freezing of relations; this
could not compel government policy, but provided a powerful signal of
Jordanian opinion. The decision to maintain the "one vote" electoral law
led to the opposition decision to boycott the 1997 elections. The elections
produced a Parliament almost devoid of opposition forces, especially the
Islamic Action Front, and dominated by tribal, non-party candidates. To the
surprise of most observers, however, this Parliament seemed determined to
demonstrate its independence and integrity, and challenged the government
on a number of issues. The controversial Press and Publications Law, for
example, passed only after long and contentious deliberations. With regard
to Israel, the new Parliament proved unenthusiastic about normalization and
skeptical about the benefits of the peace process, reflecting the mood of the
Netanyahu era of Arab-Israeli relations. During the 1998 vote of confidence
on the new Prime Minister, Fayz Tarawneh, an unprecedented unified statement by 53 Members of Parliament demanded the freezing of normalization
and the improvement of Jordan's relations with the Arab world.

State Policy

There is serious disagreement as to whether the treaty should be considered a success or a failure. While the "warm peace" hoped for by King
Hussein and Israelis has failed to materialize, security cooperation has developed and become well-entrenched, although this has been less true since

late 1997. Despite increasing disenchantment publicly expressed by the Jordanian government, Jordan has been Israel's closest ally and defender in the Arab world. Jordanian-Israeli relations since the treaty fall into three clearly identifiable stages: first, a honeymoon period of great expectations; second, a stabilizing period of positive relations, in which numerous protocols and agreements were signed, and in which relations seemed to be generally positive; third, a period of sharp decline after the attack on Lebanon, actions in Jerusalem, and the election of Netanyahu, in which relations have not been broken but in which relations have become cold and increasingly hostile, and progress toward normalization has largely stopped. There have been moments of increased warmth, but the general trend has been clear.

Since the treaty there have been several cases that allow evaluation of the impact of the peace treaty on Jordan's international behavior. Chapter 8 provides a detailed study of the transformation of Jordanian-Iraqi relations. Here, I evaluate Jordanian-Israeli relations since the treaty, which included the May 1995 Israeli confiscation of land in Jerusalem, the April 1996 Israeli assault on Lebanon, the election of Benjamin Netanyahu, and the August 1997 Misha'al Affair. Israeli actions on other tracks angered Jordanians for their own sake, in that Jordanians identified with the Palestinian and Lebanese suffering. Such actions also provided important signals about Israel's "type": was Israel the kind of state that would honor its commitments and seek peaceful, cooperative relations with Arab states, or was it the kind of state which would violate its commitments and pursue its preferences through power? Each of these events put the demands of the competing frames into sharp and unavoidable conflict. Would Jordan act as a member of the Peace Camp and put its relations with Israel and its commitment to the peace process above all other interests, or would Jordan act as an Arab state and stand with urgent Arab concerns? Could Jordan use its close relations with Israel to influence Israel behavior, vindicating the claim that engagement might change, or at least constrain, Israel?

In the first stage after the peace treaty, Israel and Jordan enjoyed something of a honeymoon at the official level and among Israelis, if not at the popular Jordanian level. Rabin and Hussein enjoyed extremely close relations, and shared a common vision of the regional order. The leaders, and other officials, met regularly to discuss the implementation of the treaty, signing a series of supplemental agreements. In April 1995, Jordan and Israel exchanged ambassadors, and regular visits between high level officials began to build personal contacts between the two sides. Shimon Peres took a highly publicized walking tour of Amman during a state visit, and was charmed at the warm reception from Jordanians. Tourism, primarily Israeli visitors to Jordan, boomed almost immediately, and plans to jointly develop Aqaba and Eilat, as well as the Jordan Valley, were drafted.

The first signal that the Israeli-Jordanian peace treaty could not be insulated from broader regional politics came in early May 1995, when Israel announced the confiscation of land in Arab East Jerusalem. The confiscation surprised nearly everyone, and outraged Jordanians who viewed Jerusalem as an issue of particular importance and sensitivity. A number of Arab states, including Jordan, announced that they would hold a mini-summit to consider unified action against the Israeli action. Rabin refused to reconsider, until the Likud opposition joined in a no-confidence motion brought by the Arab parties in the Knesset, threatening to bring down the government. A furious Rabin grudgingly froze the land confiscation and the Arab mini-summit was canceled.

This was one of the first major tests of Jordanian behavior in an Arab-Israeli confrontation after the peace treaty. The regime found its efforts to use its friendly ties to Israel to mediate the conflict ineffective, and the crisis caused a temporary but sharp deterioration in Jordanian-Israeli relations. On May 15, Foreign Minister Kabariti officially complained to Shimon Peres that "Jordan considers the Israeli measures to be directed at Jordan directly and to show a lack of respect for the Jordanian role in Jerusalem." After Israeli Ambassador Shimon Shamir informed the Jordanians that the decision would not be reversed, Prince Hassan met with the American Ambassador, again with little effect. Finally, King Hussein wrote directly to Rabin, emphasizing the importance of Jerusalem. Officials warned that "Jordan's firm commitment to the peace process . . . can not serve as cover for Israeli behavior in Jerusalem."[12] None of these efforts succeeded in modifying Israeli behavior, undercutting two major regime claims: that Jordan could use its friendship to influence Israeli behavior; and that the peace process had modified Israeli ambitions on the West Bank and Jerusalem, or that at least the desire to keep the process moving would constrain them. As Kabariti complained, "such Israeli measures cause embarrassment to all supporters of the peace process."[13]

Societal and Parliamentary reaction was less restrained than the official attempts at mediation. Where the government cast its objections in terms of its commitment to the peace process, a special session of Parliament attended by more than 60 (out of 80) deputies called informally to cancel the peace treaty. With the controversial vote on revoking boycott laws only days away, Parliament showed every indication of rejecting the revisions, which would have been a major setback for Jordanian-Israeli relations.[14] With Parliament firmly in the hands of a pro-government majority, such an action would have to be taken as an expression of societal consensus. In an interview with an Israeli newspaper, Kabariti noted that the confiscation "will not help us implement the peace process at the public level . . . how can the King now ask Parliament to abrogate the boycott laws, when the entire Jordanian public believes Israel is violating treaties?"[15] After Israel froze its decision, the pro-government deputies returned to the fold and passed the laws, but the event left a strong impression that an opposition consensus capable of overcoming regime commitments could be mobilized. It strengthened the opposition frame by providing concrete evidence that Israel had not abandoned its ambitions on the West Bank and Jerusalem. While the regime denounced the Israeli action, and therefore the popular mobilization did not directly contradict official policy, there were very clear differences in the relative priority of the Jordanian peace based on narrow Jordanian interests and Arab and Palestinian interests. The resolution of the crisis kept these contradictions from coming to a head.

The assassination of Yitzhaq Rabin in November 1995 affected all dimensions of the peace process. For Jordan, it represented a particularly damaging blow because of the close friendship and deep trust between Hussein and Rabin. While Shimon Peres shared Rabin's commitment to the peace process, his conception of Israeli interests and of Jordanian-Israeli relations differed from Rabin's. Furthermore, Rabin's murder undoubtedly evoked Hussein's own sense of personal vulnerability; the headline in the Jordanian Islamist weekly, "One Less Murderer!" reportedly infuriated Hussein. Hussein's eloquent eulogy at Rabin's funeral struck many as the ultimate example of what Arab-Israeli peace should mean: a demonstration of affection, mutual respect, and hope for the future. Jordanians reacted less positively to this articulation of the Peace Camp frame. For many Jordanians, Rabin remained the leader of an enemy state, the Israeli Chief of Staff in 1967, the harsh repressor of the Intifada. Hussein's evocation of his close, personal friendship with Rabin sharply contrasted with the public conceptions.

In March 1996, a series of suicide attacks in Israel led to the convocation of the extraordinary anti-terrorism "Summit of Peacemakers" at Sharm al-Shaykh. This Summit, while widely dismissed as a public relations stunt, did in fact serve to concretely embody the concept of the Peace Camp, so central to King Hussein's identity frame. The wide attendance of the Summit seemed to lend plausibility to the idea that there existed a moderate center committed to peace, threatened by a small, violent minority.

In April 1996, however, Israel mounted a large-scale bombing campaign on southern Lebanon. While ostensibly in retaliation for Hizbullah rocket attacks on northern Israel, most observers interpreted the attack as part of Shimon Peres's reelection campaign—proof that he could be trusted with security. World public opinion became outraged only when Western journalists revealed an Israeli bombing attack on a UN facility full of children; Arab public opinion reacted immediately. The timing of the "Grapes of Wrath" campaign could not help but recall the 1982 Israeli invasion of Lebanon, only a few years after Camp David, which helped ensure that peace treaty's failure to lead to a broad Arab-Israeli peace. For Jordanians, as for Egyptians fourteen years earlier, the Israeli attack swung the internal and regional debate over relations with Israel against the "Peace Camp" frame.

Jordanians, horrified at the Israeli assault on Lebanon, demanded government action. As in the Jerusalem crisis, the government attempted to use its diplomatic ties with Israel to mediate while refraining from public comment. To the anger of the public and Parliament, the government did not issue any public condemnation for more than a week as it attempted diplomacy behind the scenes. On April 14, Kabariti phoned Peres asking him to stop the attacks in order to "remove all causes of tension and resume the peace process." On April 16, Kabariti made an unprecedented trip to Jerusalem [rather than Tel Aviv] desperately seeking to mediate. These efforts were firmly rebuffed, angering even the pro-Israel camp. On April 18, King Hussein's frustration boiled over into his first public criticism of Israel in years, as he "strongly condemned Israel's flagrant aggression and the criminal military operations inflicted on the brotherly Lebanese people." That the language of his condemnation was among the strongest used by any Arab leader is indicative of the sense of betrayal he undoubtedly felt. Kabariti simultaneously summoned the Israeli Ambassador to register an official protest. According to the official Jordanian news agency, Kabariti "told [Ambassador] Shamir that Jordan was outraged because its quiet diplomatic efforts to mediate an end to the eight-day-old blitz were only countered by further Israeli escalation of the fighting."

The response in the Jordanian public sphere revealed the power of the opposition frame. The attack on Lebanon simply could not be reconciled with the regime frame of a new Israel, a reliable partner in peace led by Peres, a visionary of peace. The Parliamentary opposition again called on the government to abrogate the peace treaty and expel the Ambassador. The arguments of peace treaty advocates to "not abrogate the treaty . . . do not sacrifice Jordanian interests to a non-Jordanian cause" fell dangerously flat.[16] Rallies of thousands filled the streets with banners denouncing Israel and the peace treaty. Kabariti warned that "there is a sense of alarm in Jordan and within the Jordanian public. . . . the situation is really dangerous and explosive." For the second straight year, virtually all Jordanians boycotted the Israeli Independence Day festivities. The Islamist newspaper *al-Sabil* published an opinion poll of dubious scientific but considerable political value which claimed that 77 percent of Jordanians supported abrogating the peace treaty immediately.[17] Opposition writers leveled deeply effective criticism against government attempts to maintain its peace camp frame: "The Information Minister says that Jordan . . . will work to save the peace process. What about saving the Lebanese people?"[18]

These events preceded the election of Benjamin Netanyahu, which is usually blamed for the collapse of the peace process. Rabin's confiscation of Jerusalem land and the assault on Lebanon under Peres badly damaged the Peace Camp's position by demonstrating Israeli behavior inconsistent with its frame. The case for a Peace Camp identity depended upon the portrayal of Israel as sympathetic toward Jordanian interests, trustworthy, and sincerely interested in peace. The opposition frame, portraying Israel as hostile, contemptuous of international law, antipathetic to Arab interests, and more interested in regional power and domination than in peace, seemed to better account for Israeli behavior. As one palpably frustrated centrist wrote, "they don't want peace. We thought they had changed . . . but we do not find any evidence of any Israeli inclination for peace."[19] The regime's inability to influence Israeli behavior undermined the argument that Jordan could use its connection to Israel to pursue Arab interests.

The election of Benjamin Netanyahu in May 1996, while not the first crisis in Jordanian-Israeli relations, posed a serious challenge to them. The return of the Likud threatened to leave Jordan in its worst possible outcome: publicly bound to Israel and isolated from all other Arab and Palestinian actors. Jordan's strategy in the peace process had been premised on its irreversibility and the construction of new regional institutions and order. King Hussein had been careful to cultivate relationships with the Likud, and did not immediately condemn Netanyahu. Unlike most Arab leaders, Hussein called on Arabs to give the new leader a chance. In June, an Arab summit in Cairo warned against an Israeli retreat from its commitment to the peace process and advocated a freeze on normalization until the new Israeli leadership proved itself. In July, Prime Minister Kabariti met with Netanyahu for the first time, delivering four specific questions on the peace process. In

August 1996, Hussein and Netanyahu met, with discussions focusing on bilateral issues. Hussein pointedly called on the new Prime Minister to live up to Israeli commitments, a theme that would be central to Jordanian discourse.

In September, however, Israel sparked uprisings and armed confrontations between PNA and Israeli personnel by opening an archaeological tunnel in an extremely sensitive part of the Old City of Jerusalem. This Israeli action particularly infuriated King Hussein because Dore Gold, Netanyahu's close adviser, had visited Amman only two days before and had not warned the Jordanians of the tunnel opening; Jordanians felt that Israel hoped to implicate Jordan as complicit in the action. In October, a meeting in Washington called by President Clinton with Hussein, Arafat, and Netanyahu (Mubarak declined to attend) witnessed a surprising outburst from Hussein, in which he warned of his loss of trust and his deep disappointment.[20] On October 9, King Hussein warned that the Jordanian-Israeli peace treaty would be in question if Israel did not live up to its commitments to the Palestinians, and two days later Kabariti bluntly stated that the Israeli-Palestinian crisis was causing a Jordanian-Israeli crisis. On October 23, Hussein again called on Israel to live up to its agreements, warning that "the Middle East is on the brink and I fear we may all fall into it."

Throughout December 1996, Hussein had spoken publicly and met privately with Israeli officials about the need to move the peace process forward, warning that the stagnation strengthened the opposition's position and weakened the hand of the Peace Camp. In January 1997, Hussein helped to mediate the Israeli-Palestinian negotiations with a well-publicized intervention into the bargaining over the fate of Hebron. In a last-minute visit to Israel and to Gaza, Hussein personally pleaded with both sides to accept a compromise in order to prevent the peace process from collapsing completely. When Netanyahu finally agreed to a partial withdrawal from Hebron on January 25, commentators on all sides viewed it as a landmark decision, evidence that Netanyahu had changed and was now committed to the peace process.

By March 1997, these Jordanian hopes had faded. Netanyahu's obstructionist tactics in the negotiations with the Palestinians left Hussein frustrated and furious. On February 25, Netanyahu visited Amman; two days later, in a move reminiscent of the tunnel opening, Israel announced the beginning of construction of a new settlement in Jebel Abu Ghunaym/Har Homa, a move that would effectively cut East Jerusalem off from the West Bank. On March 10, Hussein sent a blistering open letter to the Israeli Prime Minister expressing his disenchantment: "I no longer believe that you are a serious partner in peace." The attack on Israeli tourists at Baqoura, as discussed above, obscured Hussein's arguments, putting him on the defensive. Hussein's framing of the Baqoura incident demonstrates the power of his commitment to the peace process. While Netanyahu exploited the situation by attempting to blame Hussein for creating a hostile atmosphere conducive to the Jordanian soldier's attack, Hussein quietly rebuked the attack by personally traveling to Israel to apologize to the bereaved Israeli parents. Hussein's words and deeds reinforced his frame: he was part of a Peace Camp threatened by Netanyahu's defection. The response of Jordanian society equally demonstrated how isolated Hussein was in this frame.

Perhaps the most provocative event was the Misha'al Affair of August 1997. A Mossad operation, evidently approved by Netanyahu, attempted to assassinate Khalid Misha'al, a Hamas leader resident in Amman. After the action went wrong, with the agents captured, Hussein demanded and received an antidote for the poison used against Misha'al; the release of Jordanian prisoners in Israeli jails; and most significantly the release of Ahmed Yassin, spiritual leader of Hamas. King Hussein viewed the operation as a direct repudiation of the very essence of the peace treaty: "it was an act against Jordan itself, its integrity and its sovereignty, and the results were devastating for the trust we had built." The attack undercut support for the treaty even among those who had believed in its strategic value; as one Jordanian politician explained, "Jordan made a strategic alliance with Israel . . . but the attack . . . demonstrates that Israel—or at least Netanyahu—does not value Jordan as a strategic ally." In February 1998, the Israeli investigation committee refused to rule out future operations in Jordan, causing the Jordanian government to lodge an official complaint, and the Minister of the Interior to state publicly that the decision would negatively affect Jordanian-Israeli relations. Jordan temporarily froze most dimensions of security cooperation, including covert channels between the intelligence agencies.[21]

The tension in the official Jordanian-Israeli relationship did not lead to a decisive break between the two states. In March and April 1998, King Hussein and Prince Hassan met with Netanyahu, attempting to restore relations and to influence Israeli policy toward the Palestinians. Their failure to convince Netanyahu to move forward on the peace process continued to chill relations. Jordan attempted to insulate security cooperation with Israel from public scrutiny. Joint exercises and maneuvers brought the Jordanian military together with American and Israeli counterparts.[22] At the same time, most Jordanians perceived the security cooperation as not involving anything beyond state interests; every such action was widely denounced by the opposition and mainstream public opinion alike. Jordanian-Israeli security cooperation was enhanced by the United States. The sale of F-16s to Jordan was a response to Jordan's new role in the security architecture of the region. In March 1996, Jordan agreed to the deployment of an American Air Expeditionary Force as part of a deal to bring F-16s to Jordan. In defending the decision to transfer these fighters, the Defense Department representative told Congress: "Jordan has worked very closely with Israel to enhance trade, tourism, diplomatic and especially military relations between the two countries in an unprecedented fashion."[23] Clashes between the Clinton Administration and the Republican Congress over U.S. aid to Jordan soured U.S.-Jordanian relations in 1996 and 1997, however. In 1997, the problem was resolved only when Egypt and Israel each agreed to allow $50 million of their own aid packages to be diverted to Jordan.

While virtually every aspect of Jordanian-Israeli relations is now routinely and heatedly debated, security relations remained a taboo topic in the Jordanian public sphere. Issues such as the military budget, defense policy, recruitment, weapons acquisition, and deployment remain strictly off limits to public debate. Even the relatively liberal Press law of 1993 forbids discussion of all aspects of the military. In this regard, military cooperation with Israel and the United States in the wake of the peace treaty has, with one exception, not been an issue of public controversy inside of Jordan. When former Prime Minister Taher al-Masri published a devastating critique of Jordanian-Israeli relations in January 1998, for example, he explicitly exempted security cooperation as "beyond the red lines which cannot be discussed." After reports that Jordan had decided to close Mossad offices in Jordan after the Misha'al Affair, Jordanian officials were forced to publicly deny that any such offices had ever existed. In June 1998, Deputy Prime Minister Jawad al-Anani bluntly asserted that Jordanian-Israeli security cooperation had virtually ended as a result of the Misha'al Affair and the stalemate on the Palestinian track.

There is one exception to this public sphere red line: the January 1998 invitation to join Israeli-Turkish naval exercises led to one of the first public debates on security related issues in the history of Jordan. This debate, like the debate on Doha discussed below, effectively captures the major themes in the interpretive struggle over Jordanian foreign policy. Since the exercises coincided with the seating of a new Parliament and a vote of confidence for the government, numerous deputies had the opportunity and the incentive to air concerns about the exercises. The government defended them as purely humanitarian in nature and as carrying absolutely no implications about Jordanian membership in a Turkish-Israeli alliance, a claim sharply challenged by a number of Deputies. Syria, feeling that the alliance was primarily aimed at it, criticized Jordanian participation, launching the harshest Syrian-Jordanian exchange since the Asad-Hussein reconciliation in June 1996. In September, the Jordanian Information Minister asserted that "Jordan will not be a party to any alliance against an Arab state or take part in any maneuvers which threaten an Arab state's security."[24] Jordan eventually sent a single observer to the exercises, a compromise between the need to demonstrate a commitment to security cooperation with Israel and a mobilized public opinion.

Civil Society and the Jordanian Public Sphere

With the peace treaty imposed from above, normalization [tatb'i] quickly became the centerpiece of political confrontation in the Jordanian public sphere. Coined in Egypt after Camp David, "normalization" meant publicly accepting Israel and Israelis politically, economically, socially, and culturally. In practice, this became a contest over the norms of the Jordanian political system and the shape of the Jordanian public sphere. Unable to resist the state's decision to accept political normalization—a peace treaty, embassies, ambassadors—the opposition concentrated on the other spheres, entrenching its resistance in civil society. The Jordanian Resistance emulated the Egyptian model for frustrating official attempts at normalization by mobilizing and organizing civil society (Baker 1990). The Professional Associations passed resolutions banning members from professional interaction with Israelis despite the revision of the laws governing such contacts. Women's organizations, university student councils, local clubs, writers associations—indeed, virtually every organization with elected rather than state-appointed leadership—quickly adopted similar resolutions. Several organizations coordinated activities, beginning with the Popular Committee to Resist Zionism and Normalization licensed in 1992; 1994's Popular Committee coordinating the anti-normalization activities of opposition political parties; the Popular Conference to Protect the Nation and Resist Normalization in 1995; the Committee to Prevent the Israeli Trade Show in 1997; and the National Conference organized by the National Reform Forces in 1998. Despite significant differences in their positive programs, the constituent members of these organizations could unite in defense of basic shared norms. For arguably the first time in Jordanian history, a semi-permanent coalition of Islamists, leftists, Arab nationalists, and Jordanian nationalists stood together in direct opposition to the government.

While the regime adopted specific political strategies in response to this opposition, in the long run it counted on economic benefits to overcome societal resistance. This strategy rested upon assumptions about human behavior consistent with rationalist premises. Because individuals primarily respond to economic incentives and narrowly defined self-interest, principled positions will change in response to shifts in economic incentives. Therefore, people would abandon Islamist movements, political opposition, and all forms of ideology if they could find more employment opportunities and a better quality of life. That Jordanians would abandon their hostility to Israel if they saw the peace treaty improving the economy was an article of faith among Jordanian policymakers [and most Western academics]. Prominent government figures argued that the success of the peace primarily depended on the extent to which the international community contributed to revitalizing the economy. The Resistance rejected the rationalist economic view of human behavior, arguing for the autonomy of norms, principles, and beliefs. Rejecting that "the people were for sale," the Resistance placed greater weight on their ability to counter regime propaganda through effective access to the public sphere. Against the rationalist world of self-interested actors, the Resistance posed identity, norms, and public discourse. In one sense, then, the normalization struggles can be seen as a direct test of the competing views of the relationship between norms, interests, public sphere structure, and behavior. In another sense, however, such a juxtaposition of interests and norms badly misrepresents the situation: the opposition consistently argued that its defense of norms also best served Jordanian interests. Since the promised material benefits did not materialize, the opposition could claim convincingly that norms and interests ran together and not against one another.

Identity Framing

The normalization debate concerned the right of the political public to contribute to the interpretation and formation of national interests against King Hussein's claim to personal sovereignty over such interpretations. The Resistance defended an image of Jordan as an Arabist state, committed to Arab ideals, and internally democratic under the wise leadership of the monarch consulting with the people. The identity claims advanced by the Resistance drew on precisely those norms which had been secured through public debate during the 1990s. The regime, on the other hand, proposed a state identity oriented toward economic development, pragmatism, condemnation of terrorism, and so forth. While the regime did not repudiate the Arab identity of the state, it contended that the norms and positions that comprised that Arab identity needed to be replaced.

These competing identity claims [Peace Camp vs. Arabist] generated widely divergent interpretations of Jordan's interests. The regime identified Jordanian interests in terms of a New Middle East of economic development and regional cooperation. Israel, from this perspective, represented no particular threat, while Syria and Iraq required great vigilance. The Resistance defended existent conceptions of interest, insisting that Israel remained the greatest threat to Jordanian and Arab security. As one centrist writer put it, "we will never believe those . . . who pretend that Jordanian interests were threatened and the treaty with Israel saved them . . . because this supposes that the danger to our interests was not from Israel but from the Arabs. . . . Whoever says this insults Jordan and its history and the meaning of its existence as a state."[25] Where the Resistance saw Jordanian security as best protected by renewed Arab coordination, the regime preferred a close alliance with Israel. The regime and the Resistance therefore advanced fundamentally different claims about both the identity of the state and its interests.

The Resistance denounced the rapid pace of normalization as the most urgent threat to Jordanian security, independence, and values. Hussein, for his part, repeatedly vented his frustration with what he considered the slow pace of normalization. One of the key battlefields of this period would be over the patriotism and even the Jordanian identity of the Resistance. Asserting personal sovereignty over the definition of Jordanian interests, Hussein increasingly resorted to denying the Jordanian identity of his opponents. When Ahmed Obaydat, a respected former Prime Minister, publicly attacked normalization, he was dismissed from the Senate. In his speech announcing the appointment of Zayd bin Shakir to form a new government in January 1995, Hussein apologized for the lack of progress in achieving normalization, an apology that hardly responded to the Jordanian public sphere's concern with the dangers of normalization. In February 1996, he replaced Sharif Zayd with Abd al-Karim al-Kabariti, reportedly because of his frustration with the slow pace of change. After Kabariti angered King Hussein with his "grandstanding" during the Baqoura incident, Hussein appointed Abd al-Salam al-Majali, the architect of the peace agreement with Israel and the politician most closely associated with the peace treaty.

The attempted reconstruction of the Jordanian polity around peace with

Israel touched on deeply held national myths. In March, Jordan celebrates the anniversary of the battle of Karameh. In 1968, the Jordanian army, in cooperation with the Palestinian resistance forces, repelled a large Israeli punitive raid on the Jordanian village of Karameh. Driving the Israeli army back and inflicting significant casualties, the combined forces claimed a major victory that helped to break the air of defeat in Arab publics after the 1967 war. While the Palestinians won the media battle with the Jordanians in the Arab, international, and even Jordanian public spheres, claiming Karameh as a victory for the Palestinian Revolution, many Jordanians felt that the victory was as much if not more their own. The anniversary of the battle became a national holiday, one of the few victories of the Jordanian army, and a symbol of Jordanian Arabist convictions.

In 1995, however, celebrating victory over Israeli aggression became rather problematic for a Jordanian government fervently striving to reverse popular hostility to Israel. The anniversary inevitably became a symbolic battlefield between the regime and the Resistance. The regime sought to impose a new reading of the battle, emphasizing Jordanian heroism and honor while downplaying the Israeli aggression: "Karameh will remain a point of honor no matter what changes."[26] Even firm supporters of the peace treaty hesitated before the bald reversal of decades of nationalist history and mythmaking. The centrist Taher al-Udwan admitted that "the pictures on TV last night stirred powerful emotions. . . . we will never forget our martyrs . . . for this is a noble part of Jordanian history."[27] This comment nicely captures the regime's dilemma. Since Jordanian history offered few events that could be appropriated to the dominant Arabist normative structure, Karameh had been seized upon and pumped up into a monumental moment in the pantheon of Jordanian nationalist history. Pride and belief in Jordanian valor that day transcended all political positions and all identities, from Jordanian chauvinists to Palestinian revolutionaries. As such, it served as one of the very few truly unifying national myths, allowing Jordanians to feel that they had contributed to the war against Israel and for Palestinian rights.

The new interpretation would reverse all that, transforming a myth of resistance to a specific national enemy into a bland celebration of national pride and heroism. Instead of celebrating a common front against an aggressor, Karameh was to represent a spirit of sacrifice and belonging in the absence of any historical memory of the actual events. Netanyahu, then leader of the opposition, was even quoted in the Jordanian press as proposing a joint memorial for the Jordanians and Israelis (though apparently not Palestinians) killed in the battle. This crass revisionism enraged many Jordanians: "he wants us to equate the aggressors with those defending themselves. . . . they behave as conquerors who may rewrite history as they wish."[28]

Throughout the normalization battles, the theme of the authority of history would recur. For example, the Jordanian school curriculum became a sensitive issue. Initially both opponents and supporters of normalization interpreted the treaty as requiring a revision of school history texts to remove all references to Israeli aggression or hostility, the creation of Israel at the expense of Palestinians, or anything else offensive to Israelis. While such revisions might be seen as an admirable attempt to overcome deeply entrenched nationalist myths reinforcing conflict, for Jordanians sensitive to the politics of history such revisions represented a direct assault on the national identity: "What we see . . . is the erasing of our history."[29] Why, they asked, were Arabs asked to surrender their national memory, while Israel's myths and prejudices remained unchallenged? Why should Arab myths be replaced with Zionist myths? When it became apparent how explosive such revisions would be, government spokesmen disavowed any such intentions. However, the issue remained: which version of history would be told? The Arab or the Israeli? Would Jordan abandon its own historical narrative? Was normalization possible without substantial modifications of that narrative?

The Resistance insisted on retaining the "real" meaning of Karameh within its authentic historical context, which of course fit neatly within the Resistance interpretive frame: the spirit of resistance to Israeli aggression and Jordanian-Palestinian cooperation against the common enemy. Rather than an anonymous national holiday, "Karameh remains an invasion of Jordan by the Zionist enemy in which we joined with the Palestinians in all heroism."[30] Beyond contesting the regime's interpretation, and beyond defending the nationalist myth, the Resistance sought to turn Karameh into a test case for the struggle to rewrite history. Karameh presented an opportunity for the Resistance to force the regime to publicly acknowledge, and to embrace, the implications of its positions in precisely a way that would offend the most loyal and patriotic Jordanians.

The annual attempt by the Israeli Embassy to host Israeli Independence Day festivities is another example. What Israelis consider Independence Day, most Arabs—and especially Palestinians—consider the anniversary of the theft of their land and their expulsion from their homes. Holding such a celebration would be a victory for normalization, to be sure, but even supporters of the peace treaty found the invitation to celebrate the loss of Palestine in Amman to be in rather bad taste. In the first opportunity, May

1995, Israel planned an extravagant celebration, inviting thousands of prominent Jordanians. The party was almost universally boycotted; the only Jordanian attendees were a few visibly unhappy government representatives and a number of tabloid journalists eager to snap pictures of whoever dared attend. In 1996, the celebration coincided with the furor over the Grapes of Wrath campaign against Lebanon, and once again Jordanians boycotted. The festivities fared no better in subsequent years. Israel's Ambassador continued to be *persona non grata* in most public events. When Israel was finally able to open an Embassy (for the first few years it operated out of a hotel in Amman), this generated accusations that the Embassy would be a "spy center" for Israeli operations in the Middle East.

The 1998 celebration of Israel's fiftieth anniversary sparked a revisiting of the historical narrative of injustice and hostility. These fiftieth anniversary celebrations could have been framed differently: the revelations of Avi Shlaim and the New Historians about the long history of Hashemite-Zionist contacts, or Moshe Zak's accounts of Hussein's personal relationship with Israeli leaders, could have been reinterpreted (as they generally were in Israel) as evidence of a long positive identification in light of current friendly relations. Instead this dimension of Jordanian history continued to be ignored and repressed in the Jordanian public sphere, and used against Jordan in the Arabist and Palestinian arenas. No new grand narrative was proposed; after two years of Netanyahu and the collapsing peace process, few Jordanians were interested in celebrating a history of Jordanian-Israeli contacts.

Battles of this kind raged across the Jordanian public sphere in the months after the signing of the peace treaty. Resistance to cultural contacts became much stronger after the moves to peace, as the official peace removed legal barriers. The Resistance needed to enforce societal conformity much more rigidly without the political system's power behind it. When the leader of a small political party, Ahmed Zu'ubi, toured Israel and met with Israeli politicians, he was expelled from the Doctors Association. When a group of dentists attended a professional conference with Israelis, they were expelled from the Dentists Association. The Doctors Association boycotted a major international medical colloquium held in Amman because Israeli doctors attended. The Professional Associations building maintained a blacklist of "normalizers," who found themselves snubbed in their professional and social activities. A New Middle East based on economic integration and joint ventures could hardly be realized if Jordanian professionals refused to deal with their prospective partners.

One of the earliest battlefields was the Jordanian Writers Association.[31]

In 1993, JWA President Fakhri Qawar protested the invitation of the well-known Arab poet and critic Adonis to participate in the Jerash cultural festival because of his publicized contacts with Israeli academics. In June 1994, Zulaykha Abu Risha came under pressure for participating in an academic conference with Israeli women. On August 19, 1994, a special session was convened to strip her of her membership. While this did not succeed, the session passed a set of bylaws governing normalization which became a model for the Professional Associations. These restrictions, passed by a democratic vote in an open meeting, would become a central object of controversy as the normalization debate expanded. As the regime insisted that the opposition should "state its positions and then respect the will of the majority," the Resistance positions adopted by genuinely democratic means posed a stark dilemma. Which majority should carry its mandate—the majority claimed by the state, or the majority elected by the citizens? While the overwhelming majority opposed normalization, sharp differences emerged over the meaning of normalization and how to implement resistance. According to hardliners, the resistance to normalization in this uncertain age required absolute, clear guidelines banning all contact with any Israelis.

Frustrated at the hard-line interpretations and blunt political tactics of the Resistance, JWA President Mu'nis Rizaz resigned on March 8, 1995. The ensuing elections became a major test of strength between the government and the Resistance. Even though Ibrahim al-Abassi was quickly constructed by the government as the alternative to the Resistance leader Salem al-Nahass, Abassi's platform equally declared opposition to normalization: "We will resist all forms of normalization with the Israeli enemy."[32] Nevertheless, for a government desperate to find some entry into civil society, Abassi represented "realism" against "narrow party doctrine."[33] The elections became a spectacle, the focus of extraordinary local, Israeli, and international media coverage. The government intervened with all its weight, with government ministers attending in their capacity as members and long-inactive members bused in from all over the kingdom to vote.[34] In the end, Abassi won a narrow victory, and his immediate assertion that he would continue the policy of resisting normalization did not prevent government supporters from jubilantly claiming—on Israeli TV—that "our side won."

That comment, however, sparked the next crisis. Hamada Fara'na, a liberal columnist outspoken in his defense of democracy, was disciplined for insulting the Association and for engaging in normalization by analyzing the election for Israeli TV. Even a publicized phone call of support by the King to Fara'na did not swing support in his favor.[35] The suggestion that there was an "our side" composed of the regime, Jordanian supporters of the peace treaty, and Israel represented a political identity claim very few Jordanians would publicly accept. Fara'na would remain a highly polarizing figure in the normalization debate. After being elected to Parliament in 1997, he and Representative Mohammed Rifa't publicly met with members of the Israeli Knesset, prompting another major debate over normalization. During a tense Parliamentary debate, one deputy reportedly yelled at Fara'na, a Palestinian and former member of both the Palestinian National Council and the Jordanian National Charter Commission, that he was not a real Jordanian, because "your place is in the Knesset, next to Netanyahu!"[36]

The Opposition Coalition

The Resistance organized itself as a coalition of political parties, societal institutions, professional associations, and independent personalities. Bahjat Abu Ghurbiya, a respected veteran Palestinian figure, headed the Popular Committee to Resist Normalization and Protect the Nation, which acted as an umbrella for the various opposition political parties. The emphasis in the name upon "Protecting the Nation" conveys the public position carved out by the Resistance, in defiance of the regime's effort to portray all opposition as servants of foreign interests. While the Islamic Action Front carried the greatest political weight, leftist and Arab nationalist groups were prominently represented in the Committee in order to convey a broad societal consensus. The coalition of opposition parties established informal links with the Professional Associations, women's and student organizations, and other civil society organizations. The government declared the Committee an illegal, unlicensed political organization, raising a series of lawsuits against newspapers for "publishing the name and statements of an illegal political organization."

In early 1995, the Resistance planned a national conference which would adopt a comprehensive strategy for resisting normalization and draft an Honor Code to guide individual behavior. This National Conference aimed at producing a national consensus outside the state and government frameworks, consciously drawing upon the language, format, and norms of the National Charter conference of 1991, which had claimed to produce a reference point for Jordanian norms and discourse for the 1990s. The appropriation of the National Charter discourse took on even greater significance in light of calls by Israeli figures for Jordan to abolish its National Charter which considers Zionism intrinsically opposed to Jordanian identity and interests.[37] It was clear that the government could not generate the public consensus necessary to legitimate any new charter in line with the treaty. The Resistance discourse emphasized that its concerns emerged not from opposition to the Jordanian nation or its interests, but out of its concern for Jordan. By surrendering to Israeli power, the government had put Jordan in great danger; the Resistance framed its mission as minimizing the impact of that surrender until such a time as it could be reversed. This emphasis upon protecting Jordanian identity, security, and interests is the most important dimension of its frame. Rather than placing itself in opposition to Jordanian identity and interests, it claimed to better represent that identity and those interests than did the government.

The government was not comforted by this Resistance appropriation of Jordanian identity and interests. If anything, such a claim was more threatening than any certifiably "foreign" opposition. The government tried to portray the Resistance as tied to foreign agents, dismissing it as primarily concerned with interests and identities other than Jordanian. The government alternately accused the Resistance of "having a Palestinian face," of being controlled by Syria and Iraq, and of being the tool of Islamic fundamentalist radicals controlled from abroad. However, the clarity and consistency of Resistance framing of the national identity and the national interest undercut this government frame. The Jordanian public therefore faced a choice not between "Jordan" and some other reference point (the PLO, Arabism, Islam), but between two competing conceptions of Jordanian identity and interests: the government, claiming that the peace treaty and normalization served Jordanian interests; and the Resistance, claiming that these changes threatened Jordanian interests.

Unable to carry the public sphere argument, the government chose to exert power instead, shutting down the public sphere outlets it could not control and systematically distorting media coverage. The National Conference had been scheduled and postponed numerous times in the first half of 1995. Finally, it was scheduled for May 29, receiving a reluctant permit from the Mayor of Amman. The government had a last-minute change of heart, and after unsuccessful midnight negotiations between the Prime Minister and Ishaq Farhan of the Islamic Action Front, the government withdrew its permit. Armed troops surrounded the building, participants were turned away, and the government issued a terse statement citing security concerns and its dissatisfaction with the text of the preliminary Conference Resolution. A smaller Conference was eventually held, with much less fanfare and public attention.

The opposition coalition achieved its most united front in January 1997 with the organization of a boycott of an Israeli Trade Show scheduled for Amman. Fronted by former Prime Minister Ahmed Obaydat, the coalition against the Trade Show rapidly achieved a critical mass and a public consensus. While the controversy over the Parliamentary elections diverted attention for most of 1997, the boycotting parties formed a coalition of National Reform Forces to propose an alternative to the rejected government policies. This National Reform coalition aspired to bring together the traditional opposition and regime loyalists who believed that the treaty threatened Jordanian security, identity, or interests. It planned a National Conference for the summer of 1998, which would present such an alternative; in foreign policy, this entailed a reorientation back toward Arabism, Syria, and Iraq, and away from the United States and Israel.

The debate over normalization has implications for the broader construction of state identity and interests. The regime position combined support for normalization with the valorization of state interest as the highest good. Jordanian identity becomes congruent with subordination to statist interpretations of the national interest; all competing interpretations become, by definition, foreign. Foreign, in turn, becomes discursively restricted to those Palestinian and Arab norms, groups, and interests that in the past had been considered part of the Self. It is the reversal of Self/Other claims that most characterizes the identity struggle inherent in the normalization debate: As liberal opposition figure Toujan Faisal asks: "How can everyone with an opinion contrary to the state be accused of having ties to foreign agents, knowing that this opinion is an Arab nationalist one, and the foreign agents are Arabs, while the 'foreign' they reject is the enemy of the Arab umma. Has the state come to consider Israel 'inside' and Arabs a hostile 'outside'?!?"[38]

Arab Identity and the New Middle East

The struggle over Jordanian identity was embedded within a larger struggle over regional identity; indeed, the transformation of Jordanian identity, institutions, and interests depended to an important degree upon a transformation of regional identity and institutions. The debate over the peace treaty and normalization invoked two sharply competing conceptions of regional order and of state interests. Jordan's embrace of peace with Israel extended to an ambitious agenda for a new regional order. While the debate over a "New Middle East" raged throughout the region, few Arab states had more tangible interests in its achievement (Khuli 1994; Salameh 1995). Were a regional order inclusive of Israel to be established, Jordan would be uniquely well-placed to exploit its close relations with Israel for political influence and to attract foreign investment and assistance. Furthermore, in a region structured around economic cooperation and shared institutions, Jordan's perennial security dilemma would be profoundly reduced. Hussein and Prince Hassan enthusiastically embraced this vision, with the November 1995 Amman Economic Summit marking an important step toward realizing such an institutional vision. This conception of Jordanian interests, in which Israel would provide security, regional influence, and access to economic prosperity, clashed sharply with conceptions of Jordanian interests based on Arabism. While some supporters suggested that Jordan could be a part of the new order without sacrificing its Arab identity, opponents posited the Arab order and the New Middle East as "not only two different concepts but contradictory ones."[39]

The New Middle East is understood in the international public sphere as an economically integrated region free of war, extremism, violence, and turmoil (Peres 1993). Proponents of this position paint grand visions of regional development projects uniting Israeli technical sophistication with Arab natural resources, manpower, and capital. This discourse is presented as a dramatic break from and diametric opposite to the nationalist, military dominant politics of the Arab-Israeli conflict. Despite its visionary image, this project rests on assumptions consistent with the neoliberal position. The envisioned international society is one of rational, sovereign, and radically individuated states pursuing absolute gains through institutionalized cooperation. Strategic interaction between states does not end, but shifts from the military sphere to the economic and cultural sphere. In the Arabist order, conflict and cooperation were mediated by the Arabist public sphere, with interaction rendered meaningful by reference to shared norms embedded in shared identity. The New Middle East would replace this international society with an interest-based community of autonomous actors pursuing common economic interests. The appeal to the common identity of Arab states has no place: cooperation is based on shared interests, not shared identity, while institutions reduce transaction costs and uncertainty rather than expressing shared commitment to norms.

State identity plays a different role in the two conceptions of regional order. In the Arabist order, the state is defined by its Arab identity or lack thereof, such that sovereignty carries different meaning for Arab and non-Arab states. The international system is composed of essentially unlike units:

Arab states differ from non-Arab states. In Middle East order, on the other hand, states are essentially similar units, despite differences in capabilities, political systems, or ethnic identity. Accepting the Middle East description rather than the Arab means abandoning the normative dimensions of the Arab state: there would be no difference between the Arab and the non-Arab state. State interests are primarily defined in economic terms, with no allowance for an articulation of interests based on political or identity considerations. Regional institutions "will encourage people living in the Middle East to see the regional framework as an entity in its own right" (Peres 1993: 111). Thus, membership in the Middle East would replace Arab identity as the source of state interests. International institutions would be built on these assumptions of state identity free of Arab specificity: "Arab states will be required to abolish . . . any agreement which allows a distinction between relations between Arab states and relations with other regional states" (Farhan 1994). In other words, the New Middle East represented a bid to construct a new regional identity, embodied in regional institutions, which would profoundly change the nature of strategic interaction.

Peres proposed replacing Arab-Israeli enmity with a new, common enemy for Israel and Arab regimes: fundamentalism. A new fault line would be drawn to replace the Arab-Israeli divide: the rational, moderate, democratic peacemakers against the fanatical, backward, violent fundamentalists. Hussein's assertion of a Peace Camp identity powerfully articulated what such a vision would look like for Arab states. Where the MENA economic conferences offered an institutional expression of the economic dimension of the New Middle East, the Sharm al-Shaykh anti-terrorism summit of November 1995 embodied the peace camp identity claim. By providing a common enemy, the Peace Camp/Enemies of Peace divide served the agenda of constructing a new shared identity. Even after the collapse of the peace process, King Hussein continued to argue that there existed a large majority in favor of peace, both in Israel and in Jordan, and that Netanyahu did not represent this large majority.

The idea of a New Middle East generated an energetic debate throughout the Arab world (Barnett 1996/1997, 1998). Arab intellectuals debated the implications of a New Middle East, holding high profile conferences and filling the pages of the prestige Arab press. Syria, as the state most profoundly outside the peace process consensus (except for Iraq), viewed the New Middle East in almost purely conflictual terms, emphasizing the dangers of Israeli expansionism and hegemony, and viewing multilateral conferences and economic development schemes as Israeli attempts to move past the unresolved political differences. Egyptian intellectuals and policymakers took a more complicated and communicatively engaged approach to the debate. Like Israel, Egypt hoped for a new regional order; also like Israel, Egypt hoped to be its leader. Egyptian intellectuals saw both dangers and opportunities in a new regional order. After 1995, Egypt increasingly began to call for a revitalized Arab order and became increasingly hostile to Israel (Gerges 1997).

Netanyahu disavowed the idea of a New Middle East, and instead advanced a traditional Realist view of regional politics. For Netanyahu, peace could only follow from the balance of power, interpreted as Israeli strategic superiority; treaties, normalization, and economic interaction could be the fruits of peace, but could not produce peace.[40] No concession should be made that was not forced by the balance of power; no treaty should be signed that might constrain Israel's ability to impose its preferences. After Netanyahu's election, moves toward normalization and a New Middle East ground to a halt. The centerpiece of this vision had been the annual MENA economic summits, which brought together Arab and Israeli officials and private-sector representatives. The first two MENA summits, in Casablanca and Amman, generated great enthusiasm and seemed to be laying the groundwork for the institutionalization and routinization of economic interaction. The third MENA conference, in Cairo, which followed the change in Israel's leadership, was far more politicized than the two earlier summits, and expressed strong condemnation of Israeli behavior. The fourth MENA conference, scheduled in Doha in 1997, generated a long and impassioned debate over whether it would even be held. Coinciding with provocative Israeli actions toward the Palestinians and with a major American-Iraqi confrontation, the Doha summit struck most Arab states as inappropriate. Despite tremendous American pressure, most Arab states boycotted the summit. Jordan attended, but it stood as a clear outlier in the Arab consensus on the issue.

The Jordanian debate over attending the Doha MENA conference powerfully captures the tension between the competing conceptions of Jordanian interests and regional order. On the one hand, most of the Jordanian public sphere embraced the Arabist frame that the MENA process represented normalization and served Israeli interests; hence, participation rewarded Israel, and should be withheld in order to punish it for its behavior in the peace process. On the other hand, Jordanian state officials saw concrete benefits in the MENA process, and wanted to attend in order to continue to attract foreign investment and in order to continue to build a regional infrastructure. These arguments held little power in the Jordanian public sphere, however, particularly given widespread frustration with the lack of economic prosperity since the treaty. The government therefore justified its participation in terms of the principle of *hiwar*: the way to influence Israeli behavior was not to ignore it, but rather to engage with it. Because Jordan had taken a strategic decision for peace, and because it had tied its interests so conclusively to the peace process, it made no sense to boycott Doha. In the end, the Jordanian regime decided to attend, and agreed to the formation of a Jordanian-Israeli industrial zone in Irbid and advanced plans to sign a trade agreement with Israel. The divergence between popular and official conceptions of Jordanian interests, the increasing difficulty of defending the official frame, and the continuing power of the state to carry out its decisions despite public opposition are all demonstrated in this debate.

Consensus Formation: The Disengagement and the Treaty

The peace treaty resembles the severing of ties in its dramatic challenge to the norms, identity, and interests of the Jordanian polity. Where the severing of ties eventually produced consensus, however, the peace treaty thus far has not. Public sphere structure is one important explanation for the variation in outcomes. The disengagement responded positively to the Arab consensus. The decision to surrender political claims to the West Bank and endorse PLO claims satisfied the public demands of an existing Arabist public sphere consensus, and served to harmonize the Jordanian position with that consensus. The peace treaty, by contrast, had an ambiguous relationship to the Arabist public sphere. Since Madrid, most Arab states had accepted the principle of peace with Israel and differed primarily over the acceptable terms of the peace. Jordan's peace move did not respond to a fully formed Arab consensus, but neither did it blatantly contradict an Arab consensus. Jordan assumed an active role in pushing a peace camp that might form a new Arab consensus.

The disengagement took place before the system shocks of the Gulf war and Oslo. While the efficacy of the Arabist sanctions had decreased markedly since the 1960s, they still played an effective role, particularly in the context of such clearly expressed a consensus as that over PLO representation of the Palestinians of the West Bank. The peace treaty, by contrast, followed the profound shocks to the Arabist system, as well as the remarkable development of the Jordanian public sphere in the 1990s, which further muffled the effective influence of Arabist debates on Jordanian behavior. The changes in the Arabist public sphere between 1988 and 1994 had important implications for the unfolding of the two cases.

The cases should also be compared in terms of their relationship to the international public sphere. The disengagement had not been welcome to American and Israeli policymakers, who clung to the idea of a Jordanian final settlement of the West Bank. These commentators stressed the reversibility and tactical nature of the disengagement. The peace, by contrast, was enormously popular in the international public sphere. The decline in the efficacy of the Arabist public sphere noted above coincided with relatively increased salience of international opinion. Much Jordanian discussion of the peace treaty was clearly oriented toward the international public sphere. The sharp contrast between discourse primarily aimed at satisfying the Arabist public [1988] and at satisfying the international public [1994] explains a great deal in the development of the contestation of these two cases. In each case, Jordanian state officials needed to prove the reality of their commitment to the new policy and to convince skeptical publics of their intentions.

The domestic public sphere gained and lost efficacy in direct relation to the shifting salience of the two primary external public spheres. The domestic print public sphere of the 1990s provided a dense, more independent, and more rational-critical national forum for public debate of the peace treaty. By 1994 the days had passed when public debate could be stifled by replacing one or two editors of state-owned newspapers. Comparable stifling of debate in 1994 required a highly contentious and difficult series of measures against numerous independent newspapers. Nevertheless, the similarities in the government–public sphere interaction in the two cases is striking. In 1988, the disengagement brought on an outpouring of impassioned public debate, which the government repressed. The repression of this debate contributed to the buildup of societal pressure which led to the April 1989 explosion of popular discontent that shook the regime. In 1994, the peace treaty brought on an outpouring of impassioned public debate, which the government attempted to repress. The riots of summer 1996 should be seen as a direct response to the growing distortions of the public sphere and the polarization of society.

In the severing of ties, an effective consensus on Jordanian external identity and interests was secured through this public debate. While this consensus did not extend to domestic identity, it provided for stability and consistency in Jordanian policies toward the West Bank itself. Bargaining in the peace process built upon this identity consensus, recasting Jordanian interests in terms of narrow state concerns. In the peace process, by contrast, the regime's vigorous efforts to achieve consensus failed. Two mutually exclusive frames, each claiming to best interpret reality and to articulate Jordanian national interests, continue to compete in the public sphere. The absence of consensus on the new conception of Jordanian identity, Jordanian interests, and the nature of regional order is the most basic fact governing the political process in this period.

8 Abandoning Iraq?

Jordan's behavior toward Iraq after the Gulf War presents an important challenge to constructivism. Between 1991 and 1995 Jordan shifted from Iraq's closest ally to one of its most outspoken critics. For the rationalist, this reversal poses little obvious challenge. As power relations, threats, and incentives shift, states change alliances. After the destruction of Iraqi power, Jordan had little choice but to rebuild its relations with the United States and Israel. Because ties with Iraq proved to be an obstacle to this, Jordan made a rational decision to change sides. For the constructivist, on the other hand, the reversal poses serious challenges. What happened to the constitutive norms and shared identity that led Jordan to side with Iraq in 1990–91? Did popular opinion cease to inform Jordanian behavior? Was a new conception of interests articulated?

In this chapter, I argue that the changes in Jordan's policy toward Iraq followed from the comprehensive redefinition of state identity and interests in the peace process. Peace involved an attempt to redefine Jordan's identity and interests, linking Jordanian policy to a transformation of regional institutions and order. Abandoning the Iraqi regime, which had been demonized by the United States and banished from the Arab order, became necessary in order to manifest this new state identity. Iraq had not become more threatening, nor had its material assets become less valuable. In terms of Jordan's attempt to redefine its international identity, however, Iraqi friendship became a burden rather than an asset. This shift set regime policy in direct opposition to the Arabist consensus secured during the Gulf crisis. Regime and opposition alike recognized that abandoning Iraq signaled a new state identity. The opposition's commitment to Iraq symbolized its mandate to preserve Jordan's Arab identity. The course of events was also deeply shaped by changes in public sphere structure. Rationalist approaches accurately describe Jordanian behavior in this period precisely because the state exerted considerable repressive power in order to insulate itself from the domestic public sphere and thereby pursue interests defined in terms of the international system. The attempt to exogenize interests generated considerable opposition: the new frame hostile to Iraq and the refusal to discuss it in the public sphere led to opposition and instability.

Mending Fences, 1991–1994

In the early 1990s, the Jordanian public sphere enjoyed efficacy, normative primacy, and a relative freedom unique in its history. The Arabist public sphere, fragmented by the Gulf war, had yet to be reformulated. Beyond the bitter resentments between states on the opposite sides of the war, the crisis affected the very existence of the Arabist order as a realm of justification. Jordan's calls for the Arab order to move beyond the ruptures caused by the war received little response. The international public sphere remained hostile because of Jordanian behavior in the Gulf War, although Jordanian participation in the Madrid peace process did begin to rehabilitate Jordan's image. Finally, the Gulf War produced an unprecedented consensus on Jordanian policy within the Jordanian public sphere which was widely credited with having influenced state behavior, which built confidence in the efficacy of public deliberation. Because Palestinians and Jordanians had agreed on Gulf War policy, it served as an important frame promoting national unity. Changes in public sphere structure, as the Jordanian public sphere opened while the international and Arab public spheres closed, shape Jordanian behavior in this period.

Government and opposition alike recognized the heavy economic and political price Jordan had paid for its Gulf War positions, but they disagreed over the appropriate response. The tension between the desire of state policymakers to restore Jordan's position with its traditional Western and Gulf allies and the strong normative commitment to Iraq became more important as Jordan moved to reestablish a place in the American camp. The contradiction manifested itself in the diametrically opposed public stances demanded by the Jordanian and the international public sphere. On the one hand, Saudi Arabia and Kuwait demanded a full Jordanian apology, a confession that its support of Iraq had been politically and even morally wrong. On the other hand, the regime's domestic legitimacy rested in no small part upon its Gulf War policies. The crisis had unified the population around a shared identity, no small achievement for Jordan's traditionally fragmented political society. The regime made much of the hardships Jordan had suffered for its principles, and sought to frame other policies from within this consensus. Jordanian policy rested upon a normative consensus that could not be lightly reversed: Jordan, unlike most other Arab states, had done the right thing during the Gulf crisis. The newly secured Jordanian identity rested upon this defining moment of unity and shared sacrifice. This consensus was reinforced in the press and in the discourse of almost every political party. Maintaining the legitimacy achieved in the Gulf crisis meant maintaining relative alignment between public opinion and foreign policy toward Iraq. Iraq policy therefore served as a leading indicator of Jordan's identity in international, Arab, and domestic public spheres. Maintaining support for Iraq signaled an Arabist identity, while reducing support for Iraq signaled motion toward a "Peace Camp" identity.

Between 1991 and 1995, the Jordanian government tried to reconcile this normative consensus with Western and Gulf demands. Throughout, Jordanian policy adhered to a set of consistently articulated principles: a commitment to maintaining the unity and integrity of the Iraqi state; nonintervention in Iraqi affairs; and humanitarian concern for the Iraqi people. Each of these norms combined interest and principle. Concern for Iraqi unity expressed a real normative commitment to sovereignty, but it also protected Jordan: "We worry about the territorial integrity and unity of Iraq because we shudder to think about the consequences of its dismemberment and the kind of black hole this would produce."[1] All states neighboring Iraq shared this general fear of the chaos that might follow an Iraqi collapse, as well as the increased Iranian power in the Gulf which would ensue.[2] Even after the turn against Iraq, King Hussein continued to emphasize Jordan's interest in Iraqi unity and territorial integrity.[3] Nonintervention in Iraqi affairs also followed a longstanding Jordanian norm, based on its struggles with the intervention of other Arab states in its internal affairs. Humanitarian concern for the Iraqi people was reinforced by the large numbers of impoverished Iraqi refugees and visitors in Amman, as well as comprehensive media coverage of the deterioration of Iraqi living standards. Norms and interest reinforced each other: security fears from an Iraqi collapse; avoiding a precedent of intervention; material economic interests. This should not obscure that these interests were articulated within a normative frame, which linked Jordanian and Iraqi identity, emphasized shared suffering, and increasingly focused on the injustice of seemingly endless international sanctions. This normative consensus, communicatively secured in the Jordanian public sphere, set the boundaries for Jordanian maneuver in the state's efforts to win back Western and Gulf support.

The normative dimension constituted the power and meaning of the interpretive frame justifying support for Iraq. Three issues in particular stand out. First, many Jordanians saw the human misery in Iraq caused by the sanctions as a moral issue. Outraged by the starvation, disease, and poverty caused by the American sanctions, Jordanians set aside personal economic concerns in solidarity with the Iraqi people. Even when Iraq took actions directly harming Jordan, such as its April 1993 declaration that 25 Iraqi Dinar notes would no longer be honored, wiping out $100 million of Iraqi currency held in Jordan, the sanctions frame directed popular anger toward the West and not toward Iraq.[4] Growing disenchantment with Saddam Hussein did not necessarily translate into a diminished identification with the suffering of the Iraqi people or the disappearance of support for Iraq as a normative focus for Arabist and Jordanian identity. The importance of the moral dimension, the outrage at the injustice of Iraqi suffering, should not be minimized; nor should the identification of Jordanians with the suffering Iraqis. Second, most Jordanians saw a double standard in this unprecedented sanctions regime. The fevered efforts to enforce these international resolutions, while dozens of United Nations resolutions related to Israel and the Palestinians remained unenforced, enhanced the "injustice" frame. Third, the blockade of the port of Aqaba struck most Jordanians as an unjustifiable infringement of Jordan's sovereignty, which unfairly singled Jordan out for punishment. Finally, the economic problems Jordan experienced due to the sanctions and the influx of refugees allowed the articulation of a frame linking Iraqi and Jordanian suffering.

Jordan generally complied with the sanctions despite popular opposition and severe costs to its own economy, estimated at $3 billion by the summer of 1998.[5] While the government determined that it could not afford to further antagonize the Americans, its compliance is explained more by compulsion than by persuasion of the normative correctness of the sanctions.[6] The sanctions never enjoyed legitimacy among the Jordanian public. American maneuverings to frustrate the easing the sanctions provided an endless source of outrage for Jordanian writers. In its attempt to balance these demands, the government adhered to the letter of UN resolutions and resisted unilateral American demands.[7] Nevertheless, in June 1993, the Congressional General Accounting Office released a report accusing Jordan of wide-spread violations of the sanctions, shortly before King Hussein was scheduled to meet President Clinton; the report prevented Clinton from approving the release of sequestered funds for Jordan.[8]

King Hussein expressed frustration at the application of sanctions to Jordan, calling the criteria for certification of compliance "vague" and noting that other neighboring countries faced far less rigid monitoring regimes. Jordanians regarded the intrusive inspection regime at the Port of Aqaba as a particular insult to Jordanian sovereignty. While resentful that their government was compelled to honor a blockade they considered unjust, Jordanians were even more outraged that Jordan was singled out as a violator of sanctions. The Aqaba inspections were seen more as punitive toward Jordan than as an instrument to increase the effectiveness of sanctions. Hussein maintained that "the blockade of Aqaba . . . from the beginning was meant to damage Jordan's credibility."[9] Writers raged that Jordan should not engage in peace talks as long as the Jordanian port remained blockaded. Aqaba became framed as "a matter of sovereignty" distinct from the question of sanctions compliance.[10]

The regime made a number of attempts to distance itself from the Iraqi regime and find a place within the international consensus without departing from these norms. In November 1992, King Hussein expressed frustration with Saddam and suggested that the time had come for Iraqis to achieve democracy.[11] While expressing dismay at developments in Iraq, he did not call for the overthrow of the Iraqi regime. In early 1993 he suggested that Saddam Hussein's "relentless grip on power" had become a burden on the Iraqi people and hinted that he personally would step down if he ever became such a burden. The distinction increasingly drawn between the Iraqi regime and the Iraqi people lay the foundations for justifying a future turn against Saddam. These moves foundered upon the reticence of the Gulf states, which did not respond to Jordanian overtures, and the ability of Saddam Hussein's regime to stay in power. Shortly after his November 1992 remarks, Hussein lashed out in frustration at the Kuwaitis and Saudis to remarkably strong public applause, which only reinforced the limited societal interest in Gulf reconciliation compared to societal concern with Iraqi suffering.[12] As long as Jordanian policy remained within the bounds of its normative consensus, it could not satisfy its Arab and international critics.

As Brand (1994) would suggest, state policymakers placed far more emphasis on the need for Gulf financial support and American approval than did most of the public. The public consensus rejected sacrificing Iraq as the price for Gulf reconciliation. As a leading Jordanian columnist put it, "the benefits which might come to Jordan from Saudi Arabia and Kuwait do not justify desecrating our country's policies in the war."[13] Kuwait and Saudi Arabia demanded a clear and unequivocal Jordanian admission that it had been wrong before full relations could be restored. Jordanian political society was intensely proud of Jordan's stance in the Gulf crisis and fiercely opposed any apology. At stake was not material interest but a normative stance. The "magic words" of apology would have likely brought a direct monetary reward. For the Jordanian public, however, such an apology meant a repudiation of precisely the normative consensus that had constituted the new political system. Until the upheaval brought on by the Jordan-Israeli peace treaty, the Jordanian public sphere enjoyed sufficient efficacy to prevent the government from making these symbolic concessions in the international public sphere, even had it wanted to. Officials found themselves on the defensive, forced to reassure the public that Jordanian-Iraqi relations remained strong.[14] The public valued Jordanian norms and its pride in Jordanian honor and courage more than it valued the potential budget subsidies from the Gulf states, to the consternation of those state officials who preferred to pursue material gain over normative values.

The divergence between the public consensus and the international orientations of state policymakers became sharper in 1994. As the peace process advanced toward a Jordanian-Israeli treaty, all other political activity, including relations with Iraq, came to be recast within that frame. Societal actors framed Iraq as the Arabist alternative to Israel and demanded support for Iraq as a signal that the peace process would not cost Jordan its Arab identity. Policymakers resented the efficacy of public opinion in binding its options on Iraq as much as they were infuriated by popular resistance to the movements to peace with Israel. This anger manifested itself in state complaints about the abuse of "responsible" press freedoms. Prime Minister Majali repeatedly "blamed the Jordanian media for continued strains in relations between the Kingdom and the Gulf states," noting that every time relations warmed, an article in the Jordanian press would set off a new crisis.[15] Officials questioned whether "it is a coincidence that just as Jordan tries to improve its relations with a Gulf country, one of our papers publishes a story offensive to it?"[16] After the peace treaty, this criticism escalated into repression, as editors began to be charged with the crime of "insulting a friendly head of state" for publishing articles critical of Gulf monarchies.[17] The strong public reaction to moves related to Iraq and the Gulf clearly revealed the existence of competing conceptions of Jordanian interests. As the peace process sharply polarized Jordanian political society, Iraq policy was invoked in both domestic and foreign policy framing. In addition to the choice between Arab identity and the "Peace Camp," Iraq policy signaled a choice between democracy, defined in terms of the government acting on publicly expressed societal preferences, and authoritarianism, defined in terms of the government acting against these societal preferences. By 1994, a semi-permanent coalition of Arab nationalists, leftists, Islamists, and "old guard" Jordanian nationalists had formed in opposition to Jordan's move to peace and to the attendant crackdown on public freedoms. Where the Gulf crisis forged a powerful state-society consensus, the peace process generated public opposition to the state: "since independence I don't remember a time when there was such complete divergence between regime policies and popular opinion."[18] From 1990–1994, the regime and the opposition engaged within the bounds of the Gulf crisis consensus. After 1994, the consensus broke down, replaced by a broad opposition between societal and state interpretations of Jordanian interests, as manifested in policy toward Israel and Iraq.

The Reversal: 1995–1996

Realism offers a straightforward rationalist explanation of the Jordanian reversal: Jordan bandwagoned with the ascendant Israeli-American pole. Jordan was not balancing against an Iraqi threat or Iraqi power by moving closer to Israel; incremental shifts in Iraqi power were only marginally relevant for Jordanian policy. The growing conviction that the blockade on Iraq would never be lifted as long as Saddam Hussein remained in power facilitated the decision by reducing the expected benefits of the pro-Iraqi policy. More importantly, as the peace process developed, the payoffs of aligning with the Israeli-American coalition seemed to outweigh the dangers of the policy change. The strategic decision to align with Israel, based on a rational calculation of Jordanian interests in a changing regional and international environment, came first. Abandoning Iraq stood as the price of admission. The goals of Jordanian policy were widely understood in three terms: as a move to cement Jordan's position with Israel and the United States and to secure a reconciliation with the Gulf states.

Jordanian policymakers clearly understood important private benefits for the Jordanian state in the new policy. Ties to the Iraqi economy, however lucrative, stood in sharp tension with conceptions of a Middle East market in which Jordan mediated between Israel and the Arab world, and developed a Jordanian-Palestinian-Israeli economic zone. The government came to view economic and political ties to Iraq as a constraint and as a threat, rather than as a benefit. Security, in this new strategic vision, would be achieved through the United States and Israel, against threats posed by Iraq and Syria. Crucially, however, the government could not, and did not, publicly justify its policy in these terms. On the contrary, Jordanian officials framed the new policy in terms of Jordan's concern for the welfare of the Iraqi people and the conviction that Saddam Hussein's regime no longer served their interests. Jordanian discourse also highlighted Iraqi behavior which revealed a lack of concern for Jordanian interests. The reason for this disjuncture between private interest and public discourse lies in the public sphere. Securing Jordan's role in a new regional order required a reformulation of state identity, which meant persuading the Jordanian public with convincing arguments. Official discourse therefore attempted to persuade Jordanians that the Iraqi regime no longer merited Jordanian or Arab support, and that the new policy in fact best served the real interests of the Iraqi people. Much of the Jordanian public rejected these arguments, arguing that Jordan's interests were better served by continued ties with Iraq and a commitment to Arab identity.

The turn against Iraq formed a major part of Jordan's bid to redefine its identity in the international public sphere. The rearticulation of Jordan's identity and interests proved far more successful there than in the Jordanian public sphere, where it remained highly controversial. Abandoning Iraq provided a costly signal of Jordan's real commitment to the peace process and to its alignment with the United States; indeed, the public opposition to the new Iraq policy could be interpreted as increasing the impact of the Jordanian move in the international public sphere, since it demonstrated the regime's commitment even in the face of high domestic costs (Fearon 1994). The success of these efforts can be seen in the appreciative analysis of *The New Republic*: "The King has well atoned for his sin [of supporting Saddam]."[19] By "atoning for his sin," the King, and his Kingdom, could now presumably be allowed back into the company of the righteous, and fit once again within the American frame.

Unable to convince the Jordanian public of its new foreign policies in Israel and Iraq, the regime moved to drastically curtail the Jordanian public sphere. The years after the peace treaty witnessed a sharp decrease of state tolerance of public criticism. The more that international society celebrated Jordanian behavior, the more alienated the Jordanian public became. Hussein complained bitterly about this disjuncture in a heated address to the nation in November 1995. He questioned the value of a public sphere in which critical voices "undermine national unity and blow up everything of value, tarnishing every achievement of this country." Denouncing the public sphere, he said: "I do not feel that there are any media in this country that identify with this country." Blanket denunciations of the Jordanian press by the King, Prime Ministers, and Cabinet officials became a regular feature of Jordanian discourse after 1995. The repressive press laws of 1997 and 1998 demonstrated the regime's determination to reclaim control of the public sphere.

The reversal of Jordanian policy crystallized around the acceptance of two Iraqi defectors on August 11, 1995. To that point Jordan had only tentatively distanced itself from the Iraqi regime. When Hussein welcomed the defectors into Jordan, allowing Saddam's son-in-law Hussein Kamil to hold a dramatic press conference from the Royal Palace, he launched an aggressive campaign to reposition Jordan in the Western camp on the Iraqi issue. Speaking to the Israeli press on August 15, Hussein declared that "the time is now for change in Iraq," a claim he would repeat often in the next few months. The use of the Royal Palace for Kamil's press conference seemed to signal Jordanian support for a campaign to overthrow Saddam Hussein.[20]

On August 23, 1995, Hussein delivered an extraordinary speech to the nation amounting to a manifesto of a new Jordanian policy hostile to the Iraqi regime: "a second White Book . . . rewriting the history of Jordanian-Iraqi relations . . . [and] banishing all the norms of Jordanian discourse."[21] After reviewing Jordanian-Iraqi ties over the years, Hussein slammed the Iraqi leadership for repeatedly ignoring his advice and breaking explicit promises by invading Kuwait. He complained that Iraq had consistently disregarded Jordanian interests, during the Gulf war and after, especially by launching SCUD missiles through Jordanian airspace and exposing Jordan to the danger of Israeli retaliation. The next day, a senior Jordanian official confirmed that "the break with Baghdad is now sealed, totally and brutally."[22] An effusion of cables of support followed, a Jordanian political tradition reserved for unpopular policy decisions. After the reversal, the King regularly attacked Iraqi behavior as deliberately harmful to Jordanian interests, in a concerted effort to disassociate Jordanian and Iraqi identity and interests and to undercut the positive identification between the two states. While always emphasizing his deep concern for the suffering of the Iraqi people, Hussein argued that the interests of the Iraqi people were no longer served by their leadership.

The United States guaranteed Jordanian security against Iraqi retaliation for this breaking of relations. This display of American deterrence bore little relation to the behavior of Iraq, which publicly and privately assured Jordan that it had no intention of attacking in revenge.[23] Tariq Aziz, the senior Iraqi diplomat, insisted that "the claims of Iraqi threats to Jordan are an American invention." Dependent on Jordan for food and medicine, and weakened by sanctions and the inspection regime, Iraq posed no real threat to Jordan. Constructing such an Iraqi threat helped to justify a closer United States-Israel-Jordan alignment, however. The Jordanian public expressed extreme skepticism, asserting that they felt no threat from Iraq and would not accept efforts at constructing such a threat.[24] The difficulty the regime faced in convincing public opinion of this threat has interesting implications for rationalist models of threat balancing; based on divergent conceptions of state identity and the social meaning of relations with Iraq, the government and the public expressed profoundly different perceptions of threat. In fact, the threat perceived by many Jordanians was that Jordan would get drawn in to an American plot to destabilize Iraq. In other words, Jordanians showed more concern that Jordan might threaten Iraq than that Iraq threatened Jordan!

The Americans pushed Jordan to go even farther, suggesting that Jordan cut economic ties with Iraq and become a base for operations aimed at overthrowing Saddam Hussein. Jordan rejected these suggestions, but still decisively moved into an anti-Iraqi position.[25] The Jordanian reversal sharply improved American-Jordanian relations, already strong in the wake of the Israel treaty. Clinton Administration officials argued that "King Hussein is demonstrating great courage as he takes a stalwart stand against the regime of Saddam Hussein . . . [he has] initiated a series of actions . . . that have decisively distanced Jordan from the Iraqi dictator."[26] Based on Jordan's new policies, Congress approved long-withheld arms sales (including F-16 fighter planes), and military and intelligence cooperation escalated dramatically.[27] Commentators in the international press agreed that the turn against Iraq, along with Hussein's embrace of a warm peace with Israel, had secured Jordan a more central role in American strategy. In 1997, Jordan became an American "major non-NATO ally," the first Arab country to enjoy such status. American aid increased to $225 million a year, in recognition of Jordan's importance as a dependable ally within America's generally crumbling Middle East policy. The United States encouraged Kuwait and Saudi Arabia to restore relations with Jordan, albeit still with limited success. Jordan allowed U.S. warplanes to be based in southern Jordan in order to train Jordanian pilots, although the government denied that there would be a permanent U.S. presence or that the planes would be used to monitor southern Iraq.[28] In April 1996, Jordanian and American forces conducted well-publicized joint maneuvers, which the public found particularly distressing because they coincided with the Israeli assault on Lebanon.

The Jordanian government took numerous practical steps to back up its new discourse. Border controls with Iraq were tightened, along with stricter enforcement of residence visa regulations for the tens of thousands of Iraqis who had sought refuge in Amman. Jordanian customs agents seized several shipments of parts allegedly intended for missiles and chemical weapons and turned them over to UN inspectors. Trade with Iraq was slashed in half, to the consternation of Jordanian business sectors. The government also took measures to "reduce Iraqi influence," including the expulsion of embassy staff and a campaign against pro-Iraq journalists.

Economic relations could not be severed as cleanly as political relations, however. Jordan's economic relations with Iraq went beyond the trade networks that bound many societal actors to the Iraqi market. State actors hoped to reduce the centrality of the Iraqi market for the Jordanian economy, but could not easily live without the oil Iraq provided at half the world market price. In August 1995, a Jordanian official claimed that Jordan had many alternatives to Iraqi oil, and over the next few weeks both Kuwait and Saudi Arabia floated proposals to replace the Iraqi supply. The Jordanian Energy Minister then pointedly canceled a planned visit to Baghdad to extend the oil protocol. Iraq reportedly made a better offer, though, and the Gulf countries proved hesitant to follow through. By late September, despite American reservations, the oil deal was quietly signed.[29] Such gambits to replace Iraqi oil recurred regularly over the next few years, often around the time of the renegotiation of the Jordanian-Iraqi oil protocols. All failed, and Jordanian-Iraqi oil relations continued.

In November 1995, Hussein met with Iraqi opposition leaders in London, and offered Jordan as a base for political (but not military) activities. Several prominent Iraqi defectors took up residence in Amman, establishing political and information offices.[30] The Iraqi National Accord [al-Wifaq] set up a radio station broadcasting violent denunciations of Saddam Hussein into Iraq. While the government insisted that no armed activities would be permitted, most observers felt that a line had been crossed and that Jordan was now actively involved in the effort to topple Saddam Hussein.[31] Press reports indicated Jordanian involvement in a failed CIA sponsored coup attempt based in the Kurdish autonomous zones. On the other hand, press reports also regularly surfaced of Iraqi attempts to subvert Jordanian stability, with

Iraq being accused for virtually every unsettling incident in the Kingdom.

In September 1995, Hussein called on the Iraqi people to unite, "restore democracy," and end their suffering. In November 1995, a flurry of activity whirled around Hussein's proposal, later disavowed, to turn Iraq into a federation of its Sunni, Shi'a, and Kurdish components with a weak central government. The proposal was interpreted in part as a bid for a Hashemite restoration, appealed to nobody in particular, and was dropped. Speculation about Jordanian ambitions in Iraq, whether through a Hashemite restoration or through a territorial partition of Iraq, circulated widely despite Jordanian denials.[32] In December 1995, Hussein noted that "I cannot see any ray of hope . . . because the [Iraqi] leadership will not enter into a dialogue which would help us lift the blockade." King Hussein stepped up his attacks on Saddam after Kamil's return to Baghdad and brutal murder in February 1996. Jordan remained within fairly clear limits, despite this heightened campaign: focusing its attacks on the Iraqi regime, justifying its opposition to Saddam Hussein on the basis of its concern for the Iraqi people, and opposing any outside intervention or partition of Iraq.

King Hussein tried to rally Arab leaders in support of an activist policy to bring about change in Iraq. These Jordanian initiatives soon foundered, however. Syria and Egypt, who both wanted Iraq to be constrained but not destroyed, issued a strong joint warning to Jordan against intervening in Iraqi affairs. Hostile media campaigns followed, reminiscent of Egyptian-Jordanian media wars over the Gulf War, until a "media ceasefire" in September 1995.[33] In February 1996, Mubarak secured a commitment from King Hussein to not intervene in Iraq. After a mini-summit convened by Egypt in May 1996, Jordan backed farther away from its calls for change in Iraq, as the Arab states looked to close ranks in the face of Israeli behavior.[34] An Arab consensus gradually emerged welcoming Jordan's denunciation of the Iraqi regime but rejecting any active efforts to bring down Saddam Hussein. Egypt seemed most worried that King Hussein's increasingly prominent role in American and Israeli strategy could come at the expense of Egyptian influence. This concern predated the Iraq reversal: Mubarak had brought together Syria and Saudi Arabia, pointedly excluding Hussein, as early as January 1995 in Alexandria to demonstrate Egyptian displeasure with the Western rehabilitation of Jordan. Syria feared the disruptive effects of upheaval in Iraq and worried about the emergence of a pro-American, anti-Syrian regime in Baghdad. Furthermore, Syria saw the American-Jordan embrace as a move to increase pressure in the Israeli-Syrian peace talks; relations between Syria and Jordan were often extremely tense in this period.

Only in the Cairo Summit (June 1996) did Asad and King Hussein meet and calm the tensions, putting a temporary end to hostile media campaigns and Jordanian accusations of Syrian subversive activities in Jordan. The Syrian-Iraqi decision to open borders in the summer of 1997 alarmed Jordan, which feared for both economic and political interests in such a reconciliation.

The Gulf states still proved unresponsive to the Jordanian gambit. Kuwait proved intransigent in its refusal to normalize relations with Jordan, sparking fierce resentment among Jordanians who saw the sacrifice of ties with Iraq going in vain.[35] Each time relations seemed to improve, some rift would reappear, usually instigated by Kuwaiti politicians or media figures whose hostility to "Iraqi allies" in the war was as normatively central to postwar Kuwaiti policy as Jordanian sympathy for Iraq was normatively central to Jordan. In September 1995, attempts at rapprochement were interrupted by sharp Kuwaiti criticism. Occasional signs of warming relations, such as the release of Jordanian prisoners or mid-level official visits, failed to bring about a general normalization between the two states. In February 1996, when Kabariti became Prime Minister, there seemed to be some progress, but it quickly faded; King Hussein announced confidently that Jordanian-Kuwaiti normalization had begun and would not stop. By June 1996, the Jordanian press was lambasting Kabariti for his embarrassingly futile efforts to win over the Kuwaitis.[36] A poll published in Kuwait's *al-Watan* in September 1995 found that Kuwaitis opposed normal relations with Jordan by a 51%-32% margin.[37] The Kuwaiti press and Parliament regularly aired harsh criticisms of Jordan that hindered the willingness of some decisionmakers to even consider reconciliation.

The emergence of an Arab consensus against external interference in Iraqi internal affairs reined in Jordanian activity. Jordan was forced to defend itself in the Arab public sphere, and ultimately adjusted its positions and its behavior in order to fit into the Arab consensus. Because of its interest in rehabilitation in the Arabist public sphere in order to restore relations with the Gulf, and because of its consistently expressed interest in restoring Arab dialogue, Jordan could not ignore the demands of Arabist argumentation. Jordan could neither ignore nor carry the Arab debates over its turn against Iraq. This is ironic, because in many ways the Jordanian reversal put it in line with rather than outside the Arab consensus. The inability of Jordanian discourse to establish its own authoritative interpretation was partly due to the counter-interpretations of others, but was also caused by its own inconsistencies. Insisting that Jordan's policy had not fundamentally changed—

both to placate domestic critics and to reinterpret Jordan's past behavior—undermined the new frame.[38]

The primary source of the redefinition of Jordanian identity and interests was the international, especially American and Israeli, public sphere. Jordan engaged with the Arabist public sphere, and attempted to place its new position within the Arabist consensus, but its policy emerged from the developing peace camp identity. Its moderation of its hostility toward Iraq coincided with the collapse of the peace process and its vision of transformed regional order and the revival of inter-Arab cooperation. After the election of Netanyahu and the crisis of the peace process, an Arab order began to reemerge. In June 1996, the first Arab summit since the Gulf Crisis convened in Cairo to discuss the implications of the change in Israeli leadership. Iraq was not invited to the summit, indicating its continuing isolation from the Arab order, but Jordan participated enthusiastically. In the summer of 1997, Syrian–Iraqi rapprochement indicated the possibility of the reincorporation of Iraq into an Egyptian-Syrian-Gulf regional order; this did not immediately happen, but speculation in the Arab media continued. During the November 1997 showdown between the United States and Iraq over the inspection of weapons production sites, no Arab state expressed willingness to join American military activity. This wholesale refusal signaled the death of Arab support for a coalition against Iraq, despite continuing hostility toward and fear of Saddam's regime. The coincidence of the Iraq crisis and the general Arab boycott of the Doha MENA economic conference with Israel demonstrated the linkage between the two arenas.

As the Arab order began to reappear, Jordan tentatively renewed contacts with the Iraqi leadership, albeit at lower levels of intimacy. Iraq's acceptance of UN Resolution 986 ("Oil for Food") made it seem less likely that Saddam's fall was nigh, as Hussein had gambled. The recognition of shared interests demanded functional cooperation, oddly reminiscent of Jordanian-Israeli relations in the past, without a return to any articulation of shared identity. Jordan's relations with Israel and close ties to the United States now represented the boundaries on its action. King Hussein attempted to use this position to mediate between Iraq and the United States, meeting with President Clinton and calling for direct American-Iraqi dialogue. In the November 1997 and the January 1998 crises, Hussein actively worked for a diplomatic solution. Jordanian officials emphasized that King Hussein was not a mediator between the two sides, since "we have no interest in it, and we have our own differences with Iraq."[39] King Hussein met with a number of high-level Iraqi officials and exchanged several letters with Saddam Hussein in this period. Even as Jordan worked to prevent the renewal of military hostilities and to bring about such a dialogue, however, it continued to work against Jordanian-Iraqi positive identification, banning pro-Iraqi rallies, arresting pro-Iraqi activists, and maintaining its discourse of distrust for the Iraqi regime. King Hussein continued to refer to Iraqi disregard for Jordanian interests, and continued to justify Jordanian behavior in terms of concern for the Iraqi people, not for the Iraqi regime.

Jordanian Public Sphere

The Jordanian public sphere seized on the reversal as not simply a decision with questionable implications for state interests but as one with profound implications for state identity. As a prominent Islamist writer noted, "this is a retreat from all declared Jordanian political norms . . . to the extent that even discussing these norms is seen as provocative!"[40] The opposition brought their objections into the public sphere and forced the government to articulate and defend its new policies: "The Jordanian public must raise their voices and repeat what they say in their private conversations. . . . The government knows that as long as the opposition continues to whisper, then the field is open for it alone to make the necessary changes by reversing the nation's constant principles, beliefs, and cultural identity."[41] Objections were framed in terms of generalizable Jordanian interests. By framing the reversal as the inevitable consequence of the peace treaty, the opposition successfully linked the two issues in the political arena. The opposition coalition regularly called for an end to the sanctions on Iraq and denounced policies hostile to Iraq almost as frequently as it denounced normalization with Israel. In this frame, Iraq stood as the leading symbol of the Arab identity abandoned by the regime in its pursuit of cooperation with Israel.

The new policy caused a split within the ruling elite, much of which had built personal, political and business ties to Iraq during the long years of close alliance.[42] Hussein's appointment of Kabariti's "White Revolution" government in February 1996 seems to have been a pointed step toward the removal of the "old guard," viewed as too closely tied to Iraq and too closed-minded with regard to relations with Israel. Kabariti, the architect of the Iraq reversal as Foreign Minister, was seen as hostile to the Iraqi regime, close to King Hussein, and well-placed to execute Hussein's vision of Jordanian interests. Kabariti's appointment was interpreted as a major departure in Jordanian politics, intimately bound to the new foreign policy and to the domestic stalemate in the struggle over foreign policy. The spokesman of the Islamic Action Front made identity his primary concern after the dismissal of Sharif Zayd's government: "We want a government that understands the identity of the *umma* [nation] and preserves this identity."[43] Kabariti's appointment, by contrast, signaled a concerted struggle for a changed conception of Jordan's identity and interests. The Parliamentary confidence debate and press discussion of the new Prime Minister focused debate on Jordan's Arab identity.

The extent of elite dissatisfaction shows the degree to which the reinterpretation of Jordanian interests came from the very top levels alone and the regime's failure to persuade the public of its strategic vision. Jordanian policymakers, increasingly oriented to the international system and hostile to the dominant trends expressed in the Jordanian public sphere, derived their conceptions of Jordan's interests from the international sphere. By 1997, especially after Abd al-Salam al-Majali replaced Kabariti, Jordanians complained that the government seemed intent on rejecting anything the public demanded, whether in foreign or domestic policy. The regime had come to view the Jordanian public sphere as a hostile entity, to be engaged in strategic battle, rather than as a partner in deliberation. The desire to forge closer ties with the United States and Israel took priority over the interest in nurturing a Jordanian consensus. The Jordanian public sphere continued to serve as a primary source of norms, identity, and interests for most Jordanians, however. The conflict over foreign policy therefore reflected a deeper struggle over the place of the public sphere and over Jordan's identity.

Opposition to the reversal considered both interests and identity. First, commentators asked what Jordanian interest was served by fomenting instability in Iraq, especially since the Jordanian government had often publicly asserted a Jordanian interest in maintaining Iraqi unity and territorial integrity. Second, the opposition cast the reversal in terms of Jordan's Arab identity, claiming that the new policy replaced Iraq with Israel and foolishly severed Jordan from its true Arab identity. The opposition reiterated the Gulf Crisis frame which defined Arab identity in terms of Iraq. Third, the opposition pointed to potential economic losses from any fallout with Iraq. Finally, the opposition asked for evidence of any positive benefits from the decision, pointing specifically to Kuwaiti and Saudi behavior as indicative.

The resistance to the reversal on Iraq encompassed virtually all sectors of public opinion, bridging most political differences: "while every salon has a different dangerous scenario, all agree that Jordan faces serious danger."[44] By positing the reversal as the logical and inevitable consequence of the peace treaty, the opposition expanded its coalition and further embedded its interpretive frame. The weekly press served as the most important channel for the expression of opinion, demanding explanations of official policy and expressing normative outrage over every deviation from the popular consensus in support of Iraq.

Civil society organizations played an important role in expressing public opinion. The Professional Associations, cultural associations, women's organizations and political parties were outspoken in their condemnation of state policy toward Iraq. Even the normally apolitical Chamber of Commerce joined in the criticism. The coalition of opposition political parties released regular statements challenging official policies and questioning their justifications, while affirming that the Jordanian public continued to adhere to its normative commitment to Iraq. In June 1996 a "Popular Jordanian Delegation" toured Iraq to express Jordanian solidarity. The Delegation, which included over seventy leading political figures from these civil society institutions, declared that it "represented most sectors of society and expressed the position of the majority of the Jordanian people."[45] Explicitly claiming that official Jordanian positions were not those of the Jordanian people, the Delegation made a powerful bid to contest state primacy in the articulation of state identity and interests. In the summer of 1998, a broad coalition of opposition forces made a central plank of their draft national charter an appeal to redirect Jordanian foreign policy away from the United States and Israel and back toward Iraq and the Arab order.[46]

Parliament, with a pro-government majority, was unable to check government decisions. It did provide a platform for heated debate, however, which forced the government to clearly articulate and defend its policies. In August 1995, Prime Minister Zaid bin Shakir explained government policy to a contentious Parliament; public sphere discussion of this session clearly indicated his failure to convince many Jordanians with his arguments. During Kabariti's confidence vote, Iraq policy occupied a central position in the debate.[47] Liberal MP Taher al-Masri warned passionately against cutting Jordan off from its Arab community. According to Masri, adhering to Jordanian norms of nonintervention and support for Iraqi unity served Jordanian security and stability: "any call to change Jordan's strategic and economic ties from Arab to Middle Eastern threatens to isolate Jordan from its Arab identity and community."[48] Islamist MP Bisam al-Amoush responded forcefully to Kabariti's definition of Jordanian interests, asserting that "we stand against this . . . and we represent the pulse of the Jordanian street, which rejects these developments toward Iraq." In an unprecedented joint statement by 53 deputies during the confidence debate over a new Prime Min-

ister in October 1998, a Parliamentary majority demanded that the government step back from its relations with Israel and restore its relations with
Iraq. Shortly thereafter, 46 MPs issued a resolution demanding specifically
that Jordan end the sanctions against Iraq and work to restore Jordan's Arab
relations. Such exchanges forced the government to publicly articulate and
defend its conceptions of Jordan's foreign policy interests, even if they could
not compel the government to alter its policies.

From the political economy perspective, the domestic conflict might be
interpreted in terms of a contradiction between the trade interests of Jordanian businessmen in Iraq against the budget-subsidy–seeking state (Brand
1994). The behavior of the state could plausibly be interpreted as rent-seeking behavior, with state actors preferring Gulf and American subsidies to the
Iraqi market. Economic sectors with interests in the Iraqi market naturally
cared more for maintaining the Iraqi market than about the Gulf. There is
substantial evidence of such a conflicting understanding of economic interests. Jordanian businessmen feared that the anti-Iraq policy would cost them
the privileged position in a reopened Iraqi market for which they had so
patiently waited. As noted above, however, the Jordanian state also had considerable economic interests in relations with Iraq, notably the access to Iraqi
oil. This complicates any direct inference of state preferences. The state
budget could not easily live without the oil Iraq provided at half the world
market price. While Jordanian officials claimed that Jordan had many alternatives to Iraqi oil, and Kuwait and Saudi Arabia floated proposals to replace
the Iraqi supply, none materialized and Jordan maintained its oil deal with
Iraq.[49]

The sanctions had a mixed impact on the Jordanian economy. On the
one hand, the sanctions cost Jordan some 25 percent of its foreign markets
in 1991 alone.[50] Despite the problems caused by the war and the mass return
of expatriates, however, the Jordanian economy in many ways boomed in
the early 1990s. The returnees placed great strain on housing and services,
but at the same time brought substantial capital and skills with them. Their
demand for housing set off a boom in construction which transformed Amman. Furthermore, the sanctions distorted the economy, especially among
those sectors geared toward the Iraqi market, by the artificial monopoly access to Iraq created by the sanctions. A report prepared by the Amman
Chamber of Commerce in January 1996 documented the development of
Iraq as a valuable trading partner, even under the weight of the sanctions.
According to this report, in the first eight months of 1995 no less than 50
percent of Jordanian manufactured exports went to the Iraqi market.[51] De-

spite the sanctions, Iraq remained Jordan's largest trading partner into 1997 despite official slashing of trade protocols over Iraqi nonpayment of debt.[52]

While trade created profits for some businesses, state decisionmakers had reservations about whether it constituted a viable foundation for Jordan's political economy. The conflict over the meaning of Jordanian-Iraqi relations extended to a reinterpretation of the value of Jordanian-Iraqi economic relations. Businessmen, who amassed considerable profits from trade with Iraq even under sanctions, had a rather different perspective than state policymakers, who expressed increasing doubts about the merits of the Iraqi market. Even in the 1980s, trade with Iraq depended on Jordan's provision of export credits, on which Iraq had amassed a billion dollar debt (Brand 1994: 223–25). While businesses prospered, the state was losing money, actively subsidizing the private sector profits. While this provides a material basis for the state-society differences over Jordanian interests, this should not be taken too far. The state also profited from the Iraqi connection through discounted Iraqi oil, bartered at prices less than half of the world market price. Therefore, a direct inference that Jordanian economic interests as interpreted by the state drove the abandonment of Iraq is difficult to sustain.

The economic dimension of the relationship with Iraq involved political and normative framing. The Jordanian-Iraqi trade relationship was both an expression of and a force in creating the shared identity of the two states: "the organic ties have formed this class into Iraqi allies who oppose any move to reorient the Jordanian economy," regardless of potential profits elsewhere.[53] Writers heaped scorn on the idea that "our brotherly relations with Iraq are based on trade or oil deals and that they will end if the trade or oil stops."[54] For these Jordanians, a common identity bound Iraq and Jordan together, rather than self-interest. In other words, economic interests took on political meaning through the process of interpretation within a master frame of shared identity.

As the struggle over state identity escalated in 1995, economic interests in Iraq took on new meaning, as the regime came to interpret economic ties to Iraq as a threat and a constraint rather than as a benefit. The search for new markets to replace the Iraqi market reflected the new identity frame, which identified Jordan's interests in building an economy oriented toward Israel and Palestine. This conception of Jordan's economic interests followed from the new positions on identity, not from overwhelming economic analysis or evidence. Ties to the Iraqi economy stood in sharp tension with the visions of an emergent Middle East market in which Jordan mediated between Israel and the Arab states and developed Jordanian-Palestinian-Israeli integration. The conflict over Jordan's economic future reflected the political struggle over Jordanian identity: Arab or Middle Eastern? Iraq or Israel?

Jordanian policymakers faced a strategic choice about the future of the Jordanian political economy, crudely summarized as a choice between facing east or facing west. The tight Jordanian-Iraqi interconnections bound the Jordanian economy to certain kinds of production and left it dependent on a single market. With the peace treaty, Jordanian planners—notably Prince Hassan—envisioned a Jordan at the center of a rapidly developing Middle Eastern regional market. "[For these] ambitions of becoming a center of regional economic activities. . . . Jordanian relations with Saddam Hussein are a major obstacle."[55] It is highly suggestive that Jordan's break with Iraq came two months before the Amman Economic Summit, heralded in Jordanian official discourse as the foundation of the Middle East market. In other words, the break with Iraq had an economic dimension, but as mediated through identity.

In August 1996, Jordan's south erupted in riots reminiscent of 1989, sparked by the government's IMF-mandated decision to remove bread subsidies. While the army controlled the riots and restored stability, the events struck deep into the political and social system. King Hussein blamed Iraqi agents for igniting the conflict, to the extreme skepticism of virtually all observers and participants.[56] Others classified the riots as a typical reaction to IMF demands. A more convincing explanation lay in the combination of escalating economic hardship, exacerbated by the closing of the Iraqi market, and the increasing repression of the public sphere. The level of political frustration over the peace treaty with Israel, the turn against Iraq, the impotence of Parliament and the harassment of press and civil society, was evident to everyone. Faced with decreasing opportunities for both economic survival and political expression, Jordanians took to the streets. It is intriguing that the government chose to frame the unrest in terms of Iraq, in order to discredit the protesters as well as to further drive a wedge between Jordan and Iraq. Iraq denied involvement, accusing Jordan of "trying to blame Iraq for its internal problems," and leaders of the protests framed their demands almost entirely in terms of domestic policy.

The relationship between the Jordanian government's commitment to new regional structures and its policies toward Iraq is demonstrated by the impact of the deterioration of the peace process on Jordan's Iraq policy. As the international consensus on the sanctions regime frayed, and the United States and Iraq engaged in a series of tense military showdowns, Jordan began to renew its calls for an end to the sanctions and for an American-

Iraqi dialogue. Relations between Jordan and Iraq remained tense, despite Jordan's diplomatic efforts in this regard, as Jordanian officials sought to prevent a resurgence of positive identification between the two states. In December 1997, the Iraqi execution of four Jordanian students for smuggling aroused considerable furor in Jordan. The government gleefully exploited the crisis, attempting to whip up popular hostility to Iraq to muster popular support for its policy. Despite the claim by an Iraqi defector that the executions were in fact in retaliation for Jordanian involvement in a foiled coup attempt, public anger did indeed mount. Several weeks later, an Iraqi diplomat and three others were murdered in spectacular fashion, in what many observers interpreted as a sign that "internal Iraqi battles are being waged on the streets of Amman."[57]

In January 1998, the Iraqi government directly appealed to the Jordanian public by releasing all Jordanians in Iraqi prisons "because of its deep respect for the Jordanian people." Rather than release the prisoners to a representative of the Jordanian government, the Iraqi government chose Layth Shubaylat, an outspoken critic of Jordanian foreign policy. While the official media could not ignore the release of prisoners, it downplayed Shubaylat's role and tried to minimize the significance of the Iraqi action.[58]

The difficulties of abandoning Iraq, and the importance of public sphere argumentation, can be seen in Jordanian policy during the U.S.-Iraqi crisis of February 1998. During this crisis, Jordan again tried to play a mediating role, warning against the use of military force and calling for a diplomatic solution. As in 1990, Jordan feared the consequences of a military confrontation, sealing the border to prevent refugee flows and working for a diplomatic solution. Unlike 1990, where the government allowed free expression to public opinion, however, in 1998 the government now tightly controlled popular mobilization. On February 11, the government announced that all rallies, under any slogan and for any purpose, would be banned. Security forces broke up a massive pro-Iraq rally at the Husayni Mosque in Amman on February 14. On February 16, Ma'an and other Jordanian cities erupted in violent uprisings which were put down by the army. Mass arrests and a round-the-clock curfew were imposed on the cities. Deputy Prime Minister Abdullah al-Nasour again blamed Iraq for the growing unrest in Jordan.[59] This restrictive policy denied the right of opposition groups to rally public opinion in support of Iraq as they had in 1990.

The February 1998 crisis showed the sharp divergence between popular and official positions toward Iraq, but it also suggested that completely abandoning Iraq might be beyond the capabilities of Jordanian policy. In No-

vember 1997, the linkage between the American confrontation with Iraq
and the collapsing Arab-Israeli peace process demonstrated the need to re-
formulate policies on both fronts. Jordan's turn against Iraq depended on
the peace process and the construction of new regional economic and security structures; the collapse of those efforts undermined Jordan's Iraq policy. King Hussein lobbied the United States to rethink its policies toward
Iraq, appealing for a direct American-Iraqi dialogue. Given the failure to
bring about a change in Iraq's regime, and the ongoing importance of Iraq
to the Jordanian economy, Jordan moderated its overt hostility. The near
collapse in the Palestinian-Israeli peace process pushed Jordan back to an
Arabist policy. As the peace process collapsed, so did the main justification
for the new policy toward Iraq.

Rationalist and Constructivist Explanations

While the rationalist perspective can explain the broad contours of the
strategic realignment, it neglects important dimensions of the Iraqi-Jordanian relationship and its role in Jordanian politics. Jordan's relations with Iraq
extended deeply into the political identity of Jordanians and into the norms
and structures of the Jordanian polity. Support for Iraq involved an expression of the Arab identity which structured Jordanian political discourse, as
well as economic and civil society institutions built around the principle of
Iraqi-Jordanian cooperation and unity. These ties transcended a convergence of interests.

Relations with Iraq stood symbolically for the Arabist identity threatened
by the move to peace with Israel and the calls for a Middle Eastern identity.
The Gulf crisis transformed the alliance with Iraq into a central dimension
of Jordan's self-interpretation of its Arab identity. Jordan's decision to stand
by Iraq consolidated the Jordanian public, giving meaning to an Arab identity even as the Arab order collapsed. Enjoying virtual consensus and universally interpreted as the expression of the popular will, the policy bound
the public together. Rallies of solidarity with the Iraqi people and calls to
lift the UN embargo could always be counted on to unite a public deeply
divided over many issues. Support for Iraq in the war served as a foundation
myth for Jordanian democracy, a moment of unity which overpowered the
potent Jordanian-Palestinian, urban-tribal, or state-society cleavages that had
always informed competing interpretations of the Jordanian polity. In this
myth—and calling it a myth does not imply that it was not largely true, but
only describes its function as a normative locus in the public sphere—the

Jordanian people were revealed as a unified whole by the consensus decision to stand by its Arabist identity and principles. Shared economic and political suffering only confirmed this identity-securing myth.

Shifting these alliances involved more than changes in the balance of power. The shift away from Iraq and toward Israel represented a bid to alter the foundations of Jordanian identity. Without winning public consensus on these new identity claims, the Jordanian government could not guarantee stability. The challenge of Jordanian politics in this period has been the struggle to find a workable consensus on Jordanian identity and interests that could legitimate the international alliances chosen by King Hussein in response to American hegemony. The fundamental question for the Jordanian polity is whether such a consensus could be reached through public sphere debate, or whether the state would have to exert power to restrict or even shut down the public sphere. The latter route, while within the short-term power of the state, would shatter the normative unity and the public sphere legitimacy gained in the first half of the decade.

The rationalist explanation of the reversal of Iraq policy specifies the shifting incentives in the international and regional system, and correctly suggests the strategic motivations behind state decisions. This explanation remains seriously incomplete, however, if it fails to consider the nature of the public contestation of the policy and the impact on the Jordanian polity of these debates. Far from representing the self-interested action of a unified Jordan, the reversal attempted to restructure dominant interpretations of Jordanian identity and interests within the Jordanian public sphere. This interpretation, by locating the dynamic of change within public sphere struggles, opens the way to considering the relative weight of multiple public spheres, in this case primarily the Jordanian and the international. In 1994, with the signing of the peace treaty, state policymakers made a clear decision to grant primacy to the international public sphere as a source of interests. The reversal of positions on Iraq continued this logic, with state decisionmakers primarily oriented toward international public spheres. In the intense struggles that followed, the Jordanian public demanded recognition of its competing definition of interests. The state chose to repress the Jordanian public sphere rather than submit its policies to public deliberation. This decision, and the ability of the state to implement it in the short term, explains why rationalist models are useful in this case.

While the rationalist perspective can explain Jordan's strategic realignment, it neglects important dimensions of the Iraqi-Jordanian relationship and its role in Jordanian politics. Positions toward Iraq and Israel extended deep into the political identity of Jordanians and into the norms and structures of the Jordanian polity. Enmity to Israel and affinity with Iraq went beyond the calculation of interests, power or threat, constituting Jordanian identities, world views, and interpretation of interests. The master frame in which these norms and identities were embedded underlay the decisions concerning the economy, the political system, and civil society. The peace treaty and the turn against Iraq failed to generate and institutionalize a new consensus. The failure of this project of transformation, along with the failure to achieve the desired international results, prevented enmity to Iraq from being institutionalized.

9   Identity and the Politics of Public Spheres

Jordan's political history in the decade following the severing of ties offers an exceptional case of the relationship among internal and external identity contestation, interest formation, and political behavior. Contested identity in the political struggles over the peace process, the severing of ties, and relations with Iraq shaped Jordanian articulation of interests and understandings of international and regional order. Changes in public sphere structure at both the domestic and regional levels clearly affected Jordan's behavior. Change and continuity alike follow from the process of consensus formation within public sphere structures. By challenging the assumption of preference stability central to rationalist models and specifying the conditions under which identity and interests are likely to change, the public sphere approach can enrich both rationalist and constructivist arguments.

The development of the public sphere concept and the close examination of the Jordanian cases aimed at establishing linkages among identity, interests, and international political behavior. Rather than either holding state identity and interests constant at all times or presenting them as in perpetual flux, I have argued that they become subject to change at those points when an open public sphere permits the appearance of public deliberation oriented toward questioning consensus norms. After the severing of ties and the democratic opening of 1989, state identity became the explicit subject of intense contestation by state and societal actors in a national public sphere. As the public sphere opened and identity emerged as a primary source of contention, actors set forth competing interpretive frames in an effort to establish and institutionalize a new consensus on the purpose of Jordanian action. Conceptions of the Jordanian national interest followed from the contestation and consolidation of state identity within a newly active, open and effective public sphere. Change in public sphere structure, in this case a nascent Jordanian public sphere uniquely insulated from frag-mented Arabist public spheres, provided the structural underpinnings of change in behavioral and discursive outcomes. The repression of the public sphere and the increasing resort to state power rather than open debate after the peace treaty, in contrast, produced no consensus on the state's identity claim, specification of interests, or policy, creating instability and divisions.

Empirically, the book involves cases of both success and failure in the production of consensus on identity and interests. The fundamental ques-tion of identity posed by Palestine represents a surprising success, which was neither predicted nor explained by competing approaches. The new con-ceptions of Jordanian external identity produced in the Jordanian public sphere after 1989 profoundly changed perceptions of threat and power with regard to the PLO. Despite continued mistrust and ongoing competitive maneuvering between Jordan and the PLO, both sides eventually recognized a public Jordanian consensus that would not bear the weight of a renewed Jordanian bid for the West Bank and changed their behavior toward one another accordingly. The peace treaty with Israel proved less successful, despite major state efforts to force consensus. The Jordanian state's bid to redefine Jordan's identity within a Peace Camp, which changed state policy across numerous issue areas, did not achieve a public consensus. Jordanian politics since 1994 have thus been consumed by an unresolved clash be-tween competing conceptions of Jordanian identity and competing articu-lations of Jordanian interests.

In this final chapter, I return to the questions raised in the opening chap-ters. First, I discuss the implications of the empirical findings about the change of identity and interests in the process of public interaction. In par-ticular, I review the findings that the depth and significance of change, and the durability of the new discourse and behavior, depended on the extent to which public debate produces a consensus that is successfully institution-alized. Second, I return to the relationship between rationalist and construc-tivist arguments, drawing out points of potential synthesis and of continuing disagreement and suggesting avenues for further research. Finally, I recon-sider the contributions of the public sphere as a structural variable for un-derstanding international behavior.

Identity and International Politics

This project began with a primary research question about the potential for and mechanism of change in state identity and interests. The empirical findings support the claim that in certain cases the process of public consensus formation produces significant changes in conceptions of identity and interests. Identity and interests were not in constant flux, but neither were preferences fixed or exogenous to the political process. In those cases where these properties were thematized in the public sphere and a workable consensus was achieved and institutionalized, behavior changed along with conceptions of Self. Even fundamental state interests proved open to change. Jordanian identity with regard to Palestine represents the major positive finding. The new identity politics after the severing of ties, in conjunction with the unprecedented opening of the public sphere after 1989, produced a new conception of Jordanian identity in which ties to the West Bank lost their status as a primary interest motivating Jordanian foreign policy. The Jordanian public sphere produced a similarly powerful consensus binding Jordanian and Iraqi identity and interests during the Gulf crisis, which paradoxically emphasized Arabist norms while rejecting the Arabist public sphere in favor of the Jordanian. The peace treaty with Israel and the reversal of ties with Iraq demonstrated the failure of the regime to obtain public sphere consensus behind its actions, despite considerable success in achieving commendation in international public spheres. While state behavior changed dramatically, the absence of a public consensus limits the depth and the likely durability of the new policy in the latter cases.

The structural relationship between national and international public spheres underlies the process of public debate. It is not public debate alone, but rather specific kinds of public debate within particular public sphere structures, which can produce change. The process of change with regard to Jordanian claims to the West Bank is particularly instructive. Prior to 1988, the Jordanian domestic public sphere stood in a subordinate relationship to multiple international public spheres. Questions of identity were resolutely excluded from the bounds of legitimate public discourse in the Jordanian public sphere, while Arabist and the Palestinian public spheres took precedence as sites of public contestation. The severing of ties, enacted primarily in response to challenges in these international public spheres, destabilized Jordanian identity norms. When the regime prevented public debate geared toward securing new identity norms, the political system became unstable, leading to the upheavals of April 1989. The liberalization that followed these upheavals opened up the Jordanian public sphere. In the next few years, the Gulf War and the Oslo accords closed off the two most influential competing public spheres, centering the Jordanian public sphere as the site for the production of new identity norms. Once the truncated and liberalized Jordanian public sphere became the dominant site of norm and identity contestation, a redefinition of identity and interests became far more likely. The Israel treaty, the reversal on Iraq, and the refusal to reengage with the West Bank all were made possible, even driven, by the changes in identity and the understanding of interests that took place within the transformed public sphere.

While some observers might contest the empirical claim that Jordan's identity and interests changed, the evidence strongly supports the assertion that such change took place. I presented abundant evidence of significant change in discourse, institutions, and behavior with regard to Jordanian-Palestinian relations. The Jordan dealing with the West Bank and with the Palestinian National Authority in 1997 carries a fundamentally different identity than the Jordan of a decade earlier, behaving differently and being treated differently by others. With the severing of ties, Jordan redefined itself both abroad and at home, and by the 1990s a very different image of Jordan emerged in the consensus positions framed in public debate. By abandoning its international claim to sovereignty over the West Bank, Jordan asserted a new identity for itself that defied the efforts of other actors to impute a Palestinian identity to the Jordanian polity. Jordan's clear support for the creation of a Palestinian state is fundamentally inconsistent with its old conception of identity and interests. The consensus on Jordanian identity, secured through meaningful public sphere debate, strongly discouraged any other interpretation. This Jordan carried different interests and behaved differently than the "old" Jordan. Relations between the two entities, while often conflictual, now revolve around distributional rather than existential concerns.

While the severing of ties produced change legitimated by a public sphere and likely to endure, the peace treaty has to this point failed to establish such consensus. After the peace treaty with Israel, Jordan asserted a Peace Camp identity at the official level which guided its articulation of interests in dealing not only with Israel, but also with Iraq and other Arab states. The justifications and explanations offered in both the international and domestic arenas for breaking ties with Iraq in 1995 revealed a state with a significantly different conception of its identity and its interests than the Jordan which refused to join the Gulf war coalition. This new conception of state interests stood in opposition to the expressed position of much of the public, however. This public rejection of the state identity frame rendered the new behavior unstable and subject to reversal. Every step, no matter how minor, became invested with great symbolic significance and encountered fierce resistance, accompanied by state efforts at public justification and explanation. As the peace process on the Palestinian and Syrian tracks collapsed, Jordan found itself unable to justify the Peace Camp frame. As King Hussein's frustration mounted, he sent increasingly bitter messages to Netanyahu, accusing him of betraying the peace process and the potential for regional transformation. While this swing is largely explained by Jordanian frustration with Israeli behavior, the failure to achieve public consensus made such reversions far easier than in the case of the renunciation of the West Bank. Reclaiming the West Bank today would involve major institutional change; freezing ties with Israel would involve important changes, especially in the realm of security cooperation, but would not be perceived by many Jordanians as a violation of Jordan's identity or interests.

The contrast between the process of consensus formation in the "Jordanized" Jordan after 1988 and "Peace Camp" Jordan after 1994 thus demonstrates the behavioral implications of public sphere debates on identity. We can predict Jordan's refusal to reassert its claim to the West Bank with far more confidence than we can predict Jordan's position on a future Arab-Israeli confrontation. The "Jordanian" identity claim succeeded in large part because it was accompanied by the extremely popular liberalization program; because it could persuasively be cast as a positive response to long-standing Arabist and Palestinian claims for an independent Palestinian identity; and because it produced a convincing articulation of Jordan's place and interests in a changing international structure. With its success, it became relatively noncontroversial for the state to articulate and enact policies based on the interests of the new Jordan. Jordan's participation in the Madrid peace process revealed a new conception of Jordanian identity and interests, as Jordan rejected every opportunity to reassert a claim to the West Bank and eventually signed a treaty based and justified exclusively on narrowly defined state interests. Most political opposition is now cast in terms of competing interpretations of the interests of this new Jordan, not in terms of rejecting the priority of narrow Jordanian interests. The identity claim of a Jordanized Jordan, once controversial, now is largely beyond debate and informs the argumentation of regime and opposition alike.

The peace treaty, by contrast, met with increasing hostility and opposition, as the Peace Camp identity failed to supplant competing identity claims to become a common, collective point of reference. Instead of liberalization and an unfettering of public debate, the peace treaty was accompanied by · repression of public discourse and a return to authoritarian behavior. Instead of a positive response to Arabist norms, the Peace Camp frame actively repudiated them and sought to discredit them. As a result, the public challenged the Peace Camp identity frame, constructed an increasingly rigid dichotomous opposition between the government professing that identity and Jordanian society, and challenged every policy taken in its name. Instead of convincingly interpreting the new international reality, the Peace Camp frame was repeatedly mocked by Israeli actions such as closures of the West Bank, the assault on Lebanon, Netanyahu's election, settlement activity and provocative actions in Jerusalem, the end of real negotiations with the PNA, the Misha'al Affair.

The focus on distinct cases should not conceal the essential interconnectedness of the processes. The struggles surrounding each of the issues contributed to a broadly contested reinterpretation of identity and interests within changing international and domestic structures. Jordanian identity with regard to the Palestinian identity, the first to be thematized, brought into question the nature of the Self in visceral, undiluted ways. The public debate over the legitimate extension of the Jordanian state over the West Bank and the meaning of the citizenship rights of Jordanians of Palestinian origin made it impossible to sustain the notion of Self that had informed Jordanian behavior. Once the self-image of Jordanian society lost the taken for granted stability of earlier decades, a new consensus on the basic dimensions of identity needed to be secured through public discourse. New claims about identity meant a rearticulation of interests, new notions of security and threat, and a new interpretive frame in which to justify and explain behavior.

The contestation of the meaning of Jordanian identity against Palestinian identity was profoundly influenced by the struggle over the meaning of Arab identity. The Gulf crisis shattered norms of the meaning of Jordan's Arab identity, while the move to peace with Israel cast doubt upon the very primacy of an Arab identity. Where the Palestinian debate threw open the internal constitution of Self, the Gulf crisis and peace process undermined and reconstructed the dominant elements of the external sources of the Jordanian Self. Even as the Gulf crisis made Arabist identity a matter of primary public concern, the Arabist public sphere closed to Jordanian participation. Support for Iraq in the Gulf crisis, in repudiation of an Arab consensus considered inauthentic, provided an essential moment of unity, grounding the opening Jordanian public sphere in Arabist identity and norms. Defense of pro-Iraqi norms and positions within the Jordanian public sphere, rather than participation in an actual Arabist consensus, came to be the operative sign of Arabism. Thus, the Gulf crisis reinforced Arabist norms and identity in Jordan, but severed them from the institutions and processes of the Arabist public sphere, recasting them within the internal—Jordanian public sphere—interpretative frame. The turn against Iraq in 1995 ironically brought Jordanian policy into line with the official Arab consensus, but for Jordanians the Arabist arena was no longer the relevant site for the evaluation of compliance with Arabist identity and norms. The development of the Jordanian public sphere after the Gulf crisis effectively changed the political meaning of Arabism by locating the site of contestation within the Jordanian rather than the Arab public.

The assertion of a new identity in the early 1990s succeeded because of the dramatic challenge posed by the severing of ties, the open public sphere, and the generation of consensus through public debate. Only after a Jordanian identity distinct from the Palestinian identity had been secured could the rearticulation of Jordanian interests be achieved. The struggle over the peace treaty revolved around competing conceptions of Jordanian interests, not around Palestinian or Arab interests. It is inconceivable that Jordan could have signed the peace treaty it did, with its focus on narrow Jordanian state interest and its total exclusion of Palestinian and Arab interests, prior to the reconstruction of Jordanian identity and the shifts in the structure of the Arabist public sphere in the early 1990s.

Once the Jordanian public sphere had developed into an effective site of contestation, state officials—even the King—could no longer simply redefine state interests. When such a sovereign assertion of new interests did take place, notably with the peace treaty and the turn against Iraq, it encountered strong and persistent resistance. Despite the power of the King, in these two key cases the outcomes—defined in terms of identity—were the opposite of his intentions. In the severing of ties, the regime intended a foreign policy tactic, which the process of public sphere debate transformed into a fundamental restructuring of identity and interests; in the peace treaty, the regime embarked upon an attempt to transform the identity and interests of the polity and encountered substantial resistance. In the latter case, the regime tried to convince the public of the validity of its new interpretations through debate, but when its arguments failed it resorted to power and shut down or ignored expressed public opinion. While the assertion of state power over rational debate permitted the regime to persist in its policies, this came at the expense of regime legitimacy and the stability of the system.

Both the external and internal facets of Jordan's identity were at stake in these debates. The internal battles over the place of Palestinians within the Jordanian identity cannot be arbitrarily separated from the external struggle to achieve international recognition of Jordanian sovereignty. The internal contestation of the peace treaty has everything to do with Jordan's assertion of an international identity as a leader of the Peace Camp. Competing conceptions of regional order—New Middle East or Arab—involve claims about state identity tied to the status of the Arabist and international public spheres. The various proposals for regional order rested upon the internal dimension of state identity as much as the external.

Rationalism and Constructivism

The sharp contrast between the rationalist and constructivist approaches may be overdrawn: rationalist explanations should import constructivist arguments, while constructivist approaches should incorporate strategic interaction. While there are important theoretical differences, the approaches complement each other at many points. The discussion of the Jordanian-Israeli peace treaty demonstrates the potential for a synthesis. A constructivist account should not ignore the importance of power imbalances, or the dynamics of two-level bargaining situations. Rationalist explanations, on the other hand, rely on assumptions about actor identity, the framing of political reality, and discourse, which constructivists render explicit. The rational bargaining account of the peace treaty assumes the definition of the situation as one of two states interested in a settlement while pursuing narrowly defined interests. Arriving at this framing of Jordanian-Israeli relations was a long, hugely contentious process, however, which remained uncompleted in the eyes of many Jordanians. Rather than ignore these political struggles, or relegate them to exogenously determined constants, an integrated theory should make them endogenous and explicit. Strategic bargaining should incorporate discursive structures and framing processes, while constructivism should recognize strategic behavior and power relations.

While the potential for theoretical synthesis is real, it is important to maintain the distinctive claims of each approach. The common proposal for a division of labor, in which rationalism provides a theory of strategic behavior while constructivism offers a theory of preference formation, demonstrates the possibilities as well as the dangers of attempts at synthesis. Such a division of labor works only when it is the case that preferences remain constant for the duration of the action to be explained. While this is a reasonable assumption in many cases, during those critical points when identity and interests are at stake in the process of political interaction, the assumption no longer holds. At these crucial junctures, institutionalized interests and identity norms come under question and become subject to change. In such situations, the specification of interests and identity is an integral part of strategic interaction, neither prior to nor exogenous from behavior. Instead of the usual division of labor, then, it is necessary to specify—independently of outcomes—those cases in which identity and interests are likely to be at stake.

The public sphere approach recognizes that not every action in international politics puts basic identities and interests at stake, but that it is necessary to account for those cases which do. When identity and interests are not thematized within an effective public sphere, strategic analysis can justifiably hold them constant. For example, during the decades of Jordanian-Palestinian rivalry prior to 1988, Jordanian identity was rigorously excluded from public sphere discussion and a working consensus on Jordanian interests successfully maintained. Analysis predicated on the relative stability of Jordanian identity and interests during those years was not unreasonable. Holding Jordan's identity, interests, or preferences constant across the decade covered in this dissertation, on the other hand, would produce incorrect analysis, misleading conclusions, and false predictions. These problems arise because of the specific conditions of the latter cases, in which identity was thematized in an effective public sphere. Such cases require a different mode of analysis, one that considers the distinctive characteristics of communicative action within a public sphere.

Beyond this argument about the division of labor between rationalism and constructivism, there are potential points of convergence. Even where identity and interests remain stable, constructivists accounts can inform modified rationalist models. Key variables in rationalist models take on political meaning through the mediation of public communication, and constructivist insights can help make this explicit. It is not necessary to deny that power, threat, or economics are crucially important for explaining behavior in order to claim that their political significance depends on framing and interpretation. For example, in the disengagement, power relations between Jordan and the PLO rested on the ability to claim convincingly to represent the Palestinians of the West Bank. In the peace treaty, American ascendance dictated the conditions of the peace process, but the response to power depends upon its social meaning. While the Resistance and the regime agreed on the fact of American hegemony in the mid-1990s, they disagreed profoundly over the appropriate response to this preponderance of power and Jordan's true interests in such a structure.

Threat even more clearly relies upon identity, framing, and the process of interpretation. In each case, change in the perception of threat followed from public contests over identity and interests rather than independently motivating changes in behavior. Ties to the West Bank became a threat rather than an interest because of the reformulation of Jordanian identity after the severing of ties. The relative threat to Jordan posed by Israel and by Iraq changed in the eyes of regime decisionmakers after (or during), not before, the changes in behavior. In the eyes of most of the Jordanian public, perception of threat had not changed at all, rendering state policy unjustifiable. Whether Israel represented a threat to Jordan after the peace treaty or Iraq threatened Jordan after Hussein Kamil's defection were profoundly political questions, the subject of rich public sphere debate, with no objective answers. The construction of threat to justify foreign policy positions more accurately characterizes Jordanian experience than does the claim that the state responded to threat.

Economic explanations also depend upon the interpretation of economic indicators within public sphere structure. The 1989 uprisings in southern Jordan, like the 1996 bread riots, were immediately sparked by economic problems and the sudden increase in bread prices. But the economic crisis was largely caused by Palestinian uncertainty about the future after the severing of ties and the closure of the public sphere, and the violent reaction was determined by the absence of a public sphere or representative institutions in which grievances could be expressed. The 1996 uprisings reflected similar political and public sphere concerns. The interpretation of the economic consequences of the Gulf crisis depended more upon the normative value of ties with Iraq than upon the probable loss of foreign budget subsidies. The economic explanation for the peace treaty and the Iraq reversal had more to do with competing visions of Jordanian state identity—Should the economy be oriented east or west? Should the region be considered Middle Eastern or Arab?—than with specific calculations or promises of economic benefits.

The rise of "Realist" behavior among Arab states in the 1980s and 1990s can be explained at least in part in terms of the shift in public sphere structure. As a set of norms and prescriptions for state behavior, Realism serves as a justification for action rather than as an objective description of action. Realism can be interpreted as the *claim* to be pursuing objective state interests within the bounds of the balance of power. This discursive strategy has great power within state-level public spheres constituted around nationalist norms. It has less appeal where dominant public spheres do not correspond with state boundaries, or where no clear consensus on national or state identity has been secured. In the Arabist public sphere, appeals to Realist justifications had little value and were rarely heard: indeed, raison d'état was the most illegitimate justification for behavior. When Jordan struggled to achieve recognition as the representative of West Bank Palestinians in the 1970s, it did not appeal to state interests. By contrast, in the 1990s, Realism emerged as the dominant mode of argumentation and justification. The observation that Realism plays a role in public sphere contestation does not, of course, necessarily mean that it is not correct as an explanation of state behavior. Indeed, a strong constructivist argument could be made that the more actors justify their action in Realist terms, the more their interpretation of reality will come to approximate the Realist vision and the more they will in fact behave according to Realist precepts. This claim contrasts with the familiar Realist assertion, that states always act as Realists although their public rhetoric changes.

Strategic Framing

This project gives a great deal of importance to interpretive frames as a power resource with relative autonomy from material power resources and as an object of political struggle. Each public sphere is characterized by a set of norms and interpretive frames that empower certain kinds of arguments and claims. These norms, though fiercely contested and often contradictory, provide the points of reference by which action is interpreted and judged. At times where a frame is thematized, opened to public contestation, actors compete to establish and to destabilize interpretive frames. The ability to successfully interpret action within the public sphere as consistent with norms is a very real dimension of political power.

Discussion of an issue is not enough for change: what is needed is discourse that challenges the dominant frame. In order to identify the potential for change, it is necessary to determine whether argumentation is oriented toward securing interests within an existing master frame or toward establishing a new interpretive frame. The severing of ties could have been framed as a tactical maneuver to undercut the PLO, as many Realists argued it "really" was. Such a frame minimizes the extent of change, which would allow for the reassertion of the Jordanian claim at any opportune time. The failure of this frame foreclosed such options. Each of the cases examined revealed similar importance for successful or failed framing. During the Gulf crisis, the dominance of the "United States vs Arabs" frame within the Jordanian arena, rather than an "Iraq vs Kuwait" or even a "Arab defenders of sovereignty vs. Iraqi violator of sovereignty" frame, strongly influenced the behavior of all actors. In the struggle over normalization, the competition between interpretive frames remains largely unresolved. In these contested processes of framing every issue and event, however minor, becomes invested with great significance, contributing to the interpretive struggle between dichotomous, competing frames. Furthermore, during such processes actors become bound by their discourse, forced to live up to their words in order to prove their sincerity.

Success in imposing an interpretive frame is influenced by material power, but cannot be reduced to the balance of material forces. There is no doubt that states endowed with great material power will have great influence in the process of argumentation, but material resources are only one dimension of power. Within any public sphere, the ability to make claims on dominant norms and values represents an important power resource not reducible to other nondiscursive resources. When an actor can justify and interpret action with reference to these norms, the action becomes more acceptable and influential. Virtuosity in constructing arguments and justifications is, as every political campaign manager would attest, a real source of power. It is not necessary to ignore material power in order to focus attention on the neglected dimension of power found in the enabling character of norms.

Norms and frames are not disembodied, and are always located within particular public spheres. Claims made toward "Islamic values" are obviously more relevant and powerful within an Arabist or Islamic public sphere than they are in the Western-dominated international public sphere. Social power depends upon the structures in which it is wielded. While the relevant public sphere in which action will be interpreted is thus a structural variable, actors attempt to influence the site of contestation to their advantage. For example, after the severing of ties, certain actors attempted to shift the relevant site of debate from the Arabist arenas into the Jordanian arena, where their norms and arguments had more resonance. When the Jordanian public sphere emerged in the 1990s, their frames and arguments did in fact dominate, above and beyond their actual numbers, wealth, or other material resources. The emergence of one or more public spheres as the most relevant site of contestation therefore produces distinctive power relations. The balance of power between Jordan and the PLO within the Arabist public sphere is not identical to the balance of power within the Jordanian or the international public spheres: not just because military or economic or even infrastructural resources have changed, but because the actors have a different relationship and ability to draw on those specific norms.

Establishing a frame is not simply a function of the balance of power, even if the conceptualization of power is expanded to encompass access to norms. An interpretive frame claims to best interpret political reality, and is judged at least in part on its ability to explain ongoing developments and to provide compelling articulations of the collective interest. For example, throughout 1995 the Jordanian regime struggled to convince the Jordanian public that Jordan had joined with the forces of moderation [Israel, the PLO, the U.S., the international community] against the forces of extremism [Iraq, Hamas, Iran, domestic opposition], and that this alliance based on the desire for peace would lead to political stability and economic prosperity. The opposition argued that Jordan had capitulated to foreign power with malevolent intentions, and that cooperation would produce only dependence. Part of the battle was over who could better claim to speak for the Jordanian identity and interests. Another part of the battle was to more convincingly interpret ongoing political events, to demonstrate which frame better explained reality. Despite the huge advantage in material power enjoyed by the regime, the Resistance was empowered by its ability to point to events that vindicated its claim of continued Israeli hostility and lack of interest in real peace. As Israel bombed Lebanon, sealed off the West Bank, elected Netanyahu, expanded settlements in Jerusalem, and carried out assassination attempts in Amman, the regime scrambled to justify its frame with little success.

International Public Sphere Theory: Future Research Questions

The public sphere approach provides a theoretical foundation for understanding observable empirical developments in Arab and Jordanian politics. I do not claim to have fully developed the concept as a theory of international politics. Nor do I claim to have resolved many of the philosophical and theoretical questions raised by Habermas's bid to develop a universal theory of communicative action. I have hardly engaged with the normative theory that has been the primary application of Habermas in IR theory to this point. I do claim to have demonstrated the usefulness of public sphere theory for explaining Jordanian behavior and Arab order, and to have begun an engagement between rationalist and constructivist explanations.

Public sphere structure allows for an operational specification of change and continuity in important dimensions of international politics which are not captured by existing models. The characterization of change in the Arab state system is radically incomplete without some concept by which to understand the dimension of discursive interaction between and across states. The rise of Arabism in the 1950s cannot simply be incorporated into models of autonomous states pursuing stable interests. Arabist ideas, forged by political communicative action into a dominant interpretive frame within a potent transnational public sphere, fundamentally reshaped Arab actors' interpretation of their identities and interests. The turn to pragmatism in the 1980s involved more than the play of disembodied ideas or the reflection of a changing balance of power. Shifts in public sphere structure accompanied and informed material changes: both in the internal contestation within the Arabist public sphere producing new interpretive frames and norms; and in the decline in the relative centrality of the Arabist public sphere in relation to state-level and Western international public spheres. There are always multiple public spheres, both within and outside of the state, and the balance among these public spheres varies. The Arabist public sphere demonstrates that there is no necessary correlation between state boundaries and the place of the public sphere. The creation of a state-bounded public sphere is a political process with important behavioral implications.

How the findings and conclusions presented here travel to other countries, regions, or historical periods should be the subject of future research. The situation of Jordan after 1989 can be characterized by the conjunction of a challenge to state identity with an opening of an underdeveloped public sphere. Such conditions can be found in the growing universe of cases of liberalizing countries, which has been the subject of the "transitions to democracy" literature, or more ominously, in the more recent literature on liberalization and ethnic conflict. The dynamic of identity and interest contestation within the emergent public sphere should reflect similar processes. The development of a unified public sphere, the thematization of identity and interests, and the success or failure of consensus formation will be crucial variables in determining change or continuity in the articulation of interests and the political behavior likely to emerge from the transition. Another avenue for future research lies in the comparison of regions. In the

Arab case, an effective transnational public sphere predated state power, with distinctive implications for patterns of identity and interest formation. How does this compare, empirically and theoretically, with the experience of other regions? A third likely area for further research lies in the contribution of transnational public spheres to international order and disorder. Does a public sphere provide a potential means for overcoming security dilemmas, or does it simply provide another institutional arena in which states can pursue their interests? What is the relationship between international public spheres and the emerging "global civil society," networks of organizations and individuals operating outside the bounds of the state?

Public sphere theory also has important implications for the debates over the appropriate response to "rogue" regimes in the international society. Realists often argue that rogue states should be contained. Since their hostility is structurally determined, and their preferences will not change, primary attention should be given to limiting their power capabilities and to manipulating their opportunities and incentives. The United States should treat China as a likely future opponent, rather than as a future partner. Iran, Libya, Cuba and other "backlash" states should be punished, subverted, and constrained. Public sphere theory, on the other hand, suggests that engagement would be a far more productive strategy. Initiating dialogue can offer the potential for changing preferences and for identifying common identities and interests. The election of Mohamed Khatemi in Iran offers an outstanding example. The election of a moderate reformer calling for a dialogue with the United States forced Americans to grapple with the possibility of change, and the significance of dialogue.

Final Remarks

I do not mean to idealize the Jordanian public sphere in the 1990s. Like any nascent public sphere, Jordan's saw its share of self-censorship, hired pens, Byzantine disputes, grandstanding, sensationalism, and "intellectual terrorism." Participants often grew disenchanted at the polarizing tendencies of public discourse and its failure to effectively influence legislation and state policy. The regime often implemented its preferred policies in the face of near complete rejection by the public sphere, seemingly vindicating power over persuasion. Nevertheless, no observer or participant should overlook that in the 1990s the Jordanian public sphere emerged as a unique, distinctive site of opinion formation, in which virtually all sectors of political society effectively participated. This public sphere identified and thematized the most controversial issues, proposed and disposed of solutions, and fiercely defended its integrity and autonomy. Writers and actors understood their actions as contributing to the creation and development of the public sphere. An effective consensus on Jordanian identity and interests forged within this public sphere in the early 1990s brought stability and legitimacy to the political system. In the last few years, this public sphere has been embattled and has not produced such a consensus. It has nevertheless proven remarkably resilient in its insistence on public dialogue in the face of state power.

As Jordan passes from the Hussein era to the Abdullah era, the strength of the Jordanian public sphere and of the monarchy will be put to the test. Without the overwhelming personality of King Hussein, a more balanced distribution of social power should emerge. Abdullah could well choose to ignore public opinion. Insecure in his position, uncertain in the face of the powerful critiques and arguments of domestic opposition, and dependent on the goodwill of powerful external actors such as Israel and the United States, Abdullah may turn to the authoritarian practices of the past in order to maintain an unpopular foreign policy. This would be a mistake. The public sphere offers an opportunity to secure a legitimate place for the new regime in a Jordanian consensus. The experiences of the 1990s have left Jordan with a self-aware public sphere, which expects to contribute to political decision making and has the capacity to articulate its preferences. A return to liberalization and engagement with Jordanian political society offers greater prospects for long term stability in Jordan than does any attempt to ignore it. A foreign policy which is justified through reasoned argument and which satisfies the identity and conceptions of interests of Jordanian society would be an essential part of such a program of reform.

Notes

Chapter 3

1. The changing of PLO preferences represents another important and interesting case that merits a study of its own. Gresh (1989) provides an overview of the internal Palestinian debates over how and where to seek a Palestinian state, and the generally shifting Palestinian consensus.

2. Assistant Secretary of State Richard Murphy testimony before House Subcommittee on Europe and the Middle East, Developments in the Middle East, July 1988 (July 27, 1988), p. 59.

3. Flora Lewis, "A Middle East advance?" *New York Times* August 3, 1988.

4. Shamir speech to Israeli Knesset, August 10, 1988: "King Husayn's speech announcing his secession from Judea, Samaria, and Gaza [sic] did not create a legal vacuum because the current apparatus in the area continues to operate." FBIS-NES-88–155, August 11, 1988, pp. 35–37. This position was also held by Yitzhak Rabin, then responsible for the Occupied Territories; see FBIS-NES-88–148, p. 28.5. Foreign Minister Hani al-Khasawneh, interview in Sawt al-Shaab, August 3, 1988 (FBIS-NES-88–149, p. 29); also see Khasawneh, interview on Dubai Radio, July 30, 1988 (FBIS-NES-88–147); Khasawneh continued to make this argument a decade later; interview published in *al-Mithaq* May 7, 1997. King Hussein regularly used this argument as well; see press conference, Amman Television, August 7, 1988 (FBIS-NES-88–152)6. Taher al-Masri, in *al-Dustur* February 2, 1995. Masri, a prominent regime figure of Palestinian origin, resigned in protest of the implementation. In a lecture delivered in September 1989, he publicly bemoaned the direction the disengagement had taken. The lack of concern for domestic implications among the

"inner circle" was confirmed by Adnan Abu Odeh, personal interview, Washington, December 1995.

7. Tessler (1994), pp. 716–17, cites reports that the revolutionary message of the Intifada was spreading through the mosques and media of Amman in the summer of 1988.8. Brynen (1991), p. 617, cites Jordanian Public Security Directorate figures that between December 1987 and August 1988 there were 117 pro-Intifada rallies of at least 100 participants; Brand (1990) cites a figure of 114 in the same period.

9. A declaration by the United National Leadership of the Intifada, calling on Palestinian members of the Jordanian Parliament to resign was swiftly retracted, and there was a general Palestinian consensus that instability in Jordan would harm the interests of the Intifada; see Abd al-Rahman and Hourani (1995).

10. Nasuh al-Majali, Minister of Information, in *al-Dustur* August 10, 1988; also see Taher al-Masri's speech to the Arab Professional Conference, in *al-Rai* May 14, 1990.

11. Zayd Rifa'i, quoted in *al-Rai* February 6, 1989 (FBIS-NES-89–024).

12. *Al-Biyadar al-Siyasi*, August 13, 1988: "We have no faith in Husayn's intentions."

13. Abu Odeh (1997) and personal interview; Khasawneh, interviewed in *al-Mithaq* May 7, 1997.

14. Virtually the entire Palestinian leadership emphasized this point, with Yasir Arafat explicitly denying the King's claim to have given him prior notice (FBIS-NES-88–154).15. Adnan Abu Odeh, then Chief of the Royal Court, interviewed in *al-Majellah* May 21, 1988, p. 17.

16. For an overview of the spectrum of Israeli politics embracing some version of "Jordan is Palestine," see David Makovsky, "Is Jordan Palestine?" *Jerusalem Post* December 15, 1988.17. Arens interview in *Jerusalem Post* February 10, 1989, in *Israeli Foreign Relations* [hereafter IFR] vol. 11, Document 12; Shamir interview in *Ma'ariv* March 24, 1989, IFR 11, Document 33.

18. The details of this argument are described by Ryan (1987). Yorke (1987) challenges the demographic figures underlying this argument, as did the Jordanian government. For skeptical reaction by prominent American Jewish commentators, see Pipes and Garfinkle (1988). For support, see Israeli (1991) and Klieman (1981). For a sample of the debate, see Yuval Ne'eman, "Why Jordan is Palestine." *Jerusalem Post* August 26, 1988; Yisrael Harel, "Clearly, Jordan is Palestine." *Jerusalem Post* February 25, 1991; and Ariel Sharon, "Jordan is the Palestinian state." *Jerusalem Post* April 4, 1991.

19. Erwin Frankel, "The Hussein illusion." *Jerusalem Post* August 12, 1988.

20. Labib Qamhawi, "A commentary on Dr.Fanik," *al-Rai* January 25, 1990.

21. Among the prominent figures involved in the East Bank First movement include Prince Hassan, Zayd bin Shakir, Ahmed Obaydat, Jamal al-Sha'ir, Sa'id al-Tal. King Hussein was generally linked with maintaining the commitment to the West Bank. See Day (1986) for discussion of these trends before the severing of ties.

22. Layne (1993) presents a fascinating discussion of the attempt to develop tribe-based identity in Jordan, but places a bit too much importance on elements of official discourse with little popular resonance. See Shryock (1997) for an alternative reading of the new tribal historians.

23. Fahd al-Fanik, "Peace treaty finally ends the threat of the Alternative Home-land," *al-Rai* October 24, 1994, and "Dangers of the Alternative Homeland," *Shihan* December 12, 1994.

24. See Mohammed Daoudiya, "National Unity," *al-Dustur* May 27, 1990; Ramadan Rawashdeh, "Who are the enemies of the people?" *al-Dustur* May 30, 1990; Abdullah al-Khatib, "National Unity" *al-Dustur* June 2, 1990; Muna Shaqir, "Mass rallies and violent behavior and national unity" *al-Dustur* June 3, 1990; and Bisam Haddadin, "National consensus on preserving democracy" *al-Dustur* June 6, 1990; for the competing interpretations.

25. Many Israeli commentators expressed this perception of shared interests, and expected Jordan to cooperate in suppressing the Intifada.

26. Khasawneh interviewed in *al-Mithaq*, May 7, 1997.

27. King Hussein speech to Arab summit, June 7, 1988. *Collected Speeches*, p. 264.

28. *al-Ahram*, August 4, 1988, FBIS-NES-88–151, August 5, 1988, p. 6.

29. Among the Palestinian leaders to publicly express this were Salah Khalaf, Jamal al-Surani, Abd al-Hamid al-Sa'ih, Yasser Abd Raboh, Nayf Hawatmeh and George Habash.30. PLO statement of August 15, 1988, in *al-Rai* FBIS-NES-88–159, pp. 3–4.

31. Assistant Secretary of State Richard Murphy, testimony before House Subcommittee on Europe and the Middle East, *Developments in the Middle East*, October 1988 (October 13, 1988), p. 9 and p. 39.

32. Arens, interviewed in *Ha'aretz* May 5, 1989, in *IFR* 11, Document 51, p. 131.

33. In *al-Rai* August 11, 1988.

Chapter 4

1. Quoted in Andoni (1991), p. 63.

2. "Jordanian measures to serve Palestinian representation." *Sawt al-Shaab* August 6, 1988 (FBIS-NES-88–155).

3. Anne Ponger, "What they're thinking on the East Bank" *Jerusalem Post* August 24, 1988.

4. Fahd al-Rimawi, "The importance of the other opinion," *al-Dustur* August 3, 1988.

5. George Haddad, "The accursed blessing and the anticipated results," *al-Dustur* August 4, 1988.

6. Mahmoud al-Sharif, "Screams of joy for the termination of unity," *al-Dustur* August 4, 1988.

7. Minister of Information Hani al-Khasawneh, interviewed in *al-Majellah* Sep-

tember 7, 1988 (FBIS-NES-88-175, p. 26); and in *al-Sharq al-Awsat* August 27, 1988 (FBIS-NES-88-171, p. 33).

8. *Sawt al-Shaab*, "A step we awaited," August 25, 1988 (FBIS-NES-88-168) Rifa'i quoted in *al-Dustur* September 1, 1988 (FBIS-NES-88-170).

9. Fahd al-Fanik, *al-Rai* August 8, 1988; Taysir Abd al-Jabir, August 13 and August 20, and Abdullah al-Maliki, August 2, in *al-Dustur*.

10. Muhadin's (1992) opinion survey conducted in 1991 found that 74% of respondents found foreign media credible, compared with 11% who felt that way about the Jordanian media. The press fared better than the electronic media, with 64% of Jordanians relying on the press as their primary source of political news, compared to 10% who most followed TV.

11. Abd al-Latif *Arabiyyat*, Parliamentary debates published in Darwish (1992), p. 377.

12. Parliamentary debate as published in Darwish (1992), and unpublished transcripts in Majlis al-Noab (Parliament) archives, Amman.

13. Asa'ad Abd al-Rahman, *al-Dustur* March 25, 1995.

14. In Hourani 1996: 168.

15. Abd al-Hadi al-Majali, *al-Rai* December 26, 1992.

16. Abd al-Hadi al-Majali, *Rasalat Majlis al-Umma*, June 1994, p. 12.

17. Majali says that any Jordanian who accepts such an identity is welcome in the party. The Amman branch of the NCP was led by Marwan Dudin, a longstanding official of Palestinian origin. Party members also frequently point to examples of ethnic tensions in other parties, especially the Islamic Action Front. See Bilal al-Tal, "The National Constitutional Party," *al-Rai* June 21, 1997.

18. Hakim al-Khayr, spokesman for the Constitutional Party, interviewed in *Shihan* December 18, 1997. After the elections, the party split repeatedly, with the dominance of *al-Ahd* being a primary complaint.

19. Interview, Ahmed Awidi al-Abaddi, Amman, May 1995. Abaddi (1986) explains his conceptions of nationalism in his study of the Jordanian tribes. For a fascinating discussion of Abaddi's belief system, see Shryock (1995, 1997). Examples of Abadd's arguments can be found in: "*Muhajarin* and *Insar*," *Shihan* October 15, 1994; "Always We Pay the Price," *al-Bilad* January 18, 1995; "Jordan Is the Most Valuable Thing We Possess," *Shihan* September 17, 1994.

20. Nahid Hattar, "Who Is the Jordanian?" *al-Hadath*, November 1, 1995.

21. Taysir al-Zibri, "On the concept of citizenship," *al-Dustur* May 12, 1993.

22. *Al-Sabil* April 23, 1996, p. 2.

23. Fahd al-Rimawi, personal interview, May 1995; "National unity," *al-Dustur* June 11, 1990.

24. Sultan al-Hattab, "Citizenship or origins?" *al-Rai* November 19, 1993, is a good example.

25. Published in *Shihan* February 7, 1997.

26. Opposition parties statement, in *al-Majd* February 11, 1997 (FBIS-NES-97-030).

27. 'Arib al-Rentawi, "Parliament and Jordanians of Palestinian Origin," *al-Dustur* November 10, 1997.

28. Interview with Interior Minister Ra'ouf al-Dajani, *al-Rai* September 10, 1988. Dajani reflects on the intentions and application of these passport laws in *al-Dustur* September 16, 1995.

29. Among many examples: " 'Bidoun' in Kuwait.. also in Jordan?" *al-Sabil* January 25, 1994; Majid al-Khadri, "Withdrawing citizens' passports is in whose interests?" *al-Sabil* July 5, 1994; "Stories from the passport office," *al-Majd* April 10, 1995; "Parliament opens the file on the confiscation of passports," *al-Sabil* September 26, 1995.

30. *Al-Sharq al-Awsat* October 23, 1995.

31. Prime Minister Zayd bin Shakir, response to a report issued by the Parliamentary Committee on Public Freedoms, September 17, 1995. Reported by Rana Sabbagh, Reuters.

32. The exchange occurs in *al-Sabil* July 11, 1995.

33. Quotes from M.Tarshishi, Director of Palestinian Affairs, in *al-Dustur* August 30, 1997, p. 8.

34. Personal interviews with Marwan Dudin and Salim Tamari, members of the Jordanian and Palestinian delegations to the multilateral refugee negotiations, June 1997; see Arzt 1995.

35. The newspaper *al-Mithaq* was most active in identifying such deviance, which may explain why it was viewed by the government as more of a threat than other opposition vehicles.

36. The article and the unpublished responses by the Association presidents are collected in *al-Urdun al-Jadid* 12/13 (1988).

37. Rakan al-Majali, "The unprofessional associations" *al-Rai* October 6, 1988.

38. Fahd al-Fanik, "Sever the ties, oh lawyers!" *al-Rai* December 3, 1992.

39. Salameh Akour, "Questions." *Sawt al-Shaab* March 9, 1993.

40. Fahd al-Fanik, "Professional Associations outside of history," *al-Rai* June 16, 1994.

41. Layth Shubaylat, "Response to Fanik," *Shihan* July 2, 1994.

42. Samih al-Mayateh, "The attack on the Associations," *al-Sabil* October 24, 1995.

43. Abdullah Rudwan, "In defence of the decision," *al-Rai* March 13, 1995.

44. Taysir al-Zibri, interviewed in *al-Rai*, February 6, 1993.

45. Fahd al-Fanik, "Citizenship, not resettlement," *al-Rai* April 19, 1991.

46. For example, see the debate between *al-Ahd* leader Abd al-Hadi al-Majali and *Hashd* leader Bisam Haddadin, published in *al-Dustur* April 12, 1992.

47. Transcripts of Parliament debates, Majlis al-Noab archives in Amman. Debate of Political Party Law in First Special Session of 11th Parliament, June 21 to July 5, 1992.

48. Salameh al-Akour, "Words on party licenses," *Sawt al-Shabb* October 3, 1992.

49. Salameh al-Akour, "Why all this crying about national unity?" *Sawt al-Shaab*

December 23, 1992. Also see Hamada Fara'na, "Party licenses and democracy," *al-Dustur* December 22, 1992. Samih al-Khalil, "National unity is not a line that can be drawn in the newspaper," *al-Dustur* December 25, 1992.

50. Fahd al-Fanik, *"Hashd* faces a choice," *al-Rai* February 13, 1993; Salem al-Nahass, "Who chooses whom?" *al-Rai* February 15, 1993.

51. To date the legal controversy has not been resolved. Mohammed al-Subayhi, "The fate of *Hashd* is in the hands of the Interior Ministry," *al-Dustur* July 13, 1995; and the half page ad taken out by *Hashd* in its defence on July 16 in *al-Dustur.*

52. Text published in *al-Sabil.*

53. *Jordan Times* April 16, 1998.

54. Fahd al-Fanik, "What about Jordan?" *al-Rai* September 7, 1993.

55. Mohammed al-Subayhi, "In whose interest?" *al-Dustur* October 4, 1995 and "Who is the chauvinist?" *al-Dustur* November 4, 1995.

56. Fahd al-Fanik, "Crisis of identity . . . who are we?" *al-Rai* November 20, 1993.

57. Samih al-Mayateh, "The Islamist movement and Jordanian-Palestinian relations," *al-Dustur* July 25, 1993.

58. Thunaybat interview published in *al-Sabil* December 5, 1995, p. 15.

59. *al-Sabil* April 16, 1994 and April 23, 1994 for the Islamist position.

60. 'Arib al-Rentawi, "Jordan and Hamas," *al-Dustur* October 5, 1997, p. 18.

61. Ibrahim Ghousha interviewed in *al-Bilad* May 17, 1995.

62. Bisam al-Amoush, interviewed in *al-Hadath*, June 23, 1997.

63. Abu Zant interviewed in *al-Hadath* May 6, 1997.

64. Jawad al-Anani, *al-Dustur* February 24, 1997.

65. Fahd al-Fanik, "Low Walls," *al-Rai* February 22, 1995; and, all in *al-Dustur*: Musa Kaylani, "The survey," February 15, 1995; Hamada Fara'na, "The survey," February 2, 1995; Mohammed al-Subayhi, "Delusions of unity," February 11, 1995.

66. Fahd al-Fanik, "Does Jordan have interests in the negotiations?" *al-Rai* November 29, 1991; Tareq Masarweh, "The joint delegation does not represent anybody.' *al-Rai* December 14, 1991.

67. Tahir al-Udwan, "The question of Palestinian representation and Jordanian national interests," *al-Dustur* July 22, 1991; Saleh al-Qullab, "Jordan is Jordan and Palestine is Palestine," *al-Dustur* July 27, 1991.

68. Muna Shaqir, "Confederation: why is it desired now?" *al-Dustur* March 22, 1992; Taysir al-Zibri, "Confederation . . . between principled position and conditional tactic." *al-Dustur* March 24, 1992.

69. Fahd al-Fanik, "So-called confederation," *al-Rai* April 1, 1992.

70. Salameh al-Akour, "Confederation once more," *Sawt al-Shaab* July 26, 1993; Nowal Abassi, "No to confederation," *Sawt al-Shaab* July 30, 1993; Samih al-Mayeteh, "Confederation: why now?" *al-Dustur* August 2, 1993.

71. Arafat Hijazi, "Confederation: a trap for Jordanians or for Palestinians?" *Sawt al-Shaab* August 15, 1993.

72. George Hawatmeh, "Caught between two moods" *Middle East International* November 17, 1995.

73. Ahmed Awidi al-Abaddi, quoted in *al-Sharq al-Awsat* November 18, 1995.

74. Text of letter published in al-Dustur, December 3, 1997; 'Arib Rentawi, "Husayn's letter to the Prime Minister," *al-Dustur* December 6, 1997; Zeev Schiff, "King Hussein's letter," *Ha'aretz* December 17, 1997.

75. CSS 1998.

76. Jarbawi (1995) offers a less sanguine view.

77. For example, Ehud Ya'ari, "The waiting game," *Ma'ariv* August 9, 1996.

78. Nahid Hatter, "Palestine for Palestinians and Jordan for Jordanians," *al-Haddath*, November 15, 1995.

79. Parliamentary debates as printed in *al-Dustur* November 1994.

80. *Christian Science Monitor* June 20, 1996.

Chapter 5

1. George Bush demonstrated his understanding of the difficulties of the Jordanian position; see "White House moderates its criticism of Jordan," *Washington Post* September 5, 1990, and Bush and Scowcroft (1998). That he nevertheless punished Jordan reveals the rigidity of the American frame.

2. Knesset session broadcast live on Israeli Radio, October 15, 1990 (FBIS-NES-90–200).

3. Phrases taken from *Jerusalem Post* editorials between November 1990 and July 1991. Representative essays include "King Hussein vs. Islamic Fundamentalism" November 16, 1990; "The Jordan connection!!" December 1, 1990; "Jordan's choice" January 1, 1991; "Is the Hashemite imbroglio getting out of control?" January 4, 1991; "Reassessing King Husayn," January 24, 1991; "Mislabeling Jordan," February 6, 1991; Moshe Zak, "Is Jordan cooperating with Iraq?" January 25, 1991; Mordechai Nisan, "Israel's political dogma on Jordan." February 20, 1991.

4. Shimon Peres interviewed on Cairo Radio, October 15, 1990 (FBIS-NES-205).

5. This non-response was immensely controversial and not inevitable, however; see Arens (1995) and Shamir (1994) for the internal Israeli debate over retaliation.

6. In The *Jerusalem Post*, January 24, 1997, p. 17.

7. David Levy on Israeli TV, August 20, 1990, in *IFR* vol.12, document 153.

8. David Levy on Israeli TV, October 18, 1990, FBIS-NES-90–204.

9. King Hussein press conference, August 8, 1990, in *Hashemite Outcries* [hereafter *HO*], p. 56; Arens (1995) on Israeli satisfaction with the response.

10. Mudar Badran in *Jordan Times*, January 12, 1991, FBIS-NES-91–009.

11. The importance of Arabist norms in eliminating Israel as a viable choice of alliance partners is itself an important point whose significance is not generally appreciated. Nothing in power or threat alone explains the consistent refusal to align with Israel by all Arab states.

12. Jamil al-Nimri, "Hussein and the diplomacy of the Arabist position." *al-Ahali* September 5, 1990.

13. "The Arab Washington does not know." *al-Dustur* February 1, 1991 (FBIS-NES-91–023)

14. Press conference at Kennebunkport, August 16, 1990, in *HO*, p. 78.

15. Interview, September 21, 1990, in *HO*, p. 98.

16. Interview, ABC TV, February 9, 1991, in *HO*, p. 232.

17. Fahd al-Fanik, quoted in *al-Ahali* September 5, 1990.

18. Amman Chamber of Commerce Report, discussed in *al-Dustur* September 4, 1995.

19. *White Book*, p. 19.

20. Harknett and VanDenBerg (1997) argue that Bush showed considerable sympathy for Hussein, misleading Congress about the extent of Jordanian alignment with Iraq.

21. Statement published in *al-Dustur* September 26, 1990 (FBIS-NES-90–191).

22. King Hussein speech to the nation, February 6, 1991, in *HO* , p. 224.

23. *White Book*, Document #1.

24. Ibid., Document #7.

25. *Shihan* cited in Barakat, p. 39. This description is repeated uncontested, in popular and official discourse, and can be taken as a consensus interpretation in the Jordanian public sphere.

26. Hamada Fara'na, "What does the Kuwaiti delegation want?" *al-Dustur* December 3, 1990 (FBIS-NES-90–232).

27. Marwan al-Qassim, Radio Monte Carlo, October 29, 1990 (FBIS-NES-90–210).

28. Hamada Fara'na, "Jordanians and Palestinians in one trench," *al-Dustur* March 12, 1991.

29. Moshe Zak, "Is Jordan cooperating with Iraq?" *Jerusalem Post* January 25, 1991.

30. Nabil Sharif, personal interview, Amman, March 16, 1995.

31. Fahd al-Rimawi, "The non-appearance of the other opinion," *Shihan* January 26, 1991.

32. Muna Shaqir, "The role and responsibility of the writer," *al-Dustur* March 31, 1991.

33. Fahd al-Fanik quoted in Barakat, p. 25.

34. Mahmoud al-Sharif, quoted in *al-Urdun*, December 3, 1990 (FBIS-NES-90–232).

35. Nabil al-Sharif, personal interview, March 16, 1995.

36. Prime Minister Zayd bin Shakir maintained his belief in such payments despite the lack of evidence because "some articles clearly show the writer is working against the interests of this country. . . . I read articles which I do not believe any loyal Jordanian could write." Interview reported in *al-Hayat* November 16, 1995.

Needless to say, opposition writers resented the implication that their opposition could only be explained by treachery.

37. Brand (1994), p. 206 and p. 212 offers a number of examples, such as Iraq's funding of a $2.7 million housing project for journalists and a 1981 gift of $100 million to the Jordanian Ministry of Information.

38. Rimawi, "The other opinion"; Shaqir, "The role and responsibility of the writer."

39. Fanik, "The other opinion."

40. Shaqir, "The role and responsibility of the writer."

41. *Jordan Times* October 7, 1990 (FBIS-NES-90–195).

Chapter 6

1. Hosni Mubarak, June 1994: "There are few differences between Israel and Jordan." Shimon Peres, December 1993: "All we need is a pen to sign a peace treaty with Jordan."

2. Shamir, Closing speech at Madrid peace conference, text in *New York Times*, November 2, 1991.

3. Not all dimensions of Jordanian-Israeli relations were open to public discussion; security cooperation remained a red line, excluded from public deliberation, as did some sensitive issues related to Israeli investment and land purchases.

4. Fahd al-Fanik, "The latest Jordanian move," *al-Rai* June 21, 1994.

5. Thouqan al-Hindawi interviews published in *Shihan* December 10, 1994 and *al-Bilad* December 14, 1994, and commentary by opposition leaders in *al-Majd* December 8, 1994.

6. Ashrawi (1994) for a Palestinian perspective on the joint delegation and Abd al-Salam al-Majali, "Memoirs" published in *al-Rai*, April 1–4, 1995 for a Jordanian view.

7. Majali, "Memoirs." Peres (1995), p. 304, claims not to have informed the Jordanians. There is evidence that King Hussein and Prince Hassan, like the Americans, were aware of the back channel negotiations, but did not take them seriously.

8. "Jordan is not Palestine!!" *al-Rai* October 24, 1994.

9. Fahd al-Fanik, "Dangers of the Alternative Homeland," *Shihan* December 10, 1994.

10. Anani interviewed on Jordan TV, June 6, 1994, *Jordanian Documents* [hereafter JD] 94/2/27.

11. Peres in joint press conference with Abd al-Salam al-Majali, July 21, 1994.

12. Bater Wardum, "The personality of Jordan after the treaty," *al-Majd* December 26, 1994.

13. Mohammed Daoudiya, "The necessity of dialogue," *al-Dustur* February 3, 1992.

14. Tareq Masarweh, "What is the Jordan we want?" *al-Ufuq* September 7, 1994.

15. Abd al-Salam al-Majali, interviewed in *al-Dustur* November 7, 1994; King Hussein press conference, August 2, 1994, *JD* 94/3/25.

16. Joint statement issued in Damascus, quoted in *New York Times* October 25, 1991.

17. Fahd al-Rimawi, "Collapses," *al-Majd* August 1, 1994.

18. *Filastin al-Thawrah* 870, December 1, 1991, skates around the identity issue, suggesting delicately that al-Masri threatened "existing power centers of which he was not a part."

19. Saleh al-Qullab, "Jordan is Jordan and Palestine is Palestine," *al-Dustur* July 27, 1991.

20. Hussein speech to Jordanian Parliament, July 9, 1994. *JD* 94/3/3.

21. Hussein interview, ABC Television, October 25, 1994, *JD* 94/4/37, p. 261.

22. Fahd al-Fanik, *al-Rai* August 10, 1994

23. The official discourse, such as the official publication *Battle for Peace* (1994), highlights this conference; few other Jordanians refer to it.

24. For example, Hussein press conference, Washington, July 29, 1994, *JD* 94/3/23; Hassan at roundtable with opposition deputies, Royal Court, August 1, 1994, *JD* 94/3/24.

25. Majali interviewed in *al-Ahram*, August 17, 1994, *JD* 94/3/41; Hussein interviewed on Radio Monte Carlo August 17, 1994, *JD* 94/3/39.

26. Center for Strategic Studies opinion survey, August 1994; Personal interviews with Mustafa Hamarneh, director of the Center, Aguust 1994.

27. Text of Parliamentary Debates as published in *al-Dustur*; summaries and text of Foreign Relations Committee report and deliberations in *JD* 94/4/48.

28. Fahd Rimawi, "The Israeli daily decision maker," *al-Majd* March 20, 1995.

29. Rimawi, "Shylock," *al-Majd* September 5, 1994.

30. Rimawi, "Blocking the Zionist dream," *al-Majd* September 12, 1994.

31. Rimawi, "The Israeli daily decision maker."

32. Fanik, *al-Rai* July 26, 1994; even more bluntly, "all principles which contradict interests must be abolished." *al-Rai* August 19, 1994.

33. Naji Allush, "Jordan and the Peace Treaty," *al-Majd* October 24, 1994.

34. Kamal Rashid, "A great day . . . but for whom?" *al-Majd* October 31, 1994.

35. Bahjat Abu Ghurbiya, "No!!!!" *al-Majd* October 24, 1994.

36. Fanik, "The government opinion," *al-Rai* October 15, 1995.

37. Fanik, *al-Rai* November 5, 1994.

38. *al-Sabil*, August 1, 1995.

Chapter 7

1. Dore Gold, Political Advisor to Prime Minister Netanyahu, interviewed on CNN, November 1997; Shimon Shamir, Israel's first ambassador to Jordan, used identical language in his "Soul Searching for Peace with Jordan," *Ha'aretz*, October 26, 1997.

2. Layth Shubaylat, interviewed in *Shihan*, January 26, 1998.

3. CSS 1994.

4. CSS 1998.

5. Nidal Mansour, "The Israeli Trade Show and Democracy," *al-Hadath* January 13, 1997.

6. Thomas Friedman, *New York Times* June 30, 1998.

7. Bisam al-Amoush, interviewed in *Shihan* June 14, 1997.

8. CSS 1998.

9. Human Rights Watch 1997.

10. *al-Hayat*, April 17, 1998

11. CSS 1997.

12. See Sultan al-Hattab, "Jerusalem for peace," *al-Rai* May 20, 1995.

13. Kabariti in *al-Aswaq* May 10, 1995, (FBIS-NES-95–090).

14. Mohammed al-Mohasina, "Freezing the land grab . . . a Jordanian role?" *al-Dustur* May 26, 1995.

15. Kabariti in *Davar* May 10, 1995 (FBIS-NES-95–091).

16. Fahd al-Fanik, "Protect Lebanon, but . . . " *al-Rai* April 23, 1996.

17. *Al-Sabil* April 23, 1996.

18. Samih al-Mayeteh, "Arabism without action," *al-Sabil* April 23, 1996.

19. Saleh al-Qullab, "They don't want peace." *al-Dustur* May 18, 1995.

20. Thomas Friedman, "Bibi and the King," *New York Times* October 9, 1996.

21. David Makovsky, "Jordan said to have frozen security ties," *Ha'aretz*, October 12, 1997; Shimon Shamir, "Soul searching for peace with Jordan," *Ha'aretz* October 26, 1997.

22. *The Jerusalem Report* November 27, 1997.

23. "Arms Transfers," p.4.

24. Samir Mutawi, in *al-Dustur* September 11, 1997.

25. Tahir al-Udwan, "Arabism is our natural surrounding," *al-Dustur* November 8, 1994.

26. Mohammed Ibrahim Daoud, "In memory of Karameh," *al-Dustur* March 22, 1995.

27. Taher al-Udwan, "The men of Karameh," *al-Dustur* March 22, 1995.

28. Bisam Haddadin, "Karameh," *al-Dustur* March 16, 1995.

29. Fahd al-Rimawi, "The Israeli daily decision maker," *al-Majd* March 20, 1995.

30. Samih al-Mayeteh, "Karameh," *al-Dustur* March 21, 1995.

31. See Musa Barhuma, "The Jordanian Writers Association reaches a decisive point," *al-Wasat* May 29, 1995.

32. Tala'at Shana'a, "What do the candidates say?" *al-Dustur* April 5, 1995.

33. Hamada Fara'na, "The JWA elections," *al-Dustur* April 8, 1995.

34. For alleged government interventions, see "What happened in the JWA elections?" *al-Ahali* April 13, 1995.

35. Hamada Fara'na, "My side of the story," *Shihan* April 22, 1995.

36. Mohammed al-Khuraysha, during Parliamentary debate over the Press and

Publications Law, quoted in *al-Hayat* July 18, 1998, and his elaboration in *al-Hadath* July 18, 1998.

37. "Israel calls on Jordan to abolish its National Charter" *al-Sharq al-Awsat* October 7, 1995.

38. Toujan Faisal, "There is confusion in our house," *Shihan May* 13, 1995.

39. Naji Allush, "New Arab nation or new Middle East?" *al-Majd* October 3, 1994.

40. For example, see Netanyahu's important speech at the graduation ceremony of the National Defense College, August 14, 1997 (http://www.israel-mfa.gov.il/mfa/speeches/netanndc.html).

Chapter 8

1. Foreign Minister Kamal Abu Jabir, interviewed in *Middle East Policy* 1992.

2. Considerable evidence suggests that similar American fears led to the decision not to invade Baghdad or to support the Shi'a and Kurdish rebellions; see Baker 1995 and Telhami 1993.

3. King Hussein speech, December 21, 1995 (FBIS-NES-95–249, pp. 22–26).

4. George Hawatmeh, *Middle East International* April 14, 1993 for details.

5. Reported in *Jordan Times*, July 18, 1998.

6. Layth Shubaylat, Yaqoub Qirsh and Mansour Murad, joint statement, text in *al-Ufuq* July 22, 1992.

7. *Middle East International* July 24, 1992.

8. *Middle East International* June 25, 1993. Marwan Mu'asher, then head of the Jordanian Information Office in Washington, objected in a letter to the *New York Times* (June 23, 1993) that there was nothing new in the report, and that it only been released only in order to harm Jordan in the eyes of the new Administration.

9. Jordan TV press conference, April 16, 1994 (FBIS-NES-94–075).

10. Tareq Masarweh's lead editorials in *al-Ufuq*: April 29, 1992, June 17, 1992, March 22, 1994, March 30, 1994, April 20, 1994, and June 15, 1994. Also see Toujan Faisal, "A question of sovereignty," *al-Bilad* April 1994.

11. Yousif Ibrahim, "Jordan's King Urges Iraqis to Put an End to the Hussein Era," *New York Times* November 8, 1992 and December 31, 1992; Mariam Shahin, "The King Lashes Out," *Middle East International* December 4, 1992, pp. 3–4.

12. Shahin, "The King Lashes Out," *Middle East International* December 4, 1992, pp. 3–4.

13. Tareq Masarweh, "Relations with the Gulf and Arab Interests," *al-Ufuq* 119, September 14, 1994.

14. *Middle East International* July 9, 1993.

15. Abd al-Salam al-Majali, January 11, 1994 (FBIS-NES-94–007). Majali made similar, and more strenuous, complaints in April 1994.

16. Abd al-Raouf al-Rawabdeh in *al-Sharq al-Awsat* December 4, 1995.

17. Fahd Rimawi of *al-Majd* became the first editor to be charged under this

obscure law in January 1996; reported in *Star* January 4, 1996; and *Human Rights Watch* (1996, 1997).

18. Mohammed al-Qadah, "When cohesion . . . when opposition?" *al-Majd* November 7, 1994.

19. "Jordan and the peace," *The New Republic* October 16, 1995.

20. For examples of this skepticism, see Mohammed al-Subayhi, 'Arib al-Rentawi and Taher al-Udwan in *al-Dustur* February 24, 1996; also Rentawi and Udwan, August 12, 1995.

21. 'Arib al-Rentawi, "The Second White Book," *al-Dustur* August 27, 1995; also see Mohammed al-Subayhi, "Readking Hussein's Speech," *al-Dustur* August 26, 1995

22. In FBIS-NES-95–164. *Al-Hayat*'s op-ed, September 28, 1995— "There is no controversy that Hussein has a new position on Iraq and Saddam Hussein."

23. On Iraqi reassurances to Jordan, see "Iraq Emphasizes Its Close Relations to Jordan," *al-Hayat* August 29, 1995; "Iraqi Letter to Prince Hassan," *al-Hayat* September 9, 1995. Tariq Aziz, quoted in *al-Dustur*, August 12, 1995, calls the Iraqi threat "an American invention."

24. *Al-Hayat*, August 20, 1995, noted that Jordanian writers were "not hiding their anger at how the US was exploiting the defection." See Taher al-Udwan, "Iraqi threat?" *al-Dustur* August 13, 1995; Mohammed Ka'oush, "America and the Arabs and us," *al-Dustur* August 18, 1995.

25. *Al-Hayat* August 19, 1995 and September 30, 1995.

26. Bruce Riedel, Deputy Assistant Secretary of Defense for Near East and South Asia, testimony during Hearing and Business Meeting of the Committee on International Relations, House of Representatives, 104th Congress, 2nd Session, March 13, 1996, p. 4.

27. Robert Pelletrau, Assistant Secretary of State for Near Eastern Affairs, Statement before the House Appropriations Committee, Washington DC, March 6, 1996, explains the American decision to sell F-16s in terms of Jordan's commitment to peace with Israel and the increased threat posed by Iraq in the wake of the reversal.

28. *Al-Sharq al-Awsat* May 3, 1996.

29. These events as reported in *al-Hayat* August 17, 1995, August 27, 1995, September 1, 1995, September 3, 1995, and September 18, 1995.

30. Minister of Information Marwan Mu'asher in *al-Sharq al-Awsat* May 6, 1996 revealed that Jordan had received 23 requests from Iraqi opposition groups to open offices in Jordan.

31. Prime Minister Kabariti quoted in *al-Hayat* March 28, 1996.

32. The ideas floated in the Western and Arab press about the possibility of a Hashemite restoration in Iraq received a remarkably negative response in Jordan; see the coverage in *al-Majellah* January 7, 1996 (FBIS-NES-96–080). Among many denials of Jordanian ambitions, Foreign Minister Kabariti, January 4, 1996, and King Hussein on December 21, 1995 (both published in *al-Dustur*.

33. See report in *al-Hayat* September 19, 1995, on talks between Kabariti and

Amru Musa. Examples of the media war include unusually prominent commentaries by Mohammed al-Subayhi (August 29), Arib Rentawi (August 30), and Ahmed Hasban (August 31) in *al-Dustur*.

34. *Al-Sharq al-Awsat* May 5, 1996.

35. For example, see *Shihan's* "Prime Minister's Office" of June 30, 1996.

36. On the brief reconciliation, see *al-Dustur* February 17, 1995 and February 20, 1995; *al-Hayat* February 16, 1995. On the breakdown see *Shihan* "Prime Minister's Office" June 30, 1996.

37. Reuters wire report, September 29, 1995. For examples of the Kuwaiti debate see FBIS-NES-95–236, 95–231.

38. For example, see Kabariti statements in *al-Hayat* September 4, 1995.

39. *Al-Hayat* March 19, 1998.

40. Hilmi al-Asmar, "Norms," *al-Sabil* August 29, 1995.

41. Layth Shubaylat, statement published in *al-Ahali* September 7, 1995 [FBIS-NES-95–175].

42. Samih al-Mayateh, "Power centers" *al-Sabil* March 1996; Saleh al-Qullab, "Tensions grow in the White Revolution," *al-Sharq al-Awsat* July 13, 1996; and Salim Nassar, "Kabiriti's Cabinet Changes the Style of Government," *al-Hayat* February 10, 1996 on the resistance to Kabariti in "old power centers."

43. Hamza Mansour, "The government we want," *al-Sabil* February 5, 1996. Also see "The meaning of the change," *al-Hayat* February 11, 1996.

44. Hilmi al-Asmar, "Norms," *al-Sabil* August 29, 1995.

45. Stories in *al-Sharq al-Awsat* June 13, 1996, June 16, 1996, and June 18, 1996. Also see Taher al-Udwan, "The Jordanian Solidarity Delegation," *al-Dustur* June 14, 1996

46. As reported in *Jordan Times*, July 15, 1998 and July 19, 1998.

47. *Al-Hayat* March 5, 1996. Parliamentary debates as published in *al-Dustur*. The 57 votes were the most received by any Prime Minister since the return of Parliament in 1989. On the other hand, victory was secured by placing an unprecedented 23 MPs in the Cabinet.

48. Taher al-Masri speech reported in *al-Hayat* March 3, 1996 and the debate recounted in detail in *al-Sabil* March 26, 1996.

49. As reported in *al-Hayat*, August 17, 1995, August 27, 1995, September 1, 1995, September 3, 1995, and September 18, 1995.

50. Amman Chamber of Commerce report, published in *al-Ufuq* 12, July 22, 1992.

51. Amman Chamber of Commerce report, in *al-Dustur* September 4, 1995.

52. *Al-Hayat* June 10, 1998 and January 8, 1996.

53. Salim Nassar, "Kabiriti's Cabinet Changes the Style of Government," *al-Hayat* February 10, 1996.

54. Mohammed Ka'oush, "Us and Iraq and America," *al-Dustur* August 15, 1995.

55. Sami Shoush, "Change in Policy and Practice," *al-Hayat* September 9, 1995;

also see *al-Hayat* op-ed, "Jordan's reliance on Iraq shackles economy," February 11, 1996.

56. Hussein speech, August 18, 1996, published in *al-Dustur*.

57. Patrick Cockburn, "Jordan at risk of becoming cockpit for proxy wars," *The Independent*, January 24, 1998.

58. Layth Shubaylat, interviewed in *Shihan*, January 26, 1998. 59. Nasour's remarks reported in *al-Rai*, February 12, 1998. For the opposition's insistence on the right to hold public rallies, see *al-Sabil* February 11, 1998, especially comments by Sulayman Arar, President of the National Committee to Support Iraq.

References

Books and Articles in English

Abbas, Mahmoud. 1995. *Through Secret Channels*. Reading, UK: Garnet.

Abedi, Mehdi and Michael Fischer. 1993. "Thinking a Public Sphere in Arabic and Persian." *Public Culture* 6: 220–229.

Abu Amr, Ziyad. 1994. *Islamic Fundamentalism in the West Bank and Gaza: Muslim Brotherhood and Islamic Jihad*. Bloomington: Indiana University Press.

Abu Jaber, Kamel and Schirin Fathi. 1990. "The 1989 Jordanian Parliamentary Elections." *Orient* 31, no.1: 67–86.

AbuKhalil, As'ad. 1992. "A New Arab Ideology? The Rejuvenation of Arab Nationalism." *Middle East Journal* 46, no.1: 22–36.

Adler, Emmanuel. 1997. "Seizing the Middle Ground: Constructivism in World Politics." *European Journal of International Relations* 3, no. 3: 319–63.

Adler, Emmanuel and Michael Barnett. 1996. "Governing Anarchy: A Research Agenda for the Study of Security Communities." *Ethics and International Affairs* 10 : 63–98.

Adler, Emmanuel and Peter Haas. 1992. "Conclusion: Epistemic Communities, World Order and the Creation of a Reflective Research Program." *International Organization* 46, no.1: 367- 390.

Ajami, Fouad. 1978/79. "The End of Pan-Arabism." *Foreign Affairs* 57: 355–73.

———. 1990/91. "The Summer of Arab Discontent." *Foreign Affairs* 69: 1–20.

———. 1991. *The Arab Predicament: Arab Political Thought and Practice Since 1967*. 2nd Edition. New York: Cambridge University Press.

Amawi, Abla. 1992. "Democracy Dilemmas in Jordan." *Middle East Report* (January–February): 25–29.

Anderson, Benedict. 1983. *Imagined Communities: Reflections on the Origin and Spread of Nationalism.* London: Verso.

Anderson, Lisa. 1991. "Absolutism and the Resilience of Monarchy in the Middle East." *Political Science Quarterly* 106, no.1: 1–15.

———. 1997. "Democratization and Foreign Policy in the Arab World: The Domestic Origins of the Jordanian and Algerian Alliances in the 1991 Gulf War." in M. Kahler, ed., *Liberalization and Foreign Policy.* New York: Columbia University Press, pp. 121–142.

Andoni, Lamis. 1991a. "Jordan." In R. Brynen, ed., *Echoes of the Intifada.* Boulder: Westview Press, pp. 165–94.

———. 1991b. "The PLO at the Crossroads." *Journal of Palestine Studies* 21, no. 1: 54–65.

Anonymous. 1987. "A Policeman on My Chest, A Scissor in My Brain: Political Rights and Censorship in Jordan." *Middle East Report* November–December: 30–4.

Arens, Moshe. 1995. *Broken Covenant: American Foreign Policy and the Crisis Between the U.S. and Israel.* New York: Simon and Schuster.

Arian, Asher. 1998. *The Second Republic: Politics in Israel.* New York: Chatham House.

Arrow, Kenneth, ed. *Barriers to Conflict Resolution.* New York: Norton.

Article 19. 1994. "Jordan: Democratization Without Press Freedom." (March 22).

Aruri, Naseer. 1985. "The PLO and the Jordan Option." *MERIP Reports* (March–April): 3–9.

Arzt, Donna E. 1997. *Refugees Into Citizens: Palestinians and the End of the Arab-Israeli Conflict.* New York: Council on Foreign Relations.

Ashley, Richard K. 1984. "The Poverty of Neorealism." *International Organization* 38, no. 2: 225–86.

———. 1987. "Foreign Policy as Political Performance." *International Studies Notes* 13: 51–54.

———. 1988. "Untying the Sovereign State: A Double Reading of the Anarchy Problematique." *Millennium* 17, no. 2: 227–62.

Ashley, Richard K. and R.B.J. Walker. 1990. "Speaking the Language of Exile: Dissident Thought in International Studies." *International Studies Quarterly* 34, no. 2: 259–68.

Ashrawi, Hanan. 1995. *This Side of Peace: A Personal Account.* New York: Simon and Schuster.

Astorino-Courtois, Allison. 1996. "Transforming International Agreements Into National Realities: Marketing Arab-Israeli Peace in Jordan." *Journal of Politics* 58, no. 4 : 1035- 1054.

Axelrod, Lawrence. 1978. "Tribesmen in Uniform." *Muslim World* 68: 25–45.

Awartani, Hisham and Ephraim Kleiman. 1997. "Economic Interactions Among Participants in the Middle East Peace Process." *Middle East Journal* 51, no. 2: 215–229.

Ayalon, Ami. 1995. *The Press in the Arab Middle East: A History*. New York: Oxford University Press.

Ayoob, Mohammed. 1991. "The Security Problematic of the Third World." *World Politics* 43, no. 3: 257–83.

Ayubi, Nazih. 1995. "Rethinking the Public/Private Dichotomy: Radical Islamism and Civil Society in the Middle East." *Contention* 4, no. 3: 79–105.

Al-Azmeh, Aziz. 1995. "Nationalism and the Arabs." *Arab Studies Quarterly* 17, nos.1–2: 1–17.

Bailey, Clinton. 1984. *Jordan's Palestinian Challenge, 1948–1983: A Political History*. Boulder: Westview Press.

Baker, James A. 1995. *The Politics of Diplomacy: Revolution, War and Peace*. New York: Putnam.

Baker, Raymond W. 1990. *Sadat and After: Struggles for Egypt's Political Soul*. Cambridge: Harvard University Press.

Baldwin, David. 1989. *Paradoxes of Power*. New York: Basil Blackwell.

———. 1993. *Neorealism and Neoliberalism: The Contemporary Debate*. New York: Columbia University Press.

Baram, Amatzia. 1990. "Territorial nationalism in the Middle East." *Middle East Studies* 26: 425–448.

———. 1991. "Baathi Iraq and Hashemite Jordan: From Hostility to Alignment." *Middle East Journal* 45, no. 1: 51–70.

Baram, Amatzia and Barry M. Rubin. 1993. *Iraq's Road to War*. New York: St. Martin's.

Barkey, Henri, ed. *The Politics of Economic Reform in the Middle East*. New York: St. Martin's.

Barkin, J.Samuel and Bruce Cronin. 1994. "The State and the Nation: Changing Norms and the rules of Sovereignty in International Relations." *International Organization* 48, no. 1: 107–130.

Barnett, Michael N. 1993. "Institutions, Roles and Disorder: The Case of the Arab States System." *International Studies Quarterly* 37, no. 3: 271–296.

———. 1995. "Sovereignty, Nationalism and Regional Order in the Arab States System." *International Organization* 49, no. 4: 479–510.

———. 1996. "Identity in Middle East Alliances." In P. Katzenstein, *Culture of National Security*. New York: Columbia University Press, pp. 400–50.

———. 1996–97. "Regional Security After the Gulf War." *Political Science Quarterly* 111, no. 4: 597–618.

———. 1998. *Dialogues in Arab Politics: Negotiations in Regional Order*. New York: Columbia University Press.

Barnett, Michael N. and Jack S. Levy. 1991. "Domestic Sources of Alliances and Alignments: The Case of Egypt, 1962–73." *International Organization* 45, no. 3: 369–92.

Bartelson, Jens. 1995. *A Geneaology of Sovereignty*. Cambridge: Cambridge University Press.

Bates, Robert H., Rui J. P. de Figueiredo Jr., and Barry R. Weingast. 1998. "The Politics of Interpretation: Rationality, Culture, and Transition." *Politics and Society* 26, no. 2: 221–256.

Baxter, Hugh. 1987. "System and Life-world in Habermas's Theory of Communicative Action." *Theory and Society* 16: 39–86.

Benhabib, Seyla. 1989. "Liberal Dialogue Versus a Critical Theory of Discursive Legitimation." In N. Rosenblum, ed., *Liberalism and the Good Life*. Cambridge: Harvard University Press, pp. 143–56.

———. 1992. "Models of Public Space." In Calhoun, *Habermas and the Public Sphere*. Cambridge: MIT Press, pp. 73–98.

———. 1996. *Democracy and Difference: Contesting the Boundaries of the Political*. Princeton: Princeton University Press.

Berger, Johannes. 1983. "Review of *Theory of Communicative Action*." *Telos* 57: 194–205.

Biersteker, Thomas J. and Cynthia Weber. 1996. *State Sovereignty as Social Construct*. New York: Cambridge University Press.

Bohman, James. 1990. "Communication, Ideology, and Democratic Theory." *American Political Science Review* 84, no. 1: 93–109.

———. 1996. *Public Deliberation*. Cambridge: MIT Press.

———. 1998. "The Globalization of the Public Sphere: Cosmopolitan Publicity and the Problem of Cultural Pluralism." *Philosophy and Social Criticism* 24, no. 2/3: 199–216.

Bohman, James and Matthias Lutz-Bachmann. 1998. *Perpetual Peace: Essays on Kant's Cosmopolitan Ideal*. Cambridge: MIT Press.

Bohman, James and William Rehg, eds. 1997. *Deliberative Democracy*. Cambridge: MIT Press.

Bookmiller, Robert. 1994. "Approaching the Rubicon: Jordan and the Peace Process." *SAIS Review* 14, no. 2: 109–123.

Bourdieu, Pierre. 1977. *Outline of a Theory of Practice*. New York: Cambridge University Press.

Bourdieu, Pierre and Loic J. D. Wacquant. 1992. *An Invitation to a Reflexive Sociology*. Chicago: University of Chicago Press.

Boyd, Douglas A. 1977. "Egyptian Radio: Tool of Political and National Development." *Journalism Monograph* 48.

———. 1993. *Broadcasting in the Arab World. 2nd Edition*. Ames: Iowa State University Press.

Brand, Laurie A. 1988. *Palestinians in the Arab World: Institution Building and the Search for State*. New York: Columbia University Press.

———. 1991a. "Liberalization and Changing Political Coalitions: The Bases of Jordan's 1990–1991 Gulf Crisis policy." *Jerusalem Journal of International Relations* 13, no. 4: 1–46.

———. 1991b. "The Intifadah and the Arab World: Old Players, New Roles." *International Journal* 45 (Summer): 501–528.

———. 1992. "Economic and Political Liberalization in a Rentier Economy: The Case of the Hashemite Kingdom of Jordan." In I. Harik and D. Sullivan, *Privatization and Liberalization in the Middle East*. Bloomington: Indiana University Press, pp. 167–88.

———. 1994a. *Jordan's Inter-Arab Relations: The Political Economy of Alliance Making*. New York: Columbia University Press.

———. 1994b. "Economics and Shifting Alliances: Jordan's Relations with Syria and Iraq, 1975–81." *International Journal of Middle East Studies* 26: 393–413.

———. 1995. "Palestinians and Jordanians: A Crisis of Identity." *Journal of Palestine Studies* 24, no. 4: 46–61.

———. 1998. *Women, the State, and Political Liberalization: Middle Eastern and North African Experiences*. New York: Columbia University Press.

Brilmayer, Lea. 1989. *Justifying International Acts*. Ithaca: Cornell University Press.

Brown, Chris. 1992. *International Relations Theory: New Normative Approaches*. London: Harvester Wheatsheaf.

Browne, Donald R. 1975. "The Voices of Palestine: A Broadcasting House Divided." *Middle East Journal* 29, no. 2: 133–50.

Brubaker, Rogers. 1996. *Nationalism Reframed: Nationhood and the National Question in the New Europe*. Cambridge: Cambridge University Press.

Brynen, Rex. 1991a. "Palestine and the Arab State System: Permeability, State Consolidation and the Intifada." *Canadian Journal of Political Science* 24, no. 3: 595–621.

———. 1991b. *Echoes of the Intifada: Regional Repercussions of the Palestinian-Israeli conflict*. Boulder: Westview Press.

———. 1992. "Economic Crisis and Post-rentier Democratization in the Arab World: The Case of Jordan." *Canadian Journal of Political Science* 25, no. 1: 69–97.

———. 1998. "The Politics of Monarchical Liberalism: Jordan." In B. Korany, *Political Liberalization and Democratization in the Arab World*, vol 2, Boulder: Lynn Rienner, pp. 71–100.

Brzezinski, Zbigniew, Brent Scowcroft and Richard Murphy. 1997. *Differentiated Containment*. New York: Council on Foreign Relations.

Bukovansky, Mlada. 1997. "American Identity and Neutral Rights from Independence to the War of 1812." *International Organization* 51, no. 2: 209–243.

Bull, Hedley. 1977. *The Anarchical Society: A Study of Order in World Politics*. New York: Columbia University Press.

Bush, George and Brent Scowcroft. 1998. *A World Transformed*. New York: Knopf.

Buzan, Barry. 1993. "From International System to International Society: Structural Realism and Regime Theory Meet the English School." *International Organization* 47, no. 3: 327–352.

Buzan, Barry, Charles Jones and Richard Little. 1993. *The Logic of Anarchy: Neorealism to Structural Realism*. New York: Columbia University Press.

Calhoun, Craig. 1988. "Populist Politics, Communications Media and Large Scale Societal Integration." *Sociological Theory* 6: 219–241.

———. 1992. *Habermas and the Public Sphere*. Cambridge: MIT Press.

———. 1993. "Civil Society and the Public Sphere." *Public Culture* 5: 267–280.

———. 1994. *Social Theory and the Politics of Identity*. New York: Blackwell Press.

———. 1995. *Critical Social Theory*. New York: Blackwell Press.

Campbell, David. 1992. *Writing Security: United States Foreign Policy and the Politics of Identity*. Minneapolis: University of Minnesota Press.

Carlsnaes, Walter. 1992. "The Agency-Structure Problem in Foreign Policy Analysis." *International Studies Quarterly* 36, no. 2: 245–270.

Chafetz, Glenn. 1996/97. "The Struggle for a National Identity in Post-Soviet Russia." *Political Science Quarterly* 111, no. 4: 661–88.

———. 1997. "An Empirical Analysis of International Identity Change." Paper presented to American Political Science Association Annual Meeting, Washington D.C.

———. 1998/99. "Identity and Foreign Policy: Introduction." *Security Studies* 8, no. 2/3.

Chambers, Simone. 1996. *Reasonable Democracy: Jurgen Habermas and the Politics of Discourse*. Ithaca: Cornell University Press.

Checkel, Jeffrey T. 1997. "International Norms and Domestic Politics: Bridging the Rationalist- Constructivist Divide." *European Journal of International Relations* 3, no. 4: 473–495.

———. 1998. "The Constructivist Turn in International Relations Theory." *World Politics* 50, no. 2: 324–48.

Claude, Inis. 1966. "Collective Legitimization as a Political Function of the UN." *International Organization* 20: 367–379.

Clark, William Roberts. 1998. "Agents and Structures: Two Views of Preferences, Two Views of Institutions." *International Studies Quarterly* 42, no. 2: 245–270.

Cobban, Helena. 1984. *The Palestinian Liberation Organization: People, Power and Politics*. New York: Cambridge University Press.

Cohen, Amnon. 1980. "Does a 'Jordanian Option' Still Exist?" *Jerusalem Quarterly* 16: 111–120.

———. 1981. *Political Parties in the West Bank Under the Jordanian Regime*. Ithaca: Cornell University Press.

Cohen, Jean L. 1979. "Why More Political Theory?" *Telos* 40: 70–94.

———. 1985. "Strategy or Identity: New Theoretical Paradigms and Contemporary Social Movements." *Social Research* 52, no. 4: 663–716.

Cohen, Jean L. and Andrew Arato. 1984. "Civil Society, Social Movements and Sovereignty." *Praxis International* 5.

———. 1992. *Civil Society and Political Theory*. Cambridge: MIT Press.

Connolly, William E. 1991. *Identity/Difference: Democratic Negotiations of Political Paradox*. Ithaca: Cornell University Press.

Cortell, Andrew and James Davis. 1996. "How Do International Institutions Matter? The Domestic Impact of International Rules and Norms." *International Studies Quarterly* 40, no. 4: 451–478.

Cox, Robert. 1981. "Social Forces, State Actors and World Orders: Beyond International Relations Theory." *Millennium* 10, no. 1: 126–55.

Creed, John. 1992. "The impact of Arab summits on conflict management." *New Political Science* 21.

Dann, Uriel. 1989. *King Hussein and the Challenge of Arab Radicalism, 1955–1967.* New York: Oxford University Press.

David, Steven R. 1991a. *Choosing Sides: Alignment and Realignment in the Third World.* Baltimore: Johns Hopkins University Press.

Davis, Uri. 1995. "Jinsiyya Versus Muwatana: The Question of Citizenship and the State in the Middle East." *Arab Studies Quarterly* 17, nos.1–2: 19–50.

Dawisha, Adeed. 1976. *Egypt in the Arab World: The Elements of Foreign Policy.* New York: Wiley.

Day, Arthur. 1986. *East Bank/West Bank: Jordan and the Prospects for Peace.* New York: Council on Foreign Relations.

Dessler, David. 1989. "What's at Stake in the Agent-Structure Debate?" *International Organization* 43, no. 3: 441–474.

Deutsch, Karl W. 1953. *Nationalism and Social Communication: An Inquiry Into the Foundations of Nationality.* New York: MIT Press.

Diwan, Ishac and Michael Walton. 1994. "Palestine Between Israel and Jordan: The Economics of an Uneasy Triangle." *Beirut Review* 8: 20–43.

Dowty, Alan. 1984. *Middle East Crisis: U.S. Decision-Making in 1958, 1970, and 1973.* Berkeley: University of California Press.

———. 1998. *The Jewish State: A Century Later.* Berkeley: University of California Press.

Ebert, Barbara. 1992. "The Gulf War and Its Aftermath: An Assessment of Evolving Arab responses." *Middle East Policy* 1, no. 4: 77–95.

Elazar, Daniel, ed. 1982. *Judea, Samaria and Gaza: Views on the Present and the Future.* Washington: American Enterprise Institute.

Elman, Miriam F. *Paths to Peace: Is Democracy the Answer?.* Cambridge: MIT Press.

Elster, Jon. 1989. *The Cement of Society: A Study of Social Order.* New York: Cambridge University Press.

———. 1993. "Constitution-making in Eastern Europe: Rebuilding the Boat in the Open Sea." *Public Administration* 71: 169–217.

———. 1995. "Strategic Uses of Argument." In K. Arrow, ed., *Barriers to Conflict Resolution.* New York: Norton, pp. 237–57.

———. 1997. "The Market and the Forum: Three Varieties of Political Theory." In J. Bohman and W. Rehg, eds., *Deliberative Democracy.* pp. 3–34.

———. 1998. *Deliberative Democracy.* New York: Cambridge University Press.

Falk, Richard. 1973. *Regional Politics and World Order*. San Francisco: W. H. Freeman.

———. 1991. "The Cruelty of Geopolitics: The Fate of Nation and State in the Middle East." *Millennium* 20, no. 3: 383–393.

Faris, Hani. 1987. *Arab Nationalism and the Future of the Arab World*. Belmont, Mass.: Association of Arab American University Graduates Monograph Series 22.

Farsoun, Samih K. and Christina Zacharia. 1997. *Palestine and the Palestinians*. Boulder: Westview Press.

Fathi, Schirin. 1994. *Jordan: An Invented Nation?* Hamburg: Deutsches Orient Institut.

Fearon, James D. 1994a. "Signaling Versus the Balance of Power and Interests." *Journal of Conflict Resolution* 38, no. 2: 236–269.

———. 1994b. "Domestic Political Audiences and the Escalation of International Disputes." *American Political Science Review* 88, no. 3: 577–592.

———. 1997. "Signaling Foreign Policy Interests: Tying Hands Versus Sinking Costs." *Journal of Conflict Resolution* 41, no. 1: 68–90.

———. 1998a. "Deliberation as Discussion." In J.Elster, ed., *Deliberative Democracy*. Chicago: University of Chicago Press, 49–68.

———. 1998b. "Domestic Politics, Foreign Policy and Theories of International Relations." *Annual Review of Political Science* 1: 259–283.

Fearon, James D. and David D. Laitin. 1996. "Explaining Interethnic Cooperation." *American Political Science Review* 90, no. 4: 715–735.

Ferejohn, John. 1991. "Rationality and Interpretation: Parliamentary Elections in Early Stuart England." In K. Monroe, *The Economic Approach to Politics*. New York: HarperCollins, pp. 279–305.

Finnemore, Martha. 1996a. "Norms, Culture and World Politics: Insights from Sociology's Institutionalism." *International Organization* 50: 325–348.

———. 1996b. *National Interests in International Society*. Ithaca: Cornell University Press.

Franck, Thomas M. 1990. *The Power of Legitimacy Among Nations*. New York: Oxford University Press.

Fraser, Nancy. 1989. *Unruly Practices: Power, Discourse and Gender in Contemporary Social Theory*. Minneapolis: University of Minnesota Press.

Freedman, Lawrence and Efraim Karsh. 1993. *The Gulf Conflict, 1990–1991: Diplomacy and War in the New World Order*. Princeton: Princeton University Press.

Frisch, Hillel. 1997. "Ethnicity, Territorial Integrity, and Regional Order: Palestinian Identity in Jordan and Israel." *Journal of Peace Research* 34, no. 3: 257–269.

Gagnon, V.P. 1994/95. "Ethnic Nationalism and International Conflict: the Case of Serbia." *International Security* 19, no. 3: 130–66.

Garfinkle, Adam M. 1992. *Jordan and Israel in the Shadow of War: Functional Ties and Futile Diplomacy in a Small Place*. New York: St. Martin's.

Garnham, Nicholas. 1993. "The Mass Media, Cultural Identity, and the Public Sphere in the Modern World." *Public Culture* 5: 251–65.

Gause, F. Gregory III. 1992. "Sovereignty, Statecraft and Stability in the Middle East." *Journal of International Affairs* 45, no. 2: 441–69.

George, Jim. 1994. *Discourses of Global Politics: A Critical (Re)Introduction to International Relations.* Boulder: Lynn Rienner.

Gerges, Fawaz A. 1996/97. "Washington's Misguided Iran Policy." *Survival* 38: 5–15.

Gerges, Fawaz A. and Tariq Tell. 1996. "When the King's Away, the Critics Play." *Christian Science Monitor* (September 20): 18.

Goldstein, Judith and Robert O. Keohane, eds. 1993. *Ideas and Foreign Policy: Beliefs, Institutions and Political Change.* Ithaca: Cornell University Press.

Green, Jerrold D. 1986. "Are Arab politics Still Arab?" *World Politics* 38, no. 3: 611–625.

Gresh, Alain. 1989. *The PLO: The Struggle Within.* London: Zed Books.

Haacke, Jurgen. 1996. "Theory and Praxis in International Relations: Habermas, Self- Reflection, Rational Argumentation." *Millennium* 25, no. 2: 255–289.

Haas, Ernst B. 1993. "Nationalism: An Instrumental Social Construction." *Millennium* 22, no. 3: 505–545.

Habermas, Jürgen. 1975. *Legitimation Crisis.* Boston: Beacon Press.

———. 1979. *Communication and the Evolution of Society.* Boston: Beacon Press.

———. 1984. *Theory of Communicative Action vol.1: Reason and the Rationalization of Society.* Boston: Beacon Press.

———. 1987. *Theory of Communicative Action vol. 2: Lifeworld and System.* Boston: Beacon Press.

———. 1989. *Structural Transformation of the Public Sphere.* Cambridge: MIT Press.

———. 1992. "Citizenship and National Identity: Some Reflections on the Future of Europe." *Praxis International* 12, no. 1: 1–19.

———. 1996. *Between Facts and Norms: Contributions to a Discourse Theory of Law and Democracy.* Cambridge: MIT Press.

———. 1998a. "The European Nation-State: On the Past and Future of Sovereignty and Citizenship." *Public Culture* 10, no. 2: 397–416.

———. 1998b. *The Inclusion of the Other: Studies in Political Theory.* Cambridge: MIT Press.

Haggard, Stephan and Beth A. Simmons. 1987. "Theories of International Regimes." *International Organization* 41, no. 3: 491–517.

Hall, Rodney Bruce. 1997. "Moral Authority as a Power Resource." *International Organization* 51, no. 4: 591–622.

Halliday, Fred. 1994. "The Gulf War 1990–1991 and the Study of International Relations." *Review of International Studies* 20: 109–130.

Hardin, Russell. 1995. *One for All: the Logic of group Conflict.* Princeton: Princeton University Press.

Harkabi, Yehoshefat. 1988. *Israel's Fateful Hour*. New York: Harper and Row.

Harknett, Richard and Jeffrey VanDenBerg. 1997. "Alignment Theory and Interrelated Threats: Jordan and the Persian Gulf crisis." *Security Studies* 6, no. 3: 112–153.

Haykal, Mohammed Hassanein. 1973. *The Cairo Documents*. New York: Doubleday.

———. 1996. *Secret Channels*. New York: HarperCollins.

Hechter, Michael. 1992. "Rational Choice Theory and Historical Sociology." *International Social Science Journal* 44: 367–73.

Hechter, Michael and Satoshi Kanazawa. 1997. "Sociological Rational Choice Theory." *Annual Review of Sociology* 23: 191–214.

Held, David. 1991. "Democracy, the Nation-state and the Global System." *Economy and Society* 20, no. 2.

Henderson, Amy. 1998. "The Trouble with Jordan." *Jerusalem Report* (April 2): 22–24.

Hinsley, F.G. 1968. *Sovereignty*. New York: Cambridge University Press.

Hiro, Dilip. 1992. *Desert Shield to Desert Storm: The Second Gulf War*. New York: Routledge.

Hoffman, Mark. 1987. "Critical Theory and the Inter-paradigm Debate." *Millennium* 16, no. 2: 231–249.

Hollis, Martin and Steve Smith. 1990. *Explaining and Understanding in IR Theory*. Cambridge: Cambridge University Press.

Holsti, Ole R. 1996. *Public Opinion and American Foreign Policy*. Ann Arbor: University of Michigan Press.

Hopf, Ted. 1998. "The Promise of Constructivism in International Relations Theory." *International Security* 23, no. 1: 171–200.

Hudson, Michael C. 1977. *Arab Politics: The Search for Legitimacy*. New Haven: Yale University Press.

———. 1988. "Democratization and the Problem of Legitimacy in Middle East Politics." *MESA Bulletin* 22: 157–171.

———. 1996. "Obstacles to Democratization in the Middle East." *Contention* 5, no. 2: 81–105.

Human Rights Watch. 1997. *Jordan: Clamping Down on Critics*. HRW/Middle East 9, no. 12 (October).

Hunt, Scott, Robert Bedford and David Snow. 1994. "Identity Fields: Framing Processes and the Social Construction of Movement Identities." In E. Larana, ed., *New Social Movements*. Philadelphia: Temple University Press.

Husayn ibn Talal. 1962. *Uneasy Lies the Head*. New York: Random House.

Ikenberry, G. John. 1998. "Constitutional Politics in International Relations." *European Journal of International Relations* 4, no. 2: 147–177.

Indyk, Martin. 1991/92. "Beyond the Balance of Power: America's Choice in the Middle East." *The National Interest* (Winter): 33–43.

Israeli, Raphael. 1991. *Palestinians Between Israel and Jordan: Squaring the Triangle*. New York: Praeger.

Jackson, Robert. 1990. *Quasi-states: Sovereignty, International Relations and the Third World*. Cambridge: Cambridge University Press.

Jankowski, James and Israel Gershoni, eds. 1997. *Rethinking Nationalism in the Arab Middle East*. New York: Columbia University Press.

Jarbawi, Ali. 1995. "The Triangle of Conflict." *Foreign Policy* 100: 92–108.

Jervis, Robert. 1970. *The Logic of Images in International Relations*. Princeton: Princeton University Press.

Joffe, George. 1993. "Middle Eastern Views of the Gulf Conflict and Its Aftermath." *Review of International Studies* 19: 177–199.

Johnson, James. 1991. "Habermas on Strategic and Communicative Action." *Political Theory* 19, no. 2: 181–201.

———. 1993. "Is Talk Really Cheap? Prompting Conversation Between Critical Theory and Rational Choice." *American Political Science Review* 87, no. 1: 74–85.

———. 1998. "Arguing for deliberation." In J. Elster, *Deliberative Democracy*. Chicago: University of Chicago Press, pp. 161–84.

Jureidini, Paul and R. D. McLaurin. 1984. *Jordan: The Impact of Social Change on the Role of the Tribes*. Washington Papers 108. Praeger.

Karsh, Efraim. 1997. *Fabricating Israeli History: The "New Historians."* London: Frank Cass.

Katzenstein, Peter J. 1996a. *The Culture of National Security: Norms and Identities in World Politics*. New York: Columbia University Press.

———. 1996b. *Cultural Norms and National Security: Police and Military in Postwar Japan*. Ithaca: Cornell University Press.

———. 1997. *Tamed Power: Germany in Europe*. Ithaca: Cornell University Press.

Katzenstein, Peter J. and Nobuto Okarawa. 1993. "Japan's National Security: Structures, Norms and Policies." *International Security* 17, no. 4: 84–118.

Keck, Margaret E. and Kathryn Sikkink. 1998. *Activists Beyond Borders: Advocacy Networks in International Politics*. Ithaca: Cornell University Press.

Kelly, Kevin. 1987. "Jordan's Plan for the West Bank." *Middle East Report* (January–February): 44–45.

Kelly, Michael. 1994. *Critique and Power: Recasting the Habermas/Foucault Debate*. Cambridge: MIT Press.

Keohane, Robert O. 1984. *After Hegemony: Cooperation and Discord in the World Political Economy*. Princeton: Princeton University Press.

———. 1989. *International Institutions and State Power*. Boulder: Westview Press.

Khadduri, Majid and Edmund Ghareeb. 1997. *War in the Gulf, 1990–91: The Iraq-Kuwait Conflict and Its Implications*. New York: Oxford University Press.

Khalidi, Rashid. 1991. "Palestinians in the Gulf Crisis." *Current History* 90, no. 1: 18–20, 37.

———. 1996. *Palestinian Identity: The Construction of Modern National Consciousness*. New York: Columbia University Press.

Khazen, Jihad and Abdul Bari Atwan. 1995. "The Arab press." *Index on Censorship*..

Khouri, Riad. 1994. "The Political Economy of Jordan: Democratization and the Gulf Crisis." In D. Tschirgi, ed., *The Arab World Today*. Boulder: Lynn Rienner, pp. 101–19.

Khoury, Nabil. 1982. "The Pragmatic Trend in Inter-Arab Politics." *Middle East Journal* 36, no. 3: 374–387.

Kienle, Eberhard. 1995. "Arab Unity Schemes Revisited: Interest, Identity, and Policy in Syria and Egypt." *International Journal of Middle East Studies* 27, no. 1: 53–71.

Kier, Elizabeth. 1997. *Imagining War*. Princeton: Princeton University Press.

Kimura, Masato and David Welch. 1998. "Specifying 'Interests': Japan's Claim to the Northern Territories and its Implications for International Relations Theory." *International StudiesQuarterly* 42, no. 2: 213–244.

Klandermans, Bert, Hanspeter Kriesi and Sidney Tarrow. 1988. *From Structure to Action: Comparing Social Movement Research Across Cultures*. Greenwich, Conn: JAI Press.

Klieman, Aharon. 1981. *In Search of a Durable Peace: Israel, Jordan, and the Palestinians*. Sage/Washington Papers.

———. 1998. "Israel's 'Jordanian Option': A Post-Oslo Reassessment." In I. Peleg, *The Middle East Peace Process*. Albany, NY: SUNY Press, pp. 178–224.

Klotz, Audie. 1995. "Norms Reconstituting Interests: Global Racial Equality and US Sanctions Against South Africa." *International Organization* 49, no. 3: 451–78.

Knight, Jack and James Johnson. 1994. "Aggregation and Deliberation: On the Possibility of Democratic Legitimacy." *Political Theory* 22, no. 2: 277–296.

———. 1997. "What Sort of Equality Does Deliberative Democracy Require?" In J. Bohman and W. Rehg, *Deliberative Democracy*. Cambridge: MIT Press, pp. 279–320.

Kocs, Stephen. 1994. "Explaining the Strategic Behavior of States: International Law as System Structure." *International Studies Quarterly* 38, no. 4: 535–56.

Korany, Baghat. 1997. "The Old/New Middle East." In L. Guazzone, ed., *The Middle East in Global Change*. New York: St. Martin's, pp. 135–52.

Korany, Baghat and Ali E. Hillal Dessouki, eds. 1991. *The Foreign Policies of Arab States: The Challenge of Change*. Boulder: Westview Press.

Korany, Baghat, Rex Brynen and Paul Noble. 1993. *The Many Faces of National Security in the Arab World*. New York: St. Martin's Press.

———. 1998. *Political Liberalization and Democratization in the Arab World*, vol. 2. Boulder: Lynn Rienner.

Koslowski, Rey and Friedrich Kratochwil. 1994. "Understanding Change in International Politics: The Soviet Empire's Demise and the International System." *International Organization* 48, no. 2: 215–47.

Kramer, Martin. 1997. "The Middle East, Old and New." *Daedalus* 126, no. 2: 89–112,.

Krasner, Stephen D. 1983. *International Regimes*. Ithaca: Cornell University Press.

————. 1985. *Structural Conflict: The Third World Against Global Liberalism.* Berkeley: University of California Press.

————. 1988. "Sovereignty: An Institutional Perspective." *Comparative Political Studies* 21, no. 1: 66–94.

Kratochwil, Friedrich V. 1990. *Rules, Norms and Decisions: On the Conditions of Practical and Legal Reasoning in International Relations and Domestic Affairs.* New York: Cambridge University Press.

————. 1993. "The Embarrassment of Changes: Neo-realism as the Science of Realpolitik Without Politics." *Review of International Studies* 19, no. 1: 63–80.

Kymlicka, Will and Wayne Norman. 1994. "Return of the Citizen: A Survey of Recent Work on Citizenship Theory." *Ethics* 104: 352–81.

Laclau, Ernesto and Chantal Mouffe. 1985. *Hegemony and Socialist Strategy.* London: Verso .

Laitin, David D. 1988. "Political Culture and Political Preferences." *American Political Science Review* 82, no. 2: 589–93.

————. 1998. *Identity in Formation: The Russian-speaking Population in the Near Abroad.* Ithaca: Cornell University Press.

Lake, Anthony. 1994. "Confronting Backlash States." *Foreign Affairs* 73, no. 2: 45–55.

Lake, David A. and Robert Powell. Forthcoming. *Strategic Choice in International Relations.* Princeton: Princeton University Press.

Lake, David A. and Donald Rothchild, eds. 1998. *The International Spread of Ethnic Conflict: Fear, Diffusion, and Escalation.* Princeton: Princeton University Press.

Lapid, Yosef and Friedrich V. Kratochwil, eds. 1996. *The Return of Culture and Identity in IR Theory.* Boulder: Lynn Rienner.

Larana, Ernesto, et al., ed. 1994. *New Social Movements.* Philadelphia: Temple University Press.

Latham, Robert. 1996. "Getting out from Under: Rethinking Security Beyond Liberalism and the Levels of Analysis Problem." *Millennium* 25, no. 1: 77–108.

Layne, Linda L. 1989. "The Dialogics of Tribal Self-representation in Jordan." *American Ethnologist* 16, no. 1: 24–39.

————. 1993. *Home and Homeland: The Dialogics of Tribal and National Identities in Jordan.* Princeton: Princeton University Press.

Lebow, Richard Ned. 1981. *Between Peace and War: The Nature of International Crisis.* Baltimore: Johns Hopkins University Press.

Legro, Jeffrey W. 1996. "Culture and Preferences in the International Cooperation Two-Step." *American Political Science Review* 90, no. 1: 118–137.

Lerner, David. 1958. *The Passing of Traditional Society: Modernizing the Middle East.* Glencoe, Il: Free Press.

Lesch, David W. 1996. *The Middle East and the United States: A Historical and Political Reassessment.* Boulder: Westview Press.

Levy, Jack S. and Michael N. Barnett. 1992. "Alliance Formation, Domestic Political

Economy and Third World Security." *Jerusalem Journal of International Relations* 14, no. 4: 19–40.

Linklater, Andrew. 1982. *Men and Citizens in the Theory of International Relations.* London: MacMillan.

———. 1990a. "The Problem of Community in International Relations." *Alternatives* 15: 135–153.

———. 1990b. *Beyond Realism and Marxism: Critical Theory and International Relations.* London: Macmillan.

———. 1992. "The question of the Next Stage in International Relations Theory: A Critical-theoretical Point of View." *Millennium* 21, no. 1: 77–98.

———. 1996. "Citizenship and Sovereignty in the Post-Westphalian State." *European Journal of International Relations* 2, no. 1: 77–103.

———. 1998. *The Transformation of Political Community: Ethical Foundations of the Post-Westphalian Era.* Columbia: University of South Carolina Press.

Lipschutz, Ronnie. 1992. "Reconstructing World Politics." *Millennium* 21, no. 3: 389–420.

Lukacs, Yehuda. 1997. *Israel, Jordan and the Peace Process.* Syracuse: Syracuse University Press.

Lustick, Ian S. Forthcoming. *Rightsizing the State.*

———. 1993a. *Unsettled States, Disputed Lands: Britain and Ireland, France and Algeria, Israel and the West Bank-Gaza.* Ithaca: Cornell University Press.

———. 1993b. "Writing the Intifada: Collective Action in the Occupied Territories." *World Politics* 45, no. 3: 560–94.

———. 1977. *Jordan and Israel: Implications of an Adversarial Partnership.* Berkeley: Institute for International Studies.

Lyons, Gene M. and Michael Mastanduno. 1993. "International Intervention, State Sovereignty and the Future of International Society." *International Social Sciences Journal* 45: 517–32.

———. 1995. *Beyond Westphalia?* Baltimore: Johns Hopkins University Press.

MacDonald, Robert W. 1965. *The League of Arab States: A Study in the Dynamics of Regional Organization.* Princeton: Princeton University Press.

MacLeod, Scott. 1991. "In the Wake of Desert Storm." *New York Review of Books,* March 7.

Maddy-Weitzman, Bruce. 1993. *The Crystallization of the Arab State System, 1945–1954.* Syracuse: Syracuse University Press.

Madfai, Madiha. 1993. *Jordan, the United States and the Middle East Peace Process, 1974–1991.* New York: Cambridge University Press.

Makovsky, David. 1995. *Making Peace with the PLO: The Rabin Government's Road To the Oslo Accord.* Boulder: Westview Press.

March, James G. and Johan P. Olson. 1984. "The New Institutionalism: Organizational Factors in Political Life." *American Political Science Review* 78, no. 4: 734–49.

Mattar, Philip. 1994. "The PLO and the Gulf Crisis." *Middle East Journal* 48, no. 1: 31–46.

McAdam, Doug, John D. McCarthy and Mayer N. Zald. 1996. *Comparative Perspectives on Social Movements: Political Opportunities, Mobilizing Structures, and Cultural Framings*. New York: Cambridge University Press.

McCain, Thomas and Leonard Shyles. 1994. *The 1,000 Hour War: Communication in the Gulf*. London: Greenwood Press.

McCarthy, Thomas. 1988. "Complexity and Democracy, or the Seducements of Systems Theory." *New German Critique*: 27–53.

———. 1996. "A reply to Georgia Warnke and David Couzens Hoy." *Philosophy and Social Criticism* 22, no. 2: 99–108.

McDaniel, Drew. 1980. "Some Notes on Political Broadcasting in the Arab World." *Middle East Review*.

McSweeney, Bill. 1996. "Identity and Security: Buzan and the Copenhagen School." *Review of International Studies* 22: 81–93.

Mearsheimer, John. 1994/95. "The False Promise of International Institutions." *International Security* 19, no. 3: 5–49.

Mercer, Jonathan. 1995. "Anarchy and identity." *International Organization* 49, no. 2: 229–252.

Miller, David. 1992. "Deliberative Democracy and Social Choice." *Political Studies* 40, no. 1: 54–67.

Miller, Judith. 1996. *God Has 99 Names: Reporting from a Militant Middle East*. New York: Simon and Shuster.

Milner, Helen V. 1991. "The Assumption of Anarchy in International Relations Theory: A Critique." *Review of International Studies* 17: 67–85.

———. 1997. *Interests, Institutions and Information: Domestic Politics and International Relations*. Princeton: Princeton University Press.

Mishal, Shaul. 1978. *East Bank/West Bank*. New Haven: Yale University Press.

Monroe, Kristen. 1991. *The Economic Approach to Politics*. New York: HarperCollins1991.

Moravcsik, Andrew. 1997. "Taking Preferences Seriously: A Liberal Theory of International Politics." *International Organization* 51, no. 4: 513–553.

Morris, Benny. 1990. *1948 and After: Israel and the Palestinians*. New York: Oxford University Press.

———. 1993. *Israel's Border Wars: Arab Infiltration, Israeli Retaliation, and the Countdown to the Suez War*. New York: Oxford University Press.

Morrow, James D. 1994. "Modeling the Forms of International Cooperation: Distribution Versus Information." *International Organization* 48, no. 3: 387–423.

———. 1997. *Game Theory for Political Scientists*. Princeton: Princeton University Press.

Mufti, Malik. 1996. *Sovereign Creations: Pan-Arabism and Political Order in Syria and Iraq*. Ithaca: Cornell University Press.

Mutawi, Samir A. 1987. *Jordan in the 1967 War*. New York: Cambridge University Press.

Nau, Henry R. 1993. "Identity and International Relations." Paper Presented to the Annual Meeting of the American Political Science Association.

Netanyahu, Benjamin. 1993. *A Place Among the Nations: Israel and the World*. New York: Bantam Books.

Neufeld, Mark. 1993. "Interpretation and the 'science' of International Relations." *Review of International Studies* 19.

Nevo, Joseph. 1980. "Is There a Jordanian Entity?" *Jerusalem Quarterly* 16: 98–110.

———. 1993. "Jordan's Relations with Iraq: Ally or Victim?" In A. Baram and B. Rubin, *Iraq's Road to War*. New York: St. Martin's, pp. 135–147.

———. 1996. *King Abdallah and Palestine: a territorial ambition*. New York: St. Martin's.

Nevo, Joseph and Illan Pappe, eds. 1994. *Jordan in the Middle East: The Making of a Pivotal State*. Essex: Frank Cass.

Nisan, Mordechai. 1982. "The Palestinian Features of Jordan." In D. Elazar, *Judea, Samaria and Gaza*. Washington: American Enterprise Institute, pp. 191–209.

Noble, Paul. 1991. "The Arab System." In B.Korany and A. Dessouki, *The Foreign Policies of Arab States*. pp. 49–102.

Norden, Edward. 1996. "The Jordan Imperative." *The New Republic* (March 18): 21–27.

Onuf, Nicholas. 1989. *World of Our Making: Rules and Rule in Social Theory and International Relations*. Columbia: University of South Carolina Press.

Owen, John M., IV. 1997. *Liberal Peace, Liberal War: American Politics and International Security*. Ithaca: Cornell University Press.

Oye, Kenneth A. 1986. *Cooperation Under Anarchy*. Princeton: Princeton University Press.

Page, Benjamin I. 1996. *Who Deliberates? Mass Media in Modern Democracy*. Chicago: University of Chicago Press.

Parekh, Bhikhu. 1994. "Discourses on National Identity." *Political Studies* 42, no. 4: 492–504.

Parker, Richard B. 1993. *The Politics of Miscalculation in the Middle East*. Bloomington: Indiana University Press.

———. 1996a. *The Six-day War: A Retrospective*. Gainesville: University Press of Florida.

———. 1996b. "The United States and King Hussein." In D.Lesch, *The Middle East and the United States*. Boulder: Westview Press, pp. 103–16.

Peres, Shimon. 1993. *The New Middle East*. New York: Henry Holt.

———. 1995. *Battling for Peace*. New York: Random House.

Picard, Elizabeth. 1996. *Lebanon: A Shattered Country*. New York: Holmes and Meier.

Pipes, Daniel and Adam M. Garfinkle. 1988. "Is Jordan Palestine?" *Commentary* (October): 35–42.

Plascov, Uri. 1981. *The Palestinian Refugees in Jordan 1948–1957*. London: Frank Cass.

Pollock, David. 1992. *The 'Arab Street'? Public Opinion in the Arab World*. Washington: Washington Institute for Near East Policy Paper 32.

Powell, Robert. 1994. "Anarchy in International Relations Theory: The Neorealist-Neoliberal Debate." *International Organization* 48, no. 2: 313–334.

Powell, Walter and Paul DiMaggio. 1991. *The New Institutionalism in OrganizationalAnalysis*. Chicago: University of Chicago Press.

Price, Richard. 1998. "Reversing the Gun Sights: Transnational Civil Society Targets Land Mines." *International Organization* 52, no. 3: 613–644.

Price, Richard and Christian Reus-Smit. 1998. "Dangerous Liaisons? Constructivism and Critical International Theory." *European Journal of International Relations* 4, no. 3: 259–94.

Putnam, Robert D. 1987. "Diplomacy and Domestic Politics: The Logic of Two-level Games." *International Organization* 42, no. 3: 427–461.

Quandt, William B. 1978. "Lebanon 1958, Jordan 1970." In B. Blechmann, *Force Without War*. Washington: Brookings Institution.

———. 1993. *Peace Process: American diplomacy and the Arab-Israel Conflict Since 1967*. Washington: Brookings Institution.

Rabin, Yitzhaq. 1996. *The Rabin Memoirs*. Berkeley: University of California Press.

Razzaz, Omar. 1993. "Contested Space: Urban Settlement Around Amman." *Middle East Report* (March–April): 10–14.

Reed, Stanley. 1990/91. "Jordan and the Gulf crisis." *Foreign Affairs* 69: 21–35.

Rengger, N. J. 1988. "Going Critical? A Response to Hoffman." *Millennium* 17, no. 1: 81–89.

———. 1992. "A City Which Sustains All Things? Communitarianism and International Society." *Millennium* 21, no. 3: 353–69.

Rescher, Nicholas. 1993. *Pluralism: Against the Demand for Consensus*. Oxford: Oxford University Press.

Reus-Smit, Christian. Forthcoming. *The Moral Purpose of the State*. Princeton: Princeton University Press.

———. 1997. "The Constitutional Structure of International Society and the Nature of Fundamental Institutions." *International Organization* 51, no. 4: 555–589.

Riedel, Tim H. 1994. "The 1993 Parliamentary Elections in Jordan." *Orient* 35, no. 1: 51–63.

Risse-Kappen, Thomas. 1991. "Public Opinion, Domestic Structures and Foreign Policy in Liberal Democracies." *World Politics* 43, no. 4: 479–512.

———. 1995. *Cooperation Among Democracies*. Princeton: Princeton University Press.

———. 1995. *Bringing Transnational Relations Back In*. New York: Cambridge University Press.

Risse, Thomas. 1996. "Exploring the Nature of the Beast." *Journal of Common Market Studies* 35, no. 1: 53–80.

————. 1997. "Let's Talk! Insights from the German debate on Communicative Behavior and International Relations." Paper presented to the American Political Science Association Annual Meeting.

Robins, Philip. 1989. "Shedding Half a Kingdom." *British Society for Middle East StudiesBulletin* 16, no. 2: 162–175.

————. 1990. "Jordan's Election: A New Era?" *Middle East Report* (May–August): 55–57.

Robinson, Glenn E. 1997a. "Can Islamists Be Democrats? The Case of Jordan" *Middle East Journal* 51, no. 3: 373–387.

————. 1997b. *Building a Palestinian State: The Incomplete Revolution.* Bloomington: Indiana University Press.

————. 1998. "Defensive Democratization in Jordan." *International Journal of Middle East Studies* 30, no. 3: 387–410.

Rogan, Eugene and Tariq Tell. 1994. *Village, Steppe and State: The Social Origins of ModernJordan.* New York: St. Martin's Press.

Rosenau, James N. 1990. *Turbulence in World Politics: A Theory of Change and Continuity.* Princeton: Princeton University Press.

Rosenberg, Justin. 1994. *The Empire of Civil Society: A Critique of the Realist Theory of International Relations.* London: Verso.

Ruggie, John Gerard. 1992. "Multilateralism: The Anatomy of an Institution." *International Organization* 46, no. 3: 562–598.

————. 1993. "Territoriality and Beyond: Problematizing Modernity in International Relations." *International Organization* 47, no. 1: 139–174.

————. 1994. "Third Try at World Order: America and Multilateralism After the Cold War." *Political Science Quarterly* 109: 553–70.

————. 1997. "The Past as Prologue? Interests, Identity and American Foreign Policy." *International Security* 21, no. 1: 89–125.

Ruggie, John Gerard and Friedrich V. Kratochwil. 1986. "International Organization: State of the Art in the Art of the State." *International Organization* 40, no. 4: 753–75.

Rugh, William. 1987. *The Arab Press.* Philadelphia: Temple University Press.

Russett, Bruce M. 1993. *Grasping the Democratic Peace: Principles for a Post-Cold War World.* Princeton: Princeton University Press.

Ryan, Curtis. 1998a. "Jordan in the Middle East Peace Process." In I. Peleg, ed., *The Middle East Peace Process.* Albany, NY: SUNY Press, pp. 161–77.

————. 1998b. "Jordan and the Rise and Fall of the Arab Cooperation Council." *Middle East Journal* 52, no. 3: 386–401.

Ryan, Sheila. 1983. *Palestine Is, but Not in Jordan.* Washington: Association of Arab-American University Graduates.

Said, Edward W. 1979. *Orientalism.* New York: Vintage.

————. 1991. "Thoughts on a War: Ignorant Armies Clash by Night." *The Nation* (February 11).

———. 1994. *The Politics of Dispossession: The Struggle for Palestinian Self-determination, 1969- 1994.* New York: Pantheon Books.

———. 1996. *Peace and Its Discontents: Essays on Palestine in the Middle East Peace Process.* New York: Vintage.

Salameh, Ghassan. 1994. "The Middle East: Elusive Security, Indefinable Region." *Security Dialogue* 25, no. 1: 17–35.

Salloukh, Bassel. 1996. "State Strength, Permeability, and Foreign Policy Behavior: Jordan in Comparative Perspective." *Arab Studies Quarterly* 18, no. 2: 39–65.

Satloff, Robert B. 1986. *Troubles on the East Bank: Challenges to the Domestic Stability of Jordan.* New York: Praeger.

———. 1992. "Jordan's Great Gamble: Economic Crisis and Political Reform." In H. Barkey, *Politics of Economic Reform in the Middle East,* pp. 129–52.

———. 1994. *From Abdullah to Hussein: Jordan in Transition.* Oxford: Oxford University Press.

———. 1995a. "The path to peace." *Foreign Policy* 100: 109–122.

———. 1995b. "The Jordanian-Israeli Peace Treaty: A Remarkable Document." *Middle East Quarterly* 2, no. 1: 47–59.

Sayigh, Yezid. 1991. "The Gulf Crisis: Why the Arab Regional Order Failed." *International Affairs* 67, no. 3: 487–507.

———. 1997. *Armed Struggle and the Search for State: The Palestinian National Movement, 1949- 1993.* New York: Oxford University Press.

Schiff, Ze'ev. 1991. "Israel After the War." *Foreign Affairs* 70, no. 2: 19–33.

Schlesinger, Philip. 1991. "Media, the Political Order, and National Identity." *Media, Culture and Society* 13: 297–308.

Seale, Patrick. 1986. *The Struggle for Syria: A Study of Postwar Arab Politics, 1945–1958.* New Haven: Yale University Press.

Sela, Avraham. 1992. "Transjordan, Israel and the 1948 War: Myth, Historiography and Reality." *Middle Eastern Studies* 28, no. 4: 623–688.

———. 1998. *The Decline of the Arab-Israeli Conflict: Middle East Politics and the Quest for Regional Order.* Albany: State University of New York Press.

Shadid, Mohammed and Rich Seltzer. 1988. "Political Attitudes of Palestinians in the West Bank and Gaza Strip." *Middle East Journal* 42, no. 1: 16–32.

Shamir, Yitzhaq. 1994. *Summing Up: an Autobiography.* Boston: Little, Brown.

Shemesh, Moshe. 1996. *The Palestinian Entity. 2nd Edition.* London: Frank Cass.

Shindler, Colin. 1995. *Israel, Likud and the Zionist Dream: Power, Politics, and Ideology from Begin to Netanyahu.* New York: St. Martin's.

Shlaim, Avi. 1987. *Collusion Across the Jordan: King Abdullah, the Zionist Movement, and the Partition of Palestine.* New York: Columbia University Press.

Shryock, Andrew J. 1995. "Popular Genealogical Nationalism: History Writing and Identity Among the Balqa Tribes of Jordan." *Comparative Studies in Society and History* 37, no. 2: 325–357.

————. 1997. *Nationalism and the Genalogical Imagination: Oral History and Textual Authority in Tribal Jordan*. Berkeley: University of California Press.

Shwadran, Benjamin. 1959. *Jordan: A State of Tension*. New York: Council on Foreign Relations.

Smith, Charles D. 1997. "Imagined Identities, Imagined Nationalisms: Print Culture and Egyptian Nationalism in Light of Recent Scholarship." *International Journal of Middle East Studies* 29, no. 4: 607–622.

Snow, David and Robert Benford. 1988. "Ideology, Frame Resonance, and Participant Mobilization." *International Social Movement Research* 1.

Snyder, Jack and Karen Ballantine. 1996. "Nationalism and the Marketplace of Ideas." *International Security* 21, no. 2: 5–40.

Somers, Margaret. 1993. "Citizenship and the Place of the Public Sphere: Law, Community, and Political Culture in the Transition to Democracy." *American Sociological Review* 58, no. 4: 587–620.

————. 1994. "The Narrative Constitution of Identity: A Relational and Network Approach." *Theory and Society* 23: 605–649.

————. 1995a. "What's Political or Cultural About Political Culture and the Public Sphere?" *Sociological Theory* 13, no. 2: 113–143.

————. 1995b. "Narrating and Naturalizing Civil Society and Citizenship Theory." *Sociological Theory* 13, no. 3: 229–273.

Strang, David. 1991. "Anomaly and Commonplace in European Expansion." *International Organization* 45, no. 4: 846–60.

————. 1994. "Institutional Accounts of Organizations as a Form of Structural Analysis." *Current Perspectives in Social Theory* (Supplement 1): 151–73.

Susser, Asher. 1990. *In Through the Out door*. Washington: Washington Institute for Near East Policy Papers 19.

Susser, Leslie. 1994. "The Secret Route to Public Dialogue." *Jerusalem Report* (August 11): 20–21.

Swidler, Ann. 1986. "Culture in Action: Symbols and Strategies." *American Sociological Review* 51: 273–86.

Tal, Lawrence. 1993. "Is Jordan Doomed?" *Foreign Affairs* 72, no. 5: 45–58.

Talhami, Ghada. 1993. "Jordan, the Ubiquitous Partner: The Jordan Option Resurrected." *Arab Studies Quarterly* 15, no. 3: 47–61.

Tarrow, Sidney. 1994. *Power in Movement: Social Movements, Collective Action, and Politics*. New York: Cambridge University Press.

Taylor, Michael. 1989. "Structure, Culture and Action in the Explanation of Social Change." *Politics and Society* 17, no. 2: 115–62.

Taylor, Philip. 1992. *War and the Media: Propaganda and Persuasion in the Gulf War*. New York: St. Martin's.

Telhami, Shibley. 1990. *Power and Leadership in International Bargaining: The Path to the Camp David Accords*. New York: Columbia University Press.

————. 1992. "Between Theory and Fact: Explaining American Behavior in the Gulf War." *Security Studies* 2, no. 1: 96–121.

————. 1993. "Arab Public Opinion and the Gulf War." *Political Science Quarterly* 108, no. 3: 437- 452.

————. 1994. "Power and Legitimacy in Arab Alliances." Paper presented to the Annual Meeting of the American Political Science Association.

Tessler, Mark A. 1989. "The Intifada and Political Discourse in Israel." *Journal of Palestine Studies* 19, no. 1: 43–61.

————. 1994. *History of the Israeli-Palestinian Conflict.* Bloomington: University of Indiana Press.

Van den Berg, Alex. 1990. "Habermas and Modernity: A Critique of the Theory of Communicative Action." *Current Perspectives in Social Theory* 10: 161–193.

Vincent, R. J. and J. D. B. Miller. 1991. *Order and Violence: Hedley Bull and International Relations.* New York: Oxford University Press.

Walker, R. B. J. 1989. "History and Structure in the Theory of International Relations." *Millennium* 18, no. 2: 163–183.

————. 1990a. *Inside/Outside: International Relations as Political Theory.* Cambridge: Cambridge University Press.

————. 1990b. "Sovereignty, Identity, Community: Reflections on the Horizons of Contemporary. Political Practice." In R. Walker and S. Mendlovitz, eds., *Contending Sovereignties,* pp. 159–85.

————. 1991a. "On the Spatiotemporal Conditions of Democratic Practice." *Alternatives* 16: 243- 62.

————. 1991b. "State Sovereignty and the Articulation of Political Space/time." *Millennium* 20, no. 3: 445–461.

————. 1994. "Social Movements/world Politics." *Millennium* 23, no. 3: 669– 700.

Walker, R. B. J. and Saul Mendlovitz, eds. *Contending Sovereignties.* Boulder: Lynn Rienner.

Walker, Stephen, ed. 1987. *Role Theory and Foreign Policy Analysis.* Durham: Duke University Press.

Walt, Stephen M. 1987. *The Origin of Alliances.* Ithaca: Cornell University Press.

————. 1991. "The Renaissance of Security Studies." *International Studies Quarterly* 35, no. 2: 211- 39.

————. 1996. *Revolution and War.* Ithaca: Cornell University Press.

Waltz, Kenneth N. 1979. *Theory of International Politics.* New York: Random House.

Warnke, Georgia. 1996. "Legitimacy and Consensus: Comments on Part of the Recent Work of Thomas McCarthy." *Philosophy and Social Criticism* 22, no. 2: 67–81.

Weber, Cynthia. 1995. *Simulating Sovereignty: Intervention, the State and Symbolic Exchange.* New York: Cambridge University Press.

Weingast, Barry R. 1995. "A Rational Choice Perspective on the Role of Ideas: Shared Belief Systems and State Sovereignty in International Cooperation." *Politics and Society* 23, no. 4: 449–64.

Weldes, Jutta. 1996. "Constructing National Interests." *European Journal of International Relations* 2, no. 3: 275–318.

Wendt, Alexander. 1987. "The Agent-structure Problem in International Relations Theory." *International Organization* 41, no. 3: 335–370.

———. 1992. "Anarchy Is What States Make of It: The Social Construction of Power Politics." *International Organization* 46, no. 2: 391–425.

———. 1994. "Collective Identity Formation in the International System." *American Political Science Review* 88, no. 2: 384–396.

———. 1995. "Constructing International Politics." *International Security* 20, no. 1: 71–81.

Wendt, Alexander and Daniel Friedheim. 1995. "Hierarchy Under Anarchy: Informal Empire and the East German State." *International Organization* 49, no. 4: 689–721.

Wilson, Mary C. 1987. *King Abdullah, Britain, and the Making of Jordan.* New York: Cambridge University Press.

World Bank. 1994. *Peace and the Jordanian Economy.*

Yee, Albert. 1996. "The Causal Effects of Ideas on Policies." *International Organization* 50, no. 1: 69–108.

Yetiv, Steve. 1997. "Peace, Interdependence and the Middle East." *Political Science Quarterly* 112, no. 1: 29–49.

Yorke, Valerie. 1988. *Domestic Politics and Regional Security: Jordan, Syria, and Israel.* New York: Ashgate Publishers.

———. 1988. "Jordan Is not Palestine: The Demographic Factor." *Middle East International* (April 16): 16–17.

Young, Iris Marion. 1989. "Polity and Group Difference: A Critique of the Ideal of Universal Citizenship." *Ethics* 99: 250–74.

Zaghal, Ali S. 1984. "Social Change in Jordan." *Middle Eastern Studies* 20, no. 4: 53–75.

Zak, Moshe. 1985. "Secret Jordanian-Israeli Meetings." *Washington Quarterly.*

———. 1997. "God Save the King." *Jerusalem Post*, January 24.

Zunes, Stephen. 1995. "The Israeli-Jordanian Agreement: Peace or Pax Americana?" *Middle East Policy* 3, no. 4: 57–68.

Zurn, Michael. 1997. "Assessing State Preferences and Explaining Institutional Choice: The Case of intra-German Trade." *International Studies Quarterly* 41, no. 2: 295–320.

Books and Articles in Arabic

Abass, Mahmoud. 1994. *Tariq Oslo.* [The Oslo Path] Beirut.

Abd al-Hadi, Mohammed. 1996. "Al-mukahymat al-filastiniyya fi al-urdun." [The Palestinian camps in Jordan] *Al-Samid al-Iqtisadi* 106: 138–153.

Abd al-Jabiri, Mohammed. 1992. *Al-khutab al-'arabi al-mu'asira* [Contemporary Arab discourse]. 4th edition. Beirut: Center for Arab Unity Studies.

Abd al-Latif, Kamal. 1994. *Qira'at fi al-falsafat al-arabiyyat al-mu'asira* [Readings in contemporary Arab philosophy]. Beirut: Dar al-Tali'ya.

Abd al-Rahman, Asa'ad. 1994. *Al-'aliqat al-filastiniyya al-urduniyya*. [Jordanian-Palestinian relations]. Nablus: Center for Palestine Research and Studies.

Abd al-Razaq, Ammar. 1990. *Azmat al-dinar al-urduni wa in'akasatiha 'ala al-iqtisad al- filastini* [The crisis of the Jordanian Dinar and its impact on the Palestinian economy]. Ramullah: Markaz al-'amal al-tanmawi.

Abidi, Awni Jadu.' 1991. *Jama'at al-ikhwan al-muslimin fi al-urdun wa filastin*. [The Muslim Brothers in Jordan and Palestine]. Amman.

Abu Amru, Ziyad. 1997. Muqawwimat wa isbab qadrat al-nizam al-urduni "ala al-ta'aqallum ma'a al-tahawwilat al-jariyya fi al-mantiqa" [Bases and reasons for the ability of the Jordanian regime to survive the changes in the region] *Al-Siyasa al-Filastiniyya* 13: 102–110.

Abu Bandoura, Isma'il. 1993. *Al-niqabat al-mihniyya al-urduniyya: azmat al-dur.* Amman: Dar al-Yanabiy'a.

Abu Nowar, Ma'an. 1992. *Fi al-dimoqratiya al-haditha.* [On modern democracy] Amman.

Abu Odeh, Adnan. 1997. "Al-aliqat al-urduniyya al-filastiniyya." [Jordanian-Palestinian relations] *Al-Siyasa al-Filastiniyya* 14: 75–88.

Abu Roman, Bashir. 1991. *Al-harakat al-islamiya wa al-barliman.* [The Islamist movement and Parliament] Amman.

Abu Roman, Husayn. 1989. Al-intikhabat al-barlamaniya al-urduniyya [The Jordanian Parliamentary elections]. *Al-Urdun al-Jadid* 14/15.

Ajluni, Ibrahim. 1992a. *Fi al-masa'ila al-dimuqratiya* [On the democracy question] Amman: Mu'assisat Ram.

———. 1992b. *Humum urduniyya* [Jordanian concerns]. Amman: Mu'assisat Ram.

"Al-Aliqat al-Urduniyya al-Filastiniyya." 1995. *al-Nadwa* 6: 1–139.

Aliyan, Mamduh. 1993. *Filastin: hatha al-hal? al-hukm al-thati, federaliyya, konfederaliyya.* [Palestine: is this the solution? Self-Rule, Federation, Confederation] Amman.

Allush, Naji. 1972. Al-mumarisat al-siyasiyya li-wasfi al-tal. [The political practices of Wasfi al- Tal] *Shu'un Filastiniyya* 7: 177–189.

Amin, Galal. 1993. "Mashru' al-suq al-sharq awsatiyya wa mashru' al-nahda al-arabiyya." [The project of the Middle Eastern market and the project of the Arab revival] *al-Mustaqbil al-Arabi* 178: 42–55.

———. 1991. *Al-Arab wa nakbat al-kuwayt.* [The Arabs and the disaster of Kuwait] Cairo.

Amman Chamber of Commerce. 1996. "Al-aliqat al-iqtisadiya wa ma'awiqat al-tabadul al- tujari al-urduni al-filastini." [Economic relations and terms of Jordanian-Palestinian trade] *Samid al-Iqtisadi* 105: 180–204.

Al-Ammar, Man'am. 1993. "Fi mustaqbil al-nizam al-arabi." [On the future of the Arab order] *Al-Mustaqbil al-Arabi* 167: 16–36.

Arar, Sulayman and Taher al-Masri. 1989. "Jordanian-Palestinian Relations." Lecture to Shuman Foundation; text in Shuman Archives.

Atibi, Subhi Jabir. 1994. *Al-wasatiyya bayn al-kalima wa al-fa'il fi tajribat al-urduniyya* [Centrism in word and deed in Jordanian experience]. Amman: Committee on Jordanian History.

Ayad, Khalid (ed). 1995. "Al-Aliqat al-Urduniyya al-Filastiniyya." [Jordanian-Palestinian relations] *Majellat al-Dirasat al-Filastiniyya* 24: 89–154.

al-Azhari, Mohamed Khalid. 1988. "Al-qadaya al-filastiniyya wa tutawwar mafhum 'al- khayar al-urduni.' " [The Palestinian issue and the development of the concept of 'the Jordan option.'] *Shu'un Filastiniyya* 189: 20–33.

Barakat, Marwan. 1992. *Harb al-khalij fi al-sihafa al-urduniyya*. [The Gulf War in the Jordanian press] Amman: Mu'assisat Ram.

Budran, Ibrahim. 1988. *Al-urdun wa al-wasatiyya*. [Jordan and moderatism] Amman.

Dajani, Ahmed Sidqi. 1994. *Fi muwajiha nizam al-sharq al-awsat* [Confronting the Middle East order]. Cairo: Dar al-Mustaqbil al-Arabi.

Dajani, Hisham. 1980. "Al-istratijiya al-sayhuwiniyya tijaha sharqi al-urdun." [Zionist strategy toward East Jordan] *Shu'un Filastiniyya* 101: 94–104.

Darwish, Sa'id. 1993. *Al-marhala al-dimoqratiyya al-jadida fi al-urdun*. [The new democratic era in Jordan] Amman: al-Mu'assisat al-Arabiyya.

Al-Fanik, Fahd. 1989. *Dawlat al-qattriyya*. [The territorial state] Amman: Arab Thought Forum.

Farhan, Hamed. 1994. "Ikhtar amliyat al-salam ala al-masarayn al-urduni wa al-filastini." [Dangers of the peace process on the Jordanian and Palestinian arenas]. *Al-Mustaqbil al-Arabi* 189: 65–75.

Ghalyun, Burhan. 1991. "Harb al-khalij wa al-muwajjiha al-istratijiyya fi al-mantiqa al- arabiyya." [The Gulf War and the strategic confrontation in the Arab region] *Al-Mustaqbil al-Arabi* (May): 4–22.

———. 1992a. "Al-arab wa al-nizam al-dawli." [The Arabs and the international order] *Jadal* 2: 4–14.

———. 1992b. *Ightiyal al-'aql*. [Murder of the mind] 6th edition. Beirut: Al-Mu'assisat al-Arabiyya lil-Dirasat wa al-Nashir.

———. 1994. "Assir al-taswiyat al-iqlimiya." [The age of regional settlement]. *Al-Wahda* 106: 7–17.

Al-Ghubra, Shafiq. 1995. "Naqd al-aqil al-arabi al-mughamira: hala azmat al-khalij." [Critique of the Arab reason: the case of the Gulf crisis] *Al-Siyasa al-Dawliya* 119: 18–38.

Ghuna'im, Ibrahim. 1980. "Al-mutam'i al-sayhuwiniyya fi suriya wa sharq al-urdun." [Zionist ambitions in Syria and East Jordan] *Shu'un Filastiniyya* 106: 33–57.

Haddad, Tariz. 1994. *Malf al-ihzab al-siyasiyya fi al-urdun 1919–1994* [The file of political parties in Jordan 1919–1994]. Amman.

Hadawi, Hassan. 1993. *Jansiyya wa ihkamiha fi al-qanun al-urduni*. [Nationality and its rules in Jordanian law] Amman.

Hamarneh, Mustafa. 1994a. *Al-iqtisad al-urduni*. [The Jordanian economy] Amman: Center for Strategic Studies.

———. 1994b. "Democracy in Jordan 1993." Amman: Center for Strategic Studies.

———. 1995a. "Istitla'a fi aliqat al-urduniyya filastiniyya" [Jordanian-Palestinian Relations] Amman: Center for Strategic Studies.

———. 1995b. "Democracy in Jordan 1995" Amman: Center for Strategic Studies.

———. 1996. "Democracy in Jordan 1996." Amman: Center for Strategic Studies.

———. 1998. "Al-aliqat al-urduniyya al-filastiniyya." Amman: Center for Strategic Studies.

al-Hamash, Munir. 1995. *Al-nizam al-iqlimi al-arabi fi zul al-mutaghayarat al-dawliyyawa al-iqlimiyya*. [The Arab regional order in light of international and regional changes] Damascus: Dar al-Mustaqbil.

Al-Hassan, Khalid. 1972. "Muthakarat tahliliya hawl mashru'u al-malik husayn" [Notes on King Hussein's project] *Shu'un Filastiniyya* 7: 258–266.

———. 1985. *Al-ittifaq al-urduni al-filastini* [The Jordanian-Palestinian agreement]. Amman.

Hattar, Nahid. 1986. *Fi al-qadayat al-urduniyyat al-arabiyya* [On the Jordanian Arab issue]. Amman: Al-Dar al-Arabiyya.

Haydari, Nabil. 1988. "Al-urdun wa mu'adilatihi al-filastiniyya." [Jordan and its Palestinian considerations] *Shu'un Filastiniyya* 186: 3–13.

Haykal, Mohammed Hassanein. 1992. *Harb al-Khalij* [The Gulf War].

Hindi, Khalil. 1971. "Al-ta'aba'iyat al-urduniyya did al-muqawimat al-filastiniyya." [Jordanian actions against the Palestinian resistance] *Shu'un Filastiniyya* 4: 31–54.

Hizb al-Shaab al-Dimoqrati al-Urduni. 1992. *Fi al-aliqat al-urduniyya al-filastiniyya*. [On Jordanian-Palestinian relations].

Hourani, Hani. 1995. *Al-aliqat al-urduniyya al-filastiniyya*. [Jordanian-Palestinian relations]. Unpublished manuscript.

———. 1997. *Al-mithaq al-watani wa al-tahawwal al-dimoqrati fi al-urdun*. [The National Charter and the democratic transition in Jordan] Amman: Al-Urdun al-Jadid.

———. 1972. Al-ittihad al-watani wa al-shakil al-rahin li-al-sulta fi al-urdun. [The National Union and the current form of the regime in Jordan] *Shu'un Filastiniyya* 14: 49–68.

Hourani, Hani and Asa'd Abd al-Rahman. 1997. *Al-aliqat al-urduniyya al-filastiniyya*. [Jordanian-Palestinian Relations] Beirut.

"Irtifa'u ayadakum an al-niqabat al-mihniyya!" [Raise your hands from the Professional Associations!]. 1989. *Al-Urdun al-Jadid* 12/13: 19–63.

Isma'il, Mohammed. 1994. "Al-huwiya al-arabiyya fi muwajiha al-salam al-isra'ili." [The Arab identity in confrontation with the Israeli peace] *Al-Mustaqbil al-Arabi* 190: 26–44.

———. 1995. "Al-nizam al-arabi wa al-nizam al-sharq awsati." [The Arab order and the Middle Eastern order] *Al-Mustaqbil al-Arabi* 196: 4–26.

Jodeh, Qassim. 1994. "Al-taswiya wa al-ta'awun al-iqtisadi al-filastini al-urduni." [The settlement and Jordanian-Palestinian economic cooperation] *Samid al-Iqtisadi* 98: 191- 207.

Khouri, Tareq. 1990. *Mustaqbal al-urdun: al-dimoqratiyya, al-huwiya, al-tahdiyyat.* [The future of Jordan: Democracy, identity, challenges] Amman.

Khulayfat, Sahban. 1993. *Al-dimoqratiyya fi al-urdun.* [Democracy in Jordan]. Amman: Dar Afaq.

Al-Khuli, Lutfi. 1995. *Arab? Na'am. Wa sharq awsatiyyun aidan* [Arabs? Yes. And also Middle Easterners.] Cairo: Markaz al-Ahram.

Khuraysha, Khalaf. 1991. *Al-malik al-husayn bin talal wa diblomasiya al-salam.* [King Hussein and the Diplomacy of Peace]. Irbid.

Lajna lil-dafa'a haquq al-insan fi al-urdun. 1989. *Haquq al-insan fi al-urdun.* [Human rights in Jordan].

Mansour, Farouq. 1992. *Al-nasher wa al-mutaba'a wa al-maktabat fi al-urdun.* [Publishers and printers and libraries in Jordan] Amman: Committee on Jordanian History.

Maqsoud, Clovis. 1972. "Al-ab'ad al-amrikiat-al-israiliya li-mashru' al-malik husayn wa kayfiya.

ihbatahu." [The American-Israeli dimension of Hussein's project and how to frustrate it] *Shu'un Filastiniyya* 9: 5–19.

Markaz Dirasat al-Wahda al-Arabiyya. 1994. *Al-tahdiyyat al-sharq awsatiyya al-jadida waal-watan al-arabi* [The challenges of the New Middle Easternism and the Arab Nation]. Beirut.

al-Maw'id, Mohammed Sa'id. 1996 "Nahu alaqat filastiniyya urduniyya bila mukhawif." [Towards Jordanian-Palestinian relations without fears] *Al-Samid al-Iqtisadi* 104: 129–140.

Mayeteh, Samih. 1994a. *'Alan washington fi al-mizan.* [The Washington Declaration in the Balance] Amman.

———. 1994b. *Al-tajriba al-siyasiyya lil-harakat al-islami fi al-urdun* [The political experience of the Islamist movement in Jordan]. Amman: Dar al-Bashir.

Muhadin, Zakriyya. 1992. *Jawlat istitla'a al-ra'i al-aam al-urduni.* [Survey of Jordanian public opinion] Amman: Mu'assisat Ram.

Muhafiza, Ali. 1990. *Al-fikr al-siyasi fi al-urdun.* [Political thought in Jordan] Amman: Markaz al-Kutb al-Urduni.

Muhafiza, Mohammed. 1983. *Al-aliqat al-urduniyya al-filastiniyya 1939–51*. [Jordanian-Palestinian Relations 1939–1951]. Amman: Dar al-Farqan.

Muharrib, Abd al-Hafiz. 1975: "Al-matlub taghayyir al-nizam wa laysa al-kiyan." [What is needed is a change in regime, not a change in entity] *Shu'un Filastiniyya* 50/51: 349–56.

Muslih, Ahmed. 1994. "Dur al-maqha fi al-hiyat al-urduniyya [Role of the coffeehouse in Jordanian life]." *Amman* 11.

Nadwa. 1996. "Qummat Sharm al-Shaykh." [The Sharm al-Shaykh summit]. *Al-Mustaqbilal-Arabi* 207: 4–21.

Nadwa. 1992. "Mustaqbil al-nizam al-iqlimi al-arabi." [The future of the Arab regional order]. *Al-Mustaqbil al-Arabi* 162: 59–81.

Nahar, Ghazi Saleh. 1993. *Al-qarar al-siasi al-khariji al-urduni tajah azmat al-khalij.* [Jordanian foreign policy decisions toward the Gulf crisis] Amman: Dar al-Majdlawi.

Naqrash, Abdullah. 1994. "Al-mawqif al-siyasi al-rasmi al-urduni min azmat al-khalij al- arabi." [The official Jordanian political position in the Arab Gulf crisis] *Dirasat* 21(a), no. 4: 319–349.

Quttub, Samir. 1997. "Niqashat hawl imlak al-laja'in al-filastinyin fi al-urdun." [Discussions about the property of Palestinian refugees in Jordan] *Al-Samid al-Iqtisadi* 108: 246–251.

Rabab'ah, Ghazi. 1989. *Al-urdun wa qadayat filastin.* [Jordan and the Palestine issue] Amman: Maktibat al-Risalat al-Haditha.

———. 1992. *Al-hashamiyyun wa al-qadayat al-filastiniyya.* [The Hashemites and the Palestinian issue] Amman: Maktibat al-Risalat al-Haditha.

Rabi'i, Ahmed Thiban. 1992. *Al-saluk al-dimoqrati fi diwa al-tajribat al-urduniyya.* [Democratic behavior in light of the Jordanian experience]. Amman.

Rashdan, Abd al-Fateh Ali. 1995a. "Musirat al-diplumisiyat 'am 1989/1990 wa tahdiyat fi al-tisa'yinat." [Diplomacy in 1989/1990 and challenges in the 1990s] *Dirasat* 22.a., no. 4: 1623–1664.

———. 1995b. "Al-nizam sharq al-awsati al-jadid." [The new Middle Eastern order] *Qira'atSiyasiyya* 5, no. 2: 51–68.

Rimoni, Issa. 1991. *Al-tariq al-tawil ila al-mithaq al-watani al-urduni* [The long road to the Jordanian national charter]. Amman.

Salameh, Ahmed Salameh. 1995. *Al-Sharq awsatiyya: hel huwa al-khayar al-wahid?* [Middle Easternism: Is it the only option?] Cairo: Markaz al-Ahram.

Saleh, Assam. 1973. "Siyasat al-malik husayn al-filastiniyya 'abir bayanatihi." *Shu'unFilastiniyya* 23: 59–84.

Sayigh, Yusif. 1987. *Al-urdun wa al-filastiniyyin.* [Jordan and the Palestinians] London: Riyad al-Ris.

Sha'ir, Jamal. 1987. *Siyasi yatathakar.* [A politician remembers] London: Riyad al-Ris.

————. 1995. *Khamsun aaman wanif.* [After 50 years] Amman: Dar al-Urdun.

Sha'ir, Wahib. 1990. "Al-mithaq al-watani." [The National Charter]. Amman.

Sharaf, Layla. 1991. "Mawqif al-urdun min ahdath al-khalij." [Jordan's position in the Gulf events]. *Al-Mustaqbil al-Arabi*: 96–103.

Sharara, Randah. 1990. "Isra'il fi azmat al-khalij: al-mawqif min al-urdun." [Israel in the Gulf crisis: the position towards Jordan] *Majellat al-Dirasat al-Filastiniyya* 4: 72–83.

Shiqaqi, Khalil. 1996. "Al-aliqat al-filastiniyya al-urduniyya wa 'amliyat al-bina al-watani" [Palestinian-Jordanian relations and the process of nation building]. *Al-Siyasa al-Filastiniyya* 9.

Suess, Salim. 1988. *Al-urdun wa haq al-filastiniyyin fi taqrir al-masir.* [Jordan and the Palestinian right to determine destiny] Amman.

Suess, Sulayman and Suhair al-Tal. 1991. "Haquq al-insan wa wasa'il al-'alam fi al-urdun" [Human rights and the media in Jordan] Unpublished paper.

Suwayd, Yasin. 1994. "Al-nizam al-sharq awsati wa khatarihi ala al-wajud al-qawmi al-arabi.". [The Middle Eastern order and its threats to the Arab national existence]. *Al-Wahda* 106: 71–79.

Tahboub, Nasir Mahmoud. 1994. *Siyasa al-kharajiyya al-urduniyya wa al-bahath an al-salam.* [Jordanian foreign policy and the search for peace] Amman.

Tal, Bilal Hassan. 1978. *Al-urdun: muhawila lil-fahim.* [Jordan: an attempt to understand]. Amman: Dar al-Liwa.

Tal, Nasrin. 1993. *Al-konfederaliyya al-urduniyya al-filastiniyya.* [Jordanian-Palestinian Confederation] Amman.

Tal, Sa'id. 1986. *Al-urdun wa filastin: wajhat nazer arabiyya.* [Jordan and Palestine: An Arab point of view] Amman: Dar al-Fikr.

————. 1993. "Alaqat urduniyya filastiniyya" [Jordanian-Palestinian relations] *Rasalat Majles al-Umma* 4.

————. 1994. *Kitabat siyasiyya.* [Political writings] Amman: Dar al-Fikr.

Tal, Tariq. 1996. "Al-astura wa siwa al-fahim fi al-aliqat al-urduniyya al-filastiniyya" [Myth and misunderstanding in Jordanian-Palestinian relations] *al-Siyasa al-Filastiniyya* 12.

Tal, Wasfi. 1962. *Al-Urdun wa al-qadaya al-filastiniyya.* Amman: Ministry of Information.

Tamari, Salim. 1996. *Mustaqbil al-laja'in al-filastiniyin.* [The future of the Palestinian refugees] Beirut: Mu'asasat al-Dirasat al-Filistiniya.

Taqrir 'an haquq al-insan wa huriya al-sahafa fi al-urdun [Report on human rights and press freedoms in Jordan]. 1989. Arab Organization for Human Rights.

"Tatbi' thaqafi" [Cultural normalization]. 1993. *Awraq* 5.

Watha'iq Filastiniyya. Institute for Palestine Studies, various years.

Watha'iq al-Wahda al-Arabiyya. Center for Arab Unity Studies, various years.

Yassin, Al-Sayyid. 1991. "Al-tahlil al-thaqafi li-azmat al-khalij." [Cultural analysis of the Gulf crisis] *Al-Mustaqbil al-Arabi*: 30–47.

Yorke, Valerie. 1994. *Mafhum al-urdun lil alaqat urduniyya filastiniyya.* [Jordan's conception of Jordanian-Palestinian relations] Nablus: Center for Palestine Research Studies.

Zaydan, Nowaf. 1988. "Al-awsat al-sha'abiyya tunazim al-nishatat al-tadamuniyya." [Popular circles organize solidarity activities] *Al-Urdun al-Jadid*: 65–72.

Jordanian Government Publications

[In Arabic unless otherwise noted]:.
The Battle for Peace. July 1994.
Collected Speeches, 1987–1990. 1990.
Hashemite Outcries: Speeches and Statements During the Gulf Crisis. 1992.
Jordanian Cabinets 1921–1992. 1992.
Jordanian Documents. 1994, Parts 1–4.
Jordan Yearbook, various years.
Political and Public Life in Jordan: Legislation and Laws. 1993.
The White Book: Jordan and the Gulf Crisis. 1991.

Newspapers and Magazines

[In Arabic unless otherwise specified].

Jordanian Dailies

[WWW addresses where internet edition exists].
Akher Khabir.
Al-Aswaq.
al-Arab al-Yom [http://www.alarab-alyawm.com.jo/].
Al-Dustur [http://www.arabia.com/Addustour/].
Jordan Times [English] [http://www.accessme.com/JordanTimes/].
Al-Rai [http://www.accessme.com/Al-Ra'i/].
Sawt al-Shaab.

Jordanian Weeklies

[WWW addresses where internet edition exists].
Al-Ahali.
Al-Ahd.
Akhbar al-Asbu'a.
Al-Ba'th.
Al-Bilad.
Al-Hadath [http://accessme.com/Al-Hadath/].
Al-Jamahir.

Al-Liwa.
Al-Majd.
Al-Masira.
Al-Mithaq.
Al-Nahda.
Nida al-Watan.
Al-Ribat.
Al-Sabil [http://www.assabeel.com/].
Sawt al-Mara.
Shihan [http://www.alarab-alyawm.com.jo/shihan/].
Star [English].
Al-Ufuq.
Al-Urdun.

Arab Dailies and Weeklies

[WWW addresses where internet edition exists].
Al-Ahram.
Al-Asbu'a al-Arabi.
Al-Bayadir al-Siyasi.
Filastin al-Muslima.
Filastin al-Thawra.
Al-Hadaf.
Al-Hawadeth.
Al-Hayat [http://www.sitecopy.com/alhayat/].
Al-Nahar.
Al-Quds.
Al-Quds al-Arabi.
Al-Sharq al-Awsat.
Al-Wasat.
Al-Watan al-Arabi.

Other

[In English unless otherwise specified]
[WWW addresses where internet edition exists].
Christian Science Monitor [http://www.csmonitor.com].
Foreign Broadcast Information Service (United States).
Ha'aretz (http://www3.haaretz.co.il/eng/htmls/1_1.htm).
Independent (London) (http://www.independent.co.uk).
Jerusalem Post [http://www.jpost.co.il/].
Jerusalem Report.
Los Angelas Times [http://www.latimes.com].
Middle East Economic Digest.

Middle East International.

Middle East Mirror.

New Middle East.

New York Times [http://www.nytimes.com].

Washington Post [http://www.washingtonpost.com].

Index

——uprisings in, April 1989: 22, 69,
83, 86, 102, 104, 106–107, 264
——uprisings in, 1990s: 22, 68–69,
191, 229, 250, 251, 264
Jordanians of Palestinian origin: 14, 22,
75, 78, 83–84, 94, 100, 102, 104–
106, 107, 112, 115–117, 124–125,
127, 134, 138, 183, 187, 232
——and domination of private sector:
105, 115–116
——Political preferences of: 104–106,
109, 112
Jordanian nationalists: 15, 24, 60, 76,
78, 94, 105, 109–112, 118–120,
123, 125, 127, 131–136, 138, 187
Jordanian Writers Association: 220–222
Jordanian "umbrella" (Madrid peace
process): 132, 172, 181–182
"Jordan is Palestine": 6, 27, 80–81, 85–
87, 91–94, 105, 108, 112, 133, 134,
144–146, 173, 177, 183, 184, 185,
193–194, 202
"Jordan Option": 82, 85, 87, 98, 184
Jordan-PLO Agreement (1985): 80, 131
"Jordastinians": 112, 113
Justifications: 5, 7, 35, 36, 38–39, 40–
42, 44, 45, 47, 50, 53, 83, 93, 167–
168, 170, 175, 189, 191, 194, 232,
240, 252, 259

Al-Kabariti, Abd al-Karim: 68, 116, 203,
208, 209, 210, 211, 212, 217, 243,
245, 246, 247
Kamel, Hussein: 239, 242, 264
Karameh: 218–219
Katzenstein, Peter: 5, 6, 9, 22, 48, 89,
115
Al-Khasawneh, Hani: 95–96, 271n
Kratochwil, Friedrich: 5, 7, 42, 43, 44
Kuwait: 1, 59, 68, 140, 142, 143, 144,
155, 156, 158, 161, 162, 176, 232,

235, 236, 239, 240, 241, 243, 246,
248

Labor Party (Israel): 82, 86–87, 92, 132
Lebanon: 8, 61, 62, 64, 91, 109, 200,
206, 207, 210–211, 220, 241, 260
Legitimacy: 16–17, 38, 39, 42–45, 47,
90, 92, 107, 151, 157, 191, 233
Levy, David: 146
Lifeworld: 35–36, 38, 51
Likud Party (Israel): 2, 82, 86, 92, 138,
177, 184, 201, 208, 211
Linklater, Andrew: 7, 47

Madrid peace conference: 8, 188, 190,
228, 232, 259
Al-Majali, Abd al-Hadi: 110–112, 118,
274n
Al-Majali, Abd al-Salam: 116, 135, 182,
192, 203, 205, 217, 236, 246
Mansour, Nidal: 202
Al-Masri, Taher: 114, 118, 127, 187,
202, 214, 247, 271n
MENA Economic Conferences: 201,
225, 227, 244, 250
——Amman, 1995: 225, 227, 250
——Doha, 1997: 201, 227–228, 244
Middle Eastern identity: 48, 140, 226,
252
Misha'al (Khalid) Affair: 128, 201, 204,
207, 213, 214, 260
Al-Mithaq (newspaper, Jordan): 111–
112, 275n
Molodet Party (Israel): 92
Monarchy, as institution: 60, 68–69,
107, 109–110
Mubarak, Hosni: 157, 158, 163, 212,
242
Muslim Brotherhood: 128, 129, 182–
183